北京高等学校"青年英才计划"

北京理工大学"双一流"建设精品出版工程

Applied English Lexicology
(2nd Edition)

实用英语词汇学
（第2版）

栗 欣 ◎ 主编

北京理工大学出版社
BEIJING INSTITUTE OF TECHNOLOGY PRESS

内 容 简 介

《实用英语词汇学（第2版）》以语言文字发展的历史为出发点，详尽介绍了英语单词与埃及象形文字、巴比伦楔形文字、腓尼基文字、希腊字母体系和拉丁字母体系之间的传承关系。通过对英语 26 个字母的形态分析，提出了运用英语字母自身象形含义学习记忆词汇的新思路；指出了英语词汇学习的三个难点：一词多义现象、同义词辨析和形近易混词区分；并举例说明如何围绕它们开展词汇学习；介绍了常用的高效英语词汇学习方法，包括词根词缀记忆法、词汇联想记忆法（替换、添加、反写、拆分、谐音）和词源典故记忆法，详细列举了最常用的 228 个英语词根词缀及其构成的高频词汇；附加了 12 组共 240 道精选词汇练习题和答案详解，对指导读者习得英语四六级、考研、托福和雅思考试中的核心词汇具有积极作用。

版权专有　侵权必究

图书在版编目（CIP）数据

实用英语词汇学 / 栗欣主编. —2 版. —北京：北京理工大学出版社，2020.12
ISBN 978-7-5682-9260-3

Ⅰ. ①实… Ⅱ. ①栗… Ⅲ. ①英语–词汇–自学参考资料 Ⅳ. ①H313

中国版本图书馆 CIP 数据核字（2020）第 229306 号

出版发行 /	北京理工大学出版社有限责任公司
社　　址 /	北京市海淀区中关村南大街 5 号
邮　　编 /	100081
电　　话 /	（010）68914775（总编室）
	（010）82562903（教材售后服务热线）
	（010）68948351（其他图书服务热线）
网　　址 /	http://www.bitpress.com.cn
经　　销 /	全国各地新华书店
印　　刷 /	三河市华骏印务包装有限公司
开　　本 /	787 毫米×1092 毫米　1/16
印　　张 /	17.25
字　　数 /	374 千字
版　　次 /	2020 年 12 月第 2 版　2020 年 12 月第 1 次印刷
定　　价 /	72.00 元

| 责任编辑 / 武丽娟 |
| 文案编辑 / 武丽娟 |
| 责任校对 / 刘亚男 |
| 责任印制 / 李志强 |

图书出现印装质量问题，请拨打售后服务热线，本社负责调换

目录 CONTENTS

1 语言文字的起源和演化 ··· 1

2 26 个英文字母的象形含义 ··· 10

3 英语词汇学习的难点 ·· 24
   3.1 一词多义现象 ··· 24
   3.2 同义词辨析 ·· 26
   3.3 形近易混词区分 ··· 27

4 英语词汇学习的方法 ·· 31
   4.1 词根词缀记忆法 ··· 31
   4.2 词汇联想记忆法 ··· 35
   4.3 词源典故记忆法 ··· 36

5 英语常用 228 个词根词缀及构成词汇 ·· 47

6 词汇练习题 ··· 225

1 语言文字的起源和演化

谈起英语词汇，就不得不先提及人类语言文字发展的历史。了解掌握语言文字的起源和演化过程是英语词汇习得与记忆的重要前提。那么语言文字到底经历了哪几个发展阶段呢？在英语语言文字出现之前，人类社会主要经历了古埃及象形文字时期、古巴比伦楔形文字时期、古腓尼基文字时期、古希腊文字时期和古罗马拉丁文字时期。这些不同时期的文字符号对英语词汇形成和发展有着深远的影响，学习掌握这些文字的基本知识对培养英语词汇学习的兴趣和提高英语词汇记忆的效率有着重要的指导意义。

文字起源和演化的第一个阶段是古埃及（Egypt）象形文字。通过认知象形文字的含义，人们可以更加快速地学习英语词汇。距今 5 000 多年前，古埃及出现了象形文字，即埃及文字，它是世界上最古老的文字之一。早在公元前 3 100 年，法老王那默尔的铠甲关节板上就刻有象形文字，这种古埃及文字后来被欧洲人称作 Hiérpglyphe，它是希腊语"神圣"与"铭刻"组成的复合词，含义是"神的文字"。在古埃及人们认为他们使用的文字是月神、计算与学问之神图特（Thoth）创造的。

Hieroglyphics 是象形文字在现代英语中的拼写形式，是由前缀 hiero-（holy 神圣的）与词根 graph-（draw 描绘，镌刻）复合而成的。象形文字是直接描绘物体外部形象的文字符号，最初的主要使用者是僧侣。这种文字通常被刻在神庙的墙上和宗教纪念物上，因而被称为"圣书"。古埃及的象形文字早已失传，直到 1799 年，拿破仑远征埃及，其部下在罗塞塔要塞挖掘战壕时首次发现了一块刻有圣书体、世俗体和古希腊文三种文字对照的纪念碑。以这块石碑为线索，在吸收了众多学者长期研究成果的基础上，1822 年法国的商博良博士终于对这三种文字释读成功，从而标志着埃及学的诞生。

图 1 中的象形文字含义表达十分精确，第一列里可以看到男人挥动着双拳准备战斗，女人跪着双膝以示顺从，法老的胡子体现着其神圣的地位，一个人手里拿着工具正在劳动，另一个人正在向嘴里送东西吃；第二列中，房子是有一个门的空间，城市是圆形的围墙包围内

部十字形的道路，沙漠呈现连绵起伏的群山形状，太阳是天上的圆环和中间圆点的结合，行走是两条腿在迈步；第三列中，书是平放的，小鸟表示虚弱，枝条的意思是树木，一个竖条表示名词的单数，三个竖条表示名词的复数。

	man		house, building		book, writing, abstract
	woman		town, village		small, bad, weak
	god, king		desert, foreign country		wood, tree
	force, effort		sun, light, time		logogram indicator
	eat, drink, speak		walk, run		plural indicator

图 1　象形文字示例（1）

古埃及象形文字对英语词汇学习有很大的启示作用。它通过英语字母的象形含义来帮助读者去理解和记忆单词。例如，图 2 中的单词 vulture（秃鹫）可理解成由字母 v 和单词 culture（文化）组合而成，字母 v 是象形意义上峡谷的开口，秃鹫则是存在于峡谷中的一种动物文化现象。秃鹫具有贪婪的天性，因此 vulture 的引申含义为"贪婪的人"。单词 valley（峡谷）、village（村庄）、vent（排气口）也都含有字母 v 的象形含义。此外，图 2 中表示"水"的波浪符号可看作字母 w，表示"水"或"弯曲"的概念，如 wine（酒），wade（涉水），woman（女人，因为女人是水做的），twist（弯曲），wrong（错误），wrench（扳手）。

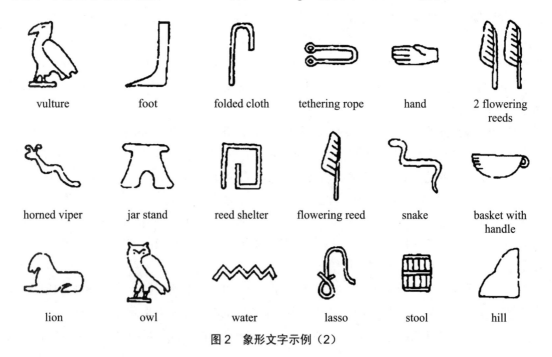

图 2　象形文字示例（2）

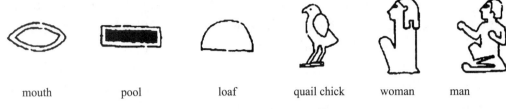

图 2　象形文字示例（2）（续）

　　文字起源和演化的第二个阶段是古巴比伦帝国（Babylon）的楔形文字（Cuneiform Script）。它是底格里斯河和幼发拉底河两河流域的古老文字，也是世界上最早的文字之一，由苏美尔人所发明。在其 3 000 多年的历史中，楔形文字以最初的象形文字系统为基础，字形结构逐渐地趋于简单化和抽象化，文字数量由约 1 000 个减至约 400 个。楔形文字多写在泥板上，少数也写在石头、金属或蜡版上。人们通常使用削尖的芦苇秆或木棒在软泥板上刻写楔形文字，因为软泥板经过晒干或烘烤后会变得坚硬，不易变形，易于保存文字。

　　公元前 18 世纪，古巴比伦王朝的君主汉谟拉比国王（公元前 1792—1750 年）编纂了一部法典，史称《汉谟拉比法典》。这部法典被认为是人类社会有史以来的第一部法典，它被雕刻在一个 2.25 米高的石柱上，由楔形文字和人像两部分组成。石柱上部是太阳神沙马什授予汉谟拉比国王象征统治权力的浮雕，下部则用楔形文字铭刻法典全文。这部法典详细规范了国王、奴隶主与自由民、奴隶之间的阶级关系，还规定了保护孤寡，将债奴期缩短为三年等。《汉谟拉比法典》不仅标志着人类社会历史性的进步，而且开创了人类社会法典领域的先河。

　　公元前 539 年，波斯征服了巴比伦王国，并从后者那里学会了楔形文字。随着波斯帝国版图的日益扩大，由于商业发展的迫切需求，伊朗高原的波斯人把美索不达米亚的楔形文字逐渐改成较为方便使用的字母文字。到了古希腊时代，腓尼基商人在埃及象形文字基础上发明了腓尼基字母文字，从此字母文字走上了历史舞台，逐渐成为西方的主流文字。楔形文字在西亚流行长达 3 000 年，迄今发现的最后一片楔形文字的泥板是公元 75 年的遗物（图 3），随后的楔形文字便再无人知晓了。

图 3　楔形文字泥板

文字起源和演化的第三个阶段是腓尼基（Phoenicia）的字母文字。腓尼基位于地中海东岸的狭长地带，南面是古埃及文明，东面是古巴比伦帝国，西面是浩瀚的地中海。传说，世界上最早的字母文字就是由古腓尼基人发明出来的。有一个叫卡德穆斯的腓尼基木匠，他的聪明远近皆知。一次，他在别人家干活，忘带了一件重要工具。他随手拿起一片木头，用刀在上面刻了点什么，然后让一个奴隶送给在家中的妻子。卡德穆斯的妻子看了木片后，什么都没说就递给了奴隶一件工具。奴隶惊呆了，以为他的主人正在使用一种神秘的方式沟通，通过木片上的符号就能表示出他需要的东西。很多人推测卡德穆斯在木片上写的就是第一次出现的腓尼基字母文字。后来，更多的人知道了这件事，他们向卡德穆斯求教，卡德穆斯就把他发明的字母文字传授给了其他人。这样，腓尼基字母逐渐传播开来。

腓尼基字母的产生并非偶然，而是实际生活的需要。腓尼基人忙于商业和航海业（图4），记账和签署文件等商业事件不可忽视。由于当时流行的象形文字和楔形文字书写起来太耗费时间，视时间如金钱的腓尼基人不能忍受。被逼无奈之下，他们只好割舍了美观的旧文字写法，从埃及象形文字中借得一点图形，又从巴比伦文字里简化了一些楔形文字，把旧写法的几个笔画重组在一起，形成了新的文字符号。可以这么说，腓尼基人既借鉴了前人的成果，又充分发挥了自己的聪明才智，终于发明了简单易用的22个腓尼基字母。

图4　腓尼基人的航海业

在腓尼基字母表（图5）中，A 在字母表上名列前茅，位于第一位。在古腓尼基时期，字母 A 叫 'aleph，意思是牛。那时 A 的写法是 V，样子像牛的双角，当中还有斜着写的一横。牛是腓尼基人的衣食之源，也是任劳任怨的劳动力，一群牛对他们来说就意味着一大笔财富。不久之后，希腊人把这个字母翻转过来，变成了现在的样子。

在腓尼基语中，B 叫 beth，意思是帐篷或房子。腓尼基字母 B 看起来就像一套两间住房。一间给男人住，一间给女人住。因为人类生存的第二个重要条件是住房，所以 B 就排在了第二位。

腓尼基的第三个字母 C 代表骆驼，它的符号像一只骆驼的头和颈部，读作 gimel。骆驼对于腓尼基人而言是很重要的旅行工具。随后希腊人把这个符号换了个方向，叫它 gamma，罗马人也借用它并赋予它一个优美的曲线，称之为 C。字母 G 也被认为象征着骆驼和它弯曲的头颈。

字母 D 在腓尼基语中叫 daleth，是从埃及象形文字借鉴过来的。在埃及象形文字中 D 的意思是门，形状也很像门，英语单词也用它描绘半圆形的物体，如 dome（半圆形屋顶，穹顶），door（门）。

腓尼基语中的字母 L 叫 lamedh，即"鞭子"。因为赶骆驼离不开鞭子，所以造了英语单词 lash（鞭子，鞭打，抨击）。

腓尼基人善于航海，把字母 M 叫作 mem，喻指海上的波浪，含义是水，创造的英语单词如 merchant（海上经商的人）。

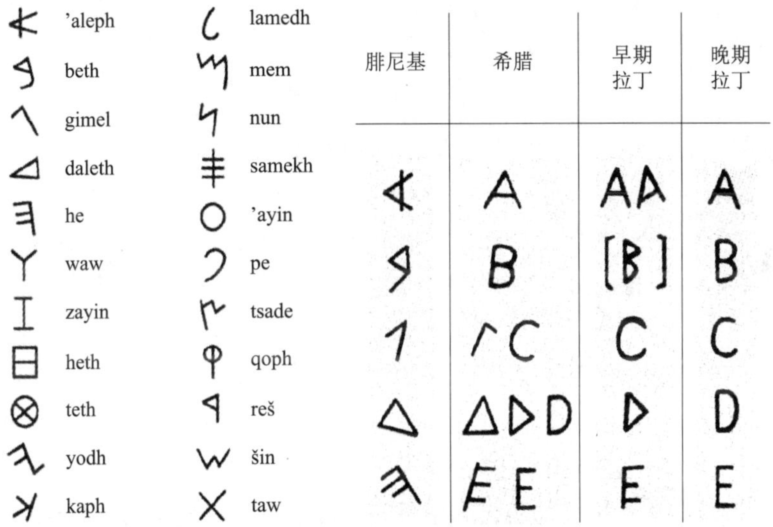

腓尼基字母		腓尼基字母		腓尼基	希腊	早期拉丁	晚期拉丁
∀	'aleph	ᒐ	lamedh	∀	A	AA	A
૬	beth	ᒣ	mem	৭	B	[B]	B
ᐸ	gimel	ᒣ	nun	٦	ᒐ	C	C
△	daleth	≢	samekh	△	△	D D	D
∃	he	O	'ayin	ᕯ	E	E	E
Y	waw	フ	pe				
エ	zayin	ᒥ	tsade				
日	heth	φ	qoph				
⊗	teth	⊲	reš				
ᕯ	yodh	W	šin				
K	kaph	X	taw				

图 5　腓尼基字母表

除了腓尼基字母表，古腓尼基人还发明了紫红色的染料（dye），其闻名历史，还令腓尼基人大发横财。连腓尼基（Phoenicia）这个单词都与紫色有关，意为"紫红色的国度"。腓尼基人发明紫红色染料纯属偶然。传说，一个腓尼基牧羊人在海边捡了一些海螺，煮好之后，扔了几个喂他的猎狗试吃。猎狗咬后，嘴边和鼻子旁都溅上了鲜红的颜色，拿水怎么冲洗都洗不掉。牧羊人仔细观察后发现是海螺中流出的红色汁水造成的。他想如果用这种颜色染布，就一定不会掉颜色。于是他又拾回一大堆这种海螺，兑水熬制，果然调出了一种紫红色的染料。凡是被这种染料染过的衣服，无论洗过多少次，还依然能够保持亮丽的紫红色，永不褪色。

这种海螺在腓尼基的浅海中特别多，人们都用它熬出的染料来染布。这种紫红色的布匹在地中海沿岸受到许多国家的欢迎，供不应求，越来越多的腓尼基人靠贩卖染料和布匹发家致富（图 6）。他们渐渐放弃了农业生产，以经商为生，腓尼基商人的足迹遍及了地中海周边的各个海港。

英语单词 purple 来自希腊语 porphyra，原指腓尼基人所生产的一种紫色染料，后来演变成"紫色"的含义。紫色代表着高贵，是古代贵族最喜爱的颜色。在古罗马时期，只有皇帝才能穿紫色的托加袍（toga），元老们的托加袍也可以配有红色或紫红色的镶边。

图 6　腓尼基染料

  文字起源和演化的第四个阶段是希腊字母的繁荣。在古希腊神话中，腓尼基王子卡德摩斯（Cadmus）为了寻找被宙斯拐走的妹妹欧罗巴（Europa）来到了希腊境内，但他因未能完成父命找到妹妹而无法回国，只能留在希腊境内居住，并建立了著名的卡德米亚城（Cadmia），也就是后来的忒拜城（Thebes），著名的俄狄浦斯王、安提戈涅和七雄攻忒拜等故事都发生在这里。当然，卡德摩斯留给希腊的不只是城市，还有一样重要的东西——文字。

  起初，卡德摩斯只为希腊带来了 16 个腓尼基字母。后来在特洛伊战争期间，希腊人又从腓尼基字母中引进了 3 个字母。他们对腓尼基字母进行了改造，使其更加适合本民族语言，创造了希腊字母。希腊人在借用了 19 个腓尼基字母之后，自己又创造了 5 个新的字母，从而完善并确立了拥有 24 个字母的古希腊字母表，该字母体系一直沿用到现在（图 7）。

图 7　古希腊字母表

  在希腊字母表中，前 19 个字母都是从腓尼基字母中改造过来的，表 1 中的字母名称体现了它们之间的衍生关系：

表 1 希腊字母与腓尼基字母的关系（前 19 个）

希腊字母序号	希腊字母	字母名称	腓尼基字母	腓尼基字母名称	腓尼基字母含义
1	Α α	alpha		'aleph	牛
2	Β β	beta		beth	屋子
3	Γ γ	gamma		gimel	骆驼
4	Δ δ	delta		daleth	门
5	Ε ε	epsilon		he	窗户
6	Ζ ζ	zeta		zayin	武器；剑
7	Η η	eta		heth	墙；围栏
8	Θ θ	theta		teth	轮子
9	Ι ι	iota		yodh	手
10	Κ κ	kappa		kaph	手掌
11	Λ λ	lamda		lamedh	刺棒
12	Μ μ	mu		mem	水
13	Ν ν	nu		nun	鱼；蛇
14	Ξ ξ	xi		samekh	鱼；支柱
15	Ο ο	omicron		'ayin	眼睛
16	Π π	pi		pe	嘴巴
17	Ρ ρ	rho		reš	头
18	Σ σ ς	sigma		šin	牙齿
19	Τ τ	tau		taw	标记

后添加的 5 个字母是希腊人自己创造的，它们分别是（表 2）：

表 2 希腊字母表（后 5 个）

希腊字母序号	希腊字母	字母名称
20	Υ υ	upsilon
21	Φ φ	phi
22	Χ χ	chi
23	Ψ ψ	psi
24	Ω ω	omega

文字起源和演化的第五个阶段是拉丁语和拉丁字母的兴盛。公元前 8 世纪左右，居住在意大利中部地区的伊特鲁里亚人（Etruscans）深受希腊殖民地的影响，借用并改造了希腊字

母，形成了伊特鲁里亚字母。到了公元前 6 世纪，伊特鲁里亚人在意大利建立了王朝，统治着罗马和其他地区。后来罗马成为意大利半岛的新霸主，罗马人沿用并改造了伊特鲁里亚字母，变成了自己民族的文字。因为罗马人最初居住在台伯河（Tiber）岸的拉丁姆（Latium）地区，所以他们所使用的字母被称作拉丁（Latin）字母，其语言也被称为拉丁语。英勇好战的罗马人通过一系列的战争统治了意大利半岛（Italian Peninsula），后又通过领土扩张将几乎整个欧洲纳入帝国版图。罗马军队和官吏把拉丁字母带到了他们所征服的土地上，并推行拉丁语以取代当地的语言。罗马帝国衰落之后，帝国各行省的拉丁语方言逐渐分化，形成了后来的意大利语、法语、西班牙语、葡萄牙语、罗马尼亚语等子语言。拉丁字母也因罗马帝国的影响，被欧洲各地纷纷采用。在大航海时代，拉丁字母又随着欧洲列强的海外殖民，由官吏、商人、传教士传到了美洲（南美洲、中美洲及墨西哥等地区因使用西班牙语、葡萄牙语等拉丁子语而被称作拉丁美洲）、大洋洲（大洋洲语言全部都使用拉丁字母书写）、非洲的大部分地区（除埃塞俄比亚和埃及外，非洲大部分地区都使用拉丁字母）、部分亚洲国家（如土耳其、越南、印度尼西亚、菲律宾等国家），就连我国也借用了拉丁字母作为文字拼音注释。拉丁字母现在已经成为世界上使用最广泛的官方文字，现今全世界约有 30 亿人使用拉丁字母作为母语文字。

现在使用的由 26 个字母组成的拉丁字母体系是 15 世纪后才最终形成的。在古罗马时期，拉丁字母表实际上只有 23 个字母，称为古典拉丁字母，常见的拉丁语文献里也一般只有 23 个字母。到了文艺复兴时期，人们又在古典拉丁字母的基础上新增了 3 个字母，它们分别是 J，U，W，并最终形成了拥有 26 个字母的拉丁字母体系。在早期的拉丁字母表中，23 个古典拉丁字母都源于希腊字母，其名称如表 3 所示：

表 3　23 个古典拉丁字母

字母序列	拉丁字母	字母拉丁名称	源自希腊字母	注释
1	A a	ā	A α	
2	B b	bē	B β	
3	C c	cē	Γ γ	
4	D d	dē	Δ δ	
5	E e	ē	E ε	
6	F f	ef		由不使用的早期希腊字母 digamma 改变而来
7	G g	gē		由拉丁字母 C 改变而来
8	H h	hā	H η	
9	I i	ī	I ι	
10	K k	kā	K κ	
11	L l	el	Λ λ	
12	M m	em	M μ	

续表

字母序列	拉丁字母	字母拉丁名称	源自希腊字母	注释
13	N n	en	N ν	
14	O o	ō	O o	
15	P p	pē	Π π	
16	Q q	qū		由不使用的早期希腊字母 qoppa 改变而来
17	R r	er	P ρ	
18	S s	es	Σ σ ς	
19	T t	tē	T τ	
20	V v	ū		由希腊字母 upsilon 改变而来，表示 u 音
21	X x	ix	X χ	
22	Y y	ī Graeca	Y y	为转写希腊文字而引入
23	Z z	zēta	Z z	为转写希腊文字而引入

2

26 个英文字母的象形含义

人们普遍认为英语是拼音文字,与象形无关。但是,即使作为拼音文字,英语的字母来源与象形文字也有着密不可分的关系。可以这么说,英语中的 26 个字母,每个都有其象形意义。它们的象形含义不但在英语构词上起到了重要的作用,还对如何记忆单词有着积极的影响。下面将举例说明如何利用 26 个英文字母的象形含义分析理解单词,提高英语词汇学习的效率。

A a

(牛头;财富;领头羊,首领;尖端,锐利;高的,高处)

字母 A a,其大写形式 A 比较常见,人们普遍认为这个字母可能源于牛头的形状。在 3 000 多年前,腓尼基字母表中的字母 A 读作 'aleph,写出来形似字母 V,中间再添加一横,代表牛头或牛角。后来古希腊人把它翻转过来写。对古腓尼基人来说,牛意味着财富,吃、穿、行和耕作都少不了它。这也许就是 A 被列为第一个字母的原因。

希腊字母中的字母 A 仍继承和保留了腓尼基字母 'aleph 的一些原始含义。希腊字母 alpha 是牛,是移动的财富,它不仅是物质财富,而且是精神财富。不但希腊人认为牛是财富,连罗马人也是这样认为的。在铸币技术传入罗马后,他们对财富价值的衡量标准就是以牛的头数来计算的。

在古代社会,牛是人类最依赖的动物之一。人们喝牛奶,吃牛肉,穿牛皮和用牛角,牛这样重要的动物是无愧于其首当其冲的地位的。在牛津大词典中 alpha 的词条下有一条对其含义的解释是 "ox or leader"。这样看来,它不仅仅是牛,还是 "领头羊,首领" 或指 "有头有脸的人物"。所以在词典中有许多表示 "鼻祖,领导,统治者" 的词都以字母 A 开头,如

author（作者），athlete（运动员），artist（艺术家），arbiter（权威人士）。

由于字母 A 本身就是尖尖的样子，所以构成了一系列和尖端、锐利有关的词汇。比如 ace 就是扑克牌里的至尊，表示"最好的，一流的"；acute（锐角的；敏锐的；疾病急性的；问题严重的）取的是字母 A 尖端的含义；acumen（敏锐，聪明，机智）可以记成一个有尖端头脑的人（men）很聪明。

此外，字母 A 还可以表示高高在上的物体外部形态，如 Alps（阿尔卑斯山），altitude（海拔），altar（圣坛）。

B b

（两间房子；棍状物；口袋，一包；负担，支持；弯曲）

字母 B b，其大写形式 B 在古时表示房子或家。在腓尼基字母表中，字母 B 读作 beth，代表房屋，意为"朝东的两间房子"。在希伯来语中，字母 B 也叫 beth，也有房屋之意。字母 B 形似原始社会的两间房屋，小写字母 b 是从大写字母 B 衍变而来的。在约旦河西岸，有一个基督教的圣地叫 Bethlehem（伯利恒，耶稣的诞生地），该单词中至今还包含着 beth 这一部分。单词 bath 则指人们经常在家（beth）中洗浴。

B 在字母表中位列第二是因为对人类来说，住的重要性是仅次于衣食的，房子也是人类生存的必需品。把 B 横过来也可以看成是一条扁担挑着两个担子的形象，所以有"木棍、扁担""口袋、一包、一捆""负担、支持、担子"和"弯、弯曲"等引申义。例如，bar（条，棒，横木，酒吧间，栅，障碍物，阻止），bark（树皮，吠声），base（底部，基础，根据地），bat（棒球球棒，蝙蝠），bean（豆，豆形果实），bed（床，基座），board（木板，甲板，伙食，董事会），bolt（门闩，螺钉，闪电，快跑），bore（使厌烦，钻孔），bail（保释，保释金），bear（负担，忍受，生育，结果实，刻字，狗熊），brace（支架，使准备），bag（袋子，眼袋，黑眼圈，猎捕动物），bale（大包，大捆），bin（垃圾箱），bind（捆，绑，装订，约束），back（背部，后面，后退，支持），bend（弯腰，路的转弯，使弯曲，专心于，屈服），bow（弓，蝴蝶结，船首，鞠躬）。

C c

（骆驼；罗马数字的 100；开口状；弯曲状；变化；
手抓物体；控制，操纵；覆盖）

字母 C c，大写的 C 在腓尼基字母中叫 gimel，表示骆驼（camel）。它在字母表中的排列顺序和希腊字母 Γ（gamma）相同，处于第三位。英语字母 C 的字形是从 Γ 演变而来的。C 在罗马数字中表示 100。

字母 c 象形半圆形，指开口状、弯腰状、手抓状，也有覆盖、变化、控制的意思。C c 字母不论大小写都是半圆形，像张开嘴巴的侧面图。如 cow（奶牛），描绘了奶牛张嘴喝水的样子，c 是侧面张开的嘴巴，o 是胖胖的身躯，w 表示水。又如 call（叫），就是张开嘴（c）叫大家（all）过来，其中 a 指人头，两个 ll 指站立的人，三人成众，所以 all 有"大家，全部"的意思。

同时，c 又如弯腰状，所以单词 curly 指弯曲缠绕的蛇身或卷曲的头发。单词 curve 指球类飞行的弧线，股票的曲线图，女性的身体曲线或道路河流的拐弯处。单词 climb（爬）描绘的是一个弯腰（c）再站立起来（l）的人（i）在爬山（m）的样子，当他到达了山顶，就静静地（b）坐在地上休息，缓解疲劳，不说话，所以 b 不发音。

字母 c 由直变弯的形状可喻指变化。如 change（变化，改变，零钱），chance（机会，机遇），challenge（挑战，质疑），climate（气候，社会风气）。

c 又像手抓物体的动作。创造出了 cat（猫），catch（抓，接住，赶上），capture（抓住，抓拍图像），captivate（吸引）等词。

c 从手抓状又可引申为控制、操纵。如 control（控制），console（控制台，安慰）。

c 的半圆形也象征着覆盖上物体。如 cover（盖上，覆盖，掩护，报道），cap（帽子，瓶盖）。

D d

（门；坐；上小下大的物品；向下；弓形；半圆形屋顶）

字母 D d，大写的 D 在古时是用来描绘拱门或呈门形形状物体的象形符号。在古腓尼基语和希伯来语中，D 叫作 daleth，具有"门"的含义，相当于希腊字母 Δ（delta）。

字母 d 的外形像一只坐着的狗，造出了英语单词 dog（狗）。

同时，d 也像上小下大的物品，如 bed（床）表示床的两旁各有一个上小下大的床架，中间躺着一个弯腰睡觉的人（e）。单词 beard（胡子）可理解为耳朵（ear）以下两边脸颊上逐渐增多的胡子，尤其指下巴上的胡子。

从字母 d 上小下大的形状可引申出"向下"之意，比如 down（向下），dip（蘸），drop（落下），decrease（下降），diminish（减少）等词。

当然，大写的 D 也形似"弓"，可转义为"发射""张开""开始"等意，比如 dart（飞镖），dash（猛冲），do（做），drive（赶走，驾驶，干劲，道路名称的命名）等词。

大写的 D 也是个半圆形，像一个屋顶，所以创造了 dome（穹顶，圆形屋顶），domestic（家庭的，国内的），dominate（支配，俯视）。

E e

(窗户；出去；眼睛；植物发芽；叶子)

字母 E e 是英语里使用最多的字母。在腓尼基语和希伯来语中，E 是代表窗户的象形符号，读作 he，相当于希腊字母 E（epsilon）。

字母 e 形容窗户打开的样子，表示出来。如 exit（出口），emerge（浮现，出现），emit（排放污染物），evade（逃避责任，躲避税收），escape（逃跑），erupt（爆发，喷发），escort（护送，护卫）。

e 又像眼睛，所以 eye（眼睛）是中间的一个鼻子 y 加上旁边的两只眼睛。单词 see（看见）表示一个人弯下了腰（s），用两只眼睛（ee）发现了某件东西。单词 weep（哭泣）描绘了泪水（w）从两只眼睛（ee）中滑落的表情。单词 deem（认为）指的是一个人站在山上（m）向下看（ee）的思考状态。单词 esteem（尊敬，敬重）是由 est-（表示最高级）与 deem（认为）合成的，指用目光关注他人的最高程度，表示尊敬、敬重。

此外，e 还有植物发芽和叶子的象形含义。单词 earth（土壤，地面，地球）指能让植物发芽生长的泥土，e 是植物刚刚发芽的样子，a 表示"正在"，有 on, in 或 at 的含义，如 asleep（睡着的），abed（在床上的），ashore（在岸上），r 表示植物向上继续分裂生长的形态，th 表示 the，在词根里 the 指神，创造了单词 theology（神学），所以名词前要求加 the 是表示神创造了万物，因此，earth 指神创造的土地能孕育植物的发芽生长；单词 leave（树叶）就是指细长的树枝上长出了许多 e 状的叶子，l 表示叶子细长，v 表示树叶交叉，指叶子很多，彼此互相交叉生长在一起的状态。

F f

(源于 V；木栓，木钉；长发；女性；飞行，飞扬，飘落)

字母 F f 是英语字母表中的第六个字母，源于腓尼基语第六个象形字母，该字母形似今天的英语字母 Y，代表木栓或木钉（peg），在腓尼基语和希伯来语中的名称为 waw。中世纪的重罪犯（felon）的左脸颊会被打上 F 的印记，以示惩戒。

字母 f 象形女性的披肩长发，许多和女性有关的词汇都以 f 开头。如 female（女性的）就是在 male（男性）一词前面加上 f（披肩长发）和大大的眼睛 e，代表女性的两大特征；feed（喂养）指女性养育后代；feel（触摸，感觉）指细腻敏感的女性（f）睁大双眼（ee）观察感知世界，并用她长长的手臂（l）去触摸，产生了 feeling（感情）；feeble（虚弱的，无力的）指女性纤弱的体质；女性的感情激烈起来会像火（fire）一样燃烧，所以 fire 表示"火"，指具有女性（f）气质的人（i）很重感情，有时会冒出火苗（r）来；生活中人们常把错事、坏事归罪到女性身上，给她们打上重罪犯（felon）的 F 印记，所以 fault（错误），flaw（缺陷）中也含有表示女性意义的字母 f。

由 f 的披肩长发状可引申出飞行、飞扬、飘落等象形含义。如 fly（飞），flag（旗帜），flutter（振翅），flare（信号弹），float（漂流），flow（流动），fall（落下），fluctuate（价格波动），flu（感冒），influence（影响）。

G g

（弯曲的骆驼头颈；走动；地球；土地；运动）

字母 G g 在古腓尼基语和希伯来语中是用来描绘骆驼的头部和颈部轮廓的象形字母，叫作 gimel。后来希腊人借用了该符号，写作 Γ（gamma）。实际上，字母 G 与字母 C 都源于同一腓尼基字母。在最初的拉丁字母表里也没有字母 G，含 g 音和含 k 音的词汇都用字母 C 表示。公元 3 世纪以后，古罗马人根据 C 创造了 G，从此 C 表示 k 音，G 则表示 g 音。字母 G 的骆驼头颈含义可指代骆驼在土地沙漠上跋涉千里的一生，赋予了这个字母"走动"的内涵。

字母 g 的小写形式描绘了太阳围绕地球旋转而带来的日夜交替现象。白天，象征着太阳的圆形在上面，夜晚，它就走到了下面，因此 g 指"地球，土地，运动"。go（走，去）就是地球（g）的自转运动（go）。great（大的，伟大的）中的 g 是土地，r 是向上分裂、农作物生长的状态，gr 组合后指在土地上长出了粮食，象征着古人的刀耕火种，eat 有吃的含义，所以 great 是"耕地"和"吃饭"两个意思的组合。对古人来说，耕地和吃饭是生活中最大（great）的事情。g 创造的单词还有 ground（地，地面），geology（地质学），grow（生长），globe（地球仪，地球，世界，球体），green（绿色），grass（草），grape（葡萄）等。

H h

（篱笆，栅栏；梯子；台阶；椅子；高，高处）

字母 H h，像其他字母一样，H 的历史也可以通过拉丁语和希腊语追溯到腓尼基语字母表。在腓尼基语中，和 H 相应的字母还有上下两条横杠，代表篱笆或栅栏，叫作 heth。

大写的 H 像梯子和台阶的正面，小写的 h 像台阶的侧面。台阶和梯子都是用于攀登的，所以英语中 h 表示"高""高处"的意思。如 high（高的）就是指登高（h）的一个人（i）走（g）到了另一高处（h）。h 看起来也像一把用来坐的椅子，chair（椅子）描绘的就是人（i）弯下腰（c）坐到椅子（h）上的动作。与 h 相关的词汇还有 hall（高耸的大厅），happy（幸福的，快乐的），hot（热），hail（高呼万岁，冰雹），hand（高举起来的手），hope（内心升起的希望），hike（徒步旅行，价格大幅度上升）。

I i

（手指；罗马数字的 1；人形；小）

  字母 I i，第九个字母 I 源于腓尼基字母表中叫作 yodh 的象形字母，该字母象征人的手指。起初，小写字母 i 没有上面的一点。i 上面的点是 11 世纪以后抄写员为区分字母 I 的连写形式（如单词 filii 中的后两个 ii）与字母 u 才加上去的。此外，在 19 世纪以前，i 和 j 的书写或印刷形式是可以互换的，词典也不把它们作为两个不同的字母进行区别对待。在 Samuel Johnson（1709—1784）编写的《英语词典》中，iambic 就排在了 jamb 和 jangle 这两个词的中间。英语字母 I 相当于希腊字母的 I（iota）。在罗马数字中 I 表示 1。

  i 象形人形，含有人的头和身体，所以 i 指人。在西方世界中，人们普遍认为最重要的人是自己（I），所以 I（我）这个词永远要大写，这反映出了西方文化中的个人主义倾向。但是，如果把 I（我）浸泡到水（water）里后，就不是大写了，它变成了 waiter（侍者），指侍者的工作与水有关，他们整天与汗水、口水、清洁用水打交道；单词 isolate（隔离）是由 i（人）加 solo（独自的）复合而成，表示一个人独处的状态就是被别人隔离；在 identity（身份）中，字母 i 也表示人的含义，指人的社会身份；单词 imitate（模仿）可理解为一个人（i）去 m（模仿）另一个人（i）的行为。

  i 也是最小的字母，具有"小"的含义。如 drip（水滴），rip（一点点地撕开，撕碎），grip（紧紧地抓住，控制，理解），miniature（微缩模型），miniskirt（迷你裙），minister（神父，大臣），minimal（极小的），microsoft（微软公司），minority（少数），minor（次要的，未成年人，辅修学科，小调）。

J j

（跳跃；连接）

  字母 J j，字母 J 是在莎士比亚时代后期（post-Shakespearean times）约 1630 年出现的，它和字母 V 并称为英语字母表中最年轻的两个字母。在英国国王詹姆斯一世于 1611 年颁行的《圣经》英译本中就没有 J 这个字母。正如 G 是基于 C 变化而来的，字母 J 是由字母 I 衍生出来的，是在 I 下面加上一条尾巴形成的。小写的 j 就像一个人（i）跳起来的样子。然而，直到 19 世纪，I 和 J 的书写形式和印刷形式仍然可以互换，并没有完全分离。

  j 是比 i 更长的线，表示人的跳跃动作或跳起去触摸东西，形成连接的状态。如 jump（跳）是指人跨越（j）大水坑（u），翻过大山（m），身体向前倾斜（p）的动作；jungle 指需要蹦蹦跳跳才能穿过的丛林；jet 表示飞机像被弹射出去一样跳到了空中；jog（慢跑）用来形容人在做跑步运动时跳跃的身姿；joy（高兴，喜悦）描绘了人们围成了一个圆圈，载歌载舞的快乐气氛。根据 j 表示连接的含义创造了 join（参加，连接），joint（关节，联合的，共同的），conjunction（连词）。

K k

（手，手掌；王冠；大，重要；打开，开口；破裂声，咔咔声）

字母 K k 的来源可追溯到古腓尼基语。在腓尼基字母表里，K 的象形符号代表人的手。在希伯来语中，它被叫作 kaph，含有"手、手掌"之意。后来希腊人把它写作 K（kappa）。在古罗马，犯诽谤罪的犯人前额会被烙上 K 的标记，即 kalumnia，是英语中 calumny（诽谤）的意思。

大小写 K k 的象形含义基本相同，把它横过来写像一个王冠，衍生出了 king（国王）一词。k 还可以转义为"大""重要"，如 kind（亲切的，和蔼的，种类）形容像国王一样拥有宽广仁慈的胸怀。

字母 k 还像一个开口的形状，表示打开、开口、张口之意。如 key（钥匙）在开门时，需要用眼睛（e）来观察；know（知道）指打开（k）门（n）后，看到里面有女人，o 和 w 都代表女人。know 原意是与女人同房，在圣经中使用的 know 就具有这个含义，后来又转义为"知道"，指同房后夫妻之间变得相知相爱。

k 又可喻指"破裂"的声音，如 speak（说话），break（打破），knife（小刀），knock（敲击声，碰撞），suck（吸，吮，啜），cock（公鸡），drink（喝），joke（开玩笑），kiss（吻）。

L l

（鞭子；男性；长形物；长时间）

在腓尼基和希伯来字母表中，字母 L l 叫作 lamedh，是表示刺棒（oxgoad）或鞭子的象形符号。希腊语中它对应的字母为 Λ（lambda）。

字母 l 象形个子高的人，因为男性一般个子较高，所以 l 通常表示男性或男人。如 love（爱，爱情）就是指男人（l）和女人（o）彼此用眼睛（e）交叉（v）望着对方，含情脉脉，爱意绵绵（love）。

l 有着细长的形状，可用来表示长形物或长时间处于某种状态之中。如 line（直线）就是先用一条直线 l 测量距离，再用眼睛（e）向里面（in）看看直不直；light（光线）描绘了天上的光线（l）直直地照射下来，照在了最需要它的人（i）身上，引导着他走到（g）高处（h）；leg（腿），loaf（面包），lace（带子），eyelash（眼睫毛），long（长），linger（徘徊，逗留），loose（松，松弛的）中的字母 l 也与细长形物体或长时间处于某种状态之中有关。

M m

(海浪；水；母亲，妈妈；罗马数字的 1 000；山，山峰；
男性；坚强，牢固；多；门牙)

字母 M m 也可追溯到古腓尼基语。腓尼基人勇于探险，以海上贸易远近闻名，曾远航至西班牙海岸。字母 M 在腓尼基字母表里是表示海浪的象形符号。希伯来语中把它叫作 mem，意思是"水"。希腊语中与其对应的字母为 M（mu）。在中世纪，犯杀人罪（manslaugter）的重犯左手拇指上往往被烙以 M 印记。M 在罗马数字中表示 1 000（拉丁语作 mille）。

M 表示水，和它有关的词汇有 marine（海洋的），mermaid（美人鱼），merchant（海上经商的人），mercury（水星）等。水是生命之母，所以人们用 mama 来称呼自己母亲，形容妈妈给儿女的滋养。如 maid（女仆）指像妈妈一样照顾主人的女仆人；maternal（慈母似的，母性的）指如母亲般的；mature（成熟的）指像妈妈一样成熟的。

大小写的 M m 都像山峰，创造了 mountain（山）和 camel（骆驼），骆驼的背上有两座驼峰（m），是吃苦耐劳、坚韧不拔的动物。m 可转指男性，因为男人（man）的性格需要坚强如山，如 manly（有男子汉气概的），male（男性），masculine（男性的，有男性特征的）。m 对应的是女人（woman）的柔情似水（water），两者山水相依，不可分离。

除了有"水""山""男性""坚强""牢固"的意思，m 还引申出了"多"的含义。人多力量大，东西多了就会变得坚强、牢固，坚不可摧。如 many（多）和 much（多），many 用于修饰可数名词，a 指牛头、人头，所以是可数的，many people（许多人）；much 修饰不可数名词，u 指装在桶里的水，水是不可数的，much water（许多水）。

m 还像嘴里的两颗门牙，创造了 mouth（口，嘴巴）一词，形容人一张嘴（mouth）就露出了牙齿（m）；还有一种牙齿（m）特别厉害的动物是 mouse（老鼠），它能用牙齿（m）把房子（house）咬出许多个洞来；mock（嘲笑）则是指人们露出门牙取笑他人的表情。

N n

(波浪；鱼；门；连接)

字母 N n 在埃及象形文字中呈波浪形，在腓尼基语中叫作 nun，意为"鱼"，在希腊语中对应的字母为 N（nu）。

N 实际上是字母 M（水）的一个变形，所以也含有水的意思。它构成的词汇有 navy（海军），navigate（海上导航），nation（建立在水边的国家），nature（有水的大自然）。

小写字母 n 像一个门形，如 in 表示一个人（i）在门（n）的里面，意思是"在……里面"；又如 inn（小酒馆），ink（能渗入纸张的墨水），innovation（从内心产生的创新）。

门有连接内部和外部的作用，所以 n 还可以引申出"连接"的意思，如 connect（连接，联系），next（接下来的）。

O o

（眼睛；圆形；滚动，转动；张开的嘴；太阳）

字母 O o，许多语言中都含有形似 O 的字母，指代人的眼睛。在一些古老的字母表中，O 中还会加个小圆点，表示瞳孔。在腓尼基语中，O 叫作 'ayin，即"眼睛"，而在古英语里 O 叫作 oedel，意思是"家"。

O o 这个字母不论大小写都是英语中最圆的字母，所以跟圆形有关的事物都和它相关。如 boot（长统靴）指大头靴（b）的形状是长筒的，从上面看就是两个圆圈（oo），穿在脚（t）上；又如 good（好的），指人能够平稳地走（g）在两个圆圈上（oo），并开始做（d）事，处于很好的状态（be in a good state）；roll（滚动，卷轴），loop（圈，环），scroll（卷轴，滚动计算机屏幕来阅读），orbit（轨道）中的字母 o 也都表示滚动或转动。

字母 o 也可表示张开的嘴。如 order（命令，秩序，订单），oral（口语的），oracle（神谕），oration（正式演讲），organism（用嘴吃东西的生物是有机物）。

O 还有太阳的含义。如 orient（太阳升起的地方是东方世界，确定方位），originate（起源于，源自）。

P p

（嘴；向前；向上、突出、顶端；象声词，啪啪声）

字母 P p，它是英语字母表的第 16 个字母，古腓尼基人和希伯来人称之为 pe，意为"嘴"。希腊语中相应的字母为 Π（pi）。lip（嘴唇）中的 l 和 p 就是形容长长的嘴。16 世纪有一位名叫 Placentius 的修道士写了一首题为 Pugna Porcorum 的诗，由 253 个六音步诗行构成，诗中每个词的首字母都是 p，这是史无前例的。

P 的外形像一个向前倾斜的人，喻指向前。如 progress（进步，进展），propel（推动），pronounce（宣布），project（投影，项目，预测），propagate（宣传）。

同时，p 还可以引申出向上、突出、顶端之意。如 up（从下往上），tip（尖端），top（顶部），cap（帽子），pile（堆），pine（松树）等。

P 也可以作为象声词使用，表示啪啪的声音。如 slap（扇脸，掌掴），flap（拍动翅膀），clap（拍手），rap（说唱，极速敲击，严厉批评）。

Q q

（猴子；好奇；女性发髻）

　　字母 Q q 在英语字母表中是第 17 个字母，它是由腓尼基语和希伯来语中的第 19 个象形字母 qoph 演变而来的。Q 的形状有点像倒挂在树上垂着尾巴的猴子，有强烈的好奇心，难怪腓尼基语把该字母叫作 qoph，意思就是"猴子"。在英语中，Q 后面几乎总跟着 U，写作 qu。Q 很少单独地出现在单词词尾，除非是外来语。

　　Q q 像女性头部的侧面，并扎有一个发髻。因此，以 q 开头的单词可能与女性或其特征有关。如 queen（王后）指王后是一个女性（q），认为自己什么都没有，两手空空（u），只能用两只眼睛（ee）替国王看守后宫的大门（n）而已；又如 quest（探索）是说女性（q），什么都不知道，头脑空空的（u），所以睁大眼睛（e），站着（st）去观察探索世界；将 quest 加上名词后缀 -tion 后会生成 question（问题），指女性好奇好问的思想状态；queer（奇怪的，难以理解的）也是说女人（q）无知，很空洞（u），瞪大两只眼睛（ee），招手（r）向别人发问，呈现出很好奇（queer）的表情；inquire（询问）指的是从内心对某事发出的疑问，如在奥林匹克运动会体操比赛中运动员所提出的评分申诉和质疑，用的就是这个词；inquisition（盘问，查问）指昔日罗马天主教会惩罚异端教徒的宗教法庭，即异端裁判所或指对不同信仰的宗教人士进行盘问审判的地方。

R r

（头部；狗叫声；火苗燃烧状；植物发芽分枝；
跑步；伸手，招手；升起）

　　字母 R r 是英语字母表中的第 18 个字母，它是由腓尼基语和希伯来语中的第 20 个象形字母演变而来的。腓尼基人称之为 reš，意思是"头"。从古罗马开始，R 就一直被称作 dog's letter 或 snarling letter，因为 R 的发音类似狗的叫声 r-r-r-r 或 gr-r-r-r。英国剧作家、诗人 Ben Johnson（1572—1637）在其所著的《英文文法》(The English Grammar) 一书中这样写道："R is the dog's letter, and hurreth in the sound, the tongue striking the inner palate, with a trembling about the teeth."。单词 roar（吼叫，咆哮）指的就是像狗一样大声叫喊。单词 rumble（发出隆隆声，打雷的隆隆声）指发出狗叫般的持续而低沉的声音。在莎翁的《罗密欧与朱丽叶》中，朱丽叶的保姆和罗密欧在谈及罗密欧的姓氏时说，Romeo 和 rosemary（迷迭香叶，一种与爱情相关的灌木叶子，原意是留住记忆）两个词都以字母 R 开头，暗示着这对情侣彼此忠贞的爱情就像狗对主人的忠诚那样坚不可摧。

　　r 的外形像火苗燃烧状。如 fire（火）形容火苗（r）一点点（i）飞起来（f）的状态；又如 ring（铃声鸣响）指失火（r）后人们立刻鸣钟示警发出的声音。

r 又像植物发芽时分枝的形状，如 branch（分支），rate（比率，比例，费用，评估，评价），root（植物的根部）。由于河流一般都有分支，所以创造了 river（河流），rush（急冲）。brother（兄弟）中的 b 上小下大，可指男性的稳固牢靠，r 则表示分枝，放在一起后指兄弟也是一个树上的两个分枝。spring（春天，泉水，跳跃，弹簧）可以形容人跳跃时的动作，包括弯腰（s），前倾（p），分开双腿起跳（r）和跳起来后动作的持续性（ing）；春天（spring）也是万物复苏（r）和孩子们蹦蹦跳跳的季节，所以 spring 有"春天"之意；弹簧（spring）的特征是有弹性，会反弹，周而复始，像人们不停跳跃的状态，所以 spring 又被赋予了"弹簧"的含义。

r 还喻指跑步，是跳跃前的准备工作。如 run（跑）表示人跑（r）过一块空地或水域（u），到达一个门（n）。

r 形似一个人做出伸手或招手的动作。如 girl（女孩）表示一个扭动着（g）身体跳舞的女孩（i）用手臂（r）做出各种舞姿，亭亭玉立的样子（l）。

r 也表示升起。如 rise（升起），rank（排名），riot（骚乱，暴动）。

S s

（牙齿；弯曲状；弯腰状；弯曲的音符；某种声响，
嘶嘶声；女性身体曲线）

字母 S s，在腓尼基语和希伯来语中，S 叫作 šin，意为"牙齿"，它的形状很像今天的字母 W。S 现在的字形是进入拉丁语之后逐渐演变形成的。在希腊语中它对应的字母为 Σ（sigma）。

S s 的大小写形式均呈弯曲状，像一条蛇（snake）。如 size（大小），shape（形状），shake（摇动，震动），sleep（弯曲身体睡觉）中的 s 都含有弯曲之意。S 也可指弯腰状，如 sit（坐），指弯下腰（s）的人（i），坐在桌子（t）旁；又如 session（会议），squat（蹲，蹲坐）。

字母 s 还可指弯曲的音符或某种声响。如 sing（唱，唱歌）和 song（歌曲）中 s 表示唱出的音符，ing 和 ong 都表示歌唱时所拖的长音，i 和 o 表示张开的嘴；又如 scissors（剪子）的读音是在模仿用剪刀裁剪纸张时发出的嘶嘶声。

此外，s 还可以用来形容女性的身体曲线，如 sister（姐妹）表示两个身材（s）较好的女子（i）间的亲属关系。

T t

（记号；树；支撑物；箭头符号；十字形）

字母 T t 是从腓尼基象形字母演变而来的，其早先的字形类似于今天英语字母的 X，叫作 taw，意思是"记号"（mark）。它在希腊语中对应的字母为 T（tau）。

T 的外形就像一棵树，创造了 tree（树）一词，r 表示分枝，ee 代表叶子。tile（瓷砖，瓦片）指树上的一片片小树叶（i）像房顶的瓦片。tent（帐篷）指用前后两棵树（t）作为支撑搭起帐篷，中间有窗眼（e）和门（n）。tense（拉紧的）则是形容固定帐篷的绳子被拉紧的状态。

T 的外形还像十字形，起到支撑的作用，可转义为支撑物，指"站立"或"工具"，如 foot（足，脚）。又如 table（桌子），stable（稳定的，马厩），statue（雕像）。stand（站立）表示一个人从坐着（s）的状态到靠脚（t）站起来的状态；tool（工具）中的四个字母分别象形各种工具的不同形状；stool（凳子）指能够支撑身体的工具。

T 的外形也像箭头符号，表示方向。如介词 to 就是指方向、方位；又如 top（上部），tip（指尖，尖端，小费，小建议），touch（触碰，使感动），torrent（湍流，急流）。

U u

（源于 V；空的装水容器；空空的；水）

字母 U u 是由字母 V 派生而来的。早在 19 世纪前的数百年间，这两个字母就如同 I 和 J 一样，可以互换使用，在英语书籍的编写上也不区分。在 16 和 17 世纪出版的图书中，upon 常拼作 vpon，而 have 也常拼作 haue。

U u 的大小写形式像一个空的装水容器，表示"空空的"或"水"的含义。如 universe（宇宙）指无限广阔、浩瀚无垠的宇宙像海水一样无边无际；cup（杯子）指人张开嘴（c），喝杯子（u）中的水，身体向前倾（p）的动作；umbrella（雨伞）指代一种用来防雨水的工具；urine（尿）用 u 开头是指尿像水一样是液体，它是人体的排泄物；tube（管子）指水在管子内部可以流动，t 表示方向，be 表示物体。

V v

（木栓，木钉；罗马数字的 5；山谷；交叉；空空的；胜利的手势；
衍生出字母 F、U、W、Y）

字母 V v 是英语字母表中两个最年轻的字母之一（另一个为 J），它在莎士比亚时代之后约 1630 年出现。V 同时又是 U，W，Y 这三个字母的祖先，甚至连 F 也是从 V 派生而来的。字母 V 源于约公元前 1000 年腓尼基字母表中的第 6 个象形字母，该字母形似今天英语字母的 Y，叫作 waw，意思是"木栓"或"木钉"。公元前 900 年后，希腊人借用了该字母，并由它衍生出两个新字母，一个后来演变成了英语字母 F，另一个则演变为 V 和 Y。19 世纪以前，V 和 U 这两个字母是不加区分的，可互换使用。V 在罗马数字里表示 5。

V v 的大小写形式像空荡的山谷（valley），同时又是交叉的样子，有"空空的"含义。如 vain（虚荣的，徒劳的）指人的虚荣心是内心空洞的表现，追求虚荣感是徒劳无获的；又如 vacant（职位空缺的，表情茫然的），vacuous（无智慧的，没有意义的），vacation（假期）中的 v 也都含有空的意思。

另外，v 也象征着胜利的手势，如 victory（胜利）。

W w

（源于 V；水波状；女性；弯曲；交叉；草生长的样子）

字母 W w 和 U, Y 一样，也是由 V 派生而来。其实 W 系双 V 连写而成的，本应读作 double V。W 之所以读作 double U 是因为在 19 世纪以前的几个世纪里 U 和 V 一直不分，可以互换。V 既是 V 的符号，也是 U 的符号，U 也常写成 V，如 upon 经常拼作 vpon。法语中的 W 就读作 double V。

W w 的大小写形式呈水波状，常与女性联系相关。女人柔情似水，所以英语中的"女人"是 woman，指女人是水做的；wash（洗）表示用水（w）冲洗掉灰尘（ash）；well（水井，好）指为了找水而挖的水井，水井像眼睛（e）一样明亮，要用长竹竿或长绳（ll）放下去取水。过去的游牧民族每到一个地方最重要的事是打井（well）取水，井出水了，生活就变好了（well），所以 well 又转义为"好"。

w 也可引申为弯曲、交叉之意。如 write（写）指用笔写出来的弯弯曲曲的各种文字；wrong（错误的）中的 w 代表走弯路，走错路；wrap（包装，总结），wrestle（摔跤），wrinkle（皱纹）和 wring（拧衣服）中的 w 都含弯曲之意。

w 又像草生长的样子，所以创造了 weed（杂草）。

X x

（鱼；罗马数字的 10；阿拉伯语的未知数；接吻的象征符号；十字交叉形状；四面八方）

字母 X x 是英语字母表的第 24 个字母，相当于希腊字母表的第 22 个字母 X（chi）。前者源于后者，后者则源于腓尼基字母表中一个表示"鱼"的象形字母 samekh。X 在罗马数字中代表 10。在代数和数学中，X 通常用来表示未知数。当数学从阿拉伯传入欧洲时，阿拉伯语中表示未知数的 shei 一词被译成了 xei，于是字母 X 就成了表示未知数的常用符号。关于字母 X 的由来，还有另外一种说法，有人认为 X 原为象征接吻的象形符号，观察 x 的左右部分，确实看起来有点像两张嘴在交叉接吻，这种解释可能出自民俗语源。

X x 的大小写形式都表示十字交叉的形状，常喻指四面八方。如 anxious（焦急的），表示一个人（a）正在门（n）口坐着，期待着四面八方（x）来的一点点消息（i），非常的焦急（anxious），-ous 是形容词后缀，表示程度过多的；Xerox（复印，复印件）指在复印机上交叉放置纸张后复印文件。Xerox（美国施乐公司）是一个著名商标和品牌。施乐公司于 1906

年成立于美国康涅狄格州费尔菲尔德县。作为商标，"施乐"只用来标识施乐公司的各种产品和服务。"施乐"商标通常放在名词前面起到形容词的作用，如施乐复印机、施乐打印机等；xylophone（木琴）是指由长短不同的长方形木块所组成的打击乐器。

Y y

（源于 V；代数中第二个未知数；分叉状；生育；生长）

字母 Y y 是从 V 派生而来，它的起源可追溯到希腊语中被称为毕达哥拉斯字母（the letter of Pythagoras）中的 upsilon。在代数中，Y 常用来表示第二个未知数。

Y y 的外形呈分叉状，表示人生的道路必有分叉，所以 way（路，道路）是指一个人（a）前面是弯曲的道路（w），后面是分叉的道路（y），需要他做出选择；yes（表示肯定）就是给别人让路（y），允许走，no（表示否定）就是在别人门（n）前放一块圆石（o），不让走。

由于分叉、分支是一种生育、生长的状态，所以 y 又可表示生育、生长。如 yield（产出，产量，屈服，让步），yeast（酵母）。

Z z

（宙斯；"之"字形；闪电状；声音词，滋滋声）

字母 Z z 的读音有三种，在英式英语中读作 Zed，在美式英语中读作 zee，在古英语中读作 izzard。Z 源于希腊字母表中的第 6 个字母 Z（zeta），而希腊语的 Z 又来源于腓尼基语。Z 象征着宇宙之主宙斯（Zeus），他的武器是闪电长矛。

Z z 的大小写字母均像"之"字形，所以 zigzag（之字形）表示一个人（i）在之字形（z）的路上行走（g）；zoo（动物园）指为了把更多的圆形笼子（oo）连接起来，便于游客参观，动物园铺设了许多之字形（z）的道路。

同时，z 又象形闪电的形状，可指眩晕、热情、狂热的状态。如 zeal（热情，热忱），zest（热情，热心），dizzy（眩晕的），dazzle（使目眩）。

此外，z 还可以表示声音，指滋滋声。如 zoom（放大或缩小图像），zip（拉链），drizzle（蒙蒙细雨）。

3

英语词汇学习的难点

在英语词汇学习过程中，词汇学习的难点主要体现在三个方面，分别是一词多义现象、同义词辨析和形近易混词区分。其中最难掌握的是一词多义现象，因为每个英语单词平均下来都有 3~5 个不同的意思，词义多的单词甚至会有 8~10 个不同的含义。下面将会围绕这三个方面进行详细的阐述。

3.1 一词多义现象

一词多义现象指词汇学习不是简单地记忆一个词义，它还涉及词义的不同层面。对词汇的理解应当是详细的、多层面的，要善于分析单词的多种含义、使用语境和固定搭配等。如 abandon（放弃，放纵）是由前缀 a-（表示"正处于某种状态"），加上 ban（禁止）和 on（表示持续的状态）三部分组成的，所以指"正在禁止某事"，即"放弃"，如 abandon ship 弃船；但它还有第二个词义是"放纵"，用作 abandon oneself to doing sth.，如 abandon oneself to drinking（放纵自己酗酒）。abandon 的第二个词义很少被关注，这反映了词汇学习中最容易忽视的一个环节，就是词义掌握不全。那么如何快速掌握这两个词义呢？最好的方式是把它们组合成一句耳熟能详的话语，例如"放纵自己就是放弃生活"，即 "To abandon oneself is to abandon one's life."。

claim 由词根 cl-（close 靠近）加 aim（目标）构成，指一个人紧盯着自己的目标，想得到它的状态。它主要有三个意思，分别是声称，领取，索赔。如 He claims that the gold belongs to his own.（他声称金子属于他自己）；baggage claim（领取行李）；insurance claim form（保险索赔表）。

game（比赛，猎物，野味）是根据字母 g（go 走）和字母 m（move 移动）组合而成的，其本义指奔跑的猎物或野味，gaze at game（凝视猎物）；比赛是它的引申义，如 Olympic Games（奥林匹克运动会）。

　　gear 的本义为"齿轮"，由于齿轮的咬合作用使机械协调运作，所以 gear 引申义为"调节、适应"，gear the policy to the international situation（调节政策以适应国际局势）；因为汽车的变速箱是通过调节齿轮转速来实现变速的，所以 gear 还引申出"挡位"的含义，shift the gear（换挡位）；另外，gear（齿轮）是所有武器的必备零件，转义为"装备"，经常在电影中看到作战之前，军队指挥官会说一句"gear up！"（带上装备，准备好战斗！）。

　　ache 的基础词义是"痛"，可作名词和不及物动词，源于字母 A，指尖锐的物体接触皮肤时的刺痛感。它的本义较易理解，但当遇到这样的句子 I am aching for him. 或 She was aching to join in the fight. 时，读者会被 ache 的词义困扰。字典里对 ache 的释义主要有"痛"和"渴望"两层意思。通过简单的联想，可以理解其"渴望"的引申义是由"思念之痛"造成的，是"痛"的心理原因，所以前一例句的句意是"我很渴望见到他"，后一例句的句意是"她渴望参加战斗"。

　　许多耳熟能详的词汇都有不为人熟知的含义，即在某个专业领域具有特殊的词义。如 dismiss 的普通含义是"解散，解雇，不理睬"，但在法律英语中，该词的意思则是"驳回案件"，The case was dismissed owing to lack of evidence.（由于证据不足，该案被驳回了）；balance 最常见的意思为"平衡"，但在金融英语中它的含义为"余额，余款"，My bank balance is not enough.（我的银行账户里余额不多了）；term 的本义为"学期，术语"，在商务英语里的含义变为"条款"，Delivery is within the terms of this contract.（合同规定要送货）；joint 的一般含义为"联合的，共同的"，但在医学英语中的含义则为"关节"，The knee joint is very crucial to a sportsman.（膝关节对运动员很重要）；非计算机专业的学生上机遇到 boot 一词时经常感到困惑，因为他们只知道 boot 是"靴子"，而对它在计算机英语中表示"启动"之意一无所知；科技英语中的 conduct 衍生出"导电、导热"的含义，conduct electricity or conduct heat，也有"进行研究、进行调查、进行实验"的意思，conduct research，conduct a survey，conduct an experiment，不再是日常英语中"指挥乐队"的词义，conduct a band，conduct an orchestra；在商务英语中 ship 的含义不再是"船"，而是"运输"，The goods are ready for being shipped.（这批货物现在可以装运了）。

　　当见到 content 时，很少有读者会注意该词重音上的变化以及这种变化给它词义带来的影响。需要提醒的是当 content 作为名词且重音在第一音节时，读作 ['kɔntent]，词义有三个，分别是"（书籍的）目录"、"（某领域的）内容"和"（某种物质的）含量"；但当 content 的重音放在第二音节上时，读作 [kən'tent]，它的词性由名词变成了形容词，意思是"心满意足的"，She is content with the result.（她对结果非常满意）。由此可见，单词重音上的变化会改变词义，使其内涵变得更加多元化。

　　一词多义现象是英语词汇中普遍存在的、最具有代表性的特征，读者应当把词汇学习的重点放在记忆单词的多层含义上，学会从上下文中推测生词词义，在语境中体会词汇的多变语义。

3.2 同义词辨析

英语同义词是指在词义上相同或相近的一组单词。然而，同义词的词义也是有差别的，它们有各自不同的词义来源。如 leap 和 plunge 都有"跳"的含义。leap 主要指"蛙跳，纵身跃下，重大历史性飞跃"，a frog leap, a cliff leap, a historical leap；而 plunge 主要指跳水时发出的声音或价格猛然下跌，plunge into the water（跳水），Price is plunging.（价格大跌）。

fabulous 和 fantastic 都有"美好的"的词义。fabulous 有寓言般美好的含义，源于 fable（寓言），如《伊索寓言》(Aesop's Fables)；fantastic 源于 fan（粉丝），强调粉丝觉得特别的好，如 She is a fabulous story teller.（她讲故事很棒），I don't think that the star's performance is fantastic.（我不认为明星的表演很棒）。

金融词汇 dividend, incentive, bonus, revenue, benefit, premium 都含有"奖励、奖金"的意思，每个词在使用搭配上却有所不同，dividend 用于股票分红，dividend policy（股利政策）；incentive 用于公司奖励，a tour incentive（旅游奖励）；bonus 用于工资以外的津贴，year-end bonus（年终奖金）；revenue 用于企业收益，sales revenue（产品销售收入）；benefit 指公共福利，benefit system（福利制度）；premium 指保险费或补偿金，insurance premium（保险费），land premium（土地补价）。

区分同义词的关键是在句子中和语境中体会单词的含义，了解其使用的固定搭配和惯用场景，掌握其在语义范围、强度、褒贬等方面的差异。如 disaster 和 catastrophe，disaster 指"灾难，灾祸"，由前缀 dis-（四散分离）加词根 -astro（星星）构成，指天上出现流星雨的现象。古希腊人认为流星雨代表着灾祸。disaster 是一般用语，语义程度较轻，而 catastrophe 指"大灾难，大灾祸"，语义程度较重。

amaze, astonish, scare, surprise 和 startle，这组同义词都含有"惊奇，惊恐"之意。amaze 源于河流 Amazon，指亚马孙河物产丰富，给人们带来许多惊喜；astonish 源于 stone，指宝石发光让人惊奇；scare 源于 scar（伤疤），指有刀疤的人惊吓到他人；surprise 由前缀 sur-（在上面），up（向上）和 rise（升起）组成，指礼物突然冒出弹出时带来的惊喜、惊讶；startle 源于 stare（凝视），指受到惊吓后导致的目光呆滞的表情。可见，只有在了解同义词的不同词源后，才能在适当的语境下准确地使用它们。

同义词的感情色彩也有不同，如 statesman（政治家）和 politician（政客），absurd（荒谬的）和 ridiculous（荒唐的），economical（节约的）和 mean（吝啬的）。在这三组同义词中，前者的情感色彩是褒义词，后者却是贬义词。又如 slim, thin 和 skinny 三个词都有"瘦"的意思。slim 是褒义词，形容女性，a slim young girl（一个苗条的年轻少女）；thin 是中性词，two thin hands（一双瘦瘦的手）；skinny 在形容人时有贬义，a skinny man（一个骨瘦如柴的男人）。

英语中许多同义词的用法是固定的，要根据其习惯搭配来使用。比如，表示"一群"含义的词汇在英语中就有许多，a flock of sheep（一群羊），a group of people（一群人），a herd of cows（一群牛），a gangster of bandits（一群强盗），a pride of lions（一群狮子），a school of whales（一群鲸鱼）。

3.3 形近易混词区分

英语词汇中存在着大量拼写相似、读音相近的单词，这类词汇叫作形近易混词，简称形近词。英语中的形近易混词种类繁多，涉及面广，十分容易被混淆、错用、误用，产生歧义。在许多文献、考卷和翻译中，错用、滥用、误用形近词的现象屡见不鲜，像把 stationery（文具）错用为 stationary（不动的），把 through（穿过）当成了 thorough（彻底的），把 rough（粗糙的，粗略的，粗鲁的，艰难的）写成了 tough（棘手的，难办的，艰难的，坚强的），等等。

英语形近易混词的构成方式比较复杂，缺乏固定的规律性，想把它们进行精确分类是比较困难的。但根据词汇的音义相近程度和音位结构特征还是能够把大多数形近易混词归纳到某一范围之内的，便于词汇学习者的区分识别，降低他们在语言应用和选取词汇上产生歧义的可能性。形近易混词主要有以下几种分类。

3.3.1 按词义相近程度，形近易混词可分为近义形近词和异义形近词

1）近义形近词。近义形近词指英语单词的拼法相近，词义基本相近的形近词。这类词汇往往容易出现错读、错用的现象，造成语义表达不确切。如 passage 和 message：passage（文章），read passages（阅读文章）；message（消息，通信），give him a message（给他带个口信）。又如 literary 和 literate：literary（文学上的），literary work（文学作品）；literate（有文化的，有阅读和写作能力的），He is musically literate.（他懂音乐）。

2）异义形近词。异义形近词指英语单词的拼法相近，词义完全不同的形近词。如 contact 和 contract：contact（联系），keep in contact with sb.（与某人保持联系）；contract（合同），sign a contract with sb.（与人签订合同）。又如 industrial 和 industrious：industrial（工业的），an independent and integrated industrial（独立完整的工业体系）；industrious（勤劳的），the brave and industrious Chinese people（勇敢勤劳的中国人民）。再如 flip, rip, tip, lip, clip 这组具有代表性的异义形近词：flip（快速翻转，抛掷硬币，浏览书报，筋斗空翻，轻率的，轻浮的），There is quite an art to flipping pancakes.（翻煎饼真是门艺术）；rip（撕，扯），rip the letter open（撕开信封）；tip（尖端，小费，小建议），He kissed the tip of her nose.（他亲吻了一下她的鼻尖）；lip（嘴唇），His bottom lip was swollen.（他的下唇肿起来了）；clip（回形针，夹子，视频片段，弹夹，修剪），a wad of money in a gold clip（用金夹子夹着的一沓钞票）。

3.3.2 按形近易混词的所属词类（即单词的词性，指形容词、副词、动词、名词、介词、连词、助词等）不同，可分为同词类形近词与异词类形近词

1）同词类形近词。如 consequent 和 subsequent 都是形容词词性，但拼写上却稍有不同，

词义也不一样。consequent（作为结果的），the rise in inflation and consequent fall in demand（通货膨胀的加剧和随之而来的需求下降）；subsequent（随后的，后来的），subsequent pages of the book（接下来的书页）。

2）异词类形近词。如 principle 和 principal：principle（原则，原理），the basic principles of business management（企业管理的基本原理）；principal（主要的，首要的），the principal character in the book（书里的主人公）。又如 grand 和 grant：grand（宏伟的，巨大的），a grand hotel（豪华的大饭店）；grant（允许，批准，资助金），grant her wish（满足她的愿望）。再如 adapt，adopt 和 adept：adapt（适应，改编）中的前缀 ad- 表示强调，apt 是 appropriate（合适的）的缩写形式，组合后强调合适、适应，adapt to the circumstances（适应环境）；adopt（采纳，收养）中的前缀 ad- 表示强调，opt 是选择的意思，组合后指先选择再采纳，adopt the one child policy（采用独生子女政策）；adept（擅长于，专家，能手）中的前缀 ad- 表示强调，ept 是 expert（专家）的缩写形式，组合后指在某方面是专家，非常擅长于该领域，be adept in speaking English（擅长说英语）。

3.3.3 按形近易混词的发音相近程度可以分为同音形近词、近音形近词和异音形近词

1）同音形近词（表 1）。这类形近词不但拼写相近，而且发音相同，经常会导致词汇的拼写和听力判断错误。同音形近词的数量不多，但应当给予特别关注。如 complement 和 compliment：complement（补足物，补充），This wine would be a nice complement to grilled dishes.（这种葡萄酒配烧烤食物会很不错）；compliment（赞美的话，夸奖，称赞），All guests paid her extravagant compliments.（所有客人都对她赞不绝口）。又如 baron 和 barren：baron（男爵，工业巨头），an oil baron（石油大王）；barren（荒芜的，不生育的），Thousands of years ago the earth surface was barren desert.（几千年以前，地球表面是一片荒漠）。再如 hare 和 hair：hare（野兔，飞奔，飞跑），He hared off down the road.（他沿着马路飞快地跑掉了）；hair（头发），a strand of hair（一缕头发）。

表 1 英语同音形近词汇表

ad/add	forth/fourth	manner/manor	raise/rays/raze	soot/suit	you're/your
affect/effect	foul/fowl	massed/mast	rap/wrap	stair/stare	you'll/yule
ail/ale	groan/grown	meat/meet	read/red	stake/steak	
aisle/I'll	guessed/guest	missed/mist	read/reed	straight/strait	
ant/aunt	gym/Jim	moan/mown	real/reel	suite/sweet	
ate/eight	hair/hare	moose/mousse	recede/reseed	tea/tee	
be/bee	hairy/Harry	morning/mourning	review/revue	team/teem	
beach/beech	hall/haul	muscle/mussel	roe/row	tense/tents	
beat/beet	halve/have	navel/naval	right/rite/write	tern/turn	

续表

bald/bawled	he'd/heed	none/nun	ring/wring	their/there/they're
bare/bear	heal/heel	not/knot	road/rode/rowed	threw/through
base/bass	hear/here	oar/or/ore	roam/Rome	throne/thrown
billed/build	heard/herd	oh/owe	role/roll	tic/tick
blew/blue	hi/high	one/won	root/route	to/too/two
by/bye/buy	him/hymn	overdo/overdue	rote/wrote	toe/tow
cell/sell	hour/our	pail/pale	rough/ruff	toon/tune
cent/scent/sent	idle/idol	pane/pain	rye/wry	urn/earn
chili/chilly	in/inn	pair/pare/pear	sachet/sashay	vain/vein
close/clothes	it's/its	passed/past	sacks/sax	vary/very
days/daze	knead/need	pause/paws	sail/sale	verses/versus
dear/deer	know/no	pea/pee	scene/seen	vial/vile
do/dew/due	knows/nose	peace/piece	sea/see	vice/vise
die/dye	lay/lei	peak/peek	seam/seem	wade/weighed
died/dyed	lead/led	pedal/peddle	sear/seer	wail/whale
doe/dough	leak/leek	pi/pie	serf/surf	waist/waste
earn/urn	lends/lens	plane/plain	sew/so	waive/wave
ewe/yew/you	lessen/lesson	pole/poll	shoe/shoo	walk/wok
facts/fax	lie/lye	pray/prey	sic/sick	war/wore
fare/fair	links/lynx	presence/presents	sighs/size	ware/wear/where
fairy/ferry	loan/lone	pride/pryed	Sioux/sue	we/wee
feat/feet	lochs/locks/lox	prince/prints	slay/sleigh	we'd/weed
fir/fur	made/maid	profit/prophet	soar/sore	weak/week
flea/flee	mail/male	pros/prose	sole/soul	whine/wine
flew/flu/flue	main/mane	quarts/quartz	some/sum	whoa/woe
flour/flower	maize/maze	racket/racquet	son/sun	wood/would
for/fore/four	mall/maul	rain/reign	sonny/sunny	yoke/yolk

2）近音形近词。此类形近词在数量上是最多的，几乎出现在所有种类的英语文献中。由于拼写相近、发音相似，它们很容易混淆。如 chef 和 chief：chef（厨师），a master chef（手艺高超的厨师长）；chief（首领，酋长，首要的），the government's chief medical officer（政

府的首席卫生官员）。又如 marrow 和 narrow：marrow（骨髓），be frozen to the marrow（冷得刺骨）；narrow（狭窄的），a long and narrow road（窄长的道路）。再如 nature，neutral 和 mature：nature（自然，本性），nature conservation（自然保护）；neutral（中立的），During World War II, Sweden was neutral.（在第二次世界大战期间，瑞典是中立国）；mature（成熟的，变成熟，债券或保单到期），a respectable mature gentleman（一位深受尊敬的成熟绅士）。

3）异音形近词。这类形近词虽然书写形式相近，但发音差别较大，数量不多，也容易发生拼写和发音上的错误。如 rough 和 tough：rough（粗糙的，粗略的，粗暴的，艰难的）源于 rock（岩石），a rough temper（粗暴的脾气）；tough（棘手的，难办的，艰难的，坚强的）源于 touch（触摸），The company admitted that it had been a tough year.（该公司承认那是艰难的一年）。又如 terrible 和 terrific：terrible（可怕的），a terrible storm（猛烈的暴风雨）；terrific（极好的），That is a terrific idea.（这个主意真棒）。再如 tune 和 tone：tune（曲调，语调，音调，协调，乐器调音，收听）中 u 的象形含义是水，喻指流水声好似歌声般的动听，sing perfectly in tune（唱得十分合调）；tone（语气，色调，基调，音色，音质）中 o 的象形含义是嘴，描绘了人说话时的语气或某种乐器特有的音色，the guitar's clean tone（吉他纯净的音色）。

异音形近词 ethic 和 ethnic：ethic（伦理，道德），work ethic（职业道德）；ethnic（种族的）中的 n 可指代 nation（国家），national ethnic conflicts（国内种族冲突）。

异音形近词 rogue, intrigue, vague, vogue 和 fatigue：rogue（流氓的，无赖的）源于 roll（滚动），指无赖在地上打滚，rogue moneylenders（胡作非为的放高利贷者）；intrigue（激起兴趣，引起好奇心，密谋，诡计），前面的 intri 是 interesting 的缩写形式，the political intrigues（政治阴谋）；vague（含糊的，不明确的，不清楚的）源于 va-，表示空，a vague outline of the tax plan（大致的税务计划）；vogue（时尚）源于 voice（声音），指好听的声音引领时尚，Short skirts are very much in vogue just now.（短裙目前非常流行）；fatigue（疲劳，疲乏）可以用 fat（肥胖）记忆，指胖子容易感到疲劳，physical and mental fatigue（身心疲惫）。

英语词汇学习的方法

4.1 词根词缀记忆法

词根词缀记忆法是英语造词的主要方法。研究词根词缀、分析英语单词的结构和构成，不仅有利于快速记忆单词，还可以加深对已知词汇的认知理解。在词汇学习中，以词根词缀记忆法为基础开展词汇的成组记忆，能让读者迅速掌握大量的相关词汇，了解词汇之间的衍生关系，快速增加词汇量。词根词缀记忆法给语言学习者开启了一扇崭新的词汇记忆大门，也为广大读者探究单词的内涵和准确应用词汇提供了可靠线索和信息来源。

4.1.1 词根词缀的形位来源和定义

词素，也称为形位（morpheme），它是构成单词的重要元素，按其类型可分为两种：第一种叫作实义形位（content morpheme），第二种叫作语法形位（grammatical morpheme）。

实义形位是把几个字母结合在一起后形成新的字母组合。该字母组合是具有实际含义的形位，是构成单词的语义基础。如 port（港口）就是实义形位，表达的意思是 carry（携带），构成的单词有 airport（机场）, portable（便携的）, transport（运输）等。有时实义形位可单独使用，变成一个词。如 formulate（规划，制定，详细说明）和 flexible（灵活的）中的 form（形成，表格）以及 flex（使弯曲），它们不但具有这两个词的中心意思，而且还可以单独作为单词使用。这种实义形位被定义为词根（root）。

语法形位与实义形位的概念不同，它只表示一种附加意义或语法意义。语法形位只能依附于实义形位，与其结合后构成单词。如 deport（驱逐）中的 de-（否定或向下）和 colorful（多姿多彩）中的 -ful（充满的），它们只具有附加意义，不是词汇构成的语义基础，且不能单独使用。一般来说，这种语法形位被称作词缀（affixes）。按照词缀的功能和位置划分，词缀可分为前缀和后缀两种类型。位于单词前面的叫前缀（prefix），比如 de-，位于单词结尾的叫后缀（suffix），比如 -ful。

要想熟练地掌握词根词缀与英语词汇的构成规律，不但需要分析词根词缀彼此间的确切含义、基本构造和组合规律，还要探究单词的基本词义，能够在综合理解后判断出单词词义的大致范围。尽管词根和词缀意思的简单叠加并不能解释所有单词的词义，但是掌握基本的词根词缀知识，还是对提高语言学习者推测生词词义的能力和提升词汇习得的效率有着积极作用。

4.1.2　词根词缀与词汇构成

词根（root）是词素的一种形式，与单词（word）的不同之处在于它不可以做进一步的分析，否则其含义的整体性就会消失。词根是构成词汇的基础元素，掌握了词根就可以利用它们成组习得单词，让词汇记忆变得更加简单高效。比如，拉丁单词 manus 在拉丁语中的含义是"手"，在英语词汇中，根据其形态创造了词根 mani- 和 manu-，均有"手"的含义。它衍生的词汇也都和"手"的意思相关。单词 manicure 的意思是"修理指甲"，其中 -cure 是由 care 衍生出的词根，意为"照顾"，那么该词的词义就变得十分明显，直译过来是照顾双手，也就是要定期地修理指甲。单词 manual，指用"手"做的某些事情或手里的物体，manual labor（手工劳动），manual gearbox（手动变速箱），a student manual（学生手册）。单词 manage，强调以管理者的身份"亲手"处理解决某事，词尾的后缀 -age 表示"一段时期"，所以其确切的含义是用手长时期地做某事，指"应对处理"。单词 manufacture 的意思是制造出来某一样东西，让人联想到"用手制作"，其中 -fact 的拉丁词根意思为 make（制作），我们最熟悉的词是 factory（工厂），两个部分合成后指用手制造工业产品。当作家亲自用手写完自己的一部作品时，出版商会查看原始的 manuscript（手稿）。它是由词根 manu- 和词根 -script（写）合成的单词，表示作品是亲手写的，有"手稿"的意思，a manuscript of a piece of music（音乐手稿）。单词 manacle 的后缀为 -cle，表达的含义是"东西或事物"，如 article（文章，物品，条款），particle（微粒，颗粒），spectacle（眼镜，精彩表演，壮观场面），tentacle（触角，触手），miracle（奇迹，意外的幸运的事），chronicle（编年史）。词根 manu- 合成该词缀后的意思为手上绑着的东西，意思就是"镣铐"，manacle 作动词的含义则为"束缚"。

词根在英语词汇构词中起到的作用是决定性的。在提到 manufacture（制造）时，我们也说到了词根 -fact 有"做"的中心意思，它也有两个变体 -fect 和 -fict，意思也是"做"。下面会列举一些和该词根相关的英语词汇。单词 faculty（大学的系，全体教员，才能天赋）是由词根 -fact 加单词 culture（文化）的缩写形式 cult 构成的，它的词义可以理解为一个研究文化的地方，或者指在文化研究领域的专门教育型人才，或者表示某人具有文化研究方面的天赋。单词 facilitate（使便利）指做出来的物品可以让许多的事情变得更加简单方便，The cars facilitate the traffic.（汽车便利了交通）。单词 affect（影响）中的前缀 af- 表示强调，它指人们做出来的行为会对外部有影响。单词 affection（爱）是在 affect 的基础上衍生出的单词，意思是 love（爱）。由于它与动词 affect 在词形上关系密切，所以名词 affection 指的是世界上最具影响力的事物，就是人类的情感，表达爱的含义。单词 effect（效应）是表示效应或影响的名词，前缀 e- 表示出来，指的是做出来的东西确实有效果、有影响，常见的词组有 butterfly effect（蝴蝶效应），greenhouse effect（温室效应）。单词 defect（缺陷），前缀 de- 在拉丁语中有"向下"或"不好"的意思，所以该词指做得不够好的事物，也就是有缺陷的事物。单词 infect（感染，传染）的前缀 in- 的意思是 inside（在内部，向内部），所以它喻指做的事情对身体内部有影响，表示传染疾病。接下来的单词都是形容词，它们除了有词根 -fict，还包括了共同的后缀 -ent（指具有某种能力）。单词 deficient（缺乏的）指的是做得不够的，不到位的，deficient food（缺乏的食物）；单词 efficient（有效率的）指的是有很强影响或效应（effect）的事物，an efficient system（有效的机制）；单词 sufficient（充足的）中的前缀 suf- 表示在下面，它的意思指在下面做了非常多的铺垫和准备工作，sufficient preparations（充足的准备）；单词 magnificent（宏伟的）中前缀 magni- 的含义为 big（大），源于 mountain（山脉），和词根 -fict 组合后的意思是做得很大的，就是壮丽的、雄伟的；单词 proficient（熟练的）中的前缀 pro- 常用在构词中，表达的意思是向前的，指做事情做到了别人的前面，一件事如果能做到了他人的前面，那么这个人做事情一定是非常熟练的。

词根 -spect 有"看"的意思，它源于 spy（侦探）。该词根能和多种前缀后缀搭配组合，构成许多单词。如单词 expect 的前缀 ex- 表示"向外"，词根 -spect 是"看"，所以合成后的含义是"向外看"，指人们推开窗子向外张望的样子，词义是"期待"，expect a joyful life（期待快乐的生活）；单词 prospect 的前缀 pro- 表示"向前"，词根 -spect 是"看"，组合后意思为"向前看"，描绘的是抬头向前看时，望见了远方美丽的景色，词义是"远方的美景"，prospect 也可引申指"美好的未来"，a student who has a great prospect（一个有美好未来的学生）；在单词 spectacle 中，-spect 表示"看"，后缀 -acle，表示"事物"，组合后指"看到的事物"，尤指"特殊的奇观景象"，如奥林匹克运动会开幕式就是 a grand spectacle（一个盛大的活动）；单词 inspect 的前缀 in- 表示"向里面"，词根 -spect 表示"看"，组合后的意思是"向里面查看"，词义是"检查"，US Boarder Inspection Station（美国边境检查站）；单词 suspect 的前缀 sus- 的意思是"向下"，词根 -spect 表示"看"，合成后指"由上向下看"，形容人的眼神由上而下地打量别人，带有怀疑的意味，其作名词指"嫌疑犯"，作动词是"怀疑"的意思，suspect one's loyalty（怀疑某人的忠心）；单词 introspect 的前缀 intro- 表示"向内心"，词根 -spect 表示"看"，指人们向自己的内心世界观察，意思是"反省，内省"，罗丹著名的雕塑"The Thinker"（思想者）中的人物形态就可用 introspect oneself（反省自己）来描绘；单词 retrospect 的前缀 retro- 表示"向后"，词根 -spect 表示"看"，组合后的意思为"向后看"，指"回顾过去"，a retrospect of college life（大学生活的回顾）；单词 spectator 中的 -spect 表示"看"，添上后缀 -or，代表"人"，指看比赛的人，即"观众"，the spectators of a spectacle（宏大场景的观众）。

词根 -ven（来）与不同前缀结合后可派生出许多同词根词汇。如 convene（召集会议），avenue（大街），revenue（收益），avenge（复仇），intervene（干涉），contravene（违反法律或法规）。

单词 apologize（道歉），dialogue（对话，对白），eulogy（颂词），prologue（开场白，序幕）和 monologue（长篇独白）中有个共同的核心词根 -log，有"话语"的意思，它被非常巧妙地融合在这些单词中。

词缀按其在词素组合中的位置可分为两种：prefix（前缀）和 suffix（后缀）。在单词 illegal（非法的）中 il- 是前缀，表示"不，非"的意思；在单词 fearless（无畏的）中 -less 是后缀，表示"没有，无"的意思。前缀在单词基础词义形态之前，通常是词根的前面。

如 be- 是单词"belittle"（轻视，蔑视）的前缀，它的意思是"正处于某种状态"，类似于现在进行时中表达正在进行某种动作状态的 be doing 形式；单词 before 的意思是"正在前面"，它由 be 加上 fore 组成，fore 的意思是 forward（向前）；单词 begin 由 be 加 gin（go）组成，表示正在走动的状态，有"开始"的意思；单词 beware 由 be 加 ware 构成，指正在意识到某事发生的概率，意思是"当心，注意"；单词 besiege 由 be 加 siege 组成，siege 的意思是"包围"，词源为 sea（大海），指大海正包围陆地的状态；单词 bewilder 由 be 加 wild（狂野）再加后缀 -er 构成，后缀 -er 表示动作的反复性，形容正处于狂野的状态，并且是持续多次的经常性反复，bewilder 的词义是"使迷惑"；单词 behold 是 be 加 hold 构成的，hold 作为动词有"认为"的意思，所以 behold 指人们正在观看的状态，有"请看，注视"的意思，它经常用在正式场合，如"Behold，the emperor."（请看，皇帝来了）。

前缀 tele-（远程的）有 far（远的）的意思，可构成的词汇有 telephone（电话），teleconference（远程会议），telemarketing（电话营销），telecommuting（家庭办公）。

单词 transport 的前缀 trans- 有"横穿，跨越"的含义，可联想到 translate（翻译），transact（交易），transcend（超越），transcribe（誊写，抄写），transverse（横向的）等词汇，它们都含有"横穿，跨越"的意思。

后缀常位于单词基础词义形态之后，也就是词根之后。如 -ish 是 childish（孩子气的）的后缀。-ish 提示单词的词性可能是形容词、名词或动词，British 作形容词时指"英国的"，作名词时指"英国人"，finish（结束，完成）则是动词。

后缀 -or、-ee、-eer、-ist、-ian、-ician、-ese、-ard、-ite、-ocrat、-wright 都是表示"人"的后缀。它们是后缀 -er 的变形，能构成的单词有 victor（胜利者），employee（雇员），volunteer（志愿者），artist（艺术家），librarian（图书馆员），physician（内科医生），Chinese（中国人），guard（守卫），elite（精英杰出人物），aristocrat（贵族），playwright（剧作家）。

单词 compete（竞争），添上不同的后缀可变成 competent（胜任的），competitive（有竞争力的），competitor（竞争者）。

后缀 -ware（部件）能构成的词汇有 hardware（硬件），software（软件），middleware（中间件），groupware（组件），freeware（免费软件）。

采用词根词缀法记忆单词具有趣味性强、规律性强、短期内能迅速增加词汇量等诸多好处。在词汇学习中要更多地使用词根词缀记忆法，把它和传统的词汇学习方法有效地结合起来。词根词缀记忆法的最终目的是让读者能在阅读文章中根据基本的词根词缀知识推测出生词的词义。当语言学习者有了一定数量的词根词缀储备后，遇到生僻词汇时就像取出了一把万能钥匙，可以轻松地推测词义，准确地理解段落内容，掌握文章的主旨大意。此外，词根词缀记忆法还可以提高英语学习者的语法能力。在英语写作中，常用的后缀能提示词汇的词性，提醒作者使用单词正确的词性，避免词性误用情况的发生。

4.2 词汇联想记忆法

词汇联想记忆法源于图式理论,它是由美国人工智能专家 Rumelhart 提出的。该理论认为人们在认识新事物时,总是设法将其与已有的或已知的事物联系起来,找到它们的相互关联,促进对新事物的信息理解,让已有的知识和知识结构对当前的认知活动产生巨大的影响。因此,在词汇记忆中可以运用联想法,即建立新词信息与旧词信息之间的联系。词汇联想记忆法可分为以下五种。

第一种联想法是"替换",指替换某个字母,让新单词变为已知词汇,找出两词之间的记忆关联。比如,ample evidence(充足的证据)中的形容词 ample(足够的,充足的),把它的第二个字母 m 替换成 p,就变成了单词 apple(苹果),读者一定认识苹果,可用 ample apples(足够的苹果)来记忆 ample;单词 linger(继续存留,徘徊,犹豫),可把它的字母 i 换成 o,变为单词 longer(时间更长久的),联想记忆 linger,指人或事物原地徘徊了更长的时间,The tax will linger on until March.(这种税还要保留到三月份。);单词 bitter(苦涩的),把字母 i 换成 e 后,就是 better(更好的),所以联想记忆 better 是"好的",而 bitter 是"苦的"。

第二种联想法是"添加",指添加某个字母或短语在新词上,让它变成已知的单词联想记忆。例如,科技英语 robot limbs(机器人四肢)中的单词 limb(四肢),可以在字母 l 前面添加字母 c,就变成了单词 climb(爬行),可联想记忆成 climb with limbs(用四肢爬行);单词 hinder(阻碍),在它前面添加 be,就变成了单词 behind(向后),-er 表示动作的反复性,可理解为阻碍就是不停地向后推某人,policies that will hinder rather than help trade(对贸易有害无益的政策);单词 heal(愈合),在它的词尾加上 -th,就变成了 health(健康),可联想记忆成伤口愈合,恢复健康。

第三种联想法是"反写",指把某个字母反过来写后变成已知的单词。例如,mild(温柔的,疾病轻微的),可把字母 m 反过来写成 w,就变成了 wild(狂野的),用 wild 联想记忆 mild,a mild form of diabetes(不严重的糖尿病);单词 harp(竖琴)是一种乐器,字母 p 反过来写成 d,就变成了 hard(艰辛的),可联想记忆在艰辛的时候倾听竖琴的音乐来放松身心。

第四种联想法是"拆分",指把新词拆分成两个已知词汇来记忆。单词 groom(新郎),可拆分成 gege(哥哥)和 room(房子),喻指有房子的哥哥才能做新郎;单词 thrift(节俭),拆分成 throw(扔掉)和 lift(举起),指把别人扔掉的东西捡起来的行为是节俭;单词 pudgy(肥胖的),可拆分成 pudding(布丁)和 guy(人),指一个肥胖的人的体态像布丁一样。

第五种联想法是"谐音",即用单词的读音记忆词义。比如,soar(翱翔,迅速上升),它的读音像汉语"嗖嗖"的发音,是个象声词,所以记住"嗖的一声"就记住了 soar, soaring unemployment(急剧上升的失业率);单词 melancholy(郁闷的)的发音类似用汉语说"卖了可怜",可联想到在卖了心爱的东西后内心郁闷的心情;单词 boom(隆隆声,激增,繁荣)的发音很像开炮时"砰"的一声,可联想记成礼炮轰鸣声, booming economy(繁荣的经济)。

词汇联想记忆法是利用人脑记忆的基本规律将新词信息与已知词汇信息相互关联的记

忆方法。新词旧词之间的联系越新奇，越生动有趣，记忆也就越深刻。除了新词与旧词的词对词联想，还可以采用由单词联想到短语，由短语联想到句子，由句子联想到对话等多元化的联想法快速记忆词汇。

4.3 词源典故记忆法

古希腊和古罗马神话故事是全世界广为传颂的人类文化瑰宝，其丰富的内涵和历史价值充分反映了古希腊和古罗马的社会生活面貌，也是形成西方文化和宗教信仰的基石。古希腊和古罗马神话一直是英美文学创作的重要素材之一，在文学作品的长期熏陶和渗透下，神话传说已经成为现代西方社会思想的重要组成部分。它们不但深刻影响着英美国家的社会发展，也对现代英语文化中的文学、语言、价值观、宗教、艺术等方面的传承创新起到了重要的作用，更推动了英语语言中词汇的演化和发展。大量源于古希腊神话和古罗马神话的单词已经融入英语语言之中，在英语词汇体系中占有不可轻视的地位。在进行英语学习和开展不同文化间的沟通交流中，语言学习者需要对神话故事有全面的了解，充分利用古希腊和古罗马神话的作用，分析词汇的来源，加深对英语词汇词源典故的印象，提高学习英语词汇的效率，培养对英语语言文化的兴趣。

4.3.1 源于古希腊、古罗马神话中天神名称的词汇

早期的古希腊、古罗马神话中的众多天神的名字都转化成了英语词汇。它们在英语中变成了普通名词，也创造了许多衍生词汇。如 Astraea（阿斯特莱姬），星辰，是正义女神，astral（星的，星状的）；Chaos（卡俄斯），最古老的神，指宇宙一片混沌，chaos（混沌，混乱），chaotic（一团糟的）；Gaea（大地女神），从 Gaea 派生出来词根 geo-，表示"土地"，geography（地理学），geopolitics（地理政治学）；Giants（巨人神），giant（巨大的），它也指捷安特自行车品牌；The Furies（希腊神话中复仇三女神），fury（暴怒），furious（暴怒的）是著名电影《速度与激情》(Fast and Furious) 的片名；Titans（泰坦巨神），titan（巨人，巨物），电影《泰坦尼克号》(Titanic)，Titanism（泰坦精神）指反对现有秩序，蔑视常规习俗的反抗精神；Uranus（乌诺诺斯），早期统治整个宇宙的天神，Uranus（天王星），uranium 是化学元素"铀"。

源于古希腊、古罗马神话中十二大天神的词汇也有很多。希腊奥林匹斯山上有十二大天神，被众神之主宙斯和天后赫拉统治着。他们和其他十大天神掌管着自然界和人类生活中的各种现象及变化，形成了以宙斯为核心的奥林匹斯天神体系。Aphrodite（阿佛洛狄特），爱与美的女神，罗马神话的 Venus（维纳斯），也指金星，Venusian（金星的）；Apollo（阿波罗），太阳神，也是音乐、诗歌和艺术的保护神。他是一个容貌英俊的年轻人，常用 like Apollo 来形容英俊潇洒。Apollo 曾拒绝了水泽仙女 Clytie 的表白，Clytie 悲痛欲绝，九天九夜凝望着太阳，她的脚扎在地上生成了根，脸庞变成了花盘，化作了一株 helianthus（向日葵），词根 helio- 就是指"太阳"，heliotherapy（日光浴治疗法）；Ares（阿瑞斯），战神，罗马神话中的 Mars（马耳斯），罗马纪年的第一个月份就献给了他，即英语中的 March（三月）。太阳系的

第四大行星火星颜色鲜红如火，也叫 Mars，Martian（火星人），martial arts（武术）；Artemis（阿尔忒弥斯），罗马神话中的 Diana（狄安娜），掌管月亮和狩猎的女神。她的另一个名字叫 Luna（卢娜），lunar（阴历的），lunatic（疯子）；Athena（雅典娜），智慧女神和雅典城的守护女神。传说她与海神波塞东同时选中了希腊南端的一块土地作为庇护地，互不相让，邀请 Zeus 仲裁，Zeus 让他们自己表达对该地区的善意，由当地居民选择。波塞冬兴风作浪，想在该地区树立海上霸权；雅典娜则把长矛向地上一掷，土地上立刻长出了象征和平的橄榄树，以此向当地人表示和平安宁。当地人最终选择拥护雅典娜为庇护神，从此该地以 Athens 命名，Athens（雅典）；Demeter（德墨忒尔），谷物女神，罗马名字是 Ceres（塞雷斯），cereals（谷类植物）；Hades（哈迪斯），罗马神话中的 Pluto（普鲁托），掌管冥界的神。Pluto（冥王星），现已由太阳系的九大行星之一降级为太阳系中的"矮行星"。由于地府有无穷矿藏，所以 Pluto 也是管理财富的天神，plutocrat（富豪）；Hephaestus（赫菲斯托斯），火和锻冶之神，罗马神话中的 Vulcan（武尔坎），volcano（火山）源于他的名字，sit on a volcano（处境危险）；Hera（赫拉），妇女和婚姻的保护神，罗马神话中的 Juno（朱诺）或 Moneta（墨涅塔）。六月是献给她的月份，叫 June。因为赫拉是女性、婚姻和母性之神，所以六月是适合结婚的月份，June bride（六月新娘）。赫拉的笔名是 Moneta，衍生出了单词 money（钱），mint（铸币厂）；Hermes（赫尔墨斯），罗马神话中的 Mercury（墨丘利），他是诸神的信使并掌管道路、商业等，Mercury（信使，水银，水星），merchant（商人），commerce（商业）；Poseidon（波塞冬），希腊神话中的海神，罗马神话中的 Neptune（涅普顿），Neptune（海王星），neptunium（化学元素"锝"）；Zeus（宙斯），希腊神话中左手拿着权杖，右手操纵雷电的众神之父，罗马神话中称为 Jupiter（朱庇特）或 Jove（朱威），指"明亮的天空"。太阳系第五大行星木星由于其硕大的外形和中心的位置，获得了以 Jupiter 命名的尊荣。Sub Jove 在拉丁语中指在光天化日之下，be in jovial mood（心情愉快）。

古希腊、古罗马神话中其他天神的名字及相关典故也创造了许多英语词汇。大力神 Hercules（赫拉克拉斯）出生后吮吸了 Hera 的乳汁，当 Hera 推开他时，用力太猛，乳汁喷到了天上，形成了 milk way（银河）；Atlas（阿特托斯）顶天巨神，他曾与其他巨神一起反对宙斯，战败后被宙斯惩罚，站在西方天地结合的地方双肩扛着天空，Atlas 喻指身负重担的人。最早的地图册封面上就绘有 Atlas 双手托天的形象，所以"地图册"叫作 atlas；Chloris（克罗莉斯），花神，罗马神话中的 Flora（福罗拉），她是春天的使者，chlorophyll（叶绿素），flora（植物群），flower（花），florist（花商）；Chronos（克洛诺斯），希腊神话的时间之神，chronicle（编年史），chronic（慢性的），chronometer（精密计时钟表）；Saturn（萨杜恩），罗马神话的农神，Saturn（土星），Saturday（星期六）；Echo（厄科），希腊神话中一位美丽的女神，因为 Zeus 贪恋 Echo 的美貌，使她遭到了 Hera 的嫉妒。Hera 对 Echo 施了魔法，让她只能重复一句话的最后三个字。Echo 后来躲到山洞里，众神只能听到她的回声，echo（回声）；Eris（厄里斯），不和女神，她用一个刻字的金苹果导致了特洛伊战争的爆发，error（错误），eristic（好争论的）；The Fates（命运三女神），fate（命运），fatal（致命的），fateful（灾难性的）；Grace（格蕾斯），赐予人们美丽和欢乐的优雅三女神，grace（优美，恩惠，宽限期），graceful（优美的）；Janus（罗马神话中守护门户的两面神），Janus-faced（两面派的），January（一月），指一年之初，往年之末，janitor（看门人）；Nike（奈基），胜利女神，罗马神话中的 Victoria（维多利亚），Nike（美国耐克牌运动鞋），victory（胜利）；Pan（潘神），人身羊足的森林之神，Pan 喜欢在山林中游荡，用自己古怪的声音和面相恐吓行人，panic（恐惧），as free as pan（逍遥自在似神仙）；Siren（塞壬），海上女妖，有着半人半鸟的外表，常用歌声诱惑过路的航海者，使他们的船只触礁沉没。它的意思是"迷人的美女，汽笛，警报，诱惑的"；Europe（欧洲）来源于希腊神话中的农神欧罗巴（Europa），她是腓尼基国王的女儿。一次她在海边采花，被宙斯（Zeus）看中，于是宙斯变作一头白色公牛，诱骗她骑在牛身上，带她奔跑到大海的对岸。从此以后，欧罗巴被宙斯带到的那块土地就以她的名字命名，称作欧罗巴大陆，后来演变成了欧洲大陆。

4.3.2 古希腊、古罗马神话对词根词缀的衍生作用

英语中众多词根词缀的产生和演化都与古希腊和古罗马神话紧密相关。古希腊神话和古罗马神话中的一大主题是关于人和神的故事。大家广为熟知的普罗米修斯（Prometheus）和人类的故事就是其中之一。他利用奥林匹亚山上的黏土（clay）和水（water）创造了人类，给予人类火种，并教会了人类如何建造房屋、驾驭船只、出海航行和治疗疾病。神话中的普罗米修斯用黏土和水捏出了人类的故事情节带来了一个常用的英语词根 -hum，表示"含水的泥土"的意思。该词根是由三个象形字母组合而成的，h 在象形符号中的意思是"高"，如 high（高）和 hill（小山），u 的象形意思为"水"，如 umbrella（雨伞）和 urine（尿液），m 的象形意思为"高山"，如 mountain（高山）和 mighty（强大的），所以词根 -hum 的含义为"高高的奥林匹亚山上含水分的泥土"。它造出的第一个单词是 human（人类），指人类是用泥土和水创造出来的。接下来又造了单词 humble，它既有"卑贱的"意思，也有"谦虚的"意思，是截然相反的两组词义。由于 humble 源于词根 -hum，具有泥土的属性，泥土又是被人踩在脚下的，所以它被理解成"被大家践踏"时就表示"卑贱的"，如经常说的"寒舍"，a humble house；泥土被践踏却依然能长出粮食，滋养着人类社会，默默无闻地奉献，具有极高的品质，因此 humble 的第二个词义为"谦虚的"，如 a humble man（一个谦虚的人）。词根 -hum 创造的另一个单词为 humid（潮湿的），-id 是表示身份（identity）的后缀，指物质的自然属性，所以 humid 指土地潮湿的属性，经常用 humid 形容水分多又潮湿的天气，如 humid weather。词根 -hum 创造的第三个单词是 humiliate，意思是"侮辱他人"。根据 -hum 表示"泥土"的含义，这种侮辱指的是古希腊和古罗马人向囚犯身上扔泥土的行为，表达对他们的蔑视，侮辱囚犯的尊严。

另一个源于古希腊神话的重要词根为 -chron，意思是"时间"，该词根源于古代希腊神话中宙斯（Zeus）的父亲时间之神克洛诺斯（Chronos）。克洛诺斯（Chronos）是希腊神话中十二位泰坦巨人（Titans）之一，他的母亲女神盖亚（Gaia）和父亲天神乌诺诺斯（Uranus）生下了泰坦巨人，总共六男六女，他是其中最小的男性泰坦天神，负责掌管天地的时间，后来他的名字被用于英语词根，用 -chron 来表示"时间"的含义。与词根 -chron 相关的词汇有单词 chronic（长期的，慢性的），chronic confusion（长期的困扰），a chronic disease（慢性疾病）；单词 chronicle 的意思为"编年史"，指的是按照时间顺序记录的历史，电影《纳尼亚传奇》

的英文名称译为 The Chronicles of Narnia；单词 chronology 为合成单词，后缀为 -ology，表示"学科"，与 -chron 合成后意思为"年代学"或"年表"，它的形容词是 chronological，指"年代顺序的"或"时间顺序的"，a chronological order 的意思是"时间顺序"或"年代顺序"。

Amour 和 Eros 分别是古罗马人和古希腊人对小爱神丘比特（Cupid）的另外两个称呼。金弓是他常用的武器，他射出的箭从无偏差，被射中者虽会饱受爱情的煎熬，但这也是种甜蜜的痛苦，谁也无法抗拒，因此爱情被认为是最可怕而又最强大的自然力量。丘比特这位可爱而又淘气的小精灵有两种神箭，分别是促使爱情走向婚姻的金头神箭和中止爱情使人分手的铅头神箭。另外，他还有一束照亮心灵的火炬。由于 Amour 是古罗马人对丘比特（Cupid）的称呼，所以词根 -am 表示"爱"的含义，amour 本身就是个指"爱"的单词，褒义时指"爱情"，贬义时指"奸情，偷情"。它有双重含义是因为维纳斯背叛了丈夫火神武尔坎（Vulcan），和战神马尔斯（Mars）偷情生下了小爱神 Amour，这份感情中既包括了爱情，又隐藏着奸情。-am 衍生出了单词 amiable，意思是"和蔼的、可亲的"，指像爱神 Amour 一样心怀爱意亲近他人，an amiable smile（亲切的微笑）；单词 amity 的意思是"国家关系上的友善或友好"，指国家关系情意绵绵，仿佛在爱恋之中，如 USA and Russia are in amity.（美国和俄罗斯关系很和睦）；单词 amateur 的意思为"业余爱好者"，an amateur photographer（业余摄影师）。此外，Eros 是古代希腊人对爱神 Cupid 的称呼，创造了形容词 erotic，含有"色情的"的意思，erotic books（色情书籍）。

Eros 除了给别人带来恋爱的滋味，也拥有属于他自己的爱情，他和普塞克（Psyche）的爱情故事是希腊神话中最为精彩的。普塞克（Psyche）是希腊神话中腓尼基王国的公主，她在结婚前答应不会偷看 Eros 的外貌，但在少女好奇心的驱使下，她点起煤油灯偷看了一眼，正在这时，Eros 突然醒来，发现 Psyche 没有履行婚前的诺言，马上离她而去。Psyche 到处寻找丈夫，来到了 Eros 母亲维纳斯（Venus）的神殿。为了惩罚她，爱神的妈妈交给她许多艰巨而又危险的任务。其中最艰难的一项任务是让她把一个空盒子交给 Persephone（冥府的王后），并从她那里带回一盒子的东西。在执行任务时，一个声音一直指引着她如何摆脱各种死亡威胁，并警告她取回盒子后，无论如何都不能打开。Psyche 克服了重重困难，终于完成了任务。但在返回途中，她的好奇心还是驱使她打开了盒子。盒子里面装的其实是地狱里的睡眠鬼，它从盒中跳出来，附在了 Psyche 身上，把她变成了一具睡尸。此时，Eros 感受到了爱人正处于危险之中，开始四处寻找，很快发现了 Psyche 僵睡在地上，Eros 立刻从她身上抓起睡鬼，重新装入盒子。Eros 用真挚的爱原谅了 Psyche 的好奇心，他的母亲维纳斯也承认了他们的婚姻，众神被 Psyche 对 Eros 执着的爱感动了，赐给她一碗长生不老羹，并封她为女神。这样，Psyche 与 Eros 终于幸福地生活在了一起。由于 Psyche 曾经失去心智灵魂，所以用她的名字创造了一个词根 -psych，意思是 heart and soul。该词根生成了单词 psychology，意思是"心理学"；psychiatrist 指"精神病学家"，如奥地利著名的弗洛伊德；psychopath 的意思为"精神病患者"，词根 -path 指"痛苦"，源于 pain（痛苦），与 -psych 合成后指精神上经受痛苦的人；psychodrama 指"心理戏剧，心理电影，心理表演疗法"；psychoanalysis 指"心理分析（治疗法）"。

古罗马神话中司掌农耕的女神塞雷斯（Ceres），因为她挚爱的女儿被冥王抢到地府而悲痛欲绝，以致大地上不再生长草木。后来由于 Zeus（宙斯）的安排，她每年能和女儿相聚一次。当母女相会时，大地变得温暖和煦，万物生长繁茂，春天来临；当女儿离开母亲后，大地则回归寒冷荒凉，冬天到来。这则神话故事不但解释了四季变换缘由，也反映了人间的悲欢离合。由于人类对春天的渴望和对食物的需求，就以女神塞雷斯（Ceres）的名字创造了两个单词 ceremony 和 cereal。单词 ceremony（仪式）表示对 Ceres 的敬意，指人类希望她能够庇护农耕生产；单词 cereal 的词义是"粮食"，表达人类希望农业女神 Ceres 能够守护人类的劳动果实，让土地肥沃，庄稼丰收。

缪斯（the Muses）是希腊神话中掌管音乐、文学、艺术、天文、科学等九位女神的总称。她们喜欢居住在希腊南部帕那萨斯山脚下以及赫利孔山上的泉水附近，因此至今仍有知识的源泉（fountain of knowledge）和灵感的源泉（spring of inspiration）之说。为了表达对缪斯女神的敬仰，古希腊人把艺术作品和有关自然科学的物品存放在缪斯神庙里。英语的 museum（博物馆）就来源于希腊词 mouseion，意思是"缪斯的神庙"；单词 music（音乐）来自古希腊语 mousike（音乐），而 mousike 则是从 mousikos 一词变化而来的，意思是"属于缪斯的"；单词 mutual（相互的，彼此的）也源于缪斯女神，指音乐、文学、艺术、天文、科学等领域是促使人类之间相互了解、共同进步的动力，mutual respect（互相尊重）。

4.3.3 古希腊、古罗马神话对常用短语和习语的衍生作用

源于古希腊和古罗马的神话故事不但带来了大量的英语词根词缀，丰富了英语词源种类，还蕴含了许多脍炙人口的英雄传说。人们以英雄的名字或事迹创造出众多常用短语和习语，显示出古希腊人和古罗马人对英雄的无比敬仰和狂热崇拜。

小爱神丘比特（Cupid）是爱神维纳斯（Venus）和战神马尔斯（Mars）偷情所生的第五个孩子，丘比特的出生带来了一个常用的短语 under the rose，但它的意思不是"在玫瑰花底下"。由于丘比特（Cupid）知道自己是个私生子，为母亲维纳斯（Venus）爱与美之神和战神马尔斯（Mars）偷情所生，所以为了维护母亲的名望，丘比特就私下找到沉默之神哈伯克拉底（Harpocrates），送给他一束玫瑰花，请他守口如瓶，不要把母亲维纳斯的风流韵事到处宣扬。哈伯克拉底接受了玫瑰花，也同时遵守了诺言，对维纳斯偷情的韵事保持缄默，成为名副其实的"沉默之神"。丘比特赠送哈伯克拉底玫瑰花的故事在罗马广为流传，古罗马人就把玫瑰花当作沉默或严守秘密的象征，并在日常生活中形成了习俗。人们去拜访做客，看到主人家的桌子上画有玫瑰花时，就知道在这张桌上所谈的一切都是秘密，不可外传。因此，短语 under the rose 有了"秘密地，私下的，暗中的"的含义。

习语 pile Pelion on Ossa 的典故出自古希腊神话故事。海神波塞东（Poseidon）有两个儿子，名字叫作 Otus 和 Ephialthes，后人合称他们为阿洛伊代（Aloidea）。这两个心高气傲的年轻人为了能飞上天庭向天后赫拉（Hera）和月亮女神阿尔忒弥斯（Artemis）表达爱意，曾尝试把伯利翁山（Pelion）叠加到奥萨山（Ossa）上。但在行动之前，他们就被太阳神阿波罗（Apollo）杀掉了，使计划落空。此后，古希腊人就用 pile Pelion on Ossa 这一习语表示"难上加难"，也可写成 heap Pelion on Ossa。

赫拉克里斯（Hercules）是古希腊最著名的英雄人物。在现代英语中，他是大力士的象

征。赫拉克里斯是宙斯（Zeus）的私生子，当他还在襁褓啼哭时，天后赫拉（Hera）就知道了宙斯有个私生子叫 Hercules，于是开始想尽办法迫害他，让他在人间经历千辛万苦。然而，由于 Hercules 遗传了宙斯的神力，所以他可以斩妖除魔，成为人间的大英雄，重新回到天神的行列。

  Hercules 名字的意思指通过完成天后赫拉的十二项艰巨任务而取得巨大成就的人。年轻时赫拉克里斯曾遇到享乐女神（Pleasure）和美德女神（Virtue）。享乐女神诱惑他走舒适的生活道路，答应给他一切肉体快乐；美德女神则教诲他不畏艰难险阻，为人类造福除害，许诺给他永生。Hercules 必须在两者之间做出抉择，他选择了后者，随后 Hercules 以非凡的胆识和智慧完成了十二项英雄业绩，被誉为希腊神话中最伟大的英雄。他在历尽人间种种磨难之后，最终被众神接纳而永生不死。Hercules' choice 的意思为"赫拉克里斯的选择"，喻指"宁愿吃苦，不愿享乐"。

  习语 Hercules' labours 也源于 Hercules 的历险故事，人们用它形容一项工作"困难重重"。按照神谕，赫拉克里斯必须完成提任斯和迈锡尼的国王欧律斯透斯吩咐他做的十二件苦差，才能擢升为神。包括① 杀死墨涅亚狮子，并取得它的皮毛；② 杀死九头水蛇许德拉；③ 生擒刻律涅亚山上有金脚铜蹄的赤牝鹿；④ 活捉厄律曼托斯山的野猪；⑤ 在一日之内清扫干净奥吉厄斯的牛圈；⑥ 射杀斯廷法罗斯湖的食肉怪鸟；⑦ 制服克吕特岛上一头发疯的公牛；⑧ 把狄俄墨得斯吃人的母马带到迈锡尼；⑨ 夺取亚马孙女王希波吕忒的腰带并献给国王欧律斯透斯；⑩ 夺走三身巨人革吕翁的牛群；⑪ 从百头巨龙那里夺取三个金苹果；⑫ 把看守冥界大门的恶犬刻耳柏洛斯从冥界带来。这些任务都是异常艰苦、几乎不可能做到的事。但是 Hercules 凭着他非凡的胆识和超人的智慧，历经了千辛万苦，最终把它们全部完成。此后，人们就用 Labour of Hercules 或 Herculean Labour 来喻指"异常艰巨的任务"或"需要极大精力才能完成的工作"。Hercules 的形容词 Herculean 也被赋予了"艰巨的"的含义，其首字母往往小写，如 a herculean task（艰巨的任务）。习语 Hercules' efforts 则表示某人具有"超出常人的能力"。

  习语 cleanse the Augean stables 和大力士赫拉克里斯也有着密切关系。它源于赫拉克里斯的十二项不可能完成的任务之一。据说，古希腊有一个国王叫奥吉厄斯（Augeas），他的牛棚 30 年未曾清扫，粪垢堆积如山。希腊英雄大力士赫拉克里斯（Hercules）引来了附近的河水，仅用一天时间就把多年的污垢冲走了，让牛舍变得整洁如新。后来，人们就用 the Augean stables 喻指"腐败肮脏（的地方）"，用 cleanse the Augean stables 一语表示"彻底清除腐败污垢"。

  荷马史诗《伊利亚特》（Iliad）和《奥德赛》（Odyssey）代表了古希腊诗歌的杰出成就，为后世提供了许多脍炙人口的习语与短语。前一部《伊利亚特》（Iliad）以其浓重的神话色彩再现了恢宏悲壮的特洛伊战争（Trojan War）。

  习语 Apple of Discord（不和的苹果）的意思是"纠纷的开端，不和的根源"。该典故讲述的是一个刻字的金苹果引起了三位女神之间的纷争。它让天后赫拉、智慧女神雅典娜和女神阿芙罗狄忒为争做天下"最美的女神"而大肆争吵。她们让特洛伊的二王子 Paris 评判，并许诺给他回报。最终，Paris 把金苹果给了允诺给他"最美丽的女人"的阿芙罗狄忒。在阿芙罗狄忒的帮助下,Paris 成功地诱拐了海伦,导致了特洛伊战争的爆发。习语 judgment of Paris（帕里斯之判）指"导致错误的裁决"。习语 Helen of Troy（特洛伊城的海伦）有两层相反的含义,"倾国倾城的美人"和"红颜祸水"。

　　Trojan horse 指（潜藏内部的）颠覆分子或（从内部进行的）颠覆阴谋。其字面意思是特洛伊木马,Trojan 为 Troy（特洛伊）的形容词。Troy 是小亚细亚西北部古城,传说特洛伊战争就发生在此地。特洛伊二王子帕里斯（Paris）诱拐了希腊绝色美女斯巴达国王墨涅拉俄斯（Menelaus）的妻子海伦（Helen）,激起了希腊诸城邦的公愤。墨涅拉俄斯的兄长阿伽门农（Agamemnon）随即率领希腊联军远征特洛伊。希腊人把特洛伊城围攻了近 10 年,但屡攻不克,佯装撤围而去,在城外丢下一个巨大木马。特洛伊人认为这是希腊人敬神的礼物,不听祭司拉奥孔（Laocoon）劝阻,将它作为战利品拖入城内,并摆宴庆功。等到夜深人静之时,木马肚子上的暗门悄悄打开,藏于内部的一支精兵偷偷爬出,与重返的希腊大军里应外合,最终攻陷特洛伊城,这就是历史上著名的木马计或特洛伊木马。Trojan horse 源于拉丁语 Equus Trojanus, 也写作 wooden horse（of Troy）,喻指（潜藏内部的）颠覆分子、颠覆集团,或（从内部进行的）颠覆阴谋、颠覆活动。

　　阿喀琉斯（Achilles）是希腊神话特洛伊（Troy）中的英雄,他是阿伽门农联军中最骁勇善战的一员战将,也是荷马史诗《伊利亚特》中的主要人物之一。传说,阿喀琉斯（Achilles）是海神的女儿忒提丝（Thetis）和希腊密耳弥多涅斯人的国王珀琉斯（Peleus）所生的儿子。阿喀琉斯出生之后,母亲忒提丝（Thetis）一心想让儿子得到永生,战无不胜,于是把他放在火里烧烤锻炼,让他先除去人类身躯上的弱点。接着又捏着他的脚踵倒置在冥河圣水里浸泡。传说凡是经过冥河圣水浸泡过的凡人躯体都会变得刀枪不入,所以阿喀琉斯的身体如钢筋铁骨般坚不可摧。但由于他的脚踵部位被母亲用手捏住,没有沾到冥河圣水,所以脚踵成了他唯一的弱点。阿喀琉斯在特洛伊战争中表现得英勇无敌,所向披靡,单枪匹马杀死了特洛伊城的大王子赫克托耳（Hector）,后来太阳神阿波罗把他的弱点告诉了赫克托耳（Hector）的弟弟二王子帕里斯（Paris）,帕里斯用计谋把阿喀琉斯引诱到城门口,并用暗箭射中他的脚踵,阿喀琉斯负伤而死。后来,习语 Achilles' heel 用来指"唯一致命弱点或要害"。

　　荷马史诗的后一部《奥德赛》（Odyssey）在神话作为大背景的烘托下,广泛地描绘了古时希腊社会生活的方方面面。其中有对上层社会和妇女圣洁情操的推崇,也有对以奥德修斯（Odysseus）为代表的男性的机智、勇敢、视荣誉为生命的英雄主义情怀的颂扬。《奥德赛》紧跟伊利亚特的剧情,讲述了希腊英雄奥德修斯在特洛伊战争胜利后返乡途中的历险故事。奥德修斯献出木马计,里应外合攻破特洛伊城之后,在返航途中用计谋刺瞎了海神波塞冬的孩子独眼巨人波吕斐摩斯,得罪了海神。因此奥德修斯屡遭波塞冬的阻挠,历经各种艰难险阻。《奥德赛》的故事讲述了奥德修斯十年海上漂泊中最后 40 天的经历。他克服艰险后到达了斯刻里亚岛,受到了国王菲埃克斯的隆重接待,酒席间应邀讲述了关于风暴、独目巨人、风袋、女妖、雷击等海上历险故事。后来奥德修斯化装成乞丐成功返乡,与家人团聚。

　　在《奥德赛》中,流浪的英雄奥德修斯曾在一个叫 lotus land 的地方发现了一种植物,叫 lotus（落拓枣,忘忧果）。当地人食用它后就会变得游手好闲、贪图安逸,外来人则会忘却家人、迷恋他乡。所以 lotus land 常用来指"安逸的地方",lotus-eater 的意思是"乐不思蜀的人"。

孟托（Mentor）是奥德修斯的挚友，他曾在英雄出征之时担负起替朋友照顾家庭和妻儿的重任，没有取而代之。现代英语中它的意思为"良师益友，可信赖的人"。

Penelope 是荷马史诗《奥德赛》中主人公奥德修斯（Odysseus）的妻子，她对丈夫忠贞不渝。佩内洛普（Penelope）以"忠诚的妻子"的含义被收录进英语词汇。在丈夫十年征战特洛伊和十年海上漂泊的漫长岁月里，奥德修斯的妻子一直苦守宫中，等待丈夫归来。在奥德修斯海外流浪的最后几年间，人们盛传他已葬身鱼腹或客死他乡，各地王公贵族纷纷登门向佩内洛普求婚，但她始终没为之所动。曾有 100 个求婚者赖在她的宫中不走，为了摆脱求婚者的纠缠，她坚持要为丈夫织一件衣服后才考虑改嫁。她白天织了衣服，夜里又拆掉衣服，每天循环反复，衣服总不能织完，一直拖延到丈夫归来，全家重聚。因此 Penelope 在英语中指"忠实的妻子"，而 Penelope's web 按字面意思是"佩内洛普的织物"，喻指"永远做不完的工作"。

Between Scylla and Charybdis 也出自希腊神话《奥德赛》。斯库拉（Scylla）和卡力布狄斯（Charybdis）两者都是希腊神话中的女海妖，分别盘踞在意大利半岛本土与西西里岛之间的墨西拿海峡两边。希腊神话中的斯库拉（Scylla）原本是一位美丽的仙女，是航海者之神格劳科斯（Glaucus）的爱人，但一名叫喀耳刻（Circe）的女巫也爱上了格劳科斯，她向格劳科斯示爱，格劳科斯不为所动，女巫恼羞成怒，嫉恨于斯库拉，就用巫术把美丽的斯库拉变成了一个有 6 个头、12 只脚、每张嘴里有 3 排利齿的怪物，随时准备撕咬猎物，格劳科斯再次见到斯库拉时仓皇逃跑，不顾昔日旧情。斯库拉痛苦万分，一个人逃到了波涛汹涌的墨西拿海峡，终日盘踞在一个岩礁上，寻找猎物。凡是船只经过，斯库拉海妖必须吞噬六名船员才能果腹息怒。在她的对面住着另一个海妖卡力布狄斯，她每日将海水吞吐三次，形成的巨大漩涡，足以毁灭所有过往船只。习语 between Scylla and Charybdis 的字面意思是从斯库拉女妖与卡力布狄斯海妖之间通过，其引申含义为进退维谷，进退两难。根据荷马史诗《奥德赛》的记述，古希腊英雄奥德修斯在取得特洛伊战争胜利后班师还朝，当他航行在斯库拉女妖岩礁与卡力布狄斯海妖漩涡之间时，进退两难。最终，奥德修斯选择了牺牲六名船员喂食斯库拉女妖（Scylla）的方式，巧妙躲避了卡力布狄斯海妖（Charybdis）的发威周期，顺利通过危险重重的墨西拿海峡。

Amalthea's horn（horn of plenty，horn of abundance）的意思是丰饶角，它是丰饶的象征。传说，古希腊神话的天神宙斯（Zeus）出生以后，他的母亲瑞亚（Rhea）怕他被父亲克洛诺斯（Chronos）吞食，就把他藏在了克里特岛的一个洞穴里，并将他托付给仙女阿玛尔特亚（Amalthea）抚养，阿玛尔特亚用山羊奶哺育他长大。另一说法是阿玛尔特亚自己就是母山羊，她用自己的乳汁哺育了宙斯。这只母山羊后来折断了一只角，她便在那只角里装满了鲜花和水果送给宙斯。在宙斯推翻了他父亲的统治，成为众神之王后，把阿玛尔特亚和这只羊角带到天上。这只羊角是件宝物，谁拥有它，就能想要什么就有什么，它被看作是无穷无尽的财富和丰饶的象征，人们称之为丰饶之角，写作 Amalthea's horn，horn of plenty 或 horn of abundance。

Have the Midas touch 指有赚大钱的本事或时时处处都能赚到钱的本领。传说，小亚细亚中西部有一古国叫弗里吉亚（Phrygia），国王迈达斯（Midas）贪恋财富，一心想成为世界上最富有的人。酒神狄俄尼索斯（Dionysus）感恩于迈达斯对他以前一位老师的帮助，答应满足迈达斯的一切请求。于是迈达斯祈求酒神赐予他点物成金的法术。他如愿以偿得到了点金术后，到处点金，凡他所触摸的东西都变成了金子。然而，变成金子的不仅只是石块、花朵和屋内的陈设，连食物、饮料和他最心爱的小女儿也都变成了金子。最后，他只好祈求酒神解除他的点金术。酒神便让他到帕克托洛斯（Pactolus）河里去洗澡，收回了他的魔力，把一切恢复了原样。此后，人们便用 the Midas touch 喻指赚大钱的本事或时时处处都能赚到钱的本领。该词组常与 have 连用，have the Midas touch（有生财之道）。

　　Rest on one's laurels 的含义是故步自封，吃老本。单词 laurel 的本义是月桂树。在古希腊和古罗马神话中，月桂树是太阳神阿波罗的圣树。传说，阿波罗爱上了女神达芙妮（Daphne）。为了摆脱阿波罗的追求，达芙妮变成了一棵月桂树。阿波罗伤感不已，摘下月桂树的枝叶，编成了冠冕戴在头上，以此表达他对达芙妮的倾慕和思念。古希腊人和古罗马人将这种冠冕授予杰出的诗人、英雄或竞技优胜者，即桂冠。后来，整个欧洲都把桂冠作为光荣称号，该习俗被沿用至今。现在 laurel 往往喻指桂冠、荣誉或殊荣，常用复数形式。习语 rest on one's laurels 指满足于既得荣誉，故步自封、吃老本，也可写作 sit（sit back）on one's laurels。

　　Under the aegis of 的含义是在……庇护或保护之下，由……主办或发起。在希腊神话中，aegis 是天神宙斯的神盾。据说，aegis 是火和锻冶之神赫菲斯托斯特意为宙斯铸造的武器。神盾上还蒙着一块曾经哺育过宙斯的母山羊阿玛尔特亚（Amalthea）的毛皮。神盾魔力无穷，宙斯只要用力晃动一下，天空就会顿时电闪雷鸣，风雨大作，敌人无不失魂落魄，惊恐万分。智慧、技艺和战争女神雅典娜（Athena）每次执行父亲宙斯的命令时，总是随身携带着神盾，因为它既象征权力，也象征神明的庇护。Aegis 原为拉丁语，来自希腊语 aigis，原义指"山羊皮"，在英语中常用喻义，具有"庇护""保护""赞助""主办"等含义，一般多用于短语 under the aegis of，意思是"在……的庇护或保护之下""由……主办或发起"。

　　Wheel of fortune 指命运或人生的变迁。罗马神话中的命运女神福尔图那（Fortuna）在绘画中或纪念碑上的形象是蒙着双眼的。她一手拿着羊角，象征着颁赐丰饶，一手握着轮子（wheel），象征着主宰命运。传说，人的命运就是随着该轮子的转动而不断变化的，捉摸不定，变幻莫测。在希腊神话中，命运女神叫提喀（Tyche），在英语中则常用 Fortune 表示。Fortune 和 Fortuna 一样，也源自拉丁语 fortuna（命运）。因此，wheel of fortune 或 Fortune's wheel 的字面含义就是命运女神之轮或命运之轮，后喻指命运或人生的变迁。

　　Accomplishment of Perseus 指的是珀尔修斯的业绩或辉煌的成就、杰出的贡献。在古希腊神话中，珀尔修斯（Perseus）是传说中的英雄。神谕预言长大成人后的珀尔修斯将会推翻外祖父的统治并把他杀死，这让他的外祖父十分恐惧，于是把他们母子二人装进了一只大箱子扔进了大海。箱子被冲到了一座小岛上，岛上的国王波吕得克忒斯（Polydectes）垂涎于珀尔修斯的母亲，开始疯狂地追求她，但受到奇迹般长大成人的珀尔修斯的阻挠。国王为了赶走他，就煽动珀尔修斯去取蛇发女怪美杜莎（Medusa）的头。渴望冒险和建功立业的珀尔修斯毅然踏上征途。蛇发女怪美杜莎面目狰狞，凡是看见她的人就会顷刻间变成石头。在智慧女神雅典娜（Athena）和信使之神赫尔墨斯（Hermes）的帮助下，珀尔修斯成功地割下了美杜莎的头。返回途中，珀尔修斯也救下了埃塞俄比亚公主安德洛墨达（Andromeda），并娶她为妻。珀尔修斯带着妻子去找母亲，发现母亲为躲避波吕得克忒斯的迫害而躲在一座破旧的神庙里，珀尔修斯就让波吕得克忒斯看美杜莎的头颅，把他变成了石头。在实现了自己的丰功伟绩（accomplishment）之后，珀尔修斯带着母亲和妻子去见外祖父。外祖父害怕神谕会应验，就躲到了外地。不久，珀尔修斯因外出路过某地，恰逢当地举办体育竞技大会，他就前去参加，在掷铁饼时，不慎将一老者打死，此人正是珀尔修斯的外祖父，神谕应验。根据帕尔修斯的传奇经历，人们用 accomplishment of Perseus 表示"辉煌的成就、杰出的贡献"。

Ambitious as Phaethon 的意思是像法厄同一样雄心勃勃，自命不凡，目空一切。法厄同（Phaethon）是希腊神话中太阳神赫利俄斯（Helios，即罗马神话中的阿波罗 Apollo）的私生子。每天清晨，法厄同的父亲赫利俄斯都驾驭着由四匹喷火快马牵引的太阳车，从东方出巡，傍晚则降落在西方，夜间再乘坐小船重返东方。法厄同非常羡慕父亲，常常夸口自己是太阳神的儿子，为了证明给别人看，他恳求太阳神让他驾驭太阳车一天。太阳神曾立誓要满足儿子的请求，只好同意。但法厄同还没等父亲讲完驾驭技巧就迫不及待地跳上了太阳车。由于换了主人，马匹根本不听法厄同的使唤，以至于缰绳脱落，太阳车脱离轨道，马匹拉着它靠近大地飞奔，地面上的森林纷纷起火，河流干涸，成千上万的人们被热死、烫死和烧死。见到此情此景，天神宙斯（Zeus）急忙用雷电轰击法厄同，法厄同被击中后浑身燃烧，一头栽进河里。法厄同的姊妹们为兄弟的死去而号啕大哭，最后都变成了一棵棵杨树（poplars），她们的眼泪则变成了琥珀（amber）。法厄同的悲剧是因为他的自命不凡，如果他能谦虚一点，谨慎一点，虚心学习驾驭太阳车的技巧，他的悲剧也许就不会发生。现在，人们用 ambitious as Phaethon 来形容"自命不凡，目空一切。"

As shy as Daphne 的含义是像达芙妮一样害羞、腼腆。达芙妮（Daphne）是河神的女儿，长得美丽动人，喜欢独处，一点儿也不喜欢被男性骚扰。太阳神阿波罗（Apollo）却是一个花心的男子，只要见到自己心仪的女性，就穷追不舍。调皮捣蛋的小爱神厄洛斯（Eros 即罗马神话中的丘比特 Cupid）有两种箭，一种是爱情的金箭（golden arrow），另一种是爱情的铅箭（lead arrow），凡是被金箭射中的人都逃脱不了热恋的冲动，凡是被铅箭射中的人就会心冷如冰。厄洛斯四处乱飞，全凭着自己的兴趣，想用箭射谁就射谁，所以被爱神之箭射中的人不分年龄、美丑、人种、国籍，甚至不分性别，随时都会投身爱情，但也随时会失去爱的感觉。小爱神用金箭射中了阿波罗，而用铅箭射中了达芙妮，于是一场爱情追逐开始了。爱火越烧越旺的阿波罗一见到达芙妮就拼命地追赶，而又羞又怕的达芙妮则夺路而逃，阿波罗真诚地求她停步，达芙妮也不予理会。最后，达芙妮累得筋疲力尽，眼看就要被追上了，于是祈求众神把自己变成一棵树。转眼间，达芙妮的模样全变了，她的身体变成了树干，两臂变成了树枝，皮肤变成了树皮，头发变成了树叶，脚变成了树根，化作了一棵芬芳怡人的月桂树。阿波罗内心痛苦异常，他抱着月桂树向达芙妮倾诉道："你虽然不能做我的妻子，但你可以做我的树，我将永远在头上佩戴你这月桂的树枝；我还要让今后的凯旋队伍戴上用你的树叶编成的花冠；我的头发将永不剃剪，而你的树叶也会永不枯萎。"从此，月桂树变成了太阳神阿波罗的圣树。在希腊语中，月桂树叫作 Daphne，在英语里，月桂树则称作 laurel，获得用月桂树枝编成桂冠的重要奖项获得者是 laureate，桂冠诗人被称为 poet laureate, as shy as Daphne 用来形容少女羞羞答答的样子。

　　古希腊和古罗马神话对英语词汇的影响已经渗透到了英语文化和英语词汇的各个方面，并极大地增强了英语语言的丰富性和完善性。学习神话典故衍生出来的词汇需要读者更多地阅读与古希腊罗马神话相关的书籍，掌握英语词汇中的神话背景知识。总之，词源典故记忆法不但能帮助语言学习者开阔视野，扩展知识领域，提高文学修养，还有利于培养持久的英语词汇学习兴趣，提高词汇记忆的效率。

5

英语常用 228 个词根词缀及构成词汇

1

1. **ab-** : away ·· 55
2. **-tain-, -tend-, -tent-** : hold, keep ························· 55
3. **-rupt-** : break ··· 56
4. **-ced-, -ceed-, -cess-** : go ································· 56
5. **aer-, aeri-, aero-** : air ······································ 58
6. **-dict-** : say ·· 58
7. **-flu-** : flow ·· 59
8. **-vert-, -vers-** : turn ·· 60
9. **-aster-, -astr-** : star ······································· 61
10. **-ag-, -ig-, -agit-, -act-** : do ······························ 61
11. **ali-, -alter-** : the other ···································· 62
12. **-arch-** : rule, ruler ·· 63
13. **-am-, -amor-, -amat-** : love ······························· 64
14. **-scrib-, -script-** : write ···································· 64
15. **-sert-** : join ··· 65
16. **ambi-** : both, around ······································ 65
17. **-scend-, -scent-** : climb ··································· 66
18. **-ann-, -enn-** : year ·· 66

19. **ante-, anti-** : 1) before, in front of   2) against, the opposite ·········· 66
20. **-sum-, -sumpt-** : take ·········· 67
21. **-audi-, -audit-, audio-** : listen ·········· 67

2

22. **-ard** : person or thing ·········· 68
23. **-it-** : go ·········· 69
24. **-circ-** : circle ·········· 70
25. **-cogn-, -cogit-** : know ·········· 71
26. **-bat-** : beat, strike ·········· 71
27. **-bel-, -bell-** : war, fight ·········· 71
28. **bene-** : well, good ·········· 72
29. **-pat-, -pass-, -path-** : feeling, pain, disease, treatment ·········· 72
30. **-pel, -pell-, -puls-** : push ·········· 73
31. **-pon-, -pos-, -posit-, -pound** : put ·········· 74
32. **bi-** : two ·········· 76
33. **-card-, cardio-, -cardia** : heart ·········· 76
34. **-log-, -logue** : word, logic, discipline ·········· 76
35. **-pend-, -pens-** : 1) pay   2) hang ·········· 77
36. **-capt-, -cept-, -ceive-, -ceipt-, -ceit-, -cip-, -cipi-** : take ·········· 78
37. **-chron-** : time ·········· 80
38. **-plex-, -plic-, -ploy-, -ply-** : fold ·········· 80
39. **-press-** : push ·········· 82
40. **-fer-** : bring, carry ·········· 83
41. **-bi-, -bio-** : life ·········· 84
42. **-ple-, -plet-, -pli-, -plish-** : cover, fill ·········· 85

3

43. **-form-** : form ·········· 86
44. **-sens-, -sent-** : perceive, feel ·········· 87
45. **-corp-, -corpor-** : body ·········· 88
46. **-rod-, -ros-** : gnaw ·········· 88
47. **-ven-, -vent-** : come ·········· 89
48. **-sequ-, -secut-, -sec-, -sue** : follow ·········· 90
49. **-st-, -sist-, -stat-** : stand ·········· 91
50. **-tang-, -tag-, -tig-, -tact-** : touch ·········· 93

51. -cred- : believe ··· 95

52. -cruci- : cross ·· 95

53. -cur- : care ·· 96

54. -cur-, -curs-, -cour- : run ··· 96

55. -duc-, -duct- : lead ·· 98

56. -fact-, -fect-, -fic-, -fit-, -feas- : do, make ······································ 99

57. -flect-, -flex- : bend ·· 101

58. -leg- : 1) law 2) appoint ·· 101

59. -lig-, -leg-, -lect- : 1) read 2) choose ··· 102

60. -sign- : sign ·· 103

61. -stru-, -struct- : build ·· 104

62. -vi- : way ·· 105

63. -dia- : 1) day 2) across ·· 105

4

64. -dom- : 1) house 2) state, realm, condition ································ 106

65. -domin- : master ··· 106

66. du- : two ··· 107

67. -dyn-, -dynam- : power ··· 107

68. -ject- : throw ··· 108

69. -lev-, -lieve, -lief : lift ·· 109

70. -loqu-, -locut- : speak ··· 110

71. -merg-, -mers- : dip, sink ·· 110

72. -migr- : move ·· 111

73. -mit-, -mitt-, -miss- : send ··· 111

74. -vid-, -vis-, -view- : see ·· 113

75. -equ-, equi- : equal ··· 114

76. -rect-, -rig- : right ··· 115

77. -spic-, -spect-, -spec- : look, see ·· 115

78. -vac- : empty ··· 117

79. -vad-, -vas- : go ··· 118

80. -voc-, -vok- : call ·· 119

81. -clud-, -clus-, -clos- : close ··· 120

82. -em-, -am-, -empt- : take, buy ·· 121

83. -ped-, -pod- : foot ··· 122

84. -plor- : cry ·· 122

5

85. **-fus-** : pour ·· 123
86. **-graph-** : record, draw ··· 124
87. **-gen-, -gener-, -genet-** : birth ·· 124
88. **-habit-** : live, dwell ·· 125
89. **-her-, -hes-** : stick, cling ··· 126
90. **-hered-, -herit-** : heir ··· 127
91. **hemi-** : half ··· 127
92. **hiero-** : holy ·· 127
93. **homeo-, homo-** : the same ·· 127
94. **-hospit-, -host-** : guest ··· 128
95. **-hum-** : ground ·· 128
96. **hydro-** : water, hydrogen ··· 129
97. **hypo-, hyp-** : below, decrease ·· 129
98. **hyper-** : extreme ··· 130
99. **-emper-, -imper-** : command ·· 130
100. **-luc-** : light ·· 131
101. **-part-** : divide, part ··· 132
102. **-cid-, -cis-** : kill, cut ··· 133
103. **-flat-** : blow ··· 134
104. **-nov-** : new ··· 134
105. **-hibit-** : hold ·· 135

6

106. **-cert-** : certain ·· 135
107. **circum-** : around ·· 136
108. **-clam-, -claim** : cry, shout ··· 136
109. **-fid-, -fess-** : faith, tell ·· 137
110. **-solv-, -solut-** : loose ··· 138
111. **-torqu-, -tort-** : twist ··· 139
112. **-tract-, -treat-** : draw, pull ··· 139
113. **-turb-** : disorder ·· 141
114. **-doc-, -doct-** : teach ·· 142
115. **-fabul-** : speak ·· 142
116. **-fall-, -fals-** : deceive ··· 143
117. **-fend-, -fens-** : strike ·· 143

118. **-frag-, -fract-** : break ··· 144
119. **-fil-** : thread, line ··· 145
120. **-fin-** : end ··· 145
121. **-flict-** : strike ··· 146
122. **-hal-** : breathe ··· 146
123. **-hap-** : chance, luck ··· 147
124. **-grav-** : heavy ··· 147
125. **-greg-** : flock ··· 148
126. **-dorm-, -dormit-** : sleep ··· 149

7

127. **-laps-** : fall ··· 149
128. **-later-** : side ··· 150
129. **-let** : diminutive ··· 150
130. **-liber-** : free ··· 151
131. **-liter-** : letter ··· 151
132. **macro-** : big ··· 152
133. **micro-** : small ··· 152
134. **-magn-, major-, maxim-** : big ··· 153
135. **mal-, pessim-** : bad ··· 154
136. **-man-** : stay, dwell ··· 154
137. **-mand-, -mandat-** : command ··· 155
138. **mani-, manu-** : hand ··· 156
139. **-mar-, -mer-** : sea ··· 157
140. **-mater-, -matr-** : mother ··· 158
141. **-medi** : middle ··· 159
142. **-memor-** : mindful ··· 160
143. **-ment-** : mind ··· 161
144. **-milit-** : army ··· 163
145. **-minent-** : hang ··· 163
146. **mini-** : small ··· 163
147. **-mir-** : wonderful, strange ··· 165
148. **-mob-, -mot-, -mov-** : move ··· 165
149. **-mon-, -monit-** : warn ··· 167
150. **mono-, mon-** : single ··· 168
151. **multi-** : many ··· 169
152. **-mony** : event or state ··· 169

153. **-nomy** : a field of study ⋯⋯⋯⋯⋯⋯⋯⋯⋯⋯⋯⋯⋯⋯⋯⋯⋯⋯⋯⋯⋯⋯⋯⋯⋯⋯⋯⋯⋯⋯⋯⋯⋯⋯ 170

154. **-nomin-** : name ⋯⋯⋯ 170

155. **-nunc-, -nounc-** : announce ⋯⋯⋯⋯⋯⋯⋯⋯⋯⋯⋯⋯⋯⋯⋯⋯⋯⋯⋯⋯⋯⋯⋯⋯⋯⋯⋯⋯⋯⋯⋯⋯⋯ 171

8

156. **-par-** : 1) equal   2) show   3) bring forth ⋯⋯⋯⋯⋯⋯⋯⋯⋯⋯⋯⋯⋯⋯⋯⋯⋯⋯⋯⋯⋯⋯⋯⋯⋯⋯ 172

157. **para-** : 1) by the side of, past, to one side, aside from   2) beyond   3) subsidiary to
     4) protection of or against ⋯⋯⋯⋯⋯⋯⋯⋯⋯⋯⋯⋯⋯⋯⋯⋯⋯⋯⋯⋯⋯⋯⋯⋯⋯⋯⋯⋯⋯⋯⋯⋯⋯⋯⋯⋯⋯ 173

158. **-pater-, -patr-** : father ⋯⋯⋯⋯⋯⋯⋯⋯⋯⋯⋯⋯⋯⋯⋯⋯⋯⋯⋯⋯⋯⋯⋯⋯⋯⋯⋯⋯⋯⋯⋯⋯⋯⋯⋯⋯⋯ 174

159. **-pet-, -peat, -petit-** : seek ⋯⋯⋯⋯⋯⋯⋯⋯⋯⋯⋯⋯⋯⋯⋯⋯⋯⋯⋯⋯⋯⋯⋯⋯⋯⋯⋯⋯⋯⋯⋯⋯⋯⋯⋯ 175

160. **-phil-** : love ⋯⋯⋯ 175

161. **-phon-** : sound ⋯⋯⋯ 176

162. **physio-** : nature ⋯⋯ 177

163. **-pict-** : paint ⋯⋯ 177

164. **-polis-, -polit-** : city ⋯⋯⋯⋯⋯⋯⋯⋯⋯⋯⋯⋯⋯⋯⋯⋯⋯⋯⋯⋯⋯⋯⋯⋯⋯⋯⋯⋯⋯⋯⋯⋯⋯⋯⋯⋯⋯⋯⋯ 178

165. **-port-** : carry ⋯⋯ 178

166. **-poss-, -pot-** : power ⋯⋯⋯⋯⋯⋯⋯⋯⋯⋯⋯⋯⋯⋯⋯⋯⋯⋯⋯⋯⋯⋯⋯⋯⋯⋯⋯⋯⋯⋯⋯⋯⋯⋯⋯⋯⋯⋯⋯ 179

167. **post-** : after, behind ⋯⋯⋯⋯⋯⋯⋯⋯⋯⋯⋯⋯⋯⋯⋯⋯⋯⋯⋯⋯⋯⋯⋯⋯⋯⋯⋯⋯⋯⋯⋯⋯⋯⋯⋯⋯⋯⋯⋯ 180

168. **-proof** : resistant to ⋯⋯⋯⋯⋯⋯⋯⋯⋯⋯⋯⋯⋯⋯⋯⋯⋯⋯⋯⋯⋯⋯⋯⋯⋯⋯⋯⋯⋯⋯⋯⋯⋯⋯⋯⋯⋯⋯⋯ 180

169. **psycho-, psych-** : spirit, soul, mind ⋯⋯⋯⋯⋯⋯⋯⋯⋯⋯⋯⋯⋯⋯⋯⋯⋯⋯⋯⋯⋯⋯⋯⋯⋯⋯⋯⋯⋯ 181

170. **-punct-** : point ⋯⋯⋯ 181

171. **-pur-** : pure ⋯⋯⋯ 182

172. **-put-** : think ⋯⋯ 182

173. **-quir-, -quisit-, -quest** : seek ⋯⋯⋯⋯⋯⋯⋯⋯⋯⋯⋯⋯⋯⋯⋯⋯⋯⋯⋯⋯⋯⋯⋯⋯⋯⋯⋯⋯⋯⋯⋯⋯ 183

174. **-rad-, -ras-** : scrape ⋯⋯⋯⋯⋯⋯⋯⋯⋯⋯⋯⋯⋯⋯⋯⋯⋯⋯⋯⋯⋯⋯⋯⋯⋯⋯⋯⋯⋯⋯⋯⋯⋯⋯⋯⋯⋯⋯⋯ 184

175. **-radic-** : root ⋯⋯ 185

176. **-rid-, -ris-** : laugh ⋯⋯ 185

177. **-rog-** : ask ⋯⋯ 185

178. **-rot-** : wheel ⋯⋯⋯ 186

9

179. **-san-** : health ⋯⋯⋯ 187

180. **-sat-, -satis-, -satur-** : enough ⋯⋯⋯⋯⋯⋯⋯⋯⋯⋯⋯⋯⋯⋯⋯⋯⋯⋯⋯⋯⋯⋯⋯⋯⋯⋯⋯⋯⋯⋯⋯⋯ 187

181. **-sci-** : know ⋯⋯⋯ 188

182. **se-** : away from, apart from, without ⋯⋯⋯⋯⋯⋯⋯⋯⋯⋯⋯⋯⋯⋯⋯⋯⋯⋯⋯⋯⋯⋯⋯⋯⋯⋯⋯⋯⋯ 189

183. **-sed-, -sid-, -sess-** : sit ⋯⋯⋯⋯⋯⋯⋯⋯⋯⋯⋯⋯⋯⋯⋯⋯⋯⋯⋯⋯⋯⋯⋯⋯⋯⋯⋯⋯⋯⋯⋯⋯⋯⋯⋯⋯⋯ 190

184. **-seg-, -sect-** : cut ⋯⋯⋯ 191

185. **-sembl-** : together ·· 192

186. **-sen-** : old ··· 192

187. **-simil-, -simul-** : similar ··· 192

188. **-sol-** : 1) alone 2) sun ··· 193

189. **-son-** : sound ··· 194

190. **-soph-** : wise, wisdom ··· 195

191. **-sort-** : select ··· 195

192. **-sper-** : hope ·· 196

193. **-stitut-** : set up ··· 196

194. **-string-, -strict-, -strain, -straint, -stress** : draw tight ····················· 197

195. **-sult-** : leap ··· 199

196. **syn-, sym-** : with, together, at the same time ·································· 199

197. **-tect-** : cover ·· 200

198. **tele-** : far or relating to television ··· 201

199. **-tempor-** : time ··· 201

200. **-text-** : weave ··· 202

201. **-tox-** : poison ··· 202

202. **trans-** : across, beyond, change into another form ······················· 203

203. **-tut-, -tuit-** : watch ··· 204

10

204. **uni-** : one ·· 205

205. **-urb-** : city ·· 206

206. **-vag-** : wander ·· 206

207. **-vari-** : change ·· 207

208. **-vir-** : man ·· 207

209. **-viv-, -vit-, -vig-** : live ·· 208

210. **-vict-, -vinc-** : conquer or overcome ·· 209

211. **-vol-, -volunt-** : will ··· 210

212. **-volv-, -volut-** : turn over ··· 210

213. **-tempt-** : test ·· 211

214. **-tend-, -tens-, -tent-** : stretch ·· 211

215. **-termin-** : border ··· 214

216. **-terr-** : 1) earth, land 2) frighten ··· 214

217. **-test-** : witness ··· 216

218. **-onym-** : name ·· 216

219. **-opt-** : 1) choose 2) eye ··· 217

220. **-ori-, -ort-** : rise ·· 218
221. **-ot** : person ·· 219
222. **pre-** : before, in front of, in advance ··· 219
223. **-preci-** : price ··· 220
224. **-prim-, prior-** : first ·· 221
225. **-spire-** : breathe ··· 222
226. **-tribut-** : give ··· 222
227. **-prob-, -prov-** : prove ·· 223
228. **-proxim-** : near ··· 224

1

1. ab- : away　巧记：a 离开 + B 两间房子 指离开房子

abnormal [æb'nɔːml] 反常的　词源：ab 离开 + normal 正常的 指离开正常的状态

abuse [ə'bjuːz] 滥用职权 abuse of power；虐待辱骂　词源：ab 离开 + use 指离开正常的使用范围　词义连记：官员滥用权力虐待辱骂犯人

abstain [əb'stein] 戒除（恶习）；弃权（投票）abstain from sth.　词源：abs 离开 + tain 拿着 指不再拿着烟酒是戒除恶习　词义连记：戒除恶习的人可以不用弃权

abstention [əb'stenʃn] 戒除（恶习）；弃权（投票）　词源：abstain 戒除 + tion 名词后缀

absurd [əb'səːd] 荒唐的　词源：ab 离开 + sure 确定 指不确定的是荒唐的

abstruse [əb'struːs] 难以理解的,过于深奥的　词源：ab 离开 + truth 真理 指远离真理是难以理解、深奥的

grab [græb] 抓,抢夺（包或财物）grab sth. from sb. / sth.；赶紧,抓紧（吃或睡）grab some sleep 抓紧时间睡一会儿；抓住（机会）；接受（邀请）；吸引（某人的注意）grab one's attention　词源：grass 草 + ab 离开 指像抓把草一样抢夺　巧记：grab bag 摸彩袋

stab [stæb]（用刀等锐器）刺,戳；（用手指或尖物）戳,捅,刺；试图（做某事）have / make / take a stab at (doing) sth.　词源：sting 叮咬 + ab 离开 指像叮咬般的刺痛别人后马上离开

backstabbing ['bæk,stæbiŋ] 背后中伤别人的名誉　词源：back 后面 + stab 刺 + ing 名词后缀 指背后中伤别人

2. -tain-, -tend-, -tent- : hold, keep　巧记：touch 触碰

abstain [əb'stein] 戒除（恶习）；弃权（投票）abstain from sth.　词源：abs 离开 + tain 拿着 指不再拿着烟酒是戒除恶习　词义连记：戒除恶习的人可以不用弃权

abstention [əb'stenʃn] 戒除（恶习）；弃权（投票）　词源：abstain 戒除 + tion 名词后缀

attain [ə'tein] 达成（目标）；获得（职位）　词源：at 强调 + tain 拿着

contain [kən'tein] 包含,包括　词源：con 共同 + tain 拿着

container [kən'teinə] 容器（箱, 盆, 罐, 壶, 桶, 坛子）tea leaves in a small metal container 小金属容器里的茶叶；集装箱　词源：contain 包含 + er 名词后缀

content [kən'tent]（书、讲话、节目或网站等的）内容；目录 a table of contents 目录；含量 protein content 蛋白质含量；心满意足的 be content with sth.　词源：contain 的名词形式 指包含了很多内容　词义连记：书的目录内容丰富信息含量高让人十分满意的　反义词：discontent

discontent [diskən'tent] 不满意的 be discontent with sth.　词源：dis 否定 + content 心满意足的 指不满意的

detain [di'tein] 拘留；推迟 be detained on urgent business 因紧急事务耽搁　词源：de 向下 + tain 拿着 指向下拿住别人拘留　词义连记：拘留老板推迟会议

entertain [entə'tein] 款待，招待；使娱乐 entertain sb. with sth.；怀有某种想法，希望，看法 entertain an idea / hope / thought　词源：enter 进入 ＋tain 拿着　指进屋拿着好吃好喝招待客人

entertainment [entə'teinm(ə)nt] 招待；娱乐　词源：entertain 招待 ＋ment 名词后缀

maintain [mein'tein; mən'tein] 维持关系；养家养车；坚持说，坚持认为 sb. maintain that…　词源：main 停留 stay ＋tain 拿着　指停留并保持拿着不动的状态是维持　巧记：mountain 指像山一样维持不动

obtain [əb'tein]（尤指通过自身的努力、技能或工作）达成，获得 obtain advice / information / permission from sb. / sth. 获得（某人或某机构）的忠告/信息/许可　词源：ob 强调 ＋tain 拿着

pertain [pə'tein] 有关于，与……相关 petain to sth.　词源：per 一直 ＋tain 拿着　指一直与某事物相关联

retain [ri'tein] 留住（客户）；留用（员工）；保留（记忆、头衔或物品所有权）；聘请（律师或专家）　词源：re 重复 ＋tain 拿着　指重复拿着是保留

sustain [sə'stein] 维持（生命）；维持（发展）；遭受（打击）；证实（观点）；支撑，承受住（重量）　词源：sus 在下面 ＋tain 拿着　指在下面顶着东西维持原有状态

sustainable [sə'steinəb(ə)l] 可持续的 sustainable development 可持续发展　词源：sustain 持续 ＋able 形容词后缀（表示可以……的）

3. -rupt- : break　巧记：r 分裂 ＋pt 声音　指植物生长时分裂发出的声音

abrupt [ə'brʌpt] 突然的 an abrupt change / halt / departure 突然改变/停顿/离开；唐突的（话语）　词源：ab 离开 ＋rupt 破裂　指突然破裂的声音　词义连记：突然说出唐突的话

bankrupt ['bæŋkrʌpt] 破产者；使破产；破产的 go bankrupt 破产；完全缺乏（某种美德或有价值的东西）的 be bankrupt of sth.　词源：bank 银行 ＋rupt 破裂

corrupt [kə'rʌpt] 腐败的；使腐败　词源：cor 一起 ＋rupt 破裂　指一起道德破裂是腐败的

disrupt [dis'rʌpt] 使（活动）混乱，扰乱（交通）　词源：dis 分离 ＋rupt 破裂　指四散分裂的状态

erupt [i'rʌpt]（皮疹）突然出现；（火山）爆发，喷发；（岩浆、烟等）喷出；（活动或情绪）爆发；（搏斗、暴力事件、噪声等）突然发生　词源：e 出来 ＋rupt 破裂　指破裂开口后喷发出来

interrupt [intə'rʌpt] 打断（谈话）；中断（信号）；暂停（节目）　词源：inter 两者间 ＋rupt 破裂　指在两者间打破联系

rupture ['rʌptʃə]（船体）裂缝；（管道）突然爆裂 ruptures of the water pipelines 输水管道的爆裂；（关系）破裂　词源：rupt 破裂 ＋nature 性质

4. -ced-, -ceed-, -cess- : go　巧记：c 弯腰 ＋seed 种子　指在田里弯腰边走边播种

cede [si:d] 割让（领土），转让 cede sth. to sb.　词源：ced 走　指离开原来的地方

accede [ək'si:d]（尤指最初不同意后）同意 accede to sth.；（国王）就职，即位 accede to the throne　词源：ac 强调 ＋ced 走　强调一起走同样的路　词义连记：同意就职做国王

access ['ækses] 路径，入口；（计算机文件）权限；进入（电子系统） 词源：ac 强调 + cess 走 强调能走的路是路径

accessory [ək'ses(ə)ri] （项链，手镯，围巾，眼镜，包等女性随身）装饰品；（汽车或手机）零件，配件；同谋犯 词源：ac 强调 + cess 走 + ory 名词后缀 指和女性一起走的是身上的装饰品 词义连记：一个女性同谋犯偷装饰品和手机零件

ancestor ['ænsestə] 祖先；（现代机器、车辆等的）原型 词源：an 否定 + ces 走 + or 人 指已经不在世上走的人是祖先

ancestry ['ænsestri] 祖先；血统 be of British ancestry 祖籍英国

concede [kən'siːd] 勉强承认（比赛或选举的失败）concede defeat；让步 concede sth. to sb. 词源：con 共同 + ced 走 指聚集的人一起走开是让步 词义连记：选举人勉强承认失败向对手让步

concession [kən'seʃ(ə)n] 让步；（资源如石油，水，木材，矿物）特许经营权；（大型建筑物或商场中的）销售点，摊位；营业摊点上出售的商品；（对特殊群体，如学生、军人、老人或儿童，在票价等费用上的）优惠价，减价票 词源：con 共同 + cess 走 + ion 名词 指完全走开让步给别人经营摊位和售卖特许商品

exceed [ik'siːd; ek-] 超出（期待）；超速；超越（规则或法律的规定） 词源：ex 出来 + ceed 走 指比别人走得快

excess [ik'ses; ek-; 'ekses] 过多量（中性词）；过量的，过多的 excess baggage / luggage 超重行李 词源：ex 出来 + cess 走 指跑出来的是过多的

exceedingly [ik'siːdiŋli; ek-] 极度地 exceedingly kind 太好了 同义词：extremely

excessive [ik'sesiv; ek-] 过度的（贬义词）excessive drinking 过度酗酒 词源：ex 出来 + cess 走 + ive 形容词后缀（表示充满活力的 active）指比过多量还多的程度是过度的

incessant [in'ses(ə)nt] 连续的 incessant rain 连绵不断的雨 词源：in 在内部 + cess 走 + ant 形容词后缀（表示具有……能力的）指内心里走来走去连续不停的

intercede [ˌintə'siːd] 求情 intercede with sb. for sth. 词源：inter 两者间 + cede 走 指走到两者间说情

precede [pri'siːd] 在……之前 a type of cloud that precedes rain 下雨前出现的一种云 词源：pre 在前面 + cede 走 指走在别的前面

preceding [pri'siːdiŋ] 先前的，前面的 income tax paid in preceding years 前几年缴付的所得税 词源：precede 在……前面 + ing 形容词后缀

precedent ['presid(ə)nt] 先例 set a precedent for sth. 创造先例；惯例 break with precedent 打破惯例 词源：precede 在……前面 + ent 名词后缀（表示具有……能力的）

unprecedented [ʌn'presidentid] 空前的，前所未有的 an event that is unprecedented in recent history 近代历史上没有先例的事件 词源：un 否定 + precedent 先例 指没有先例的

proceed [prə'siːd] 继续 proceed with sth. / proceed to do sth.；（机场）前进（到登机口）；proceed against sb. 起诉（某人），对（某人）提起诉讼 词源：pro 向前 + ceed 走 指不停向前走是继续

process ['prəuses] 过程；加工（产品）；处理（数据）；冲印（照片）　词源：pro 向前 + cess 走　指向前走的一步步加工产品的过程

procedure [prə'si:dʒə] 步骤 the procedure for applying for a visa 申请签证的手续　词源：pro 向前 + ced 走 + nature 性质

procession [prə'seʃ(ə)n]（游行）行列，（军队）队伍；一连串（游客）　词源：pro 向前 + cess 走 + sion 名词后缀　指队伍向前走

recess [ri'ses; 'ri:ses]（议会或法庭）休会；课间休息　词源：re 向后 + cess 走　指走回去休息

recession [ri'seʃ(ə)n] 经济衰退　词源：re 向后 + cess 走 + ion 名词后缀　指经济情况往后退

recede [ri'si:d] 洪水消退；（声音、图像、记忆）逐渐消失；（头发）从前额往后脱落　词源：re 向后 + cede 走　指向后退

supersede [,su:pə'si:d; ,sju:-]（产品）替代　词源：super 上面 + sede 走　指在上面走过覆盖过原来的事物

succeed [sək'si:d] 成功　词源：suc 下面 + ceed 走　指成功都是在下面努力默默走出来的

success [sək'ses] 成功；成功的人，成功的事　词源：suc 在下面 + cess 走　指成功都是在下面努力默默走出来的

successive [sək'sesiv] 连续的（胜利）successive victories　词源：success 成功 + ive 形容词后缀（表示充满活力的 active）指成功的事物是连续的

successor [sək'sesə] 继任者 a successor to the post 职位的接替者　词源：success 成功 + or 指把成功继续下去的人

predecessor ['pri:disesə]（职位的）前任　词源：pre 在前面 + de 否定 + cess 走 + or 人　指在前面曾经走过现在不再走职业道路的人

5. aer-, aeri-, aero-：air　巧记：air 空气

aerospace ['eərəspeis] 航空和航天（工业）的，宇航的　词源：aero 空气 + space 太空

aerosphere ['eərəsfiə] 大气层　词源：aero 空气 + sphere 球体　指空气组成的球体

atmosphere ['ætməsfiə] 大气层；气氛　词源：atom 原子 + sphere 球体　指空气原子构成的球体

aerial ['eəriəl] 空中的 the aerial acrobatics 空中杂技表演；从飞机上的 aerial photographs 航空照片；（电视或收音机）天线；（滑雪的）空中技巧（常复数）　巧记：aer 空气 + l 一根长棍　指空中的一根竖立的长棍是天线

aerobatics [,eərə'bætiks] 特技飞行，航空表演　词源：aero 空气 + bat 蝙蝠 + ics 学科　指像空气中的蝙蝠飞行般的航空表演　形近易混词：acrobatics

acrobatics [ækrə'bætiks] 杂技　词源：acro 高 + bat 蝙蝠 + ics 学科　指像塔尖上的蝙蝠倒立平衡做杂技动作

aerobics [eə'rəubiks] 有氧运动，有氧健身操　词源：aero 空气 + bio 生命 + ics 学科　指和空气、生命有关的运动

6. -dict-：say　巧记：di 指滴滴嗒嗒说话 + ct 声音

addict ['ædikt] 上瘾的人；使上瘾 be addicted to sth. 词源：ad 强调 + dict 说 原指说话会上瘾

contradict [kɔntrə'dikt] 反驳；使相矛盾 contradict oneself 自相矛盾 词源：contra 相反的 + dict 说 指反着说话

contradiction [kɔntrə'dikʃ(ə)n] 反驳；矛盾 词源：contradict 反驳 + tion 名词后缀

dedicate ['dedikeit] 献身，致力于事业 dedicate oneself to sth.；作品献给某人 dedicate sth. to sb. 词源：de 向下 + dict 说 指向下说话投身教育事业 形近易混词：delicate

delicate ['delikət] 精致的（蛋糕）；纤弱的（身体）；易碎的（瓷器） 巧记：delicious 美味的 指美味的都是精致的

dictionary ['dikʃ(ə)n(ə)ri] 词典 词源：dict 说 + ary 名词后缀

diction ['dikʃ(ə)n] 吐字，发音方式 clear diction 清晰的吐字；措辞，用词，（尤指文学中的）遣词用字 巧记：dictionary 字典是教措辞用词的

dictate [dik'teit] 口述（信件）dictate a letter to the secretary 向秘书口述信件；让（某人）听写；（尤指以令人不快的方式）命令，指示，强制规定；支配，决定 词源：dict 说 + ate 动词后缀

dictation [dik'teiʃ(ə)n] 口述；听写 词源：dict 说 + tion 名词后缀

dictator [dik'teitə] 独裁者 词源：dict 说 + or 名词后缀

dictatorship [dik'teitəʃip] 独裁 词源：dict 说 + ship 名词后缀（表示关系）

edict ['iːdikt]（皇帝或政府）布告，法令 词源：e 出来 + dict 说 指说出来的法令 巧记：米兰敕令（拉丁文：Edictum Mediolanense，英文：Edict of Milan），又译作米兰诏令或米兰诏书，是罗马帝国皇帝君士坦丁一世和李锡尼在 313 年于意大利的米兰颁发的一个宽容基督教的敕令。此诏书宣布罗马帝国境内有信仰基督教的自由，并且发还了已经没收的教会财产，也承认了基督教的合法地位。

indicate ['indikeit] 暗指 词源：in 内部 + dict 说 + ate 动词后缀 指内心所表达的话

indict [in'dait] 起诉，控告 indict sb. for sth. 词源：in 内部 + dict 说 指内心说对方不好 巧记：谐音 indict 读作[in'dait] 指内心中想逮捕他

predict [pri'dikt] 预言，预测 词源：pre 在前面 + dict 说 指提前说出

verdict ['vəːdikt]（法庭或陪审团作出的）裁决 reach / return a verdict of not guilty 作出无罪裁决；（上级的）正式决定，裁决 await the verdict of the umpire 等待裁判的裁决；（经过检验或认真考虑后的）决定，结论，意见 give (sb.) one's verdict (on sth.) 词源：ver 真实的 + dict 说 指法庭裁决里面说的是真话

7. -flu- : flow 巧记：flow 流动 + u 水

affluent ['æfluənt]（家庭或社会等）富裕的 affluent nations 富裕的国家 词源：af 强调 + flu 流动 + ent 形容词后缀（表示具有……能力的）指有流动的水或石油的地方

influence ['influəns] 影响 词源：in 内部 + flu 流动 指流入到内部的影响

influenza [influ'enzə] 感冒 词源：in 内部 + flu 流动 指感冒是流行性的

fluent ['fluːənt]（语言）流利的，流畅的 词源：flu 流动 + ent 形容词后缀（表示具有……能

力的）

fluid ['fluːid] 流体（指化学液体）a powerful cleaning fluid 一种强力清洁液；流动的，流体的；（动作、设计、音乐等）流畅优美的；（局势）易变的，不稳定的 a fluid political situation 不稳定的政治局势　词源：flu 流动 ＋id 身份　指有流动的身份特性

flush [flʌʃ]（用水）冲厕所；（因生气或尴尬而引起的）脸红；一阵强烈情感 a flush of anger / embarrassment / enthusiasm / guilt / excitement 一阵愤怒/尴尬/热情/内疚/兴奋；（纸牌戏中的）同花牌　词源：flu 流动 ＋sh 闪光　指冲刷时水反射的光线

fluctuate ['flʌktʃueit; -tju-]（价格）波动　词源：flu 流动 ＋ct 声音 ＋ate 动词后缀　指流动波动的状态

superfluous [suːˈpəːfluəs; sjuː-] 多余的 superfluous decoration 多余的装饰　词源：super 上面 ＋flu 流动 ＋ous 形容词后缀（表示过多）指从上面流出来的多余的

overflow [əuvəˈfləu] 溢出；充满，有许多 overflow with colour 色彩缤纷；（人）挤满　词源：over 在上面 ＋flow 流动　指从上面流出来

8. -vert-, -vers- : turn　巧记：v 峡谷口形状 ＋t 方向　指峡谷里的河流或路径转来转去

avert [əˈvəːt] 转移（目光）；避免（冲突）　词源：a 正在 ＋vert 转向　词义连记：转移尴尬目光，避免正面冲突

advert [ˈædvəːt] 提及 advert to sth.；广告（＝ad＝advertisement）词源：ad 强调 ＋vert 转向　词义连记：转身看广告提及的内容

advertise [ˈædvətaiz] 做广告 advertise sth. on televsion 电视上做广告；宣扬（自己的事）　词源：ad 强调 ＋vert 转向

adverse [ˈædvəːs] 逆境的；（自然条件）不利的 adverse wind 逆风　词源：ad 强调 ＋vers 转向　指像峡谷里的河流一样转来绕去不直接的

adversary [ˈædvəs(ə)ri] 对手　词源：adverse 逆境的 ＋ary 人　指给别人带来逆境的人

convert [kənˈvəːt]（宗教）皈依；（功能或能量）转化 a sofa that converts into a bed 可改作床用的沙发；（货币）兑换　词源：con 共同 ＋vert 转向　指全部转化成其他形式

converse [kənˈvəːs] 谈话 converse with sb.；相反的（事例或陈述）a converse example 反例　词源：con 共同 ＋vers 转向　指大家转向同一话题聊天　词义连记：和别人谈话讨论反例　巧记：converse 匡威诞生于 1908 年，创办以来 Converse 坚持品牌的独立性设计，不追随他人，最初只生产"橡胶鞋"，但很快就开始做网球和篮球鞋。

divert [daiˈvəːt; di-]（河流或道路）转向改道；改变（资金、材料等的）用途 divert more resources into research 把更多的资源用于研究；转移（注意力）divert sb.'s attention；使娱乐　词源：di 分离 ＋vert 转向　指分散转向改变路线

diversion [daiˈvəːʃ(ə)n; di-]（河流或道路）转向改道；注意力（转移）；消遣娱乐　词源：divert 转向 ＋sion 名词后缀　巧记：修路时立在路中间的警示牌上写的是 diversion

diverse [daiˈvəːs; ˈdaivəːs]（语言或文化）多样的　词源：di 分离 ＋vers 转向

diversity [daiˈvəːsiti; di-]（语言或文化）多样性　词源：diverse 多样的 ＋ity 名词后缀

diversify [dai'və:sifai; di-] 使多元化　词源：diverse 多样的 + fy 动词后缀
invert [in'və:t] 使内部颠倒 invert an hourglass 颠倒沙漏　词源：in 内部 + vert 转向 指从内部颠倒
extrovert ['ekstrəvə:t] 外向的人　词源：extro 外部 + vert 转向 指性格向外的人
introvert ['intrəvə:t] 内向的人　词源：intro 内部 + vert 转向 指性格向内的人
obverse ['ɔbvə:s]（物体，硬币或奖牌）正面的　词源：ob 否定 + vers 转向 指不转向，保持正面的
overt [əu'və:t; 'əuvə:t] 公开的　词源：over 在上面 指在上面都看得见的
covert ['kʌvət; 'kəuvə:t] 隐蔽的　词源：cover 覆盖
pervert [pə'və:t] 变态者；走歪路，腐蚀（心灵）　词源：person 人 + vert 转向 指人一直变来变去像蝙蝠侠里的小丑性格
perverse [pə'və:s] 变态的，任性的，一意孤行的　词源：person 人 + vers 转向
revert [ri'və:t]（建筑）恢复原状；重提（旧话题）；归还（房屋地产）；（手机系统）恢复原版本；拨回钟表时间　词源：re 向后 + vert 转向 指向后转回到原有状态
subvert [səb'və:t] 暗中破坏　词源：sub 下面 + vert 转向 指在下面改变原有政府或制度
reverse [ri'və:s]（物体）反面的；颠倒（图片）；倒车；取消（决议、裁决或法律等）；逆袭 reverse the tide　词源：re 向后 + vers 转向 指汽车向后转向　巧记：倒挡的缩写字母 R 是 reverse
versatile ['və:sətail]（手机或电子产品）多功能的 a versatile key 万能钥匙；（人）多才多艺的　词源：vers 转向 + ile 形容词后缀（表示容易……的）指功能上容易转换的、多样的
traverse ['trævəs; trə'və:s] 跋涉，横跨，横穿 traverse the national park 横穿国家公园　词源：travel 旅行 + vers 转向 指像马可波罗一样在欧亚大陆旅行，转向经过不同的国家

9. **-aster-, -astr-** : star　巧记：a 正在 + star 星星 指正在天上的星星
astroboy ['æstərbɔi] 阿童木　词源：astro 星星 + boy 男孩 指阿童木可以在星星中穿越飞行
asteroid ['æstərɔid] 小行星；小行星的 asteroid belt 火星和木星间的小行星带　词源：aster 星星 + id 身份
catastrophe [kə'tæstrəfi] 大灾难　词源：cata 向下 + astro 星星 + phone 声音 指天上落下流星雨的声音，预示大灾难
disaster [di'zɑ:stə] 灾难　词源：dis 分散 + aster 星星 指天上四散的流星，表示灾难
astronomy [ə'strɔnəmi] 天文学　词源：astro 星星 + nomy 名词后缀（表示学科）
astronomer [ə'strɔnəmə] 天文学家　词源：astronomy 天文学 + er 名词后缀
astrology [ə'strɔlədʒi] 占星术（指研究星体位置和运动对人的运势和事件的影响）　词源：astro 星星 + ology 名词后缀（表示学科）指观察星星算运势
astronaut ['æstrənɔ:t] 宇航员　词源：astro 星星 + navy 海军 指在星空中航行的人
asterisk ['æstərisk] 星号（*）　词源：aster 星星 + sky 天空 指天上的星星

10. **-ag-, -ig-, -agit-, -act-** : do　巧记：a 正在 + g 地球转动 指球体做运动的状态

activate ['æktiveit]（新手机开机）激活；激励 activate sb. to do sth. 词源：act 做动作 + ate 动词后缀 指使机器激活动起来能够做动作

activist ['æktivist] 积极活动分子 词源：activity 活动 + ist 人名后缀

agile ['ædʒail]（动作）敏捷的，灵活的；（思维）机敏的 词源：ag 做动作 + ile 形容词后缀（表示容易……的）指容易做各种不同动作的状态

agility [ə'dʒiləti]（狗或马过障碍）灵活，机敏 词源：agile 敏捷的 + ity 名词后缀

agitate ['ædʒiteit] 煽动，鼓动 agitate for higher pay 煽动加工资；使焦虑不安；搅动，摇动（液体） 词源：ag 做动作 + it 走 go + ate 动词后缀 指让液体在容器中走动搅动起来 词义连记：示威的人搅动着手里的酒精瓶煽动罢工引起了人们的不安

agitated ['ædʒiteitid] 不安的，焦虑的 词源：agitate 使不安 + ed 形容词后缀

agitation [ædʒi'teiʃ(ə)n] 煽动；不安；（液体）搅动，摇动 词源：agitate 搅动 + tion 名词后缀

agency ['eidʒ(ə)nsi] 机构（CIA = Central Intelligence Agency 美国中情局）；公司 ad / model / travel agency 广告公司/模特公司/旅行社 词源：ag 做动作 + cy 名词后缀 指做事情的组织或做出各种举动的团体

agent ['eidʒ(ə)nt]（旅行社，房地产）代理人；特工；化学药剂；原因，因素 词源：ag 做动作 + ent 人或物名词后缀 指频繁做各种动作、迎合客人的人是商业代理人

agenda [ə'dʒendə] 会议议程，（政府、机构等的）待办事项一览表 词源：agency 机构 + da 做 do 指机构或公司每天按时间安排做的事情

enact [i'nækt; e-] 扮演角色；制定法律 词源：en 使动词化 + Act（act 大写含义是法案）指制定法案

exacting [ig'zæktiŋ] 苛求的，要求高的 词源：exact 精确的 + ing 形容词后缀 指比做得精准的要求还高是苛刻的 同义词：demanding

interact [intər'ækt] 互动，互相来往；互相影响 词源：inter 两者间 + act 做动作 指两者间做互动的行为

react [ri'ækt] 化学反应；做出反应 react to sth.；反作用 词源：re 向后 + act 做动作 指相反方向做动作是反应

reaction [ri'ækʃ(ə)n] 反应；反作用力 词源：react 反应 + tion 名词后缀

reactionary [ri'ækʃənri] 反动派，反动分子；反动的 词源：reaction 反作用 + ary 人 指起到反作用的人

transact [træn'zækt; trɑ:n-; -'sækt] 交易，交换；业务办理 词源：trans 穿越 + act 做动作 指做以物易物的交易动作

sanction ['sæŋ(k)ʃ(ə)n]（对某国的）制裁 impose sanctions on sth.；（正式）许可，批准，接受 sanction the king's second marriage 批准国王的第二次婚姻 词源：say 说出 + not 否定 + action 动作 指和别国说不能做贸易动作是制裁

11. **ali-, -alter-** : the other 巧记：all 最后字母 l 变成 i 指有一部分变为其他的

alias ['eiliəs] 别名 词源：ali 其他的 + as 作为 指用其他的名字作为名字

alien ['eiliən] 侨民 illegal aliens 非法外侨；外星人；海外的，异域的 alien cultures 异域文化；（环境）陌生的，不熟悉的 an alien environment 陌生的环境；（思想、理念或信仰）不相容的，格格不入的 be alien to sb. / sth. 词源：ali 其他的 + en 人 巧记：Alien 系列电影《异形》；Alienware 北美顶级的电脑商，采用了最高端、顶级的配置，在业界是高端、高品质的代名词，机箱的外观十分前卫，使 Alienware 的产品极受欢迎

alienate ['eiliəneit]（家庭关系或与某群体）疏远，使格格不入 alienate sb. from sth. 词源：alien 海外的 + ate 动词后缀 指疏远的远方

alter ['ɔːltə; 'ɒl-]（使）变化，（使）改变；改（服装使更合身）have the dress altered for the wedding 把礼服改一下婚礼上穿 词源：ali 其他的 + er 动词后缀（表示动作的反复）指不停地改变成其他状态 巧记：sb.'s alter ego 指某人的第二自我，某人个性的另一面

alternate ['ɔːltəneit; 'ɒl-] 使（不同情绪）轮流出现 alternate between happiness and depression 一会儿高兴一会儿沮丧；（昼夜，四季）交替；交替的 a dessert with alternate layers of fruit and cream 水果层和奶油层相间的甜点 词源：alter 改变 + ate 动词后缀

alternation [ˌɔːltə'neiʃən] 交替 the alternation of day and night 日夜交替 词源：alternate 交替 + tion 名词后缀

alternative [ɔːl'tɜːnətiv; ɒl-] 二选一的 an alternative route 另一条路线；标新立异的，非传统的，可替代的（能源，指太阳能、风能、水能等）alternative energy；可供选择的事物 词源：alternate 交替 + tive 形容词后缀（表示充满活力的 active）

12. -arch- : rule, ruler 巧记：a 正在 + r 向上 + c 弯曲 + h 高 指向上弯曲的高高的拱门

anarchy ['ænəki] 无政府状态 词源：an 否定 + arch 统治 + y 名词后缀

anarchist ['ænəkist] 无政府主义者 词源：anarchy 无政府状态 + ist 人

anarchism ['ænəkizəm] 无政府主义 词源：anarchy 无政府状态 + ism 主义

autarchy ['ɔːtɑːki] 自给自足，闭关政策 词源：auto 自己 + arch 统治管理 + y 名词后缀

arc [ɑːk] 弧，（鼠标或彩虹的）弧形 词源：arch 拱门的弧形

arcade [ɑː'keid] 拱廊商业街；（电子游戏）游艺厅 词源：arch 拱门 + ade 名词后缀（表示强调）指市场建筑拱形结构下许多商店组成的商业街

arch [ɑːtʃ] 拱（支撑如桥梁或房屋上部的弧形结构）；拱门 the triumphal arch 凯旋门；足弓，足背 词源：arch 统治 指拱门是统治的象征

archer ['ɑːtʃə] 弓箭手 词源：arch 拱门 指弓箭手站在拱门上射箭 形近易混词：anchor

archery ['ɑːtʃəri] 箭术 词源：archer 弓箭手 + y 名词后缀 指弓箭手的射箭技术

anchor ['æŋkə] 锚；使（船）停泊；使（架子）固定；（家庭）支柱，靠山；新闻主播 词源：arch 指船锚的形状像拱门坚毅不动

archeology [ˌɑːki'ɒlədʒi] 考古学 词源：arch 拱门 + e 出来 + ology 名词后缀（表示学科）指把拱门发掘出来的学科

archeologist [ˌɑːki'ɒlədʒist] 考古学家 词源：archeology 考古学 + ist 人

architecture ['ɑːkitektʃə] 建筑；建筑风格，建筑式样；建筑学 词源：arch 拱门 + tect 覆盖 +

nature 名词后缀 指覆盖着拱门的建筑
architect ['ɑːkitekt] 建筑师 词源：architecture 建筑 指设计建筑的人
oligarchy ['ɔligɑːki] 寡头政治 词源：oligos 少的（only 的变形）+ arch 统治 指由少数人统治

13. -am-, -amor-, -amat- : love 巧记：l'amour 法语词 表示爱恋，爱情
amour [ə'muə(r)] 爱情；风流韵事，偷情 词源：l'amour 法语词表示爱恋，爱情
amorist ['æmərist] 情人 词源：amour 爱 + ist 人
amorous ['æm(ə)rəs] 多情的；色情的 词源：amour 爱 + ous 形容词后缀（表示过多的）
amiable ['eimiəb(ə)l] （性格）亲切的，（人）和蔼的 词源：am 爱 + i 人 + able 形容词后缀（表示可以……的）
amicable ['æmikəb(ə)l] （彼此关系）友好的，友善的 词源：am 爱 + c 国家 country + able 形容词后缀（表示可以……的）指国家关系可以友爱和睦的
amity ['æmiti] （国家关系）和睦，友好 词源：am 爱 + ity 名词后缀 巧记：谐音"暧昧它" 指国家关系和睦暧昧，作 amicable 的名词形式，但拼写中没有字母 c
amateur ['æmətə; -tʃə; -tjuə; ˌæmə'təː] 业余爱好者；外行，生手 词源：am 爱 + teur 人 指有业余爱好的人
amateurish ['æmətəriʃ] 外行的，不熟练的 词源：amteur 业余爱好者 + ish 形容词后缀

14. -scrib-, -script- : write 巧记：s 弯曲的路 + crab 螃蟹 指螃蟹在沙滩上走像写字
ascribe [ə'skraib] 归因于 ascribe sth. to sth. 词源：a 正在 + scribe 写 指正在写总结报告归结原因
conscribe [kən'skraib] 征兵；吸纳新成员 词源：con 共同 + scribe 写 指把新兵的名字写在一起
conscript [kən'skript , 'kɔnskript] 征兵 conscript sb. into sth.；吸纳新成员；被征召入伍者 词源：con 共同 + script 写 指把新兵的名字一起写下来
conscription [kən'skripʃn] 征兵 词源：conscript 征兵 + tion 名词后缀
describe [di'skraib] 描绘 词源：de 向下 + scribe 写 指向下写
circumscribe ['səːkəmskraib] 周围画圈，画线；限制，约束 词源：circum 围绕 circle + scribe 写 指画圆圈约束别人自由 比如孙悟空给唐僧画圈
inscribe [in'skraib] 雕刻题写，题词题字 词源：in 内部 + scribe 写 指刻在物体表面内的词句
inscription [in'skripʃ(ə)n] 碑文铭文；（名人）题词，题字 词源：inscribe 题字 + tion 名词后缀
prescribe [pri'skraib] 开药方，开处方；规定 词源：pre 在前面 + scribe 写 指提前写好了药方
prescription [pri'skripʃ(ə)n] 药方，处方；解决方法，诀窍 词源：prescribe 开药 + tion 名词后缀
prescript ['priːskript] 官方指示，命令，规定，条例 词源：prescription 处方药 指处方药要按

医生的命令规定服用

subscribe [səb'skraib] 同意 subscribe to sth.；订阅（杂志或报纸）；定期交会费或捐款；认购股份　词源：sub 下面 + scribe 写　指在文件下面签好名字是同意订阅

subscriber [səb'skraibə(r)] 用户　词源：subscribe 订阅 + er 人

scribe [skraib] 抄写员　词源：scribe 写

script [skript] 字体；剧本；听力原文　词源：script 写　指写出来的剧本

manuscript ['mænjuskript] 手稿　词源：mani 手 + script 写　指亲手写出来的文本

postscript ['pəus(t)skript]（信件）附言；（书籍）后记　词源：post 向后 + script 写　指写在信件后面的补充内容，缩写为 PS

transcript ['trænskript; 'trɑːn-] 抄本；（大学的）学生成绩单　词源：trans 穿越 + script 写　指经过别人传抄作者的原稿

15. **-sert-** : join　巧记：拟声词 指插入卡片时发出的连接声

assert [ə'səːt] 固执己见，坚决主张　词源：as 强调 + sert 连接　指紧紧连接自己的观点

assertive [ə'səːtiv] 坚定自信的　词源：assert 固执己见 + tive 形容词后缀（表示充满活力的 active）　相关词：self-assertive 非常自信的，极有主见的

insert [in'səːt] 插入 insert the key into the lock 把钥匙插进锁里；（夹在书报或杂志中的）插页广告，广告附加页 a two-page insert on cosmetics 两页化妆品插页广告　词源：in 内部 + sert 连接　指把银行卡插入连接取款机　巧记：键盘上的插入按键

desert ['dezət; di'zəːt] 沙漠；放弃　词源：de 否定 + sert 连接　指不再连接是放弃

dessert [di'zəːt]（饭后）甜点　词源：desert 放弃　指甜品吃多了不好需要放弃

exert [ig'zəːt; eg-] 尽全力，全力以赴 exert oneself to do sth.；全力施加控制或影响 exert control / impact on sth.　词源：ex 出来 + sert 连接　指出城作战不再和城内联系是全力以赴破釜沉舟对战争局势施加控制影响

16. **ambi-** : both, around　巧记：am 爱 + bi 两个 指两种感情围绕的

ambiguous [æm'bigjuəs] 暧昧的；歧义的，模棱两可的　词源：ambi 两种情感 + go 走 + ous 形容词后缀（表示过多的）指两种情感围绕是模棱两可的

ambiguity [æmbi'gjuːiti] 暧昧；歧义，模糊　词源：ambiguous 歧义的 + ity 名词后缀

ambience ['æmbiəns]（舒适，放松或友好的）气氛，情调，环境　词源：ambi 两种感情围绕的 + ence 名词后缀　指围绕着感情的氛围

ambient ['æmbiənt] 周围的（温度，光线，音乐，声音）　词源：ambi 环绕的 + ent 形容词后缀

ambivalent [æm'bivələnt] 爱恨交加的，心情矛盾的 be ambivalent about sb. / sth.　词源：ambi 两种情感 + value 价值观　指对人或事物有两种价值观的

ambitious [æm'biʃəs] 有抱负的；有野心的　词源：ambi 两种情感 + ous 形容词后缀（表示过多的）指有二心的、有野心的

17. -scend-, -scent-: climb   巧记：scale 攀登 指向上攀登

ascend [ə'send] 攀登山峰；高度上升；登上王座；职位晋升　　词源：a 正在 + scend 攀爬 指正在登山

ascent [ə'sent]（气球）上升；上坡路；（职位）上台 the President's ascent to power 总统的上台　词源：a 正在 + scent 攀爬

descend [di'send] 下降；突然降临；降序排列　词源：de 向下 + scend 攀爬

descent [di'sent] 下降；下坡；出身血统；沦落，堕落　词源：de 向下 + scent 攀爬　形近易混词：decent

decent ['diːs(ə)nt]（衣着）得体的，不暴露的；（工作）体面的；（举止行为）正派的　词源：cent 美分 指赚些小钱的工作是体面的

descendant [di'send(ə)nt] 子孙后代　词源：de 向下 + scend 攀爬 + ant 名词后缀 指向下繁衍的后代

transcend [træn'send; trɑːn-] 超越，胜过　词源：trans 穿越 + scend 攀爬 指翻山越岭的功绩超越他人

transcendence [træn'sendəns] 卓越　词源：transcend 超越 + ence 名词后缀

transcendent [træn'send(ə)nt; trɑːn-] 卓越的　词源：transcend 超越 + ent 形容词后缀（表示具有……能力的）

condescend [kɔndi'send] 自视优越,居高临下对待别人 condescend to sb.；屈尊 condescend to do sth.　词源：con 共同 + descend 下降 指完全降低身份是屈尊

condescending [ˌkɔndi'sendiŋ] 高傲的,居高临下的　词源：condescend 居高临下对待别人 + ing 形容词后缀

18. -ann-, -enn- : year   巧记：古罗马历史学家塔西佗（Tacitus）的著作《编年史》Annales

annual ['ænjuəl] 每年的；一年生植物；儿童年册，年刊，年报　词源：ann 年 + ual 形容词后缀

annals ['æn(ə)lz] 编年史；年鉴，年报　词源：塔西佗（Tacitus）古代罗马历史学家著名的两本书《编年史》Annales 和《历史》Historiae

anniversary [ˌæni'vɜːs(ə)ri] 周年纪念日　词源：ann 年 + vers 转向 + ary 名词后缀 指每年日期都会转到某天过纪念日

annuity [ə'njuːiti] 年金，（每年）养老金　词源：ann 年 + ity 名词后缀　同义词：pension

biannual [bai'ænjuəl] 一年两次的　词源：bi 两个 + ann 年 指每年两次的

centennial [sen'teniəl] 一百周年纪念　词源：cent 百 + enn 年 + ial 名词后缀 指一百年一次的

millennium [mi'leniəm] 千年　词源：million 百万 + enn 年 + ium 名词后缀 用百万年喻指千年

perennial [pə'reniəl] 常年的；长久的，持续的；植物多年生的　词源：per 一直 + enn 年 + ial 形容词后缀 指常年存在的

19. ante-, anti- : 1) before, in front of   巧记：ant 蚂蚁 指蚂蚁冲在同伴前面

anteroom ['æntiru:m] 接待室，前厅　词源：ante 在前面 + room 房间

antedate [,ænti'deit] 早于……出现　词源：ante 在前面 + date 日期

antique [æn'ti:k] 古董，古物；古老的　词源：anti 在前面 + unique 独一无二的　指以前独一无二的有价值的物品是古董

anticipate [æn'tisipeit] 预料，预测 anticipate doing sth.；期待（好事）　词源：anti 在前面 + cip 获得 + ate 动词后缀　指提前获得了消息就会有所期待

2）against, the opposite　巧记：an 否定 + t 方向 to　指与原方向相反的

antics ['æntiks] 古怪可笑的举动　词源：anti 相反 + cs 名词后缀　指和正常举动相反的行为

Antarctica [æn'tɑ:ktikə] 南极洲　词源：ant 相反 + Arctic 北极的　指与北极相反的是南极

antiwar ['æntiwɔ:] 反战的　词源：anti 相反 + war 战争

antonym ['æntənim] 反义词　词源：ant 相反 + onym 名字 name

antidote ['æntidəut] 解毒剂 the antidote to the poison 解毒药；缓解之物　词源：anti 相反 + dote（药物的）一剂 dose　指起反作用的药剂

20. -sum-, -sumpt- : take　巧记：sum 一笔钱　指拿一笔钱

assume [ə'sju:m]（无根据）假设，猜想；承担（责任或风险）assume responsibility for sth. 承担责任；呈现（某种状态、表情或样子）assume an air of indifference 表现出无动于衷的样子　词源：as 强调 + sum 拿　指得到点不实消息就胡乱猜测　词义连记：无乱猜测别人就必须承担猜错的风险

assumption [ə'sʌm(p)ʃ(ə)n]（胡乱）假设，猜想；（责任、控制或权力的）承担，取得，就任　词源：assume 猜测 + tion 名词后缀

presume [pri'zju:m]（有根据的）假设，猜想　词源：pre 在前面 + assume 猜测　指有前提的猜测

presumption [pri'zʌm(p)ʃ(ə)n]（有根据的）假设，猜想　词源：presume 猜测 + tion 名词后缀

consume [kən'sju:m] 消耗（能源，资源，燃料，能量或时间等）；消费；吃，喝，饮 consume alcohol in moderation 适度饮酒　词源：con 共同 + sum 拿　指完全拿走是消耗

consumer [kən'sju:mə] 消费者　词源：consume 消费 + er 人

consumption [kən'sʌm(p)ʃ(ə)n]（能源、油、电、食物、饮料或烟草等的）消耗量；购买，消费　词源：consume 消费 + tion 名词后缀

resume [ri'zju:m]（中断后）继续（做某事）resume doing sth.；（文章或讲话等的）摘要，概述，概要（读音[,rezju'mei]）；个人求职简历（读音[,rezju'mei] 同义词：CV = curriculum vitae）　词源：re 重复 + sume 拿　指重复拿起一件事情做是继续　词义连记：投简历继续找工作

21. -audi-, -audit-, audio- : listen　巧记：德国 Audi 奥迪车　指听发动机的声音来鉴别车

audience ['ɔ:diəns] 听众，观众　词源：audi 听 + ence 名词后缀

audible ['ɔ:dib(ə)l] 可听到的　词源：audi 听 + able 形容词后缀（表示可以……的）

inaudible [in'ɔ:dib(ə)l] 听不到的　词源：in 否定 + audible 可听到的

audio ['ɔ:diəu] 音频的，声音的 audio and video equipment 音频视频设备　词源：audi 听

audit ['ɔ:dit] 审计，审查 a tax audit 税项审计；查……的账目；旁听（大学课程）　词源：audi 听 + it 它　指听下属汇报财务情况后再亲自核实的过程是审计

auditing ['ɔ:ditiŋ] 审计学　词源：audit 审计 + ing 名词后缀

auditor ['ɔ:ditə] 审计员，查账员　词源：audit 审计 + or 人

auditory ['ɔ:dit(ə)ri] 听觉的 auditory organs 听觉器官　词源：audi 听 + ory 形容词后缀

audition [ɔ:'diʃ(ə)n] 试听，试跳，试唱，试演 have an audition for sth.　词源：audi 听 + tion 名词后缀

auction ['ɔ:kʃ(ə)n] 拍卖会；拍卖 auction sth. off　词源：audi 听 + action 动作　指听价格做报价动作

auditorium [ɔ:di'tɔ:riəm]（剧院、音乐厅等的）听众席，观众席；大礼堂；音乐厅　词源：audi 听 + ium 名词后缀（表示地点 place）指听音乐、看演出或举办活动的礼堂

audacious [ɔ:'deiʃəs]（决定或行动）大胆的 an audacious decision / operation 大胆的决定/行动　词源：auda 听 audi + i 人 + ous 形容词后缀（表示过多的）指一个人敢于倾听意见做大胆决定进行大胆行动

audacity [ɔ:'dæsəti] 大胆，无礼，冒昧，放肆 have the audacity to ask for money 厚着脸皮要钱　词源：audacious 大胆的 + ity 名词后缀

2

22. -ard : person or thing　巧记：ar, er, or 指表示人或事物名词后缀

bastard ['bɑ:stəd; 'bæst-] 私生子　词源：bad 坏 + ast 最高级 + ard 名词后缀　指私生子的性格坏

coward ['kauəd] 胆小鬼，懦夫　词源：cow 奶牛 + ard 名词后缀　指像奶牛一样胆小

cowardice ['kauədis] 胆小，怯懦　词源：coward 懦夫 + ice 名词后缀

drunkard ['drʌŋkəd] 醉汉　词源：drink 喝酒 + ard 名词后缀

laggard ['lægəd] 迟缓（落后）的人或物　词源：leg 腿 + ard 名词后缀　指拖后腿的

tankard ['tæŋkəd]（有柄的）金属大啤酒杯　词源：tank 容器（如水箱油箱）+ ard 名词后缀

tanker ['tæŋkə] 油轮，油船；油罐车　词源：tank 容器（如水箱油箱）+ er 名词后缀

wizard ['wizəd] 男巫，术士；奇才，能手 a financial wizard 金融奇才　词源：wise 聪明的 + ard 名词后缀　巧记：Wizard 美职篮奇才队

blizzard ['blizəd] 暴风雪；大量（需要处理的事）a blizzard of documents 一大堆文件　词源：blow 风吹 + zz 滋滋声 + ard 名词后缀　巧记：著名的游戏公司暴雪娱乐 Blizzard Entertainment

ward [wɔ:d] 病房；（英国城市中可选出一位地方议员的）选举区；被监护人（受法院或监护人保护的人，尤指儿童）；避免，阻止（危险、疾病或攻击等）ward sth. off　词源：war

战争 +ard 名词后缀 指在战争中躲到病房避免伤害

steward ['stjuːəd]（飞机、轮船或火车上的）男乘务员；（赛马、聚会、资源、公共财产和钱财等的）负责人，主管 词源：stew 炖肉 +ard 名词后缀 指负责给客人炖肉的服务人员

stewardess ['stjuːədis; ˌstjuːə'des]（飞机、轮船或火车上的）女乘务员 词源：steward 男乘务员 +ess 人（指女性或雌性）

mustard ['mʌstəd] 芥末 词源：must 必须 +ard 名词后缀 指吃饭时必须有的佐料

hazard ['hæzəd] 危险，隐患，风险 the health hazard posed by air pollution 空气污染对健康构成的危险 词源：haze 雾霾 +ard 名词后缀 指雾霾带来污染风险隐患

23. -it- : go 巧记：i 人 +t 方向 to 指人往某个方向走

agitate ['ædʒiteit] 煽动，鼓动 agitate for higher pay 煽动加工资；使焦虑不安 agitate sb.；搅动，摇动（液体）agitate the solution 摇动溶液 词源：ag 运动 +it 走 go +ate 动词后缀 指让液体在容器中走动搅动起来 词义连记：示威者摇动着手里的酒精瓶煽动罢工引起了人们的不安

agitated ['ædʒiteitid] 不安的，焦虑的 词源：agitate 使不安 +ed 形容词后缀

bandit ['bændit]（袭击旅行者的）强盗，土匪；赌博机，吃角子老虎机 a one-armed bandit 词源：band 一群人 +it 走 指走在路上的一群劫匪

committee [kə'miti] 委员会 词源：come 来 +it 走 +ee 眼睛 指来来去去看彼此眼睛发表意见

commit [kə'mit] 投身于（某项事业）commit to sth.；犯罪 commit a crime；犯错 commit an error 词源：committee 委员会 指委员会致力于某项事业

commitment [kə'mitm(ə)nt]（用心的）承诺或义务 commitment to family 家庭义务 词源：commit 投身致力于 +ment 名词后缀（表示思想 mind）

commission [kə'miʃ(ə)n] 犯罪；回扣，佣金，手续费（例如化妆品销售提成、房地产中介费或银行手续费等）；委员会，调查团 Federal Trade Commission 美国联邦贸易委员会；委托做某事 commission sb. to do sth. 词源：commit 犯罪犯错 +sion 名词后缀 词义连记：委员会委托他人收佣金是犯罪

circuit ['səːkit] 环形道路，环行 make a circuit of the city walls 绕城墙走一圈；赛车道；电路 an electrical circuit；网球巡回赛 the tennis circuit；（法官或宗教领袖的）巡回判案 a circuit judge 巡回法官 词源：circ 圆圈 cycle +it 走 指走了一圈

exit ['eksit; 'egzit] 出口 词源：ex 出来 +it 走 指能走出来的地方

initial [i'niʃəl] 最初的（阶段、反应、诊断或调查等）initial assumptions 最初的猜测；首写字母 词源：in 内部 +it 走 +special 特殊的 指走到内心特殊的东西是最初的想法 巧记：Initial D 动漫《头文字 D》

initiative [i'niʃiətiv; -ʃə-] 自主决断的能力，主动性 use one's initiative 自己想办法；主动，主动权 take the initiative to do sth. 主动做某事；首创精神；计划，措施，倡议 an education initiative 一项教育倡议 词源：in 内部 +it 走 +active 活跃的 指走到内心活跃的东西是主动性

initiate [i'niʃieit] 开创，开始实施，发起（重要的事）initiate a debate 发起辩论；（通过特殊或秘密仪式）使加入（组织、俱乐部或团体等）initiate sb. into sth.；（向某人）传授（技能）initiate sb. into the art of golf 教授某人打高尔夫的技巧；初学者；新入会的人　词源：in 内部 + it 走 + ate 动词后缀　指走进团体内部入会并发起活动

orbit ['ɔ:bit]（天体、卫星、航天器等运行的）轨道 a space station in orbit round the earth 绕地球运行的一个航天站；绕轨道运行 orbit the sun 绕太阳运行；势力范围　词源：orb 天体球体 + it 走　指天体绕着恒星在轨道上走

transit ['trænsit; 'trɑ:ns-; -nz-] 运输 goods damaged in transit 在运输中损坏的货物；交通运输系统 the city's public transit system 城市的公共交通运输系统　词源：trans 穿越 + it 走　指人或货物穿越城市移动

transition [træn'ziʃ(ə)n; trɑ:n-; -'siʃ-] 过渡，转变，变迁 the transition from school to work 从学校到工作的过渡　词源：trans 穿越 + it 走 + tion 名词后缀

transient ['trænziənt] 短暂的，一时的 transient fashions 短暂的时尚；（逗留时间）很短的　词源：trans 穿越 + ent 形容词后缀（表示具有……能力的）

visit ['vizit] 拜访，访问，参观，游览，看望　词源：vis 看 + it 走　指去看看某人　巧记：vis 看 + it 它　指去看它

flit [flit] 轻快的飞过，掠过 flit from one job to another 频繁跳槽　词源：fly 飞 + it 走　巧记：fly 飞 + it 它　指飞过它

slit [slit] 狭长的切口，狭缝，裂口 a long skirt with a slit up the side 侧开衩的长裙；切开，撕开 slit open the envelope 拆开信封；眯眼　词源：sl 滑动 slide + it 走　指移动划过　巧记：slide 滑动 + it 它　指划过它

spit [spit] 唾液；吐痰　词源：sp 喷射 + it 走　指走路喷口水　巧记：sp 喷射 + it 它　指喷出它

split [split]（衣物或木头）裂口，裂缝 a big split in the coat 外衣上撕了一个大口子；（意见的）分歧，（派别的）分裂；（钱的）均分，分配；分手，离婚；（使）劈开，分开（木板或水果等）；划破，碰破（头或嘴唇）；（舞蹈）劈腿，劈叉 do the splits 做劈叉　词源：sp 喷射 + l 长 + i 短 + it 走　指走过去把长的 l 劈成一截截短的 i　巧记：sp 喷射 + l 长 + i 短 + it 它　指把它从长的 l 劈成一截截短的 i

24. **-circ-** : circle　巧记：circle 圆圈的缩写形式

circular ['sə:kjulə]（桌子、楼梯或建筑）圆形的 a circular building 圆形建筑物；环绕的 a circular tour of the city 环城游览；（群发给多人的）广告印刷品，广告　词源：circ 圈 + lar 形容词后缀

circuit ['sə:kit] 环形道路，环行 make a circuit of the city walls 绕城墙走一圈；赛车道；电路 an electrical circuit；网球巡回赛 the tennis circuit；（法官或宗教领袖的）巡回判案 a circuit judge 巡回法官　词源：circ 圆圈 cycle + it 走　指走了一圈

circus ['sə:kəs] 马戏团；乱哄热闹场面 a media circus 一群乱哄哄的媒体；（街道汇集的）圆形

广场（常用于地名）；（古罗马）圆形竞技场或赛车场 Circus Maximus 马克西穆斯竞技场　词源：circ 圈 + us 名词后缀

circulate ['sɜːkjuleɪt]（使液体或气体）循环；流传，散布（谣言）；传播（信息）；（聚会）应酬，来回周旋　词源：circ 圈 + l 长 + ate 动词后缀　指长期转圈循环

encircle [ɪnˈsɜːk(ə)l; en-] 围绕，环绕 the island encircled by a coral reef 周围都是珊瑚礁的岛　词源：en 使动词化 + circ 圈 + cle 名词后缀

25. -cogn-, -cogit- : know　巧记：co 共同 + git 理解明白 get it 的缩写形式

cognitive ['kɒɡnɪtɪv]（只做定语）认知的 cognitive power 认知能力　词源：cogn 知道 + ive 形容词后缀（表示充满活力的 active）

cognizant ['kɒɡnɪzənt]（只做表语）知道的，了解的 sb. be cognizant of sth.　词源：cogn 知道 + ant 形容词后缀（表示具有……能力的）

precognition [ˌpriːkɒɡˈnɪʃn] 预知，预感 precognition in dreams 梦中预知　词源：pre 在前面 + cogn 知道 + tion 名词后缀　指提前知道

recognition [ˌrekəɡˈnɪʃ(ə)n] 认出；识别；表彰，赞扬 achieve recognition 获得表彰　词源：re 重复 + cogn 知道 + tion 名词后缀　指反复让别人知道是认出

26. -bat- : beat, strike　巧记：bat 蝙蝠 指蝙蝠攻击的状态

acrobatics [ˌækrəˈbætɪks] 杂技　词源：acro 高 + bat 蝙蝠 + ics 学科　指像塔尖上的蝙蝠倒立平衡做杂技动作

aerobatics [ˌeərəˈbætɪks] 特技飞行，航空表演　词源：aero 空气 + bat 蝙蝠 + ics 学科　指像空气中的蝙蝠飞行般的航空表演

bat [bæt] 蝙蝠；棒球棒　词义连记：batman 蝙蝠侠用棒球棒打击罪犯

batter ['bætə]（面粉、鸡蛋、牛奶做的）面糊（比如做煎饼用的糊状物）；连续重击 batter at the door with fists 用拳头砸门；（棒球）击球手　词源：bat 击打 + er 动词后缀（强调动作的反复性）指不停地击打

battle ['bæt(ə)l] 战役，战斗　词源：bat 击打 + tle 强调

baton [bəˈtɒn] 权杖，官仗；（管弦乐队指挥的）指挥棒；（行进中军乐队队长的）指挥杖；（接力赛的）接力棒；警棍　词源：bat 击打 + on 在上面　指在上面举着警棍击打

batch [bætʃ] 一批，一组（人或物）a new batch of graduates 一批新毕业生；（食物、药物等的）一批生产的量 a batch of bread 一批面包；计算机成批处理的作业　词源：bat 蝙蝠 + ch 名词后缀　指蝙蝠成批出现

combat ['kɒmbæt; 'kʌm-] 战斗；格斗 cage combat 笼中格斗；防止，抑制 combat inflation 抑制通胀　词源：com 共同 + bat 打击　指一起战斗

combatant ['kɒmbətənt] 战士，战斗人员　词源：combat 战斗 + ant 人

27. -bel-, -bell- : war, fight　巧记：bell 钟 指战争的钟声；也可指 Bellona（贝罗纳）罗马神

话中的女战神，被认为是战神 Mars（玛尔斯）的姐妹或妻子

bellicose ['belikəus] 好斗的，好战的，好争吵的 make bellicose statements 发表好战的宣言　词源：bell 战斗 + close 紧密地　指很近于战斗状态

belligerent [bə'lidʒərənt] 敌对的，好战的，好斗的，好寻衅的 a belligerent attitude 敌对的态度；（国家）处于交战状态的 the belligerent countries 交战各国　词源：bell 战斗 + ger 生成（指基因 gene 的生成）+ ent 形容词后缀（表示具有……能力的）

bellow ['beləu]（公牛的）吼叫；咆哮，怒吼；（送风的或管风琴的）风箱（常复数）　词源：bell 战斗 + low 低声的　指公牛发出战斗的低声怒吼

rebel ['reb(ə)l] 反叛；反叛者；叛逆者，不守规矩者；（胃、腿、头脑等）不听使唤　词源：re 向后 + bell 战斗　指向反方向战斗是反叛

rebellious [ri'beljəs] 反叛的 rebellious tribes 叛乱的部落；叛逆的 rebellious teenagers 叛逆的青少年　词源：rebel 反叛 + ous 形容词后缀（表示过多的）

rebellion [ri'beljən] 反叛，造反　词源：rebel 反叛 + ion 名词后缀

28. bene- : well, good　巧记：bene 意大利语表示好

benefit ['benifit] 益处，好处；（政府给病人、失业人士或穷人等提供的）救济金，补助金 unemployment / housing / child benefit 失业/住房/子女补贴；（公司或工作单位提供的）福利，补贴；有益于 sb. benefit from sth. / sth. benefit sb.　词源：bene 好 + fit 合适　指又好又合适

beneficial [beni'fiʃ(ə)l] 有益的　词源：benefit 益处 + cial 形容词后缀（表示特殊的 special）

beneficiary [beni'fiʃ(ə)ri] 受益者，受惠者；遗产继承人　词源：benefit 益处 + i 人 + ary 名词后缀

benign [bi'nain]（人）和蔼的，慈祥的，善良的；（肿瘤）良性的　词源：bene 好 + nice 好　指性格特别好　巧记：谐音 be nice

benevolent [bi'nev(ə)l(ə)nt]（人）慈善的，乐善好施的；（笑容或态度）和蔼的 a benevolent smile / attitude　词源：bene 好 + vol 意愿 + ent 形容词后缀（表示具有……能力的）指有好的意愿的　同义词：charitable　反义词：malevolent

29. -pat-, -pass-, -path- : feeling, pain, disease, treatment　巧记：pain 疼痛

patience ['peiʃ(ə)ns] 耐心；忍耐力　词源：pat 疼痛 + ence 名词后缀　指耐心就是忍着疼痛

patient ['peiʃ(ə)nt] 有耐心的 be patient with sb. / sth.；病人　词源：pat 疼痛 + ent 人　指疼痛的人

passion ['pæʃ(ə)n] 激情；（耶稣受难的）痛苦（需大写 the Passion）　词源：pass 疼痛 + sion 名词后缀　指钉在十字架上的巨大痛苦　后指部分心理变态的人把痛苦当激情

passionate ['pæʃ(ə)nət] 激情的；热爱的，酷爱的　词源：passion 激情 + ate 形容词后缀

pathetic [pə'θetik] 可怜的 a pathetic and lonely man 可怜又孤独的人；无用的，差劲的，窝囊的　词源：path 疼痛 + tic 形容词后缀　指疼痛的人是可怜的

compassion [kəm'pæʃ(ə)n] 怜悯，同情 show compassion for sb. / sth.　词源：com 共同 + pass

疼痛 + sion 名词后缀 指大家一起有心痛的感觉是同情心

compassionate [kəmˈpæʃ(ə)nət] 有同情心的　词源：compassion 同情 + ate 形容词后缀

sympathy [ˈsɪmpəθi] 同情 have sympathy for sb. / sth.；（尤指政治方面的）赞同，支持 be in sympathy with sth.；（与某人的）同感，共鸣　词源：sym 相同（same 衍生出来的前缀）+ path 疼痛 指感到相同的痛是同情　同义词：compassion

sympathetic [sɪmpəˈθetɪk] 有同情心的；赞成的，支持的 be sympathetic to sth.；合意的，合适的（环境）；招人喜欢的（人或人物角色）　词源：sympathy 同情 + tic 形容词后缀

apathy [ˈæpəθi] 冷漠，不关心 public apathy 公众的冷漠　词源：a 否定 + path 疼痛 指对事物没有疼痛感

apathetic [ˌæpəˈθetɪk] 无兴趣的，冷淡的，无动于衷的 be apathetic about sth.　词源：apathy 冷漠 + tic 形容词后缀

empathy [ˈempəθi] 同感，共鸣 have empathy with sb. 和某人有共鸣　词源：e 出来 + path 疼痛 指看到别人的经历后从自己内心释放出来的感同身受的痛苦

telepathy [təˈlepəθi]（双胞胎的）心灵感应，传心术　词源：tele 远 + path 疼痛 指能感受到远方别人的疼痛

30. **-pel, -pell-, -puls-**：push　巧记：p 人 person + e 出来 + l 棒子 指人拿出棒子推搡驱赶

compel [kəmˈpel] 强迫 compel sb. to do sth.；引起（注意）compel the audience's attention 吸引观众注意力　词源：com 共同 + pel 推动 指共同推动某人做某事

compulsory [kəmˈpʌls(ə)ri] 必须的；义务的 compulsory education 义务教育　词源：compel 强迫 + ory 形容词后缀

compelling [kəmˈpelɪŋ] 吸引人的，引人入胜的，扣人心弦的 a compelling legend 引人入胜的传说；（理由、论点或论据）令人信服的；（愿望、需要或冲动）强烈的　词源：compel 强迫 + ing 形容词后缀 指强迫别人回来看的让人流连忘返的

dispel [dɪˈspel] 驱散（咒语）dispel a magic spell；消除（信仰，理念，观念，或感觉）dispel worries 消除忧虑　词源：dis 分散 + pel 推动 指推动四散分离

expel [ɪkˈspel; ek-] 驱逐出境 expel foreign journalists and diplomats 驱逐外国记者和外交官；学校开除 expel sb. from school；排出（液体或气体）expel air from the lungs 呼出肺里的气体　词源：ex 出去 + pel 推动 指推某人出去

impel [ɪmˈpel] 内心驱使，促使 impel sb. to do sth.　词源：im 内部 + pel 推动 指内心推动某人做某事

impulse [ˈɪmpʌls] 内心冲动 impulse buying / shopping 冲动消费；神经脉冲；推动　词源：im 内部 + puls 推动 指内心的推动力

pulse [pʌls] 脉搏；（音乐的）拍子，律动　词源：puls 推动 指心脏跳动

manipulate [məˈnɪpjuleɪt] 推拿正骨，推拿治疗；（暗中）操纵，控制（某人的思想和行为）manipulate children into seeking fame 操纵孩子追求名望；熟练巧妙地操控（信息或系统）manipulate knobs and levers 操纵旋钮和控制杆　词源：mani 手 + pul 推动 + ate 动词后缀

指用手推动身体的部位进行推拿按摩

propel [prə'pel] 推动，驱动 a boat propelled by a motor 由马达驱动的小船；推搡（某人走向特定方向） 词源：pro 向前 + pel 推动 指向前推动船只或飞机前进

propeller [prə'pelə(r)] （飞机或轮船的）螺旋桨，推进器 词源：propel 推动 + er 名词后缀

repel [ri'pel] 击退（进攻或入侵）repel an attack / invasion；驱逐蚊虫；使厌恶；（电极）不导电，（磁极）排斥 词源：re 向后 + pel 推动 指向后推动敌人防线

31. -pon-, -pos-, -posit-, -pound：put 巧记：pon 拟声词 指放东西砰的一声

post [pəust] 粘贴；（路灯）杆，柱；邮递；岗位，职位 词源：pos 放置 + st 最高级 指把某人放到某个岗位 词义连记：邮递员在路灯杆上粘贴广告求职

position [pə'ziʃ(ə)n] 姿态，姿势；处境；职位；立场 词源：post 放置 + tion 名词后缀

posture ['pɔstʃə] （坐、立的）身姿；态度，立场 adopt a conservative posture towards new ideas 对新思想采取保守的态度 词源：position 姿势 + nature 性质 指身体姿态或心中立场 词义连记：不同的坐立身姿体现出不同的态度立场

pose [pəuz] 姿势；（照相）摆姿势；装腔作势；导致，引起（问题、危险、困难等） 词源：pos 放置 词义连记：指摆姿势装腔作势导致出现问题

poise [pɔiz] 镇定自若 poise and confidence；（优雅的）体态，姿态 the poise of a dancer 舞蹈演员的体态；使保持平衡，使稳定 词源：pose 摆姿势 + i 人 指舞蹈演员的优雅姿态

compose [kəm'pəuz] 由……组成 be composed of sth.；作曲作诗；使冷静 compose oneself 词源：com 共同 + pos 放置 指把音符或文字放在一起是作曲作诗 词义连记：作曲作诗时需要冷静

composite ['kɔmpəzit] 合成的 composite metals 复合金属；复合物；合成照片（尤指帮助警方捉拿罪犯用的画像或照片）a composite sketch 合成人像素描 词源：compose 组成 + ite 形容词后缀 指信息放在一起后合成的

composition [kɔmpə'ziʃ(ə)n] 组成，构成 complex chemical compositions 复杂的化学成分构成；音乐乐曲；（诗歌或文字）作品；作文 词源：compose 组成 + tion 名词后缀

composure [kəm'pəuʒə(r)] 冷静，镇定 词源：compose 冷静 + nature 性质 指人冷静的特性

compound ['kɔmpaund] 复合物（如水或二氧化碳）；（四周有围墙的）建筑群 a prison compound 监狱大院；使加剧，加重 compound a problem 加剧问题；（昆虫）复眼的 词源：com 共同 + pound 放置 指把不同元素放置在一起组成的

component [kəm'pəunənt] 组成部分，成分；（汽车、手机或电脑）零件，配件 词源：compose 组成 + ent 形容词后缀（表示具有……能力的）

expound [ik'spaund; ek-] 详细说明 expound on sth. 词源：ex 出来 + pound 放置 指把观点拿出来表达

propound [prə'paund] 提议，提出观点 词源：pro 向前 + pound 放置 指走到前面提出看法

decompose [di:kəm'pəuz] （使）腐烂，分解 词源：de 否定 + compose 组成 指不再组成

depose [di'pəuz] 罢免，废黜（领袖或统治者）词源：de 否定 + position 职位 指让某人不再在

职位上

dispose [di'spəuz] 部署（军队）dispose troops for withdrawal 部署军队撤退；排列，布展（展品）dispose vases in the gallery 在画廊布展摆放花瓶；处理，丢弃（垃圾、污水、核废料或炸弹等）dispose of sth.；应对，解决（问题）disposes of the immediate problems 解决迫切的问题；转让，变卖（股票、房产、企业或土地） 词源：dis 分散 + pose 放置 指分散放置好是排列布展

disposal [di'spəuz(ə)l] 丢弃，处理；被某人支配 at sb.'s disposal；变卖，转让；污物碾碎器（装在厨房洗涤槽下面把菜叶果皮等弄碎的机器） 词源：dispose 处理 + al 名词后缀

disposable [di'spəuzəb(ə)l] 可支配的（收入）disposable income；一次性的（筷子）disposable chopsticks 词源：dispose 处理 + able 形容词后缀（表示可以……的）

disposition [dispə'ziʃ(ə)n] 性情；意向；军队部署 词源：dispose 排列 + tion 名词后缀 指地图上摆放军队模型列阵 词义连记：指挥官的性情决定军队部署

depot ['depəu] 仓库；火车站，公共汽车站 词源：de 向下 + po 放置 指放东西的地方 巧记：The Home Depot 美国家得宝公司为全球领先的家居建材用品零售商，是排在沃尔玛、家乐福之后的全球第三大零售集团。

deposit [di'pɔzit]（银行）存钱，存款；（购房或租房）订金，押金；（河流、洪水、液体等的）沉积物，淤积物 词源：de 向下 + posit 放置 指把钱放在银行柜台下面

expose [ik'spəuz; ek-]（身体部位）暴露；揭发，揭露；使面临，使遭受（危险或不快）expose oneself to ridicule 使某人自己受到嘲笑；（胶卷）曝光 词源：ex 出来 + pose 放置 指把东西拿出来放在桌子上让大家看

exposure [ik'spəuʒə; ek-]（身体部位）暴露；揭发，揭露；报道，关注；接触，体验；（照片）底片中的一张；（照片）曝光时间；（建筑、山或房间的）朝向 a bedroom having a southern exposure 朝南的卧室 词源：expose 暴露 + nature 性质

exposition [ekspə'ziʃ(ə)n] 博览会 World Exposition 世博会；（理论、计划等的）详细说明 a lucid exposition of the theory 对理论的详尽阐述 词源：expose 暴露 + tion 名词后缀 指曝光最新产品设计的展会

exponent [ik'spəunənt; ek-]（想法、信仰等的）倡导者，鼓吹者；能手，大师 the most famous exponent of the art of magic 最著名的魔术表演艺术大师；（数学）指数，幂 词源：exposition 博览会 + ent 人 指博览会上鼓吹自己产品的人

oppose [ə'pəuz] 反对，对抗 oppose doing sth. 词源：op 相反 + pose 摆姿势 指摆姿势唱反调

opponent [ə'pəunənt]（竞争或比赛的）对手；反对者 词源：oppose 反对 + ent 人

opposite ['ɔpəzit; -sit] 在……对面；（方向或效果）相反的 have the opposite effect 效果完全相反；对立物 词源：oppose 反对 + ite 形容词后缀

postpone [pəus(t)'pəun; pə'spəun] 推迟，延迟 postpone doing sth. 词源：post 向后 + pon 放置 指向后放置安排

propose [prə'pəuz] 提议 propose a motion 提出动议；求婚 propose marriage；祝酒 propose a toast (to sb.) 词源：pro 向前 + pose 摆姿势 指走上前去单膝下跪摆姿势求婚

proposal [prə'pəuz(ə)l] 提议，建议 reject a business proposal 拒绝商业提议；求婚　词源：propose 提议 ＋al 名词后缀

32. **bi-** : two　巧记：B 两间屋子 指字母 B 的象形含义表示两间屋子

bicycle ['baisikl] 自行车　词源：bi 两个 ＋cycle 圈 指两个轮子的车

bilingual [bai'liŋgw(ə)l] 双语的 a bilingual dictionary 双语词典；会说两种语言的　词源：bi 两个 ＋lingua 长长的舌头（language 的词源）指能说两种语言的

bikini [bi'ki:ni] 比基尼泳衣　词源：美国 1946 年比基尼岛原子弹爆炸试验 指女性穿比基尼释放的魅力像原子弹爆炸

binoculars [bi'nɔkjuləz] 双筒望远镜　词源：bi 两个 ＋ocularis 眼睛 指像两只眼睛的双筒望远镜

bias ['baiəs] 偏爱，天赋 have a strong artistic bias 有很高的艺术天分；偏见，成见 political bias 政治偏见　词源：bi 两个 ＋as 名词后缀 指两个里面更喜欢其中一个

bilateral [bai'læt(ə)r(ə)l] 双边的（关系或谈判），双方的　词源：bi 两个 ＋lateralis 边

33. **-card-, cardio-, -cardia** : heart　巧记：cord 心（希腊语）　单词 core 核心为其衍生词

cardiac ['kɑːdiæk] 心脏的 cardiac surgery 心脏手术　词源：card 心 ＋ic 形容词后缀

cardiology [ˌkɑːdi'ɔlədʒi] 心脏病学　词源：cardio 心 ＋ology 名词后缀（表示学科）

cardinal ['kɑːd(i)n(ə)l] 红衣凤头鸟，北美红雀（游戏《愤怒的小鸟》里面最基本的红色小鸟的原型）；（天主教会的）红衣主教，枢机主教；基本的 The Four Cardinal Principles 四项基本原则　词源：card 心 ＋al 名词后缀 指像心一样鲜红颜色的小鸟

cardiologist [ˌkɑːdi'ɔlədʒist] 心脏病专家　词源：cardiology 心脏病学 ＋ist 人

electrocardiogram [iˌlektrəu'kɑːdiəugræm] 心电图　词源：electric 电的 ＋cardio 心 ＋diagram 图表

34. **-log-, -logue** : word, logic, discipline　巧记：log 原木 指原木上刻的字

apology [ə'pɔlədʒi] 道歉　词源：apo 离开 ＋log 话语 指因为需要提早离开活动而说的话

apologize [ə'pɔlədʒaiz] 道歉，谢罪 apologize to sb. for sth.　词源：apology 道歉 ＋ize 动词后缀

analogy [ə'nælədʒi] 类同，相似；类比 explain the movement of light by analogy with the movement of water 用水的运动作比拟来解释光的运动　词源：analyze 分析 ＋log 话语 指分析相似的事物来说明未知事物

analogize [ə'nælədʒaiz] 以类推法说明解释　词源：analogy 类比 ＋ize 动词后缀

analogous [ə'næləgəs] 类似的，相似的 be analogous with / to sth.　词源：analogy 类比 ＋ous 形容词后缀（表示过多的）

catalogue ['kæt(ə)lɔg] 商品目录，购物指南；接二连三的（不好的事）a catalogue of errors 一连串的错误　词源：cata 向下 ＋log 话语 指向下写的介绍每个商品的文字 如购物网站上显示的某品牌的各种服饰或鞋

dialogue ['daiəlɔg]（书、戏剧或电影的）对白；（组织或国家间为解决问题的）对话　词源：

dia 穿越 + logue 话语 指每天穿越于两者间的对话

eulogy ['juːlədʒi] 颂词；悼词　词源：eu 好的 + log 话语 指歌颂人生前事迹的好话

eulogize ['juːlədʒaiz] 歌颂，称赞，颂扬　词源：eulogy 颂词 + ize 动词后缀

logic ['lɔdʒik] 逻辑；逻辑学　词源：log 话语 + ic 名词后缀 指说话表达有逻辑

logical ['lɔdʒik(ə)l] 合乎逻辑的；合情合理的　词源：logic 逻辑 + cal 形容词后缀

monologue ['mɔn(ə)lɔg]（戏剧或电影的）独白；独角戏；滔滔不绝的讲话，个人的长篇大论　词源：mono 单一 + log 话语 指一个人在说话

35. **-pend-, -pens-**：1）pay　巧记：penny 便士，美分 指金钱

compensate ['kɔmpenseit] 补偿，赔偿 compensate sb. for sth.　词源：com 共同 + pens 钱 + ate 动词后缀 指完全给别人金钱补偿

depend [di'pend] 依靠，依赖　词源：de 向下 + pend 钱 指屈身向下依靠别人的钱

dependent [di'pendənt] 依赖的；有瘾的；依赖者　词源：depend 依靠 + ent 名词后缀

dispense [di'spens]（以固定数额）分发 a vending machine that dispenses drinks and snacks 发售饮料和小吃的自动售货机；施与，提供（服务）dispense free health care to the poor 给穷人提供免费医疗；配药，发药 dispense a prescription 按处方配药　词源：dis 分散 + pens 钱 指像发钱一样分发

indispensable [indi'spensəb(ə)l] 不可缺少的　词源：in 否定 + dispense 分发 + able 形容词后缀（表示可以……的）指不可以分发的　同义词：essential

expend [ik'spend; ek-] 花费，支出 expend sth. in / on (doing) sth.　词源：ex 出来 + pend 钱 指拿出来钱花

expenditure [ik'spenditʃə; ek-]（大笔的）花费，开销 public / government / military expenditure 公共/政府/军费开支；（精力、时间、材料等的）消耗，耗费 the expenditure of time and emotion 时间和感情耗费　词源：expend 花钱 + nature 名词后缀

expense [ik'spens; ek-]（小笔的）花费 legal / medical / living / travel expenses 律师费/医疗费/生活费/旅行费；代价 at the expense of sb. / sth. 以损害某人或某物为代价　词源：ex 出来 + pense 钱 指拿出来花的钱

expensive [ik'spensiv; ek-] 昂贵的　词源：expense 花费 + ive 形容词后缀（表示充满活力的 active）

independence [indi'pend(ə)ns] 独立　词源：in 否定 + depend 依靠 + ence 名词后缀 指在钱上不依靠别人

spend [spend] 花钱；度过，消磨（时间）；花费，消耗（精力）　词源：s 方式 + pend 钱 指以某种方式花钱

spending ['spendiŋ]（政府或机构组织的）花费，开销 public / military spending 公共/军费开支　词源：spend 花钱 + ing 名词后缀

sponsor ['spɔnsə] 资助者，赞助商；赞助（体育赛事、演出活动或节目）；倡议，提交（法案）sponsor a bill　词源：spend 花钱 + or 人 指花钱的赞助人

pension ['penʃ(ə)n] 养老金，退休金　词源：pen 钱 ＋sion 名词后缀

penalty ['pen(ə)lti]（因违反法律、规则或合约而受到的）处罚；罚款，罚金；（在体育运动中对犯规者的）判罚，处罚；罚球 penalty kick 足球点球　词源：pen 钱 ＋ty 指罚钱

penalize ['pi:nəlaiz] 处罚；（体育运动中）判罚　词源：pen 钱 ＋lize 动词后缀

2）hang　巧记：把 p 向上变成 d 向下 指放置在上面倒挂

appendix [ə'pendiks]（书末的）附录；阑尾　词源：ap 强调 ＋pend 悬挂 ＋i 小 ＋x 没有 指倒挂在人体盲肠上的部分

impending [im'pendiŋ]（尤指不愉快的事）迫近的 impeding failure 近在咫尺的失败　词源：im 内部 ＋pend 悬挂 ＋ing 形容词后缀 指即将破门而入的不好的事物

pending ['pendiŋ] 迫近的，将要发生的 the pending election 即将举行的选举；悬而未决的，待定的 pending trade disputes 悬而未决的贸易争端；在……期间（介词）pending further research / inquiries 等待进一步研究/调查　词源：pend 悬挂 ＋ing 形容词后缀

pendulum ['pendjuləm] 钟摆　词源：pend 悬挂 ＋l 钟摆的长棍

peninsula [pi'ninsjulə] 半岛　词源：pen 悬挂 ＋insula 岛屿 island 指悬挂在陆地外像岛屿似的土地

suspend [sə'spend]（像蜘蛛侠般的）倒挂，悬挂；暂停，延缓；停学，停职　词源：sus 下面 ＋pend 悬挂 指在下面倒挂

suspense [sə'spens]（悬疑小说或电影的）悬念，焦虑，紧张感　词源：sus 下面 ＋pens 悬挂 指悬挂在心里的未决疑虑

suspension [sə'spenʃ(ə)n] 倒挂，悬挂 a suspension bridge 悬索桥，吊桥；暂停，中止；停学，停职；汽车悬架，减震装置；悬浮液　词源：suspend 悬挂 ＋sion 名词后缀

36. -capt-, -cept-, -ceive-, -ceipt-, -ceit-, -cip-, -cipi- : take　巧记：cap 帽子 指抓帽子的动作

captive ['kæptiv] 被俘的；战俘　词源：capt 抓拿 ＋tive 形容词后缀 指被抓住的

capture ['kæptʃə] 俘获（敌人）；捕获（动物）；夺得，抢占（市场份额）；（用文字或图片）记录，描绘，捕捉　词源：capt 抓拿 ＋nature 性质

captivate ['kæptiveit] 使着迷，吸引 be captivated by sb. / sth.　词源：capt 抓拿 ＋ate 动词后缀 指抓住别人兴趣

capricious [kə'priʃəs]（人）反复无常的，任性的；（天气或气候）变化莫测的　词源：cap 抓拿 ＋ous 形容词后缀（表示过多的）指什么东西都想抓一把不定性的　巧记：小说 Gone with the Wind《飘》（改编成电影叫作《乱世佳人》）中的女主角 Scarlett 的性格就是 capricious

caption ['kæpʃ(ə)n]（图片、照片或漫画的）说明文字　词源：cap 抓拿 ＋tion 名词后缀

accept [ə'ksept] 接受；忍受　词源：ac 强调 ＋cept 抓拿 指抓住接受

acceptable [ək'septəb(ə)l] 可接受的；合意的，令人满意的　词源：accept 接受 ＋able 形容词后缀（表示可以……的）

susceptible [sə'septib(ə)l] 易受影响的；易得病的 be susceptible to infections 容易受感染；好动感情的　词源：sus 下面 ＋acceptable 可接受的 指在下面接触概率大、易受影响的

conceive [kən'siːv] 怀孕；构想（主意、计划等）sb. conceive of sth. 词源：con 共同 + ceive 拿 指完全拿出新想法

conceit [kən'siːt] 自负，自高自大 词源：conceive 怀孕 + it 名词后缀 指怀孕的女性会感觉到自己伟大、有点自负

conceited [kən'siːtid] 自以为是的，自满的 词源：conceit 自负 + ed 形容词后缀

concept ['kɔnsept] 概念，理念，观念，想法 词源：conceive 构想 + cept 名词后缀

conception [kən'sepʃ(ə)n] 概念，观念；构想；受孕 词源：conceive 构想 + tion 名词后缀

deceive [di'siːv] 欺骗 deceive sb. into doing sth.；自欺欺人 deceive oneself 词源：de 以不好的方式 + ceive 抓拿 指以不好的手段获得

deceit [di'siːt] 欺骗，欺诈 词源：deceive 欺骗 + it 名词后缀

deception [di'sepʃ(ə)n] 欺骗 词源：deceive 欺骗 + tion 名词后缀 巧记：Decepticons 变形金刚里面的反派霸天虎

perceive [pə'siːv] 认知；认为 词源：per 穿越 + ceive 抓拿 指通过拿物品了解世界

perception [pə'sepʃ(ə)n] 认知；洞察力 词源：perceive 认知 + tion 名词后缀

except [ik'sept; ek-] 除了 词源：ex 出来 + cept 抓拿 指把某个东西从一堆东西里拿出来排除它

exception [ik'sepʃn] 例外，除外 词源：except 除了 + tion 名词后缀

exceptional [ik'sepʃ(ə)n(ə)l; ek-] 例外的；杰出的 词源：exception 例外 + al 形容词后缀

intercept [,intə'sept] 中途拦截；侦听电话 intercept phone calls 词源：inter 两者间 + cept 抓拿 指拿走两者间某个东西

inception [in'sepʃ(ə)n]（组织或机构的）开端 词源：in 内部 + accept 接受 + tion 名词后缀 指内心接受是喜欢某事物的开始 巧记：电影 Inception《盗梦空间》 指梦境的开端

receive [ri'siːv] 收到；接受 词源：re 向后 + ceive 抓拿 指拿着返回的事物是收到

receiver [ri'siːvə] 电话听筒；接管人；无线电接收机，收音机，电视机；橄榄球接球手 词源：receive 接受 + er 名词后缀

receipt [ri'siːt] 收到；收据，收条 词源：receive 收到 + it 名词后缀

reception [ri'sepʃ(ə)n] 欢迎，接待；接待处，前台；招待会 词源：receive 收到 + tion 名词后缀

receptionist [ri'sepʃ(ə)nist] 接待员 词源：reception 接待 + ist 人

recipient [ri'sipiənt] 接受者；领奖者 the recipient of the Nobel Peace Prize 诺贝尔和平奖得主

receptive [ri'septiv] 善于接受的,愿意倾听的 a workforce that is receptive to new ideas 乐于接受新观念的员工 词源：receive 接受 + tive 形容词后缀（表示充满活力的 active）

reciprocal [ri'siprək(ə)l] 互惠的 reciprocal trade agreements 互惠的贸易协定 词源：reci 接受 receive + pro 提议 proposal + cal 形容词后缀 指能接受彼此提议的是互惠的

anticipate [æn'tisipeit] 预料,预测；期待好事 词源：anti 在前面 + cip 获得 + ate 动词后缀 指提前获得了消息就会有所期待

participate [pɑː'tisipeit] 参与 participate in sth. 词源：part 部分 + cip 抓拿 + ate 动词后缀 指 take part in sth.

precipitate [pri'sipiteit] 仓促的,草率的 a precipitate decision 草率的决定；导致,促成 precipitate a crisis 促成危机；使（某人或某物）突然陷入（某种状态）precipitate the country into war 使国家突然陷入战争状态；沉淀物（通过化学或物理变化从溶液或悬浮液中分离出来的物质，比如过滤后得到的物质） 词源：pre 在前面 + cip 抓拿 + it 它 + ate 动词后缀 指提前拿东西的动作是草率的行为 词义连记：草率的决定导致河流中堆积有害的沉淀物进而使环境陷入危机

precipitation [pri,sipi'teiʃ(ə)n]（雨、雪、冰等）降水,降水量 a slight chance of precipitation 降水概率不大；沉淀 obtain the compound by precipitation 通过沉淀获得化合物；仓促,轻率 词源：precipitate 沉淀物 + tion 名词后缀 指从天上落下来的沉淀物是降水

37. -chron- : time 巧记：Cronus 克洛诺斯 希腊神话中掌管时间之神

synchronize ['siŋkrənaiz] 使时间同步 synchronized swimming 花样游泳 词源：syn 相同 + chron 时间 + ize 动词后缀 指使时间节点相同

chronicle ['krɔnik(ə)l] 编年史 The Chronicles of Narnia 电影《纳尼亚传奇》 词源：chron 时间 + cle 名词后缀

chronic ['krɔnik]（疾病）慢性的 chronic bronchitis / arthritis / asthma 慢性支气管炎/关节炎/哮喘；（问题或困难）长期的 chronic unemployment 长期的失业 词源：chron 时间 + ic 形容词后缀 反义词：acute

chronology [krə'nɔlədʒi] 年代顺序；年表 词源：chron 时间 + ology 名词后缀

chronological [,krɔnə'lɔdʒikl] 按时间先后顺序排列的 arrange the documents in chronological order 把这些文件按时间顺序排列 词源：chronology + cal 形容词后缀

38. -plex-, -plic-, -ploy-, -ply- : fold 巧记：play 玩 指玩折叠玩具（字母 x，c，y 表示折叠）

complex ['kɔmpleks] 复杂的；（众多大楼或一座主楼和许多辅楼组成的）综合楼群 the White House Complex 白宫建筑群；综合体,多元体 a complex of sth.；情结 inferiority complex 自卑情结,自卑感 词源：com 共同 + plex 折叠 指完全地折叠起来的

complexion [kəm'plekʃ(ə)n] 形势，局面 put a different / new / fresh complexion on sth.使形势改观；（人的）肤色，面色 a pale / fair / ruddy complexion 苍白/白皙/红润的面色；（事物的）性质，特性（常单数）chang the complexion of the legislative branch 改变立法部门的性质 词源：complex 复杂的 + ion 名词后缀 指人的面色复杂多变

complicate ['kɔmplikeit] 使（问题，局面）更复杂；使（疾病）恶化 词源：com 共同 + plic 折叠 + ate 动词后缀

complicated ['kɔmplikeitid] 复杂的；难懂的 词源：complicate 使复杂 + ed 形容词后缀

complication [,kɔmpli'keiʃ(ə)n] 使更复杂的问题（情况），新困难；（疾病）并发症 词源：complicate 使复杂 + tion 名词后缀

perplex [pə'pleks] 使长期困扰,使困惑 a perplexing question 令人困惑的问题 词源：per 一直 + complex 复杂的 指使一直复杂

perplexity [pə'pleksiti]（不可数名词）困扰，茫然 stare at the sky in perplexity 茫然地凝视着天空；（可数名词）复杂的事物 the perplexity of Rubik's cube 魔术方块的困惑　词源：perplex 使困惑 + ity 名词后缀

plastic ['plæstik] 塑料；信用卡 take plastic 接受信用卡付款；塑料制的 plastic bags 塑料袋　词源：ply 折叠 + ast 最高级 + ic 形容词后缀

plaster ['plɑːstə(r)]（涂抹墙壁和天花板用的）灰泥；熟石膏 a plaster bust 半身石膏塑像；膏药，（窄条）橡皮膏，创可贴，护创伤胶布　词源：ply 折叠 + ast 最高级 + er 名词后缀 指可以涂抹折叠成任意形状的液体

ploy [plɔi]（欺骗性的）计策，手段，花招 a smart marketing ploy 机智的销售策略　词源：ploy 折叠 指折叠出一层又一层的计策　巧记：play 玩 指玩手段花招

deploy [di'plɔi] 部署，调动（士兵、部队或武器装备）deploy troops / weapons；（有效）利用，调动 deploy resources / staff / skills / talents 利用资源/人员/技能/才能　词源：de 向下 + ploy 折叠 指向下折叠开地图部署军队

employ [im'plɔi; em-] 雇佣；使用，利用 employ a novel teaching method 利用新颖的教学法　词源：em 使动词化 + ploy 折叠 指折叠好简历招员工

explicate ['eksplikeit] 详细解释，详细分析（想法或文学作品）explicate the traditional notion of marriage 解释传统的婚姻观念　词源：ex 出来 + plic 折叠 + ate 动词后缀 指打开折叠的文件详细说明

explicit [ik'splisit; ek-] 清晰的，直接的；（描绘性或暴力的语言或画面）清晰露骨的　词源：explicate 说明 + it 它 指详细说明它的

imply [im'plai] 暗指 implied satire 隐含的讥讽　词源：im 内部 + ply 折叠 指折叠在纸张内部的话语

implicit [im'plisit] 暗含的 implicit criticism 含蓄的批评；完全的 have implicit faith / trust / belief in sb. / sth. 完全相信某人或某事　词源：imply 暗指 + it 它 指暗指是它

implicate ['implikeit] 暗指（某人）牵连（犯罪或不诚实行为）implicate sb. in sth.；说明（某物）是导致（不好或有害的事）的原因　词源：im 内部 + plic 折叠 + ate 动词后缀 指折叠在内部的关联行为

implication [impli'keiʃ(ə)n]（行动、事件、决定等的）影响，后果 the implications of business proposals 商业提议的影响；牵涉，牵连 the implication of the former president in a scandal 前任总统卷入一宗丑闻；含意，暗示　词源：implicate 牵连 + tion 名词后缀

apply [ə'plai] 涂抹（化妆品），敷药 apply hand lotion 涂抹护手液；使用，应用 apply technology to farming 应用科技到农业；申请（工作或大学）apply for a job / apply to a university　词源：ap 强调 + ply 折叠 指把药膏或化妆品折叠后涂抹

applicant ['æplik(ə)nt]（高校）申请人；（工作）求职人　词源：apply 申请 + ant 人

application [,æpli'keiʃ(ə)n] 涂抹（化妆品），敷药；使用，应用；申请　词源：apply 涂抹 + tion 名词后缀　巧记：手机 APP 应用软件的简称

appliance [ə'plaiəns] 家用电器　词源：apply 应用 + ance 名词后缀 指可以被使用的是家用

电器

applicable [ə'plikəb(ə)l; 'æplik-] 适合的，适用的 sth. be applicable to sth. 词源：apply 应用 + able 形容词后缀（表示可以……的）

applied [ə'plaid] 应用的 applied science / physics / linguistics 应用科学/物理学/语言学 词源：apply 应用 + ed 形容词后缀 指应用性的学科

comply [kəm'plai] 遵守，服从 comply with the regulations 遵守规则 词源：com 共同 + ply 折叠 指折叠在一起形状符合 巧记：com 共同 + play 玩游戏 指玩游戏遵守规则

compliant [kəm'plaiənt]（对他人的意愿和要求）服从的，顺从的，百依百顺的，俯首帖耳的 a compliant and dutiful wife 一个顺从尽职的妻子；（与规定或标准）符合的，一致的 be compliant with the industry standard 与工业标准相一致 词源：comply 服从 + ant 形容词后缀（表示具有……能力的）

compliance [kəm'plaiəns]（对规则、协议或要求）服从，听从，遵守 in compliance with sth. 词源：comply 遵守 + ance 名词后缀

reply [ri'plai] 回复 词源：re 向后 + ply 折叠 指把信折叠后寄回

39. -press- : push 巧记：press 按压

compress [kəm'pres]（用以止血或止痛的）敷布，压布；压紧，压缩 compressed air / gas 压缩空气/气体；压缩（计算机文件）compress a computer file；压缩，精简（文字或话语）compress pages of notes into paragraphs 把许多页笔记精简成段落；压缩（做某事的时间） 词源：com 共同 + press 按压 指完全按压在上面

decompress [ˌdiːkəm'pres] 使减压，减少……的气压 decompress the cabin by breaking the plane window 打碎飞机玻璃给机舱减压；（计算机文件）解压缩（将压缩文件等恢复到原大小） 词源：de 否定 + compress 压缩 指不压缩

depress [di'pres] 使沮丧，使抑郁，使失去信心；使（经济）不景气，使萧条；降低（价格），减少（工资）；按下，压下，推下 depress the clutch pedal 踩离合器踏板 词源：de 向下 + press 按压 指被按压的心情

depression [di'preʃn] 抑郁症；忧伤，沮丧，消沉；大萧条（20 世纪 30 年代经济萧条大量失业的时期）the (Great) Depression；经济萧条期，不景气时期；洼地，坑 depressions in the ground 地面上的坑；低气压 词源：depress 使沮丧 + sion 名词后缀 词义连记：经济萧条让人沮丧抑郁，道路失修坑坑洼洼

express [ik'spres; ek-] 快速的，特快的；快递 Federal Express 联邦快递公司；（火车或公共汽车的）快车；表达 词源：ex 出来 + press 按压 指不再按压快速释放出来

expressive [ik'spresiv; ek-] 富于表现力的 expressive eyes 丰富表情的眼睛 词源：express 表达 + ive 形容词后缀（表示充满活力的 active）

impress [im'pres] 留下印象 impress sb. with / by sth.；压印，盖印于 词源：im 内部 + press 按压 指内心里有按压的记忆痕迹

impression [im'preʃ(ə)n] 印象；印记，压痕；印数（指一本书一次印刷的总册数） 词源：impress

留下印象 + sion 名词后缀

impressive [im'presiv] 令人赞叹的，令人敬佩的，给人深刻印象的 an impressive performance 印象深刻的演出　词源：impress 留下印象 + ive 形容词后缀（表示充满活力的 active）

oppress [ə'pres]（阶级）压迫 tribes oppressed by the colonists 受殖民者压迫的部落；（气氛）使压抑，使烦恼　词源：op 上面 up + press 按压　指在上面高压压迫

repress [ri'pres] 忍住，抑制（痛苦的情感、回忆、冲动、愤怒、笑声等）repress a smile 忍住不笑；镇压，压制（抗议）　词源：re 重复 + press 按压　指不停地按压情绪

suppress [sə'pres]（用武力）镇压 suppress the rebellion 镇压叛乱；禁止发表，查禁，封锁（消息或言论）suppress evidence / information 隐瞒证据/消息；忍住，控制，抑制（感情）suppress anger 按捺住怒火；抑制（生长、发展、起作用等）medicine that suppresses the appetite 抑制食欲的药　词源：sup 下面 + press 按压　指向下面暴力按压反抗　词义连记：人们对军队武力镇压游行和警方封锁消息抑制不住怒火，吃药绝食抗议

40. **-fer-**: bring, carry　巧记：f 鸟儿飞翔 + e 出来 + r 植物　指小鸟嘴里叼着筑巢用的植物飞进飞出；fer 也可理解为短语 fetch and carry（做杂务，打杂）的缩写　指做携带东西跑腿的杂活儿

interfere [ˌintə'fiə] 干涉，干预 interfere with sth. / sb.；信号干扰（广播或电视播放）　词源：inter 两者间 + fer 带来　指给两者间强行带来加入新事物　同义词：intervene in sth. / meddle (in / with) sth.

refer [ri'fə:] 提到，谈到，谈及 refer to the matter 提及这件事；涉及，关于 figures referring to sales 涉及销售额的数字；参考，查看，查阅 refer to the dictionary 查阅字典；把某人介绍给某人/把某事物交给某人 refer sb. / sth. to sb.　词源：re 向后 + fer 带来　指把东西带给别人

referee [ˌrefə'ri:] 裁判　词源：refer 查看 + ee 人　指跑回去查看后作出判罚的人

reference ['ref(ə)r(ə)ns] 参考书；推荐信，介绍信；（申请留学或求职的）介绍人，推荐人　词源：refer 参考 + ence 名词后缀

confer [kən'fə:] 商讨，讨论 confer with sb. on / about sth.；授予（称号、学位、荣耀、奖项或权利等）confer a title / degree / honour on sb. 授予某人称号/学位/荣耀　词源：con 共同 + fer 带来　指大家都带来自己的提议来商量　词义连记：开会商讨授予学位

conference ['kɔnf(ə)r(ə)ns] 会议　词源：confer 讨论 + ence 名词后缀

defer [di'fə:] 屈服，顺从 defer to sb. / sth.；推迟，延迟 defer repayment on the loan 推迟贷款还款　词源：de 否定 + fer 带来　指否定带来的建议、推迟讨论　巧记：谐音"低服"指低头服从　词义连记：屈服于某人推迟会议

differ ['difə] 与……不同 differ from sth.　词源：dif 分散 + fer 带来　指带着东西四散分离，道路不同

different ['difrənt] 不同的　词源：differ 不同 + ent 形容词后缀（表示具有……能力的）

differentiate [ˌdifə'renʃieit] 区分，识别 differentiate sth. from sth.；区别对待（尤指不公平对待）　词源：different 不同的 + tiate 动词后缀

indifferent [in'dif(ə)r(ə)nt] 冷漠的；平庸的 be indifferent to sb. / sth.　词源：in 否定 + different 不同的　指对待事物的态度没有不同的立场，都是一样的冷漠

indifference [in'dif(ə)r(ə)ns] 冷漠，不关心 show indifference to material luxuries 对物质享受缺乏兴趣　词源：indifferent 冷漠的 + ce 名词后缀

infer [in'fə:] （像侦探般根据资料）推断，推定　词源：in 内部 + fer 带来　指内心带来的推测判断

inference ['infərəns] 推论，推断的结果　词源：infer 推断 + ence 名词后缀

offer ['ɔfə] 提供（建议、帮助、支持或机会等）offer sb. sth.；开价，报价 make (sb.) an offer (for / on sth.)；特价 special offers　词源：of 强调 + fer 带来　指带来价格好的东西或好建议

prefer [pri'fə:] 更喜欢，偏爱　词源：pre 在前面 + fer 带来　指带到最前面的是更喜欢的

preference ['pref(ə)r(ə)ns] 偏爱；优待，优惠，优先（权）　词源：prefer 偏爱 + ence 名词后缀

preferential [ˌprefə'renʃ(ə)l] 优先的，优待的，优惠的 preferential credit terms 优惠信贷条件　词源：preference 优待 + tial 形容词后缀（表示特殊的 special）

transfer [træns'fə:; trɑːns-; -nz-] 调动工作；学生转学；地点转移，搬运迁移；运动员转会；账户转账；转移感情；电话转接；交通工具换乘 transfer station 换乘站；传染疾病　词源：trans 穿越 + fer 带来　指带着物品转移

fertile ['fə:tail] 肥沃的 fertile cropland 肥沃的耕地；能繁殖的；想象力丰富的　词源：fer 带来 + ile 形容词后缀（表示容易……的）指容易带着丰富营养的　形近易混词：futile

futile ['fjuːtail] 无用的，徒劳的 a futile attempt / effort 徒劳之举　词源：fut 脚 foot + u 水 + ile 形容词后缀　指双脚站在水里基本动不了的是徒劳无用的

ferry ['feri] 渡船 take a ferry across the river 坐渡船过河；摆渡，渡运 ferry sb. / sth. (from sth.) to sth.　词源：fer 带来 + ry 名词后缀　指带着人们往返两岸的船只　巧记：在美国纽约乘坐从曼哈顿到史丹顿岛免费轮渡 Staten Island Ferry 游览自由岛 Liberty Island 上的自由女神像 The Statue of Liberty

41. **-bi-, -bio-** : life　巧记：bi 两个 + o 太阳　指两个太阳滋润生命

aerobics [eə'rəubiks] 有氧运动，有氧健身操　词源：aero 空气 + bio 生命 + ics 学科　指和空气、生命有关的运动

antibiotic [ˌæntibai'ɔtik] 抗生素（比如青霉素、盘尼西林 Penicillin）；抗生素的　词源：anti 相反 + bio 生命 + tic 形容词后缀　指抵抗细菌生长的药品

autobiography [ˌɔːtəbai'ɔgrəfi] 自传　词源：auto 自己 + bio 生命 + graph 描写　指对自己生活的描绘

biology [bai'ɔlədʒi] 生物学　词源：bio 生命 + ology 名词后缀（表示学科）

biography [bai'ɔgrəfi] 人物传记　词源：bio 生命 + graph 描写　指对他人生活的记录

biosphere ['baiə(u)sfiə] 生物圈　词源：bio 生命 + sphere 球体　指由动植物生命体组成的生存圈

biochemistry [baiə(u)'kemistri] 生物化学　词源：biology 生物学 + chemistry 化学

42. -ple-, -plet-, -pli-, -plish- : cover, fill　巧记：place 地方；放置　指把大量物品摆放安置，充满整个地方

plenty ['plenti] 充足，大量，众多　plenty of eggs / money / time 充裕的鸡蛋/钱/时间　词源：ple 充满 +n 门 + ty 名词后缀　指物品充足，多得都堆到了门口

plus [plʌs] 加号；（算数中加减乘除的）加；和，外加，加上；（温度）零度以上，零上；有利因素（条件）；有利的，好的　plus points 优点；（学生考试或作业成绩）略高于（A、B 等）get B plus (B+) in the test 考试得了个 B+　词源：pl 充满 + us 名词后缀　反义词：minus

surplus ['sɜːpləs] 过剩，剩余额　produce food surpluses 生产过剩的食物；（贸易）顺差，（预算）盈余 a trade surplus / a budget surplus；过剩的，剩余的，多余的　surplus cash 多余的现金　词源：sur 上面 + plus 加　指多到附加到表面的

accomplish [ə'kʌmpliʃ; ə'kɔm-] 完成，达成　mission accomplished 大功告成　词源：ac 强调 + com 共同 + ple 充满 + ish 动词后缀　指通过努力完成　巧记：ac 强调 + complete 完成

accomplice [ə'kʌmplis; ə'kɔm-] 同谋犯　词源：accomplish 完成　指共同完成坏事的人

ample ['æmp(ə)l] 充足的，充裕的，绰绰有余的　ample time 充裕的时间；（房间或空间）宽敞的 ample room / space；（女性胸部）丰满的 an ample bosom　词源：am 爱 love；获取 take + ple 充满　指充满爱的　巧记：apple 苹果充满的

amplify ['æmplifai] 放大（声音，音乐声或信号）an amplified guitar 带有扩音设备的电吉他；增强（某种感受）amplify the feelings of regret and fear 增加懊悔和恐惧感；详述，（进一步）阐述 amplify a statement 详述声明　词源：ample 充足的 + ify 动词后缀

amplifier ['æmplifaiə(r)] 放大器，扩音器　词源：amplify 放大声音 + er 名词后缀

complete [kəm'pliːt] 完全的；完成；填写（表格）　词源：com 共同 + ple 充满　指全部圆满完成

complement ['kɔmplim(ə)nt] 补充物（比如美酒配佳肴）；补充，使相配，使完美，使取长补短 use photographs to complement texts 用照片补充文本；（语法）补语；足额，全数 have a full complement of trainees 接收的实习生全额满员　词源：complete 完成 + ment 名词后缀

complementary [kɔmpli'ment(ə)ri] 补充的，互补的，相辅相成的 be complementary to sth.　词源：complement 补充 + ary 形容词后缀

compliment ['kɔmplim(ə)nt] 恭维，称赞 compliment sb. on sth.　词源：complement 补充 + i 人　指对人的话语补充是恭维

complimentary [kɔmpli'ment(ə)ri] 恭维的，赞美的 complimentary remarks 赞美的话；（演出票、香槟等）免费赠送的 complimentary Wi-Fi 免费无线上网　词源：compliment 恭维 + ary 形容词后缀　词义连记：说恭维的话是免费赠送给别人的

implement ['implim(ə)nt] 贯彻，执行，实施（变革，决议，政策，计划，改革，建议）implement changes / decisions / policies / plans / reforms / recommendations；（尤指用于户外体力活的）工具 farm implements 农具　词源：im 内部 + ple 充满 + ment 思想 mind 指内心和思想中充满指导精神　词义连记：用农具实行耕作方式变革

deplete [dɪ'pliːt] 大量减少，削减，损耗 deplete natural resources 消耗自然资源　词源：de 否定 + ple 充满　指使不充满

replete [rɪ'pliːt] 充满的，充足的 be replete with sth.；吃饱喝足的　词源：re 重复 + ple 充满　指反复使充满

supplement ['sʌplɪm(ə)nt]（维他命或饮食）营养补品 vitamin / dietary supplements；补充 supplement one's income by tutoring 做家教来补充收入；（报纸、杂志等的）增刊；（书籍的）补编，补遗，附录；（服务、旅馆房费等的）附加费　词源：supply 供应 + ple 充满 + ment 名词后缀

supplementary [ˌsʌplɪ'ment(ə)rɪ] 补充的 supplementary information 补充信息　词源：supplement 补充 + ary 形容词后缀

3

43. -form- : form　巧记：form 形式

conform [kən'fɔːm] 从众；遵守，遵从（法律、规定）conform to / with sth.　词源：con 共同 + form　指遵守共同的规则

deform [dɪ'fɔːm]（使）变形 an empty deformed coke can 一个空的变形的可乐罐　词源：de 否定 + form 形式　指不是原有形状

forge [fɔːdʒ] 锻造车间，铁匠铺；形成，缔造（尤指与其他的人、团体或国家形成牢固的关系）；伪造（尤指文书、笔迹）；稳步前进 forge through the streets 稳步走过街道　词源：form 形式 + ge 走 go　指保持稳定形式向前走　巧记：谐音"仿制"指仿造

format ['fɔːmæt]（计算机硬盘）格式化；（书信）格式　词源：form 形式 + it 在　指把它格式化

formation [fɔː'meɪʃ(ə)n] 形态；形成，组成；（足球队）队形，阵型　词源：form 形式 + tion 名词后缀

formula ['fɔːmjʊlə] 方案 a peace formula 和平方案；公式；分子式；（药品、燃料或饮料等）配方；（赛车的）一级/二级/三级方程式 a Formula One car 一级方程式赛车；客套话，惯用语句　词源：form 形式 + la 持续 last　指持续存在的形式

formulate ['fɔːmjʊleɪt] 简要说明；规划制定　词源：formula 方案 + ate 动词后缀　指说明方案

formal ['fɔːml] 正式的　词源：form 形式 + al 形容词后缀

formality [fɔː'mælɪtɪ] 礼节仪式；正式手续 go through the formalities 办手续；例行公事　词源：formal 正式的 + ity 名词后缀　指办正式手续

inform [ɪn'fɔːm] 正式通知 inform sb. of sth.　词源：in 内部 + form 形式　指在内部告知各种形式的信息

informed [ɪn'fɔːmd] 消息灵通的，见多识广的　词源：inform 通知 + ed 形容词后缀

perform [pə'fɔːm] 表演；表现；贯彻，执行，实行 perform a study 进行研究　词源：per 一直 +

form 形式 指一直保持某种形式

reform [ri'fɔːm] 改革重组；改过自新　词源：re 重复 + form 形式 指反复改变形式

transform [træns'fɔːm; trɑːns-; -nz-] 使改变；使变形　词源：trans 穿越 + form 形式 指穿过一个过程后改变形态　巧记：Transformers 变形金刚

uniform ['juːnifɔːm] 全部相同的，一致的 a uniform size 相同大小；（学生，军人，服务员，志愿者）制服　词源：uni 唯一 + form 形式 指唯一的形式

44. -sens-, -sent- : perceive, feel　巧记：sense 感觉，感知

assent [ə'sent] 赞成，同意 assent to sth.　词源：as 强调 + sent 感知 指感觉上是一致的

absent ['æbs(ə)nt] 缺席的 absent from school 缺课；心不在焉的 an absent look 心不在焉的神情　词源：ab 离开 + sent 感知 指感觉有人离开的

consent [kən'sent] 一致同意，允许 consent to sth.　词源：con 共同 + sent 感知 指共同的感知是一致的

consensus [kən'sensəs] 共同意见，共识 reach (a) consensus on / about sth. 达成一致　词源：consent 同意 + us 名词后缀

dissent [di'sent]（官方决定或公认观点的）不同意，异议 dissent from sth.　词源：dis 分离 + sens 感知 指感觉不一致

resent [ri'zent]（因受委屈而）愤恨不满 resent being treated like a child 厌恶被当成孩子一样对待　词源：re 向后 + sens 感知 指感觉往回走

resentment [ri'zentm(ə)nt] 愤恨不满，憎恶 feel / harbour / bear resentment towards / against sb. 对某人心怀不满　词源：resent 愤恨 + ment 名词后缀（指人的思想 mind）

essence ['es(ə)ns] 本质，实质 in essence 从本质上说；精华，精髓；（烹饪用的）香精，精油 vanilla essence 香草香精　词源：e 出来 + sens 感知 + ence 名词后缀 指从感知中提炼出的精华感觉

essential [i'senʃ(ə)l] 精华的；本质的，根本的 essential difference 本质区别；必须的，必不可少的 an essential part / ingredient / component of sth. 必不可少的一部分；要点，要素 the essentials of business English 商务英语基础；必需品　词源：essence 精华 + tial 形容词后缀

sentiment ['sentim(ə)nt] 意见，观点 public sentiment 公众的意见；多愁善感　词源：sens 感知 + ment 名词后缀（指人的思想 mind）指复杂的感觉和思维是多愁善感

sentimental [senti'ment(ə)l]（故事、电影、书等）伤感的；感情用事的，非理性的　词源：sentiment 多愁善感 + al 形容词后缀

sense [sens] 感觉 a sense of achievement 成就感；意义 make sense 有意义/是明智的/有道理；感觉到，意识到 sense one's anger 觉察出某人的愤怒　词源：sens 感知

sensor ['sensə] 传感器，感应装置（如感应水龙头）　词源：sens 感知 + or 名词后缀

sensitive ['sensitiv] 敏感的，易生气的 be sensitive to criticism 一听批评就急；善解人意的，体贴的 a sensitive and caring husband 体贴的丈夫；（对温度、光、食物等）易过敏的 be sensitive to milk 对牛奶过敏；（对光、温度、位置等的变化）灵敏度高的 a highly sensitive electronic camera 高敏感度的电子摄像机　词源：sens 感知 + tive 形容词后缀（表示充满活力的 active）　巧记：sensitive plant 含羞草

sensible ['sensɪb(ə)l] 明智的, 合理的 sensible advice 合理的建议；感知某事, 察觉某事 be sensible of sth.；可以感知的, 明显的 a sensible increase in temperature 温度的明显上升　词源：sens 感觉 + able 形容词后缀（表示可以……的）指感觉上是对的

sensory ['sens(ə)ri]（视觉, 味觉, 听觉, 触觉, 嗅觉）感官的 sensory stimuli such as music 音乐的感官刺激　词源：sens 感知 + ory 形容词后缀

sensuous ['senʃuəs]（音乐或绘画）给人美感的, 给人以快感的 sensuous music 悦耳的音乐；性感的, 肉感的 sensuous lips 性感的嘴唇　词源：sens 感知 + ous 形容词后缀（表示过多的）指特别有感觉的

45. -corp-, -corpor- : body　巧记：core 核心 指人的主体核心部分是身体

corps [kɔː] 军团；特殊兵种 the medical corps 医疗部队；（一起工作的）一群人, 一组人 the diplomatic corps 外交使团　词源：corp 身体 + s 名词后缀 指由肉身组成的军队

corpse [kɔːps] 尸体　词源：corp 身体 + se 名词后缀　巧记：Corpse Bride 电影《僵尸新娘》

corporal ['kɔːp(ə)r(ə)l] 肉体的 corporal punishment （尤指学校和监狱中的）体罚；（陆军、空军等的）下士　词源：corpor 身体 + al 形容词后缀

corpulent ['kɔːpjələnt] 肥胖的, 臃肿的 a corpulent seal 一只肥胖的海豹　词源：corp 身体 + pul 推动 + ent 形容词后缀（表示具有……能力的）指肥胖的身体只能推着走

corporation [kɔːpə'reɪʃ(ə)n] 集团公司, 大企业 News Corporation 新闻集团（全球最大的媒体企业集团之一, 它的主要股东是 Rupert Murdoch 鲁伯特·默多克）　词源：corpor 身体 + tion 名词后缀 指由几个不同业务主体的公司组成的集团公司

corporate ['kɔːp(ə)rət] 公司的, 企业的 corporate culture 企业文化；共同的 corporate responsibility 共同的责任；法人的　词源：corporation 集团公司 + ate 形容词后缀

incorporate [ɪn'kɔːpəreɪt] 兼并 incorporate sth. into / in sth.；包含, 包括　词源：in 内部 + corporation 集团公司 指成为集团公司的一员

46. -rod-, -ros- : gnaw　巧记：谐音"咬的"

corrode [kə'rəʊd]（化学）腐蚀；损害 Corruption corroded the public confidence in the police force. 腐败现象损害了公众对警察机关的信任。　词源：cor 共同 + rod 咬 指完全地咬去某部分

corrosive [kə'rəʊsɪv] 腐蚀性的；起损害作用的 the corrosive effect of money in sport 体育运动中金钱的破坏作用　词源：corrode 腐蚀 + ive 形容词后缀（表示充满活力的 active）

erode [ɪ'rəʊd]（气候）侵蚀, 风化 eroded rocks 风化的岩石；逐步损害, 削弱（权力或信心）erode confidence 削弱自信心　词源：e 出来 + rod 咬 指咬出一些来

erosion [ɪ'rəʊʒ(ə)n]（气候）侵蚀 soil erosion 水土流失；（权力或信心的）逐步损害, 削弱　词源：erode 侵蚀 + sion 名词后缀

rodent ['rəʊd(ə)nt] 啮齿动物（如老鼠、兔子等）　词源：rod 咬 + ent 名词后缀（表示具有……

能力的）

rodenticide [rəu'dentəˌsaid] 灭鼠药　词源：rodent 啮齿动物 + cide 杀　指杀掉啮齿动物的药

rot [rɒt] 腐败，腐烂 Candy will rot teeth. 糖会蛀坏牙齿。　词源：rod 咬　指咬后会腐烂

rotten ['rɒt(ə)n] 腐烂的，变质的；非常糟糕的，恶劣的；刻薄的　词源：rot 腐坏 + en 形容词后缀（表示由某种物质制成的）

47. **-ven-, -vent-**：come　巧记：v 开口的 V 字形 + e 出来 + n 门　指开门出来进来；古罗马恺撒的名言"我来，我看见，我征服。"中的三个拉丁语词根就是 veni, vidi, vici，指恺撒来到的世界的任何地方，看到的土地都可以被他征服

vent [vent] 通风口 a blocked air vent 堵塞的通风口；（衣服后面的或侧边的）开衩；发泄，宣泄 vent one's anger on the referee 把气撒在裁判身上　词源：ven 来 + t 方向 to 指来风的地方

ventilate ['ventileit] 使通风 a well-ventilated room 通风良好的房间；公开表达（感情或意见）；（用呼吸机）给……供氧 ventilate the patient 给病人上呼吸机　词源：vent 通风口 + l 长 long + ate 动词后缀　指长时间通风

advent ['ædvent]（重要事件、人物、发明等的）出现，到来 the advent of the computer 计算机的问世；（基督教的）基督降临，基督降临节（圣诞节前的四个星期）　词源：ad 强调 + vent 来　指强调来临

adventure [əd'ventʃə] 冒险，奇遇 an adventure story 历险故事　词源：ad 强调 + vent 来 + nature 大自然　指来到大自然冒险　巧记：The Adventures of Tintin: The Secret of the Unicorn 电影《丁丁历险记：独角兽号的秘密》

circumvent [ˌsɜːkəm'vent] 改道，绕过 circumvent the mountains 绕过这些山；（尤指巧妙或不诚实地）回避，规避 circumvent the tax laws 规避税法　词源：circum 圈 + vent 来　指绕着圈来通过

event [i'vent] 重要事件，大事；公开活动 a fund-raising event 筹款活动；（体育运动的）比赛项目（例如跳高、跳远、100 米赛跑等）　词源：e 出来 + vent 来　指必须出来参加的大型活动　巧记：evening 晚上　指晚上发生的大事件

invent [in'vent] 发明，创造 invent the steam engine 发明蒸汽机；编造，虚构 invent an excuse 编造借口　词源：in 内部 + vent 来　指内心出来的创造构想

prevent [pri'vent] 阻止，预防 prevent sb. / sth. (from) doing sth.　词源：pre 在前面 + vent 来　指提前到来阻止他人

convene [kən'viːn] 召集，召开（正式会议）convene a meeting；（为正式会议而）聚集，集合　词源：con 共同 + ven 来　指大家共同来开会

convention [kən'venʃ(ə)n] 大会，会议 National Convention Center 国家会议中心；（国际性的）公约 the Geneva Conventions 日内瓦公约；风俗，惯例 defy social conventions 无视社会习俗　词源：convene 召集会议 + tion 名词后缀　词义连记：定期开大会制定公约形成了惯例

conventional [kən'venʃ(ə)n(ə)l]（行为、观点）传统的，循规蹈矩的；（部队或武器）常规的

conventional forces / weapons　词源：convention 惯例 + al 形容词后缀

contravene [ˌkɔntrə'viːn] 违反（法律，法规）contravene state law 违反州法律　词源：contra 相反 + ven 来　指反着来

intervene [intə'viːn] 干涉，插手 intervene in sth.　词源：inter 两者间 + ven 来　指来到两者间干预　同义词：interfere with / meddle in (with)

avenue ['æv(ə)njuː] 林荫道；大街（美国纽约市的街道称呼都缩写为 Ave，例如著名的 Broadway Avenue 百老汇大街）；方法，途径　词源：a 正在 + ven 来　指在来的路上

revenue ['revənjuː]（政府）税收 the Internal Revenue Service（美国）国内税务局；（公司、机构的）收益，收入　词源：re 向后 + ven 来　指返回来的收益

venue ['venjuː] 举办地点，举行场所，会场 a sporting / conference / concert venue 体育比赛场馆/会议地点/音乐会演出地点　词源：ven 来　指来举行活动的地方

venture ['ventʃə] 风险项目，风险投资 business / commercial / capital venture 商业风投；冒风险（去某处）；小心说，谨慎做（会使人烦恼或不快的事）venture to do sth.　词源：ven 来 + nature 性质　指出来冒险的性质

48. **-sequ-, -secut-, -sec-, -sue**：follow　巧记：second 秒　指像秒针计时一样一秒一秒跟随

consecutive [kən'sekjutiv] 连续的，不间断的 consecutive rain 连续下雨　词源：con 共同 + sec 跟随 + tive 形容词后缀（表示充满活力的 active）指完全跟随的

consequence ['kɔnsikw(ə)ns] 重大后果 have far-reaching consequences 有深远的影响；重要性 be of no consequence 无关紧要　词源：con 共同 + sequ 跟随 + ence 名词后缀　指一件件事接着发生共同造成的严重后果　比如火山爆发→地震→海啸→瘟疫

consequent ['kɔnsikw(ə)nt] 随之发生的，作为结果的 the rise in inflation and consequent fall in demand 通货膨胀的加剧和随之而来的需求下降；由……引起的 be consequent upon / on sth.　词源：consequene 重大后果 + ent 形容词后缀（表示具有……能力的）

consequently ['kɔnsikw(ə)ntli] 结果是，因此，所以（= as a consequence）　词源：consequent 作为结果的 + ly 副词后缀　同义词：therefore / accordingly / thus / hence

execute ['eksikjuːt] 处决；贯彻，执行（政策，方针，计划，法律文件）execute a plan 实施计划；完成，表演（高难度动作）；创作（绘画、书、电影、艺术品等）；执行（计算机程序或指令）　词源：ex 出去 + sec 跟随 + cut 切　指出去跟着犯人执行处决

execution [ˌeksi'kjuːʃn] 处死，处决；（政策、方针、计划、法律文件的）实施，执行；（高难度动作的）表演；（乐曲的）演奏 a perfect execution of the violin piece 完美的小提琴曲演奏；（绘画、书、电影、艺术品的）创作；（计算机程序或指令的）执行　词源：execute 执行 + tion 名词后缀

executive [ig'zekjətiv]（机构或公司的）主管，经理 CEO（首席执行官 Chief Executive Officer）；行政的，管理的 an executive decision 行政管理的决策；高档的，豪华的 executive cars / homes 豪华汽车/豪宅　词源：execute 执行 + tive 形容词后缀

obsequious [əb'siːkwiəs] 谄媚的，奉承的，奴颜婢膝的 an obsequious smile 谄媚的微笑　词源：

ob 强调 ＋ sequ 跟随 ＋ i 人 ＋ ous 形容词后缀（表示过多的）指紧紧跟随别人的

pursue [pə'sjuː] 追求（事业、兴趣、目标或喜欢的人）；追捕，追击；继续进行 pursue the matter 追究某件事 词源：pur (per) 一直 ＋ sue 跟随 指一直跟随理想

pursuit [pə'sjuːt] 追求；追捕，追赶，追踪；嗜好，爱好 pursuits such as swimming and tennis 比如游泳和打网球之类的爱好 词源：pursue 追求 ＋ it 名词后缀 巧记：The Pursuit of Happyness 电影《当幸福来敲门》

persecute ['pəːsikjuːt]（宗教或政治）迫害；骚扰 词源：per 一直 ＋ execute 处决 指一直跟进处理信念不同的人

prosecute ['prɔsikjuːt] 继续（做某事）prosecute the investigation 继续调查；起诉 prosecute sb. for (doing) sth. 词源：pro 向前 ＋ execute 处决 指走上前劝法官给犯人判刑处决

sequence ['siːkw(ə)ns] 顺序，次序 in a logical sequence 以逻辑顺序；一串相关事件 a sequence of business failures 一连串生意失败；（电影中一段）连续镜头 词源：sequ 跟随 ＋ ence 名词后缀

subsequent ['sʌbsikw(ə)nt] 接下来的，随后的 subsequent book pages 接下来的书页 词源：sub 下面 ＋ sequ 跟随 ＋ ent 形容词后缀（表示具有……能力的）指在下面跟随的 同义词：following

ensue [in'sjuː] 继而发生，因而产生 problems that ensue from food shortages 食品短缺引起的问题 词源：en 使动词化 ＋ sue 跟随 指跟随发生

ensuing [in'sjuːiŋ] 随后的，因而发生的 the ensuing days / months / years 接下来的几天／几个月／几年 词源：ensue 继而发生 ＋ ing 形容词后缀

sue [suː]（尤指为要求赔偿金而）控告，起诉 sue sb. for sth. 词源：sue 跟随 指跟进别人的违法行为进行起诉 同义词：indict / charge / prosecute / accuse

lawsuit ['lɔːsuːt] 诉讼 file a lawsuit against city 对市政府提起诉讼 词源：law 法律 ＋ sue 起诉 ＋ it 名词后缀

49. **-st-, -sist-, -stat-** : stand 巧记：stand 站立 ＋ ist 最高级 指坚毅的站立不动

assist [ə'sist] 协助 assist (sb.) with / in sth.；（足球，篮球，排球等）助攻 词源：as 强调 ＋ sist 站立 指协助站立不动

consist [kən'sist] 包含，包括，由……组成 consist of sth. 词源：con 共同 ＋ sist 站立 指大家站在一起

consistent [kən'sist(ə)nt]（态度）一贯的，一致的 the consistent performance of the football team 足球队始终如一的表现；与……一致的，吻合 be consistent with sth. 词源：con 共同 ＋ sis 站立 ＋ ent 形容词后缀（表示具有……能力的）指始终如一站立状态保持不变的

exist [ig'zist; eg-] 存在；维持生存 词源：ex 出来 ＋ sist 站立 指站立存在 stand out

existing [ig'zistiŋ] 现存的，正在使用的 词源：exist 存在 ＋ ing 形容词后缀

insist [in'sist] 内心坚持某种信念，坚称 insist on sth. / that… 词源：in 内部 ＋ sist 站立 指站立在内心的坚定信念

persist [pə'sist] 坚持不懈 persist in (doing) sth. / with sth.；继续存在（发生） 词源：per 一直 + sist 站立 指像士兵一样一直站立不动

persistent [pə'sist(ə)nt] 坚持不懈的；持续的 persistent rumours 持续流传的谣言 词源：persist 坚持不懈 + ent 形容词后缀（表示具有……能力的）

resist [ri'zist] 反抗，抵抗 resist arrest 拒捕；忍住，按捺（吃食物、有金钱、买东西等的诱惑或做某事的欲望）sb. cannot resist (doing) sth. 抵挡不住诱惑去做某事；抵抗（伤害）resist heat 耐热 词源：re 重复 + sist 站立 指反复站起来不被打倒

constant ['kɔnst(ə)nt]（数学）常数，常量，恒量（比如圆周率 π）；经常的 constant visits 无休止的拜访；固定不变的，恒久不变的 travel at a constant speed 以恒定的速度行驶；（朋友）忠实的 a constant friend 忠实的朋友 词源：con 共同 + st 站立 + ant 形容词后缀（表示具有……能力的）指大家共同站着面对困难是彼此忠诚的 词义连记：一个数学家经常拜访他忠实的朋友讨论数学常数问题

instant ['inst(ə)nt] 立即的 an instant response 即时回应；（食物、咖啡）速食的，速溶的 instant noodles 方便面 词源：in 否定 + st 站立 + ant 形容词后缀（表示具有……能力的）指站立不住的会马上溶于液体的

instantaneous [ˌinst(ə)n'teiniəs] 瞬间的，即时的 modern methods of instantaneous communication 现代的即时通信方法 词源：instant 立即的 + ous 形容词后缀（表示过多的）

instance ['inst(ə)ns] 例子，实例；例如，以……为例 for instance 词源：instant 立即的 + ance 名词后缀 指立即举出来的事例 同义词：example

static ['stætik]（价格或人口）不变的，静态的 static house prices 不变的房价；（电视）无信号，雪花噪点；（头发或衣物摩擦产生的）静电（= static electricity） 词源：stat 站立 + ic 形容词后缀 指站立不动的 反义词：dynamic 动态的；精力充沛的

status ['steitəs] 法律地位（或身份）refugee status 难民身份；社会地位 low-status jobs 社会地位低下的工作；状态，状况 the current status of the trade talks 贸易谈判目前的进程 词源：stat 站立 + us 名词后缀 指站立的方式体现身份地位 巧记：stat 站立 + us 我们 指我们的身份地位 巧记：marital status 填表中一栏的婚姻状况

statue ['stætjuː; -tʃuː] 雕像，塑像 The Statue of Liberty 自由女神像 词源：stat 站立 + u 水 指水边站立的雕像

stature ['stætʃə] 身高，（高的或矮的）身材 be short in stature 身材矮小；名声，声望 a musician of world / international / national stature 享誉世界/国际/国内的音乐家 词源：statue 雕像 + nature 性质 指雕像身材高矮的自然属性

statute ['stætjuːt; -tʃuːt] 法令，成文法 lay down sth. by statute 法律明文规定某事；（机构或组织的）条例，章程 college statutes 大学校规 词源：statue 雕像 + ute 名词后缀 指雕像上面雕刻的法令 巧记：The Statute of Westminster 威斯敏斯特法案（标志着英帝国转变为英联邦）

circumstance ['səːkəmst(ə)ns] 周围环境 in / under … circumstances 在……情况下；（经济）境况，状况 词源：circum 圈 + st 站立 + ance 名词后缀 指站在中间周围的一圈是环境

distance ['dɪst(ə)ns] 距离；人际关系疏远　词源：dis 分离 + st 站立 + ance 名词后缀　指站得分散

distant ['dɪst(ə)nt] 遥远的；不友好的，冷淡的；远亲的　词源：distance 距离 + ant 形容词后缀（表示具有……能力的）

station ['steɪʃn] 车站；使驻扎　词源：stat 站立 + tion 名词后缀　指站立等车的地点

stationary ['steɪʃ(ə)n(ə)ri] 物体不动的，静止的 a stationary vehicle 一辆停着的车　词源：station 驻扎 + ary 名词后缀

stationery ['steɪʃ(ə)n(ə)ri]（一般指有信封配套的）信纸，信笺 a letter on school stationery 用学校信纸写的信；文具 a stationery store 文具店　巧记：station 站立 + e（eraser 橡皮）+ ary 名词后缀　带 e（eraser 橡皮）的是文具

stable ['steɪb(ə)l] 马厩；（底座、支架等）稳固的；（价格、工作等）稳定的 have a stable job 有稳定的工作；（人）镇静的，稳重的　词源：st 站立 + able 形容词后缀（表示可以……的）指可以站得住的

establish [ɪ'stæblɪʃ; e-] 设立，建立（机构、委员会等）；建立（正式关系或联系）；确定，证实（事实）establish that / if / whether…；使确立地位，使立足 establish sb. as a star 确立某人的明星地位　词源：e 出来 + stable 稳定的 + ish 动词后缀　指稳定地竖立起来

establishment [ɪ'stæblɪʃmənt] 公司，机构，单位（尤指企业、商店等）an educational establishment 教育机构；统治集团，权势集团 rebel against the establishment 反抗当权者；建立，设立 the establishment of a new business school 新商学院的成立　词源：establish 建立 + ment 名词后缀

obstacle ['ɒbstək(ə)l] 障碍物，绊脚石 natural obstacles such as streams and bogs 像小溪和泥潭一样的天然障碍物；障碍，阻碍 overcome an obstacle 克服障碍　词源：ob 强调 + st 站立 + cle 名词后缀　指站在身前碍事的东西　巧记：an obstacle course 障碍赛跑道，障碍赛赛场地，军事训练场地

substance ['sʌbst(ə)ns] 物质 harmful substances in the atmosphere 大气中的有害物质；药品 substance abuse 药物滥用；（论点、文章的）主旨；重要性 matters / issues of substance 重大问题　词源：sub 下面 + st 站立 + ance 名词后缀　指在下面有腿脚支撑的站立的东西是物质

substantial [səb'stænʃ(ə)l] 大量的 a substantial salary 丰厚的薪水；大而结实的（家具）a substantial piece of furniture　词源：substance 物质 + tial 形容词后缀（表示特殊的 special）指物质是大量存在的　同义词：considerable

substantiate [səb'stænʃɪeɪt]（用实物）证明，证实 substantiate one's claims 证明某人的说法　词源：substance 物质 + tiate 动词后缀　指用大量的物质实物来证实

50. **-tang-, -tag-, -tig-, -tact-**：touch　巧记：ta 触碰 touch

attach [ə'tætʃ] 系，绑，贴 attach sth. to sth.；附属，附加；喜欢，依恋 be attached to sb. / sth.；重视 attach importance / significance to sth.　词源：at 强调 + tach 触碰　指通过触碰让物品贴在一起

attachment [əˈtætʃm(ə)nt]（电子邮件）附件 email attachments；附加条款；依恋 one's attachment to sb.；信仰忠诚 one's attachment to sth.　词源：attach 系 + ment 名词后缀

detach [diˈtætʃ] 拆下部件 detach sth. from sth.；使自己摆脱某人/某物 detach oneself from sb. / sth.　词源：de 否定 + tach 触碰 指触碰把部件卸下

contagious [kənˈteidʒəs]（疾病）传染的；（艺术）有感染力的　词源：con 共同 + tag 触碰 + ous 形容词后缀（表示过多的）指一起触碰过多会传染　形近易混词：contiguous

contiguous [kənˈtigjuəs] 毗邻的，相邻的 contiguous states 相邻的州　词源：con 共同 + tig 触碰一点点 + ous 形容词后缀（表示过多的）指在一起的事物只相互触碰一点点是彼此毗邻的　巧记：continuous 连续的 指连续进行的是相邻的

contaminate [kənˈtæmineit]（水或放射性）污染，弄脏；玷污　词源：con 共同 + ta 触碰 + mini 小的 + ate 动词后缀 指共同触碰一点点就受到污染　巧记：contain 包含包括 + mini 小的 指包含一点点其他物质是污染

tact [tækt]（语言或行为）机智，得体，乖巧，机敏　词源：ta 触碰 + act 动作 指做触碰的动作体现主动学习的机智

tactful [ˈtæktful; -f(ə)l] 机智的，乖巧的，圆通的　词源：tact 得体 + ful 形容词后缀（表示充满……的）指语言或行为充满机智的是圆通的

tactics [ˈtæktiks] 手法，策略；战术，兵法　词源：tact 机智 + ics 名词后缀（表示学科）指研究机智的学科

intact [inˈtækt] 完好无损的，未受损伤的　词源：in 否定 + tact 触碰 指不去触碰的是完好的

contact [ˈkɔntækt] 接触，联系 contact lens 隐形眼镜；联系人；联络点　词源：con 共同 + tact 触碰 指人与人彼此触碰，进行接触和联系

tap [tæp] 轻叩门；利用，开发（能源、资金或专业知识等）tap into sth.；（水、煤气等管道或容器的）龙头　词源：拟声词（指指尖敲打手机屏幕操作的声音或水龙头滴水的声音）　巧记：tap dancing 踢踏舞（指脚尖敲击地面的舞蹈）

tag [tæg] 标签，标牌；电子跟踪器；儿童撕名牌游戏；称呼，诨名；牌照，车牌　词源：touch 触碰 指手可以触碰的是标签　巧记：撕名牌就是 tear off the tags　形近易混词：tug

tug [tʌg] 拖船；猛拉，拽，拖；拔河 tug-of-war　词源：t 方向 to + u 水 + g 走 go 指在水里拉动轮船进出港口的拖船

tame [teim]（动物）驯服的；平淡乏味的；控制，驾驭 tame the trade unions 掌控工会　词源：ta 触碰 + m 摸 指动物可以摸的是驯服的

tangible [ˈtæn(d)ʒib(ə)l] 可触摸的，可触知的；（财产资产）有形的 tangible assets / property；计划确凿的，实在的（证据）tangible evidence / proof　词源：tang 触碰 + ible 形容词后缀（表示可以……的）指可以触碰到的事物是有形的

intangible [inˈtæn(d)ʒib(ə)l] 难易描绘的；无形　词源：in 否定 + tangible 有形的 指不可触摸的是无形的

tangle [ˈtæŋg(ə)l]（头发、线等的）纠结，缠绕，乱成一团；和……争吵（打架）tangle with sb.　词源：tang 触碰 + gle 动词后缀

tack [tæk] 大头钉；方针，思路；（船）抢风行驶　词源：ta 触碰 + ck 声音　指在地图上按下大头钉触碰的声音表示确定方针

tackle ['tæk(ə)l] 处理解决（难题）；（足球、曲棍球等比赛中）断球铲抢；（美式足球或橄榄球比赛中）擒抱；（钓鱼）渔具　词源：touch 触碰 + kle 动词后缀（表示 little 是 tle 的变形）指一点点的触碰就将对方放倒是铲断抢球解决防守问题

51. -cred-：believe　巧记：cry 叫喊　指大声叫喊说出鼓励的话来增加自信

credit ['kredit] 相信（某人）give credit to sb.；信用 buy sth. on credit 赊账购买；荣誉赞许 take credit for hardwork 因努力得到赞许；（大学毕业需要的）学分；归因于 credit sth. to sth.；（账户）存钱 credit money to one's account；（电影或电视节目开头或结束时播放的）全体制作者，致谢名单 the credits　词源：cred 相信 + it 它　指信任是最好的荣誉、赞许

accredited [ə'kreditid] 认证鉴定合格的 an accredited language school 一所鉴定合格的语言学校；（作为本国政府代表）被派驻国外的 the UK accredited representative 英国的官方驻外代表　词源：ac 强调 + cred 相信 + ed 形容词后缀　指被大家相信的是经过鉴定认证的

discredit [dis'kredit] 无信用，名誉丧失 bring discredit on / upon / to sb. / sth.；不相信 discredit sb./sth.；损害名声　词源：dis 否定 + credit 相信　指不再相信

credo ['kri:dəu] 信条，教义　词源：cred 相信 + do 做　指相信并可以指导做事情的信念　巧记：克雷多（Credo）是动作游戏《鬼泣 4》（Devil May Cry 4）的角色，魔剑教团的"教团骑士（Holy Knight）"骑士长，是姬莉雅（Kyrie）的哥哥，也是尼禄（Nero）的上司。其性格严肃公正，武器是只有骑士长才能使用的杜兰德尔之剑（Durandal），具备高超的剑术与统领数百名部下的领导能力。

creed [kri:d] 信条，教条 a religious creed 宗教信条　词源：cred 相信　巧记：Assassin's Creed 动作冒险类游戏《刺客信条》

decree [di'kri:]（国家统治者颁布的）法令；（法院）判决裁定 a divorce decree 离婚判决　词源：de 向下 + cre 相信　指向下发布让臣民相信的法令

credential [kri'denʃ(ə)l] 资格证书，（记者或警官）证件（常复数）press credentials 记者证；资格，资历 have excellent credentials for the job 具备出色的资历做这份工作　词源：cred 相信 + tial 形容词后缀（表示特殊的 special）

credulous ['kredjuləs] 轻信的，易上当的 credulous investors 易上当的投资者　词源：cred 相信 + l 长时间 + ous 形容词后缀（表示过多的）指长时间过分相信别人的是易上当的

incredible [in'kredib(ə)l] 难以置信的 an incredible achievement 难以置信的成就　词源：in 否定 + cred 相信 + ible 形容词后缀（表示可以……的）

52. -cruci-：cross　巧记：cross 十字架，十字勋章，十字标记，叉号，横穿，横渡，横跨

crucial ['kru:ʃ(ə)l] 至关重要的　词源：cruci 十字架+ ial 形容词后缀（表示特殊的 special）指像宗教信仰的十字符号一样重要的　巧记：谐音"可如手"指像手一样重要的

crucify ['kru:sifai] 钉死在十字架上；（当众）严厉指责　词源：cruci 十字架 + fy 动词后缀　指

把犯人钉在十字架上折磨

cruciform ['kruːsifɔːm] 十字形的 a cruciform sword 一把十字形的剑　　词源：cruci 十字 ＋ form 形式　指物品像十字形状的

crusade [kruː'seid]（发生于 11、12、13 世纪的）十字军东征；改革运动　　词源：crus 十字 ＋ ade 名词后缀（表示强调）指十字军东征的士兵胸前和臂上都佩戴十字标记

cruise [kruːz]（乘船）巡游游览 cruise missile 巡航导弹；平稳行驶；开车兜风　　词源：cru 横穿 ＋u 水 ＋ ise 动词后缀　指驾船穿过河流

cruiser ['kruːzə] 巡洋舰；游艇；警车　　词源：cruise 巡航 ＋ er 名词后缀

crutch [krʌtʃ]（腋下）拐杖 be on crutch 拄拐；（尤指不好的）依靠 use alcohol as a crutch 借酒消愁　　词源：cru 十字 ＋ catch 抓住　指抓住十字形的拐杖作为行走依靠

excruciating [ik'skruːʃieitiŋ]（关节）极疼痛的；令人极不愉快的　　词源：ex 出来 ＋ cruci 十字架 ＋ ing 形容词后缀　指钉在十字架上带来极大痛苦的

53. **-cur-**：care　巧记：care 照顾 ＋u 水　指像水一般温柔对待

cure [kjuə] 治愈（疾病）；解决（问题）cure unemployment 解决失业；药剂，疗法；对策，措施　　词源：cur 照顾

curio ['kjuəriəu] 漂亮的小玩意；珍品　　词源：cur 照顾 ＋o 圆形物品　指摆在玻璃柜里的圆形盘子、花瓶、水晶球等装饰物

curious ['kjuəriəs] 好奇的；稀奇古怪的　　词源：cur 照顾 ＋ ous 形容词后缀（表示过多的）指需要过多关注照顾的事物是让人好奇的

curator [kjuə'reitə(r)] 艺术馆、博物馆馆长；动物园园长　　词源：cur 照顾 ＋ it 它 ＋ or 人　指照顾珍贵艺术品或珍稀动物的人

secure [si'kjuə; si'kjɔː] 固定的，牢靠的；可靠的，安全的；有安全感的；保证安全；用资产为（债务或贷款）作抵押　　词源：se 分离 ＋ cur 照顾　指某人离开后还一直照顾他

insecure [ˌinsi'kjuə; ˌinsi'kjɔː] 不安全的；无自信的；没有把握的；不牢靠的　　词源：in 否定 ＋ secure 安全的　指不安全的

security [si'kjuərəti] 安全；安保措施；保障；抵押品 use a house as security for the loan 用房子作为贷款抵押　　词源：secure 安全的 ＋ ity 名词后缀

securities [si'kjuəritis] 证券　　词源：security 的复数形式　指能带来安全感的保值增值的股票证券

procure [prə'kjuə] 获得，取得（获得难以得到的东西）；采购 procure weapons 采购武器　　词源：pro 向前走 ＋ cur 照顾　指走上前给喜欢的物品照顾非常想得到它购买它

54. **-cur-, -curs-, -cour-**：run　巧记：c 覆盖 cover ＋u 水 ＋r 植物生长分裂　指水分支流淌

course [kɔːs] 当然；课程；航线 on / off course 航向正确/偏离航向；进程过程 the course of evolution 进化过程；场地 golf course 高尔夫球场；一道菜 main course 主菜　　词源：cour 跑　指船只航行的路线

concourse ['kɔŋkɔːs]（飞机场火车站）大厅；聚集的人群 a concourse of audience 一群观众　词源：con 共同 + cour 跑　指跑到一起的一群人

discourse ['diskɔːs; -'kɔːs] 讲演，论述 a discourse on art 有关艺术的演讲；（严肃的）谈话，交谈 serious political discourse 严肃的政治对话　词源：dis 分离 + course 课程　指对课程内容的分别论述

intercourse ['intəkɔːs] 沟通，交际 social intercourse 社交　词源：inter 两者间 + cour 跑　指两者相互跑到对方家里交流

recourse [ri'kɔːs]（实现或解决某事的）手段，途径 have recourse to sth.　词源：re 重复 + cour 跑　指反复跑到别人家门口感动别人是解决问题的途径

court [kɔːt] 宫廷；法庭；球场 tennis court 网球场；求爱；奉承讨好 court the media 讨好媒体　词源：cour 跑　指宫廷面积大能跑来跑去

curtain ['kɜːt(ə)n] 窗帘；幕布　词源：court 宫廷　指宫廷悬挂的窗帘

current ['kʌr(ə)nt] 水流，气流，电流；思潮；目前的　词源：cur 跑 + ent 形容词后缀（表示具有……能力的）指奔跑流动的水流

currency ['kʌr(ə)nsi] 货币；被接受 gain currency　词源：current 水流 + cy 名词后缀　指货币像水流一样具有流动性

cursory ['kɜːsəri] 匆忙的，粗略的，草率的，仓促的 a cursory glance / look 粗略地看一下　词源：cur 跑 + ory 形容词后缀　指跑过去匆忙地看了一眼

discursive [dis'kɜːsiv]（文章）跑题的，东拉西扯的　词源：dis 分散 + cur 跑 + ive 形容词后缀（表示充满活力的 active）指文章内容分散的

excursion [ik'skɜːʃ(ə)n; ek-]（集体）短途旅行，短途出行 a shopping excursion 购物游　词源：ex 出去 + cur 跑 + sion 名词后缀　指跑出去短途出行

concur [kən'kɜː] 同时发生；意见一致 concur with sb. in sth.　词源：con 共同 + cur 跑　指在一起共同跑是达成一致

incur [in'kɜː] 招致，导致，带来（成本、债务或罚款）　词源：in 内部 + cur 跑　指让不好的事物跑进来，引狼入室

occur [ə'kɜː] 出现，发生　词源：oc 强调 + cur 跑　指洪水出现

occurrence [ə'kʌr(ə)ns] 出现，发生；发生的事　词源：occur 出现 + ence 名词后缀

precursor [pri'kɜːsə]（事物的）前身，先驱 a precursor of modern jazz 现代爵士乐的先驱　词源：pre 在前面 + cur 跑 + or 人　指在前面跑过这条路的人

recur [ri'kɜː] 再次发生　词源：re 再次 + occur 发生　指再次出现

curl [kɜːl]（蛇）盘绕，（植物）缠绕；（头发）卷曲；（锻炼肌肉的）弯曲运动　词源：cur 跑 + l 长　指植物如同奔跑般向上生长时的缠绕

curly ['kɜːli]（头发）卷曲的 curly hair；（动物角）弯曲的 curly horns　词源：curl 卷曲 + ly 形容词后缀

curve [kɜːv]（女性优美的 S 型）曲线；（股票）曲线图；（棒球）曲线球；（道路、河流的）转弯　词源：cur 跑 + v 字形　指跑出 V 字形的形状

curb [kə:b] 路边，路缘；抑制，约束 curb emission 控制排放　词源：curl 弯曲 + B 两间屋子 指房子旁边的路缘是弯曲的，用路缘控制停车　巧记：谐音"磕巴"指说话磕巴抑制表达

curriculum [kə'rikjuləm] 全部课程 curriculum planning 课程安排　词源：cur 跑 + column 圆柱 指学生绕着圆柱跑看刻在上面的文字知识是学习课程

55. **-duc-, -duct-** : lead　巧记：d 向下 + u 水 + ct 声音 指古罗马城用来引水的高架水渠

abduct [əb'dʌkt] 拐卖；绑架　词源：ab 离开 + duct 引导 指引导人离开房子　同义词：kidnap

conduct [kən'dʌkt; 'kɔndʌkt] 导电，导热 conduct electricity / heat；带领，导游 conduct sb. to sth.；指挥（乐队）conduct an orchestra；进行（调查、研究、实验）conduct an investigation / a survey / research / an experiment；（尤指在公开场合、岗位上等的）行为举止 an inquiry into the conduct of the senator 对参议员行为的调查　词源：con 共同 + duct 引导 指把能量完全引导到其他地方

conducive [kən'dju:siv] 有益于某事 be conducive to sth.　词源：conduct 引导 + ive 形容词后缀（表示充满活力的 active）

deduce [di'dju:s]（侦探）推断，推论 infer and deduce；演绎　词源：de 向下 + duce 引导 指由 A→B→C→D→E 的层层引导推论

deduct [di'dʌkt] 减去，扣除 deduct sth. from sth.　词源：de 向下 + duct 引导 指向下滴滴答答按计算器扣钱的按键声

educate ['edjukeit] 教育；教导某人做某事　词源：e 出来 + duc 引导 + ate 动词后缀 指教育引导学生走出无知

educated ['edjukeitid] 有教养的；（猜测）有根据的 make an educated guess　词源：educate 教育 + ed 形容词后缀

induct [in'dʌkt] 征召入伍；（举行仪式）使正式就职 induct sb. to / into sth.；使正式加入（荣誉组织）induct sb. into the Basketball Hall of Fame 使某人加入篮球名人堂　词源：in 内部 + duct 引导 指引入团体内部　巧记：正式加入团体 induct 后需要按时扣除会费 deduct membership fee

induce [in'dju:s] 诱导（尤指似乎不明智的事）induce sb. to do sth.；导致，引起，诱发（身体反应）a drug-induced coma 药物引起的昏迷；为（产妇）催生，引产　词源：in 内部 + duc 引导 指引起身体内部的问题　词义连记：不正确地诱导孕妇引产会引起身体不良反应

induction [in'dʌkʃ(ə)n] 入职，就职 a two-day induction course 两天的入门课程；引产，催生；电磁感应 induction cooker 电磁炉；归纳法　词源：induce 引发 + tion 名词后缀 指电场和磁场相互作用

seduce [si'dju:s] 诱奸，勾引；诱惑，引诱，诱使 seduce sb. into doing sth.　词源：se 离开 + duc 引导 指引导某人离开去做某事

introduce [intrə'dju:s] 介绍；引进（制度或产品）　词源：intro 内部 + duc 引导 指引入内部

produce [prə'dju:s] 生产；生育；农产品　词源：pro 向前 + duc 引导 指引导生产线前进组装产品

reduce [ri'djuːs] 减少；降低；减肥　　词源：re 向后 + duc 引导　指向后引导是减少产量

viaduct ['vaiədʌkt]（架于山谷上的公路或铁路）高架桥　　词源：via 路 + duct 引导　指高架桥引导交通起到路的作用

56. -fact-, -fect-, -fic-, -fit-, -feas- : do, make　　巧记：f 飞 + act 动作　指小鸟筑巢的动作

factory ['fækt(ə)ri] 工厂　　词源：fact 做 + ory 名词后缀　指做产品的地方

factor ['fæktə] 因素；系数 factor 10 suntan oil 防晒系数为 10 的防晒油；因子，因数　　词源：fact 做 + or 名词后缀　指起到作用的要素

facility [fə'siləti] 设施，设备 leisure facilities 休闲设施；场所，建筑 a top-secret research facility 一个绝密的研究中心；天赋，才能 have an amazing facility for languages 有惊人的语言才能；厕所 use the facilities 去一下洗手间　　词源：fac 做 + ability 能力　指做某事的天赋能力

facilitate [fə'siliteit] 使容易便捷 Apps that facilitate language learning 方便语言学习的应用软件　　词源：facility 设施 + ate 动词后缀　指设施使便利

faculty ['fæk(ə)lti] 天赋，才能 have a faculty for sth.；（大学的）系，部，院；（大学的）全体教师　　词源：fac 做 + culture 文化 + ty 名词后缀　指做文化的地方是学院的系

manufacture [mænju'fæktʃə]（用机器大量）制造；编造（虚假情况、借口等）manufacture stories 编故事　　词源：manu 手 + fact 做 + nature 性质　指动手制作

manufacturer [ˌmænju'fæktʃ(ə)rə(r)] 制造商，制造公司　　词源：manufacture 制造 + er 名词后缀

manufacturing [ˌmænju'fæktʃəriŋ] 制造，制造业　　词源：manufacture 制造 + ing 名词后缀

fabric ['fæbrik] 纺织品，织物，衣料；（社会或建筑）结构 social fabric 社会结构　　词源：fa 做 + br 带来 bring + ic 名词后缀　指工厂最早制造的布料

fabricate ['fæbrikeit] 制造生产 fabricate discs 制造磁盘；编造捏造 fabricate evidence 捏造证据　　词源：fabric 衣料 + ate 动词后缀　指制造衣料

benefit ['benifit] 益处；救济金；福利；有益于　　词源：bene 好 + fit 合适　指又好又合适

beneficial [beni'fiʃ(ə)l] 有益的　　词源：benefit 益处 + cial 形容词后缀（表示特殊的 special）

beneficiary [beni'fiʃ(ə)ri] 受益者，受惠者　　词源：benefit 益处 + i 人 + ary 名词后缀

profit ['prɔfit] 利润；有益于，对（某人）有好处 profit sb. to do sth.；获利　　词源：pro 向前 + fit 做　指做的超前有好处

profitable ['prɔfitəb(ə)l] 有利可图的，能赚钱的　　词源：profit 利润 + able 形容词后缀（表示可以……的）

feasible ['fiːzib(ə)l] 可行的，行得通的　　词源：f 做 + easy 容易的 + ible 形容词后缀（表示可以……的）指容易做出来的是可行的

affect [ə'fekt] 影响；假装 affect a foreign accent 假装外国口音　　词源：af 强调 + fect 做　指做任何事都会产生影响

affectation [ˌæfek'teiʃn] 装模作样，矫揉造作　　词源：affect 假装 + ta 其他（谐音）+ tion 名词后缀　指假装成其他样子

affection [ə'fekʃ(ə)n] 喜爱，慈爱，挚爱，钟爱 show affection for sb. 词源：affect 影响 指最有影响的是爱

affectionate [ə'fekʃ(ə)nət] 表示爱的，深情的 词源：affection 爱 + ate 形容词后缀

defect ['di:fekt; di'fekt] 缺陷，缺点，毛病 a genetic defect 遗传缺陷；叛逃，投敌 defect from…to… 词源：de 否定 + fect 做 指做得不好的是有瑕疵的

deficient [di'fiʃ(ə)nt] 缺乏的，不足的 be deficient in vitamin 缺乏维生素 词源：de 否定 + fic 做 + ent 形容词后缀 指做得不充分的

deficit ['defisit; 'di:-] 逆差，亏损，赤字 budget deficit 预算赤字/ trade deficit 贸易逆差 词源：de 否定 + fic 做 + it 名词后缀 指财务做得差的 反义词：surplus

effect [i'fekt] 影响，作用，效应 greenhouse effect 温室效应；引起，使发生 effect change in sth. 在某方面引起改变 词源：e 出来 + fect 做 指做事情所产出的影响或效应

efficient [i'fiʃ(ə)nt] 有效率的；高效能的，节能的 energy efficient lighting 照明设备 词源：e 出来 + fect 做 + ent 形容词后缀（表示具有……能力的）指做事的能力体现在效率

infect [in'fekt] 疾病传染 sb. be infected with sth.；（情绪）感染（他人） 词源：in 内部 + fect 做 指病毒细菌作用于体内

infectious [in'fekʃəs]（疾病）传染的；（情感或笑声）有感染力的 an infectious smile 有感染力的微笑 词源：infect 传染 + ous 形容词后缀（表示过多的）指传染性过强的

magnificent [mæg'nifis(ə)nt] 宏伟的，壮丽的，富丽堂皇的 a magnificent performance 气势恢宏的演出 词源：magni 大 + fic 做 + ent 形容词后缀（表示具有……能力的）指做得非常大的是宏伟的

proficient [prə'fiʃ(ə)nt] 精通的，熟练的 be proficient in sth. 词源：pro 向前 + fic 做 + ent 形容词后缀（表示具有……能力的）指技能熟练能做到别人前面去的

sufficient [sə'fiʃ(ə)nt] 足够的,充足的 sufficient time 充足的时间 词源：suf 下面 + fic 做 + ent 形容词后缀（表示具有……能力的）指在下面做好充足准备的

suffice [sə'fais] 足够，满足要求 A light lunch will suffice. 一小份午餐就够了。 词源：suf 下面 + fic 做 指在下面做好充足准备

fiction ['fikʃ(ə)n] 虚构的事；小说 词源：fic 做 + tion 名词后缀 指小说是虚构做出来的故事 形近易混词：friction

fictional ['fikʃənl] 虚构的，编造的 fictional characters 虚构的人物 词源：fiction 小说 + al 形容词后缀

friction ['frikʃ(ə)n] 摩擦力；（人们之间的）不和，冲突 cause / create friction 造成矛盾 词源：F（物理上的）摩擦力

artifact ['ɑːtəˌfækt] 手工艺品，人工制品（指有史学价值的武器、工具等）ancient Greek artifacts 古希腊手工艺品 词源：art 艺术 + fact 做 指做出来的具有艺术价值的物品

artificial [ɑːti'fiʃ(ə)l] 人造的，假的 artificial flowers 假花；虚假的，不真挚的 an artificial smile 假笑 词源：art 艺术 + fic 做 + cial 形容词后缀（表示特殊的 special） 巧记：AI（Artificial Intelligence）人工智能

57. -flect-, -flex- : bend 巧记：fly 飞 + ect 做 act 指鸟类做飞行动作弯曲翅膀

deflect [di'flekt]（使）转向，（使）偏斜 deflect the blow 避开击打；转移（关注或批评）deflect attention；使改变（目标）deflect sb. from (doing) sth. 词源：de 以不好的方式 + flect 弯曲 指在空中以非正常方式偏离原有路线

reflect [ri'flekt]（光、热或声音）反射；反映问题；仔细思考 reflect on sth. / that… 词源：re 向后 + flect 弯曲 指光线向后折叠弯曲回去

reflection [ri'flekʃ(ə)n] 反射；反映；倒影；思考 词源：reflect 反射 + tion 名词后缀

reflective [ri'flektiv]（物体表面）能反光的；深思的；反映……的 be reflective of sth. 词源：reflect 反射 + tive 形容词后缀（表示充满活力的 active）

flex [fleks] 弯曲（肢体）；收紧（肌肉） 词源：flex 弯曲

flexible ['fleksib(ə)l] 灵活的，变通的；易弯曲的，有弹性的 flexible rubber soles 弹性橡胶鞋底 词源：flex 弯曲 + ible 形容词后缀（表示可以……的）

flexibility [ˌfleksi'biliti] 灵活性；弹性柔性 词源：flexible 灵活的 + ity 名词后缀

58. -leg- : 1) law 巧记：log 原木，日志 指原木上刻的需要遵守的文字是法律

allege [ə'ledʒ]（未证实下）硬说 词源：al 强调 + leg 法律 指从法律的角度硬说

liege [liːdʒ]（中世纪的）君主，领主 词源：leg 法律 指制定执行法律的人是领主

allegiance [ə'liːdʒ(ə)ns]（对领袖、国家、信念等的）忠诚，效忠 词源：al 强调 + liege 君主 + ance 名词后缀 指对中世纪君主的忠诚 巧记: al 强调 + leg 法律 + ance 名词后缀 指对法律的忠诚

pledge [pledʒ]（公开或正式作出的）誓言 the Pledge of Allegiance 宣誓效忠（美国人站在国旗前右手贴左胸宣誓）；捐款承诺 make a pledge of $100 to the school 向学校捐款 100 美元的承诺；抵押，典当 词源：please 请求 + leg 法律 指在法律面前宣誓请求被相信

oblige [ə'blaidʒ]（因形势、法律、义务等关系而）迫使 oblige sb. to do sth.；帮忙，答应（某人）请求 oblige sb. with sth. / oblige sb. by doing sth.；感谢，感激 be obliged to sb. for sth. 词源：ob 强调 + lig 法律 指法律上强迫做的事 词义连记：小时候被迫答应父母学习某种技能，长大以后会感激这段经历

obligation [ɔbli'geiʃ(ə)n] 义务，职责 have an obligation to do sth.有义务做某事 词源：oblige 强迫 + tion 名词后缀

legal ['liːg(ə)l] 法律的 a legal dispute 法律纠纷；合法的 词源：leg 法律 + al 形容词后缀

legitimate [li'dʒitimət] 合法的；合法婚姻所生的；合情合理的，正当的 词源：leg 法律 +it 去 go + mate 配偶 指在法律面前成为配偶是合法的

legislate ['ledʒisleit] 制定法律，立法 legislate on sth.；预防 词源：leg 法律 + is 是 be + l 长 long + ate 动词后缀 指法律立法具有长期性

legislature ['ledʒislətʃə] 立法机构，立法机关 state / national / federal legislature 州/国家/联邦立法机构 词源：legislate 立法 + nature 性质 指具有立法性质的机构

legislation [ledʒis'leiʃ(ə)n] 法规,法律 the legislation on alcohol 关于饮酒的法规 词源: legislate

立法 + tion 名词后缀

2）appoint　巧记：leg 法律　指法律上委派任命

legacy ['legəsi] 遗产；遗留问题 a legacy from the colonial period 殖民时期遗留下来的问题　词源：leg（法律上的）委派 + cy 名词后缀　指法律上委派的指定继承的财产

delegate ['deligət] 代表（可数名词）；委派工作 delegate sb. to do sth.；下放（权力）delegate power to sb.　词源：de 向下 + leg（法律上的）委派 + ate 动词后缀　指合法下放权力

delegation [deli'geiʃ(ə)n] 代表团 trade delegation 贸易代表团；授权 the delegation of authority 授权　词源：delegate 代表 + tion 名词后缀　指由代表组成的团体

legate ['legət] 使节；教皇使节　词源：leg（法律上的）委派 + ate 名词后缀

59. -lig-, -leg-, -lect- : 1）read　巧记：leg 法律　指法律条款供人们阅读和选择应用

college ['kɔlidʒ] 大学；学院　词源：col 共同 + leg 读说　指大家共同读书的地方

colleague ['kɔli:g] 同事，同僚　词源：college 大学　指大学里的同事

elegant ['elig(ə)nt]（女性）优雅的；（想法或计划）巧妙的，简洁的　词源：e 出来 + leg 读说 + ant 形容词后缀（表示具有……能力的）指文字能读出来的是优雅的　形近易混词：eloquent

eloquent ['eləkwənt] 雄辩的；（图片不用文字）清楚表明的　词源：e 出来 + loqu 说话 + ent 形容词后缀（表示具有……能力的）指能说清楚话的

elicit [i'lisit] 套出信息，诱导说话 elicit sth. from sb.　词源：e 出来 + lic 读说 + it 它　指诱导别人读出一段话

solicit [sə'lisit] 请求，恳求，乞求 solicit sth. from sb.　词源：sol 单独 solo + lic 读说 + it 它　指一个人在一直说话是请求别人

illicit [i'lisit] 非法的, 违禁的, 社会不容许的 illicit drugs 违禁药品　词源：il 否定 + lic 读说 + it 它　指不能读的书或不能说文字

dialect ['daiəlekt] 方言，土语，地方话　词源：dia 穿越 + lect 读说　指每天在人们间穿越的话语

intellect ['intəlekt] 智力；才智出众的人　词源：in 内部 + tell 区分 + lect 读说　指内心的辨别区分和读说的能力

intellectual [,intə'lektʃuəl; -tjuəl] 智力的，脑力的 intellectual development 智力开发；（人有）知识的，高智力的 intellectual property 知识产权；知性的；知识分子　词源：intellect 智力 + ual 形容词后缀

intelligence [in'telidʒ(ə)ns] 智力；聪明；情报 Central Intelligence Agency（CIA）美国中情局　词源：in 内部 + tell 区分 +gen 基因　指内心里先天基因带来的辨别能力

neglect [ni'glekt]（无意地）忽略 neglect to do sth.；被忽略的人或事（尤指家人或孩子）　词源：ne 否定 no + lect 读说　指不读不说

negligible ['neglidʒib(ə)l] 可忽视的，微不足道的　词源：neglect 忽略 + ible 形容词后缀（表示可以……的）

negligence ['neglidʒ(ə)ns] 疏忽；玩忽职守　词源：neglect 忽略 + ence 名词后缀

legible ['ledʒib(ə)l]（字迹）可辨认的，清晰易读的　词源：leg 读说 + ible 形容词后缀（表示可以……的）

lecture ['lektʃə] 讲演；讲课；讲座；训斥告诫　词源：lect 读说 + nature 性质　指讲课具有读说的性质

lectern ['lektən]（教堂的）诵经台；（桌面倾斜的）讲演台　词源：lect 读说 + ern 名词后缀　指读说的站的地方

legend ['ledʒ(ə)nd] 传说，传奇；联想集团（联想曾将其英文标识从 Legend 变为 Lenovo）　词源：leg 读说 + end 终点　指让人们从头说到尾的是传奇　巧记：谐音 legend "来真的" 指传奇是把不可能的变成真的

legendary ['ledʒ(ə)nd(ə)ri] 传奇般的，大名鼎鼎的　词源：legend 传奇 + ary 形容词后缀

2) choose　巧记：leg 法律 指法律条款供人们选择应用

collect [kə'lekt] 收集，收藏；收货；聚集，增加；收缴欠款；接人；对方付款的　词源：col 共同 + lect 选择 指把类似的物品挑选共同聚集在一起

collection [kə'lekʃ(ə)n] 收藏品；收账收债；（时装公司季节性推出的）时装 spring collection 春季时装；（故事、诗歌、音乐）集；一群聚集的人或事物　词源：collect 收集 + tion 名词后缀

elect [i'lekt] 选举；选择做某事 elect to do sth.　词源：e 出来 + lect 选择 指选择出来领袖

elective [i'lektiv] 选举的；非必需的；（课程）选修的；选修课　词源：elect 选择 + tive 形容词后缀（表示充满活力的 active）

elite [ei'liːt] 社会精英；上层人士；出类拔萃的　词源：e 出来 + lit 选择 指选出来的精英

eligible ['elidʒib(ə)l] 有资格的 be eligible to do sth.；可竞选的；（作为婚姻对象）合适的，合意的　词源：e 出来 + lig 选择 + ible 形容词后缀（表示可以……的）

select [si'lekt] 精选；精选的；奢华的，一流的　词源：se 分离 + lect 选择 指分离出其他后精选出的

selection [si'lekʃ(ə)n] 精挑细选；精品；挑选，选择，选拔 natural selection 自然选择　词源：select 精选 + tion 名词后缀

60. **-sign-**：sign　巧记：sign 标识

sign [sain] 标记，标识，标牌 road signs 路标；征兆；手势；手语 sign language；符号，记号；星座（也作 star sign）What sign are you? 你是什么星座？；签名，签署 sign a contract 签署合同　词源：sign 标识

signal ['sign(ə)l] 信号，讯号，暗号；发信号；信号灯；表明 signal that…；标志着，预示（开始或结束）signal the start / beginning / end of sth.；重要的 signal honour 极大荣誉　词源：sign 标识 + al 名词后缀

signature ['signətʃə] 签名；特征特色 signature singing style 标志性的演唱风格　词源：sign 标识 + nature 性质 指签名具有代表自己身份的性质

signify ['signifai] 象征，意味着；要紧，有重要性　词源：sign 标识 + fy 动词后缀　指标识象征

assign [ə'sain] 委派分配（任务或作业）assign sb. to do sth.；确定（时间、价值、地点）　词源：as 强调 + sign 标识　指给某人画上标识后委派他去做某事

consign [kən'sain] 弃置（尤指准备丢弃）consign the letter to the waste basket 把信丢进了废纸篓；把……置于（尤指不好的境地）；运送，托运（尤指为了卖掉）　词源：con 共同 + sign 标识　指全部贴上标识签上字托运货物

consignment [kən'sainm(ə)nt] 发送的货物，运送物 a consignment of medicines 运送的一批药物　词源：consign 托运 + ment 名词后缀

design [di'zain] 设计；设计图　词源：de 向下 + sign 标识　指向下画标识

designate ['dezigneit]（用符号或名字来）标明，表示；任命，指派 designated driver 指定的司机（指外出聚会、上酒吧等时同意开车接送朋友因而不饮酒的人）　词源：design 设计 + ate 动词后缀　指特意指定某个设计师设计作品

insignia [in'signiə]（军衔）徽章 military insignia 军队标志；（机构）标志　词源：in 内部 + sign 标识 + ia 名词后缀　指放在衣服里面的标识表示人的身份

resign [ri'zain] 辞职；使自己不得不顺从接受某事，安于某种状态 resign oneself to (doing) sth.　词源：re 向后 + sign 标识　指退回原有标识是辞职

resignation [rezig'neiʃ(ə)n] 辞职 hand in / tender your resignation 递交辞呈；辞职信；顺从　词源：resign 辞职 + tion 名词后缀

61. **-stru-, -struct-**：build　巧记：structure 结构，构造

structure ['strʌktʃə] 结构；建筑物；组织安排　词源：struct 建立

structured ['strʌktʃəd] 有条理的　词源：structure 结构 + ed 形容词后缀

construct [kən'strʌkt] 建造；作图；概念，构想　词源：con 共同 + struct 结构　指共同建造

destruction [di'strʌkʃ(ə)n] 破坏，摧毁 weapons of mass destruction 大规模杀伤性武器　词源：de 否定 + struct 建立 + tion 名词后缀　指不建立

destructive [di'strʌktiv] 破坏性的 the destructive power of modern weapons 现代武器的破坏力　词源：de 否定 + struct 建立 + tive 形容词后缀（表示充满活力的 active）

instruct [in'strʌkt] 命令，指示 instruct sb. to do sth.；教授，指导 instruct sb. in sth.；通知 instruct sb. that...　词源：in 内部 + struct 建立　指给别人内心建立正确的价值观

instruction [in'strʌkʃ(ə)n] 用法说明，操作指南；命令，指示；教导，指导　词源：instruct 指导 + tion 名词后缀

instrument ['instrum(ə)nt]（科学、医学等工作用的小巧的）仪器设备 surgical instruments 外科（手术）器械；仪表 flight instruments 飞行仪表；乐器；手段，方法　词源：in 内部 + stru 建立 + ment 名词后缀　指用来指导工作的仪器设备

instrumental [instru'ment(ə)l] 乐器的；对某事起重要作用的 be instrumental in (doing) sth.　词源：instrument 器械 + tal 形容词后缀　指仪器的作用是辅助性的

obstruct [əb'strʌkt] 阻塞（道路或通道）；阻止阻隔 obstruct the peace process 阻挠和平进程　词源：ob 强调 + struct 建立　指违建阻挡道路

infrastructure ['infrəstrʌktʃə] 下部构造；基础设施（如公路、铁路、银行等）　词源：infra 下面 + structure 结构　指在下面建的起到支撑作用的部分

superstructure ['suːpəstrʌktʃə(r)] 上部构造；上层建筑　词源：super 上面 + structure 结构　指在上面部分的建筑结构

62. **-vi-**：way　巧记：v 峡谷 + i 小的　指峡谷里的小路

via ['vaiə] 经过，取道；借助于 via the Internet 通过网络　词源：vi 路

deviate ['diːvieit] 偏离（路线或计划）deviate from sth.　词源：de 以不好的方式 + vi 路 + ate 动词后缀　指不好好走原来的路

deviant ['diːviənt]（行为）反常的，变态的 deviant behaviour 变态的行为　词源：deviate 偏离 + ant 形容词后缀（表示具有……能力的）指偏离正路的

devious ['diːviəs]（路线）迂回的，绕远的 a devious route 迂回的路线；欺诈的，不诚实的 a devious politician 一名不诚实的政客　词源：de 以不好的方式 + vi 路 + ous 形容词后缀（表示过多的）指不正确的路走得过多的

obvious ['ɔbviəs] 明显的　词源：ob 强调 + vi 路 + ous 形容词后缀（表示过多的）指在大路上走是明显的

previous ['priːviəs] 以前的；返回上级菜单　词源：pre 在前面 + vi 路 + ous 形容词后缀（表示过多的）指以前走过的路

viable ['vaiəbl]（想法、计划或方法）切实可行的　词源：vi 路 + able 形容词后缀（表示可以……的）指可以走的路

viaduct ['vaiədʌkt]（架于山谷上的公路或铁路）高架桥　词源：via 路 + duct 引导　指高架桥引导交通起到路的作用

63. **-dia-**：1）day　巧记：day 的词形变化　指时间上过一天

diary ['daiəri] 日记　词源：dia 天 + ry 名词后缀　指每天写的日记　形近易混词：dairy / subsidiary

dairy ['deəri] 牛奶场；牛奶公司；乳制品 dairy products / produce　巧记：Dairy Queen（DQ 冰淇淋）指牛奶制品女皇

subsidiary [səb'sidiəri] 子公司，附属公司；附带的，连带的 be subsidiary to sth.　词源：sub 下面 + side 边 + ary 名词后缀　指在下边的机构

dial ['daiəl] 日晷；表盘；拨电话　词源：dia 天 + l 一根长长的棍子　指在地上竖立根棍子观察影子看时间

meridian [mə'ridiən] 子午线，经线　词源：mer 中间的 middle + dia 天　指一天的中间点

antemeridian [æntimə'ridiən] 上午的　词源：ante 前面 + meridian 子午线　指在子午线之前

postmeridian ['pəustmə'ridiən] 下午的　词源：post 后面 + meridian 子午线　指在子午线之后

diaper ['daɪəpə] 尿布，尿片　词源：dia 天 + per 人 person　指每天给一个小宝宝换尿布

diabetes [ˌdaɪə'biːtiːz] 糖尿病　词源：dia 天 + beat 揍　指每天被糖尿病折磨像挨揍

2）across　巧记：day 一天　指过一天是时间上的跨越

diagnose ['daɪəgnəʊz; -'nəʊz] 诊断；判断　词源：dia 穿越 + nose 鼻子　指通过鼻子闻的味道判断

diagnosis [ˌdaɪəg'nəʊsɪs] 诊断；判断　词源：diagnose 诊断 + sis 名词后缀

dialogue ['daɪəlɒg]（书、戏剧或电影的）对白；（组织或国家间为解决问题的）对话　词源：dia 穿越 + logue 话语　指每天穿越于两者间的对话

dialect ['daɪəlekt] 方言，土语，地方话　词源：dia 穿越 + lect 读说　指每天在人们间穿越的话语

diagram ['daɪəgræm] 图表，示意图　词源：dia 穿越 + gram 写　指每天在地上走来走去画的图形

diameter [daɪ'æmɪtə] 直径　词源：dia 穿越 + meter 测量 measure　指穿越圆周测量直径

diamond ['daɪəmənd] 钻石；菱形；扑克牌中的方片　词源：dia 穿越 + mond 坚毅的（adamant 的变化，源于 Adam 亚当，指像亚当般的坚毅的）指钻石穿越时间恒久不变的

4

64. **-dom-**：1）house　巧记：D 半圆　指半圆形的屋顶

dome [dəʊm] 圆屋顶，穹顶 planetarium dome 天文馆穹顶；半球形　词源：dom 房子

domestic [də'mestɪk] 家庭的 domestic chores 家庭琐事；国内的 GDP（gross domestic product）国内生产总值　词源：dom 房子 + tic 形容词后缀　指房子里的是家庭的

domesticate [də'mestɪkeɪt] 驯养（动物）　词源：domestic 家庭的 + cat 猫 + ate 动词后缀　指让动物像猫一样家养化　同义词：tame

domesticated [də'mestɪkeɪtɪd]（动物）驯化的；喜爱家庭生活的，乐意操持家务的　词源：domesticate 驯养动物 + ed 形容词后缀

domesticity [ˌdəʊme'stɪsəti] 家庭生活 a scene of happy domesticity 一派幸福家庭的景象　词源：domestic 家庭的 + ity 名词后缀

2）state, realm, condition　巧记：D 半圆形屋顶　指半圆形屋顶房子的覆盖范围

freedom ['friːdəm] 自由　词源：free 自由的 + dom 状态

kingdom ['kɪŋdəm] 王国　词源：king 国王 + dom 状态

serfdom ['səːfdəm] 农奴身份；农奴制　词源：serf 农奴 + dom 状态

stardom ['stɑːdəm] 明星的地位　词源：star 明星 + dom 状态

wisdom ['wɪzdəm] 智慧，学识　词源：wise 聪明的 + dom 状态

65. **-domin-**：master　巧记：dome 圆屋顶　指住在圆屋顶下面的有权势的人

domain [də(u)'mein] 领地，领土，版图 the extent of the royal domain 皇家领地的范围；（活动、兴趣或知识的）领域，范围，范畴 the domain of medical science 医学范畴；（网站）域名（例如 .org / .net / .com / .cn） 词源：domin 掌控 ＋ main 居留 stay 指居住的领地

dominate ['dɔmineit] 支配，主宰；（建筑）比……高，俯视，俯瞰 词源：domin 掌控 ＋ ate 动词后缀

domination [dɔmi'neiʃ(ə)n] 支配，操纵 词源：dominate 支配 ＋ tion 名词后缀

dominant ['dɔminənt] 支配的 dominant position 支配地位；（基因）显性的 词源：dominate 支配 ＋ ant 形容词后缀（表示具有……能力的）

predominant [pri'dɔminənt] 支配的；占优势的 词源：pre 在前面 ＋ dominant 支配的 指在前面的将军是处于支配地位的

domineering [dɔmi'niəriŋ] 作威作福的，专横霸道的 a domineering mother 专横的母亲 词源：domin 掌控 ＋ ee 眼睛 指眼神是控制欲强的

domino ['dɔminəu] 多米诺骨牌 词源：domin 掌控 指多米诺骨牌产生连锁倒下的反应 指一张牌的倒下掌控着下张牌的倒下

dominion [də'miniən] 统治权，管辖权 have / hold dominion over sb. / sth.；领地，领土，版图 the king's dominions 国王的领地；（英联邦的）自治领地 词源：domin 掌控 ＋ on 正在 指正在统治的领地

66. du- : two 巧记：double 的缩写形式

dubious ['djuːbiəs] 可疑的，靠不住的 dubious eyes 怀疑的眼神；无把握的，不确定的 be dubious about sth.；质量不好的 dubious decoration 质量差的装修 词源：du 两个 ＋ bi 两个 ＋ ous 形容词后缀（表示过多的）指比四个还多的是可疑的 词义连记：用怀疑的眼神表示对于劣质产品的无把握

dual ['djuːəl] 双的，双重的，两部分的 dual core CPU 双核处理器 词源：du 两个 ＋ al 形容词后缀

duel ['djuːəl]（旧时两人为解决争执的）决斗；（双方进行的）斗争，对抗 a verbal duel 舌战 词源：du 两个 ＋ e 出来 ＋ l 长剑 指两个人拔出长剑决斗

duet [dju'et] 二重奏（曲）；二重唱（曲） 词源：du 两个 ＋ et 名词后缀

dub [dʌb] 给（电影或电视节目）配音 a British film dubbed into French 一部被配成法语的英国影片；起绰号 sb. / sth. be dubbed sth.；混合录音；封……为爵士 词源：du 两个 指有第二个声音 巧记：谐音"嘚啵"指人嘚啵嘚啵说话是配音

duplicate ['djuːplikeit] 复制；复制的 a duplicate key 复制的钥匙；复制品 词源：du 两个 ＋ plic 折叠 ＋ ate 动词后缀

duplicity [djuː'plisiti; dju-] 口是心非，两面派，欺骗行为，奸诈行径 词源：du 两个 ＋ play 玩 ＋ city 城市 指两个城市间玩两面派

67. -dyn-, -dynam- : power 巧记：dye 染色 指古罗马有权势的人才能穿染上色彩的衣服

dynamic [dai'næmik] 动态的，不断变化的 a dynamic and unstable process 动态的、不稳定的过程；精力充沛的，有活力的 dynamic and ambitious people 精力充沛及雄心勃勃的人；音乐力度　词源：dynam 力量 + ic 形容词后缀

dynamite ['dainəmait] 炸药，黄色炸药 a dynamite blast 炸药爆炸；会惹出大麻烦的事物或人；极好的顶呱呱的人或事　词源：dynam 力量 + ite 名词后缀　指有巨大动态力量的物品是炸药

dynamo ['dainəməu]（直流）发电机；工作积极且精力充沛的人；原动力　词源：dynam 力量 + o 太阳　指像太阳一样有能量的发电机

dynast ['dainəst] 世袭君主　词源：dyn 权力 + ast 名词后缀　指有权势的人

dynasty ['dinəsti] 王朝，朝代　词源：dynast 君主 + ty 名词后缀　指君主建立的朝代　巧记：Dynasty 王朝干红葡萄酒

aerodynamics [ˌeərə(u)dai'næmiks] 空气动力学　词源：aero 空气 air + dynamic 动态的 + ics 学科后缀

68. -ject-: throw　巧记：j 跳起来 + e 出来 + ct 声音　指扔出来的声音

abject ['æbdʒekt] 可怜的 abject poverty / misery / failure 赤贫/凄苦/惨败；自卑的，自惭形秽的 an abject apology 低声下气的道歉　词源：ab 离开 + ject 扔　指被扔出家门的人是可怜的

adjacent [ə'dʒeis(ə)nt] 邻近的，毗连的 the building adjacent to the library 紧挨着图书馆的建筑　词源：ad 强调 + jac 连接 join + ent 形容词后缀（表示具有……能力的）指连接在一起的

dejected [di'dʒektid] 抑郁的，沮丧的　词源：de 向下 + ject 扔 + ed 形容词后缀　指摔跤被扔到下面心情是沮丧的

eject [i'dʒekt] 弹射，喷射 eject fuel 喷出燃料；（武力）驱逐；强迫离职 eject sb. from sth.；光盘弹出　词源：e 出来 + ject 扔　指弹射的状态是扔出东西　巧记：ejector seat（飞机上的）弹射座椅

inject [in'dʒekt] 注射打针 inject sth. into sb. / sth.；增添（气氛、兴趣）；投入（资金、设备）　词源：in 内部 + ject 扔　指扔进内部

injection [in'dʒekʃ(ə)n] 注射打针 an injection of insulin 胰岛素的注射；资金注入（为了改进某事）a massive injection of public funds 大量注入公共基金；（液体）注入 a fuel injection system 燃料注入系统　词源：inject 注册 + tion 名词后缀

interject [ˌintə'dʒekt] 突然插嘴，插话　词源：inter 两者间 + ject 扔　指在两个通话的人之间突然扔入一些话语

object ['ɔbdʒikt; -dʒekt] 客体，物体 UFO（unidentified flying object）不明飞行物；目标，宗旨；反对 object to (doing) sth.　词源：ob 强调 + ject 扔　指把东西直接扔掉表示反对

objection [əb'dʒekʃ(ə)n] 反对，异议 have no objection (to sth.)（对某事）没有异议　词源：object 反对 + tion 名词后缀　巧记：objection! 反对！抗议！（一方律师在法庭上向法官提出，用于反对另一方律师刚说的话）

objective [əb'dʒektiv] 客观的 objective assessment 客观的评价；目标 set an objective 制定目标

词源：object 客体 + tive 形容词后缀

project ['prɒdʒekt] 投影 project the slide onto the wall 幻灯片投射到墙上；计划，项目，课题；预测 the projected closure of the hospital 计划关闭这所医院；凸出 projecting teeth 突出的牙齿　词源：pro 向前 + ject 扔　指把图像扔到屏幕上是投影

projector [prə'dʒektə] 投影仪　词源：project 投影 + or 名词后缀

projection [prə'dʒekʃ(ə)n] 投影；预测；凸出；形象化　词源：project 投影 + tion 名词后缀

subject ['sʌbdʒekt; 'sʌbdʒikt] 臣民 a British subject 英国国民；对象，主体 subjects of this experiment 实验的对象；（绘画、摄影等的）主题；学科；受限于 be subject to sth.　词源：sub 下面 + ject 扔　指在社会底层被扔被抛弃的人们

subjective [səb'dʒektiv] 主观的 subjective judgment 主观判断；（语法中）主语的　词源：subject 主体 + tive 形容词后缀（表示充满活力的 active）

reject [ri'dʒekt] 拒绝；嫌弃；次品 a shop selling cheap rejects 销售便宜次品的商店　词源：re 反复 + ject 扔　指反复扔掉的物品

69. -lev-, -lieve, -lief : lift　巧记：l 一根长棍 + e 出来 + v 开口　指棍子翘起开口

alleviate [ə'li:vieit] 缓解减轻（痛苦）alleviate the symptoms of flu 减轻流感症状　词源：al 强调 + lev 升起 + ate 动词后缀　指提升舒适水平

believe [bi'li:v] 相信；认为　词源：be 强调 + lieve 升起　指相信是精神水平的提高

belief [bi'li:f] 信念，信仰；信心　词源：be 强调 + lief 升起　指信念是精神水平的提高

elevate ['eliveit] 升起，抬起；升职，提拔　词源：e 出来 + lev 升起 + ate 动词后缀　指让物品的位置在水平方向上提升

elevator ['eliveitə] 电梯　词源：elevate 升起 + or 名词后缀

escalator ['eskəleitə] 自动扶梯　词源：e 出来 + scale 攀登 + or 名词后缀　指斜着向上升高的商场或地铁的扶梯

lever ['li:və]（机器或设备的）控制杆，操纵杆 car shift lever 汽车变速杆；杠杆；（影响局势的）方法，手段；撬起 lever the stone 翘起石头　词源：lev 升起 + er 名词后缀

leverage ['li:v(ə)ridʒ; 'lev(ə)ridʒ] 杠杆作用；影响 diplomatic leverage by the US 美国施行的外交影响　词源：lever 杠杆 + age 名词后缀（表示时间长）指杠杆发明对世界的长期影响

levy ['levi] 征税；税款 levy a tax / charge / fine (on sth.)；税款，税额 impose a levy on landfill waste 对填埋的废弃物征税　词源：lev 升起 + y 名词后缀　指税费提高

levitate ['leviteit]（靠魔力）飘浮空中　词源：lev 升起 + it 它 + ate 动词后缀　指让它升起在空中

relieve [ri'li:v] 缓解（疼痛）relieve the pain；执勤换班 relieve the guard；排遣调剂（无聊）relieve the boredom；解围城市　词源：re 反复 + lieve 升起　指反复提升健康水平

relieved [ri'li:vd] 宽慰的，不再忧虑的，释怀的 a relieved smile 宽心的笑容　词源：relieve 缓解 + ed 形容词后缀

relief [ri'li:f] 缓解；宽慰，轻松；救济品 relief center（大灾难如地震、海啸、洪水等过后的）

救济中心；换班人 a relief driver 换班司机；浮雕 figures carved in relief 浮雕人像；解围 the relief of the city 城市解围　词源：re 反复 + lief 升起　指从水平面升起凸出的雕刻艺术品

70. -loqu-, -locut- : speak　巧记：lot 许多 + question 问题　指说许多提问的话

eloquent ['eləkwənt] 雄辩的，能言善辩的 an eloquent appeal for support 能打动人心的求助呼吁；清楚表明的　词源：e 出来 + loqu 说 + ent 形容词后缀（表示具有……能力的）指能滔滔不绝说话的

eloquence ['eləkwəns] 雄辩，口才　词源：e 出来 + loqu 说 + ence 名词后缀

elegant ['elig(ə)nt] 优雅的；巧妙的，简洁的　词源：e 出来 + leg 读 + ant 形容词后缀（表示具有……能力的）指读出来的文字优雅的

grandiloquent [græn'diləkwənt]（计划）浮夸的，华而不实的，不切实际的　词源：grand 宏大的 + loqu 说 + ent 形容词后缀（表示具有……能力的）指说大话的

loquacious [lə'kweiʃəs] 健谈的；多嘴的，话多的　词源：loqu 说 + ous 形容词后缀（表示过多的）指说很多话的　同义词：talkative

obloquy ['ɔbləkwi] 谩骂，痛责；丧失尊严，耻辱　词源：ob 否定 + loqu 说 + y 名词后缀　指说不好的话

soliloquy [sə'liləkwi]（戏剧）独白　词源：soli 单独的 solo + loqu 说 + y 名词后缀　指一个人独自说话

71. -merg-, -mers- : dip, sink　巧记：谐音"没之"指淹没到水中

merge [mə:dʒ] 合并，融合 merge with sth.　词源：merg 下沉

emerge [i'mə:dʒ]（太阳）浮现，出现 the sun emerging from the clouds 云层后露出来的太阳；走出困境；兴起　词源：e 出来 + merg 下沉　指从水下升出来

emergence [i'mə:dʒ(ə)ns] 浮现，出现 the emergence of new evidence 新证据的出现；（困境的）摆脱　词源：emerge 浮现 + ence 名词后缀

emergency [i'mə:dʒ(ə)nsi] 紧急情况 emergency exit 紧急出口　词源：emerge 浮现 + ency 名词后缀

immerge [i'mə:dʒ] 浸入液体 The diver immerged in the icy sea. 潜水员潜入冰冷的海中。　词源：im 内部 + merg 下沉　指沉入液体中

immerse [i'mə:s] 浸入液体 immerse sb. / sth. in sth.；专心做某事 sb. be immersed in sth. / immerse oneself in sth.

immense [i'mens] 巨大的　词源：im 否定 + mens 测量 measure　指不能测量出来的是巨大的

immersion [i'mə:ʃn] 浸入液体；（做某事的）专心投入 one's immersion in music and culture 对音乐和文化的潜心研究　词源：immerse 浸入 + sion 名词后缀

submerge [sʌb'mə:dʒ] 使浸没，淹没；（潜艇）没入水中，下潜；掩盖，遮掩（感情、想法或观点）　词源：sub 下面 + merg 下沉　指下沉入水中

72. -migr- : move 巧记：m 移动 move + i 人 + gr 生长 grow 指人移动到别的地方生长

migrate [mai'greit; 'maigreit]（鸟或兽）迁徙；移居 词源：migr 移动 + ate 动词后缀

migration [mai'greiʃ(ə)n]（鸟或兽）迁徙；（一大群人为找工作的）移居，迁移 词源：migrate 迁徙 + tion 名词后缀

migrant ['maigr(ə)nt] 候鸟，迁徙动物；迁徙者，移居者 词源：migrate 迁徙 + ant 名词后缀

immigrate ['imigreit] 入境移民，（为定居而从外国）移居，移入 词源：im 内部 + migrate 迁徙 词源：指移居进入本国

immigrant ['imigr(ə)nt]（外来）移民 词源：immigrate 入境移民 + ant 名词后缀

emigrate ['emigreit] 出境移民，移居外国 词源：e 出来 + migrate 迁徙 指移居迁出本国

emigrant ['emigrənt] 出境移民，（移居外国的）移民 词源：emigrate 移居国外 + ant 名词后缀

73. -mit-, -mitt-, -miss- : send 巧记：m 移动 move + it 它 指把它移动发送到其他地方

admit [əd'mit] 勉强承认；允许进入，加入 admit sb. to / into sth.；入院收治 be admitted to the hospital；接收入学 词源：ad 强调 + mit 发送 指发送进入

admission [əd'miʃ(ə)n] 勉强承认；允许进入加入；录取录用 admissions policy 招生政策；入院收治；入场费 free admission to parks 免费进公园 词源：admit 允许进入 + sion 名词后缀

admittance [əd'mit(ə)ns] 进入权 gain admittance to the club 获取俱乐部进入权 词源：admit 允许进入 + ance 名词后缀

dismiss [dis'mis] 解散 Class dismissed. 下课；解雇 dismiss sb. from the post 从职位上解雇；不予理睬 dismiss a proposal 拒绝提议；驳回诉讼 dismiss a case 驳回案件 词源：dis 分散 + miss 发送 指把别人提交的文件撒到地上 词义连记：国王不理睬、建议驳回诉讼、解散议会

dismissal [dis'misl] 解散；解雇；不予理睬；驳回诉讼 词源：dismiss 解散 + al 名词后缀

dismissive [dis'misiv]（神情或姿势）蔑视的，轻视的 be dismissive of sth. 词源：dismiss 解散 + ive 形容词后缀（表示充满活力的 active）

emit [i'mit] 发光，发热，排气 词源：e 出来 + mit 发送 指发送出来的气、热、光、声音等

emission [i'miʃ(ə)n] 发光，发热，排气；排放量 cut emissions of carbon dioxide 减少二氧化碳排放 词源：emit 散发 + sion 名词后缀

emissary ['emis(ə)ri] 特使，密使 词源：e 出来 + miss 发送 + ary 名词后缀 指派出来完成任务 mission 的人

hermit ['hɜːmit] 宗教隐居者，独居修道士 词源：her 她 + mit 发送 指把她送走像小龙女一样去隐居

intermit ['intə'mit] 中断，暂停 词源：inter 两者间 + mit 发送 指中断比赛时发送给观众小礼物

intermittent [intə'mit(ə)nt] 断断续续的，间歇的 intermittent showers 断断续续的阵雨 词源：intermit 中断 + ent 形容词后缀（表示具有……能力的） 巧记：term 学期 指学期是断断续续的

intermission [ˌintə'miʃn] 间歇；(比赛)中场休息；(戏剧、音乐会等的)幕间休息　词源：intermit 中断 + sion 名词后缀

missile ['misl; 'misail] 导弹 cruise missile 巡航导弹；投掷物　词源：miss 发送 + ile 名词后缀(表示容易……的)指导弹是容易发射的　巧记：谐音"没了，嗖的一声"是导弹

mission ['miʃ(ə)n] 任务；使团；传教，布道　词源：miss 发送 + sion 名词后缀 指发送派遣人员出去完成传教任务

missionary ['miʃ(ə)n(ə)ri] 传教士；传教的 a missionary hospital 教会医院　词源：mission 任务 + ary 名词后缀 指完成传教任务的人

omit [ə(u)'mit] 忽略，遗漏 omit to do sth.　词源：o 否定 + mit 发送 指忘记而没有发送某部分　巧记：谐音"哦，没它"指忽略

omission [ə(u)'miʃ(ə)n] 忽略，省略；省略的东西　词源：omit 忽略 + sion 名词后缀

permit [pə'mit] 允许 permit sb. to do sth.；许可证 work permit 工作许可证　词源：per 穿越 + mit 发送 指穿越大门一直发送货物

premise ['premis] 前提；(商店、餐馆、公司等使用的)房屋及土地 business premises 企业经营场所　词源：pre 在前面 + mis 发送 指需要提前发送的条件是前提　巧记：promise 承诺是合作的前提 premise

remit [ri'mit] 免除(债务或处罚)；把(建议、计划或问题)发回重新决定 remit the matter to the agency for reconsideration 把此事转回事务处作重新考虑；汇款 remit payment by cheque 用支票汇付货款　词源：re 反复 + mit 发送 指重复发送钱款

remittance [ri'mitns] 汇款；汇款金额　词源：remit 汇款 + ance 名词后缀

submit [səb'mit] 提交，呈上；屈服顺从 submit to sb. / sth.；建议，主张 submit that...　词源：sub 下面 + mit 发送 指从下向上发送呈交　形近易混词：summit

summit ['sʌmit] 山顶 reach the summit 到达山顶；顶点 the summit of one's career 事业顶峰；首脑峰会　词源：sum 总结 sum up + mit 见面 meet 指领导人见面总结工作的会议

submissive [səb'misiv] 屈服的，顺从的　词源：submit 屈服 + ive 形容词后缀(表示充满活力的 active)

submission [səb'miʃ(ə)n] 提交，提交书；屈服，顺从 a gesture of submission 投降的手势；(向法官提出的)意见，看法　词源：submit 提交 + sion 名词后缀

transmit [trænz'mit; trɑːnz-; -ns-] 传送信号；传授知识；传承文化；传染疾病；传播(声、热或光)　词源：trans 穿越 + mit 发送 指穿越时间空间发送信息

transmitter [trænz'mitə; trɑːnz-; -ns-] (无线电或电视信号的)信号发射机；(价值观或病毒)传播者，传播媒介　词源：transmit 发送信号 + er 名词后缀

transmission [trænz'miʃ(ə)n; trɑːnz-; -ns-] (电子信号、信息等的)传送；(疾病)传播；(文化)传承；(电视、广播等的)节目播送；(汽车)传动装置，变速器　词源：transmit 传送 + sion 名词后缀

vomit ['vɔmit] 呕吐；呕吐物　词源：vo 发声(指嘴发出声音 voice) + mit 发送 指从嘴里发声发送出呕吐物

74. **-vid-, -vis-, -view-**：see 巧记：v 峡谷开口 +i 人 +d 向下 指人站在峡谷向下看风景；古罗马恺撒的名言"我来，我看见，我征服。"中的三个拉丁语词根就是 veni，vidi，vici，指恺撒来到的世界的任何地方，看到的土地都可以被他征服

video ['vidiəu] 视频录像 video materials for language teaching 语言教学的影像素材 词源：vid 看

visual ['viʒuəl; -zj-] 视觉的 visual effect 视觉效果；视觉画面 the film's stunning visuals 这部电影令人震撼的画面 词源：vis 看 + ual 形容词后缀

visualize ['viʒuəlaiz] 设想，想象 visualize sb. doing sth. 词源：visual 视觉的 + ize 动词后缀 同义词：imagine

visible ['vizəbl] 可见的 visible outline 清晰的轮廓；明显的，显然的；引人注目的 highly visible politicians 十分引人注目的政治家 词源：vis 看 + ible 形容词后缀（表示可以……的）

invisible [in'vizib(ə)l] 隐形的 invisible plane 隐形飞机；无形的 invisible earnings / exports / trade 无形收益/输出/贸易 词源：in 否定 + visible 可见的

visibility [vizi'biliti]（尤指受天气状况影响时的）能见度 good / poor visibility；关注程度 the visibility of women artists 女性艺术家的知名度 词源：visible 可见的 + ity 名词后缀

visit ['vizit] 拜访，访问，参观，游览，看望 词源：vis 看 + it 它 指去看它

visa ['viːzə] 签证 work / student / tourist visa 工作/学生/旅游签证 词源：vis 看 指签证是去国外看看的证件

vista ['vistə]（大片区域内的）景色 stunning vistas of the coast 海岸迷人的景色；街景；（对新经历、想法、事件等的）展望，前景 词源：vis 看 巧记：windows 操作系统 vista 不要与维塔斯（Vitas）弄混 后者是俄罗斯流行音乐领域著名男歌手

advise [əd'vaiz] 建议，劝告 advise sb. to do sth. 词源：ad 强调 + vis 看 指拿出建议让别人看

devise [di'vaiz] 设计，想出 devise a method for quick communications 发明出一种快速通信方法 词源：de 向下 + vis 看 指向下看设计图纸

device [di'vais] 装置设备 digital device 数码设备；特殊方法手段 a useful device for studying 一种有效的学习方法；诡计花招；修辞手段 词源：devise 设想 指设计出来的物品

vision ['viʒ(ə)n] 视力 night vision 夜视能力；视野；远见卓识；设想，构想 a grand vision for the country 对国家的宏伟构想；（宗教经历的）幻像；极美的人或事物；（电视）图像（质量） 词源：vis 看 + sion 名词后缀

envision [en'viʒ(ə)n] 想象，展望（美好的事） 词源：en 使动词化 + vision 视野

envisage [in'vizidʒ; en-] 展望，设想 envisage doing sth. 词源：en 使动词化 + vis 看 + age 一段时间 指对未来一段长时间的展望

evidence ['evidəns] 证据，证明 词源：e 出来 + vid 看 + ence 名词后缀 指看得出来的证据

evident ['evid(ə)nt] 明显的，明白的 self-evident truths 不言自明的真相 词源：evidence 证据 + ent 形容词后缀（表示具有……能力的）指证据明显的

prevision [priː'viʒən] 预知，先见 词源：pre 在前面 + vision 视野 指提前看见未来

provide [prə'vaid] 提供 provide sb. with sth.；（法律或规章）规定 provide that…；预防，防备，

防止 provide against sth. 词源：pro 向前＋vid 看 指走上前把物品给别人看

provision [prə'vɪʒ(ə)n] 提供，供应；（为旅行储备的）粮食，食物；（为将来做的）准备 make provisions for sb. / sth.；（协议或法律中的）条款，规定 under the provisions of the contract 按合同条款规定　词源：provide 规定＋sion 名词后缀 指条款是一条条规定　词义连记：把提供粮食援助写入条款规定

providence ['prɒvɪd(ə)ns] 天意，天命 divine providence 天意　词源：pro 向前＋vid 看＋ence 名词后缀 指人要学会向前看明白过去的一切都是天意　巧记：天意 providence 就是上天提供 provide 的规定 provision

provident ['prɒvɪd(ə)nt] 有远见的，未雨绸缪的，深谋远虑的　词源：providence 天意＋ent 形容词后缀（表示具有……能力的）

improvident [ɪm'prɒvɪdənt] 目光短浅的　词源：im 否定＋provident 有远见的

preview ['priːvjuː]（戏剧或电影）预演预映；（电影、电视节目）预告片；预审；预习　词源：pre 在前面＋view 看 指提前看一遍

interview ['ɪntəvjuː]（求职、入学等的）面试；（对名人的）采访，访谈　词源：inter 两者间＋view 看 指两者相互看对方面试或访谈

review [rɪ'vjuː] 回顾；复习；审查；（电影）评论 a film review 影评；（军队）检阅 a naval review 海军检阅　词源：re 反复＋view 看 指重复看

view [vjuː] 景色；观点；认为　词源：view 看

viewer ['vjuːə] 观看者；电视观众　词源：view 看＋er 名词后缀

revise [rɪ'vaɪz] 修订书籍；修改计划；考前复习　词源：re 反复＋vis 看 指反复看稿件修订

revision [rɪ'vɪʒ(ə)n] 修改修订（文稿）；修订稿；温习

supervise ['suːpəvaɪz; 'sjuː-] 监督，管理，指导 supervise the research 指导研究　词源：super 上面＋vis 看 指在上面盯着看

improvise ['ɪmprəvaɪz] 即兴创作，即兴表演 an improvised performance 即兴表演；临时拼凑制作　词源：im 内部＋provide 提供＋vis 看 指内心里即兴提供给别人看的想法素材

75. -equ-, equi- : equal　巧记：equal 平等的

equal ['iːkwəl] 平等的 equal rights 平等权利；相等的 an equal number of votes 相等票数；能应付难题的 be equal to the challenge 应对挑战；同等的人　词源：equ 平等的

equality [ɪ'kwɒlɪti; iː-] 平等 equality between men and women 男女平等　词源：equal 平等的＋ity 名词后缀

adequate ['ædɪkwət] 尚可的，过得去的；足够的 adequate sleep 充足睡眠；胜任的　词源：ad 强调＋equ 平等的＋ate 形容词后缀

inadequate [ɪn'ædɪkwət] 不足够的 inadequate resources 资源缺乏；不胜任的 feel inadequate 觉得能力差　词源：in 否定＋adequate 足够的

equilibrium [ˌiːkwɪ'lɪbrɪəm; ˌekwɪ-] 平衡 upset the economic equilibrium 打乱经济平衡；（心态）平静 recover one's equilibrium 恢复平静　词源：equ 平等的＋Libra 天秤座＋ium 名词后缀

equivalent [i'kwiv(ə)l(ə)nt] 等价物；等价值的 be equivalent to sth. 词源：equ 平等的 + val 价值 value + ent 形容词后缀（表示具有……能力的）

equivalence [i'kwivələns] 等价值 词源：equivalent 等价的 + ence 名词后缀

equation [i'kweiʒ(ə)n] 等式，方程式；（涉及平衡的）影响因素；关联 词源：equ 平等的 + tion 名词后缀

equator [i'kweitə] 赤道 a small village near the equator 赤道旁的小村庄 词源：equ 平等的 + or 名词后缀 指赤道把地球分为两个等同部分

equivocal [i'kwivəkl] 模棱两可的，含糊的 equivocal answer 模棱两可的回答 词源：equi 平等的 + vocal 声音的 指发出两种同等相似的声音让人听起来含糊 同义词：ambiguous

equivocation [i,kwivə'keiʃn] 模棱两可，含糊的话 词源：equivocal 含糊的 + tion 名词后缀

76. -rect-, -rig- : right 巧记：r 植物向上分裂的状态 + e 出来 + ct 声音 指植物竖直生长发出分裂的声音

reckon ['rek(ə)n] 估算 reckon sth. up；认为 reckon sth. to be sth. / reckon that…；指望 reckon on sth. 词源：rect 正确的 + on 在某种状态下 指正在认为某事是正确的状态

reckless ['reklis] 鲁莽的，不计后果的 be reckless with money 花钱大手大脚的 词源：reck 正确的 + less 否定 指不考虑正确与否的

direct [dai'rekt] 直接的；直率的；针对；指示，命令；指路；指引；指导；指挥；导演 词源：di 分散 dis + rect 直的 指在分散的路口指出正确的方向

correct [kə'rekt] 正确的；行为得体的；纠正；批改作业 词源：cor 共同 + rect 正确的 指一起做正确的事

incorrect [inkə'rekt] 错的；不合礼节的 词源：in 否定 + correct 正确的

erect [i'rekt] 勃起；竖起 erect barriers 设立路障；搭起 erect a tent 搭帐篷；建立 erect a town hall 建市政府；雄起；竖直的 stand erect 笔直站立 词源：e 出来 + rect 直的 指竖立直挺的

erection [i'rekʃ(ə)n] 勃起；竖立；建立 the erection of a new temple 建造新寺庙 词源：erect 竖立 + tion 名词后缀

resurrection [,rezə'rekʃn] 耶稣复活；复兴，恢复 a resurrection of old jealousies 昔日嫉妒心的再次出现 词源：re 反复 + sur 上面 + rect 直的 + tion 名词后缀 指重新站立起来的

rectitude ['rektitju:d] 正直，公正，诚实（像包青天） 词源：rect 正确的 + tude 名词后缀

rectify ['rektifai] 纠正，矫正，拨乱反正 rectify the situation 整顿局面 词源：rect 正确的 + fy 动词后缀

rectangle ['rektæŋg(ə)l] 矩形，长方形 词源：rect 直的 + angle 角度 指都是直角的图形

77. -spic-, -spect-, -spec- : look, see 巧记：spy 间谍 指间谍般的窥探

aspect ['æspekt] 外表,外观；方面 aspects of family life 生活的各个方面；房屋朝向 a south-facing aspect 朝南方向 词源：a 正在 + spect 看 指正在看到的部分是外表

circumspect ['sə:kəmspekt] 小心谨慎的 词源：circum 围绕 circle + spect 看 指绕着圆圈察看

周围的环境　同义词：cautious

conspicuous [kən'spikjuəs] 明显的；显眼的 a bird with conspicuous red feathers 一种长着显眼红色羽毛的鸟　词源：con 共同 + spic 看 + ous 形容词后缀（表示过多的）指大家都能看到的

despise [di'spaiz] 鄙视，轻视　词源：de 向下 + spi 看 指眼神向下看别人

despicable [di'spikəb(ə)l; 'despik-] 卑鄙的，可鄙视的 despicable deceit 卑鄙的欺骗　词源：despise 鄙视 + able 形容词后缀（表示可以……的）

expect [ik'spekt; ek-] 期待，预料　词源：ex 出去 + spect 看 指从窗户看出去期待

expectation [ekspek'teiʃ(ə)n] 期待，指望　词源：expect 期待 + tion 名词后缀

expectancy [ik'spekt(ə)nsi; ek-] 期待，预期；（人或动物的）预期寿命 life expectancy　词源：expect 期待 + ancy 名词后缀

inspect [in'spekt] 仔细检查 inspect the damage 检查损坏；检阅视察 inspect the troops 检阅部队　词源：in 内部 + spect 看 指向内部看

inspector [in'spektə] 检查员，督察员 ticket inspectors 查票员；警队督查　词源：inspect 检查 + or 名词后缀

inspection [in'spekʃn] 仔细检查；巡查，视察 border inspection station 边境检查站　词源：inspect 检查 + tion 名词后缀

introspect [ˌintrəu'spekt] 自省，反省　词源：intro 内部 into + spect 看 指向自己的身上查看问题

introspection [ˌintrə(u)'spekʃ(ə)n] 自省，反省　词源：introspect 反省 + tion 名词后缀

prospect ['prɔspekt]（尤指从高处看到的）景色，远景 a delightful prospect of the lake 令人心旷神怡的湖上风光；前景，未来 an exciting prospect 令人兴奋的前景；探矿，勘探（以寻找金、银、石油等矿藏）prospect for gold 淘金；寻求（商机）prospect for new customers 寻找新客户　词源：pro 向前 + spect 看 指向前看寻求机会

prospective [prə'spektiv] 有前途的 prospective employee / candidate / buyer 可能成为雇员的人/可能成功的候选人/潜在的客户　词源：prospect 前景 + tive 形容词后缀（表示充满活力的 active）

perspective [pə'spektiv] 透视法，透视效果；角度，观点 from sb.'s perspective；（尤指由近而远的）景观，远景　词源：per 穿越 + spect 看 + tive 名词后缀 指绘画穿过平面的透视画法 如在纸上画一条向内延伸的具有立体感的街道

respect [ri'spekt] 尊敬；方面 in one respect / in some respects 在某个/某些方面　词源：re 反复 + spect 看 指反复注视是尊重

respective [ri'spektiv] 各自的 respective life 各自的生活　词源：respect 方面 + tive 形容词后缀（表示充满活力的）指各个方面的

respectable [ri'spektəb(ə)l] 体面的，正派的，受人尊敬的 a respectable family 正经人家；好的，令人满意的 a respectable income 不错的收入　词源：respect 尊重 + able 形容词后缀（表示可以……的）

respectful [ri'spek(t)ful; -f(ə)l] 有礼貌的，恭敬的，尊敬他人的 be respectful of authority 尊重权威　词源：respect 尊重 + ful 形容词后缀（表示充满的）

retrospect ['retrəspekt] 回顾，回想 in retrospect　词源：retro 向后 return + spect 看　指向过去看

specious ['spiːʃəs] 华而不实的，似是而非的 a specious argument 貌似有理的论据　词源：spec 看 + ous 形容词后缀（表示过多的）指看起来好像可行的　形近易混词：spacious

spacious ['speiʃəs] 宽敞的；广阔的 a spacious living area 宽敞的居住空间　词源：space 空间 + ous 形容词后缀（表示过多的）指在空间上过多的

specify ['spesifai] 详细说明　词源：spec 看 + fy 动词后缀　指边看边说明

specific [spə'sifik] 详细精准的 specific instructions 明确的指示；特效药　词源：spec 看 + ic 形容词后缀

specification [ˌspesifi'keiʃ(ə)n] 详述 job specification 工作职责说明；产品规格 engineering specifications 工程设计规格　词源：specific 具体的 + tion 名词后缀　指具体的产品规格说明

spectacle ['spektək(ə)l] 壮观的景象（比如古罗马斗兽场的竞技表演）；出洋相，出丑 make a spectacle of oneself；（常复数）眼镜 a pair of spectacles 一副眼镜　词源：spect 看 + cle 名词后缀　指看到的非凡景象

spectator [spek'teitə]（活动或体育比赛的）比赛观众　词源：spect 看 + or 名词后缀

spectacular [spek'tækjulə] 宏伟的，壮观的 a spectacular success 辉煌的成就　词源：spectacle 壮观景象 + lar 形容词后缀（表示特殊的 particular）指特别壮观的

spectrum ['spektrəm] 光谱；频谱；范围，幅度 the ethnic spectrum of America 美国的各种族　词源：spect 看 + um 名词后缀　巧记：spect 看 + u 水 + m 山　指可看到的山水景色范围

speculate ['spekjuleit] 推测，猜测 speculate on / about sth.；商业投机 speculated in stock 投机炒股票　词源：spec 看 +l 长时期 long + ate 动词后缀　指看到长期形势

suspect [sə'spekt] 嫌疑犯；怀疑　词源：sus 下面 + spect 看　指眼神向下看怀疑别人

suspicious [sə'spiʃəs] 怀疑他人的 be suspicious of / about sth.；可疑的 a suspicious package 一个可疑的包裹　词源：suspect 怀疑 + ous 形容词后缀（表示过多的）

suspicion [sə'spiʃ(ə)n] 怀疑，不信任　词源：suspect 怀疑 + sion 名词后缀

78. **-vac-**：empty　巧记：v 峡谷开口 valley

vacuum ['vækjuəm] 真空；真空吸尘器；空虚 leave a vacuum in one's life 生活变得空虚　词源：vac 空 + um 名词后缀　指山水间的空旷

vacate [vei'keit; və'keit] 腾空（房间）vacate rooms 腾房；腾出（职位）vacate the position 离职　词源：vac 空 + ate 动词后缀

vacancy ['veik(ə)nsi] 职位空缺 fill the vacancy 填补职缺；空房间 No vacancies 客满；无聊空虚 the look of vacancy 茫然若失的神情　词源：vac 空 + ancy 名词后缀

vacant ['veik(ə)nt]（座位、房屋、土地）空的，未被占用的 a vacant lot 一块空地；（工作或职位）空缺的；茫然的 vacant expression / look / stare 茫然的表情/神情/凝视　词源：vac 空 +

ant 形容词后缀（表示有……能力的）

evacuate [i'vækjueit] 排泄（粪便）；紧急疏散，撤离 evacuate sb. from / to sth. 词源：e 出来 + vac 空 + ate 动词后缀 指排空出来

vacation [və'keiʃ(ə)n; vei-] 休假，假期 take / have a vacation 休假 词源：vac 空 + tion 名词后缀 指空闲时间是休假

vacuous ['vækjuəs]（表情）茫然的 a vacuous expression 茫然的表情；（文字）无意义的 a vacuous romantic novel 空洞的爱情小说 词源：vac 空 + ous 形容词后缀（表示过多的）

vacuity [və'kjuːəti] 空虚，茫然 mental vacuity 精神空虚 词源：vac 空 + ity 名词后缀

vain [vein] 徒劳的 in vain；虚荣的,自负的 词源：va 空 + in 内部 指虚荣的是内心空虚的 形近易混词：vein / veil

vein [vein] 静脉；（干酪、石头等的）纹路；（说话、写作）风格 poems in a serious vein 更为严肃的诗 词源：v 峡谷开口 valley + e 出来 + in 内部 指像峡谷般蜿蜒的静脉

vanity ['vænəti] 自负虚荣；梳妆台 a vanity table 词源：vain 自负的 + ity 名词后缀

veil [veil] 面纱 a bridal veil 新娘的面纱；遮掩；一层云雾 a veil of mist / cloud / smoke 一层薄雾/云/烟雾 巧记：reveal 揭露 指反复揭开面纱 re 反复 + veil 面纱

vase [vɑːz] 花瓶 词源：va 空 指空空的花瓶

van [væn] 大篷车；厢式小货车，运钞车，救护车 词源：va 空 + n 大篷车车顶的形状 指有空间和顶棚可以运货的车

vanish ['væniʃ]（尤指莫名其妙地）突然消失 vanish without a trace 消失得无影无踪；（突然）灭绝消亡 词源：va 空 + ish 动词后缀 形近易混词：varnish

varnish ['vɑːniʃ]（尤指刷在木制品上的）清漆彩釉；上清漆；涂指甲油 varnishing nails 涂指甲油 巧记：涂上清漆 varnish 就不会消失 vanish

vapor [veipə] 水汽，蒸汽 词源：va 空 + por 倒水 pour 指倒水后蒸发

evaporate [i'væpəreit] 使蒸发；（感觉）逐渐消逝 词源：e 出来 + vapor 水蒸气 + ate 动词后缀 指使液体变为蒸汽释放出来

79. **-vad-, -vas-**: go 巧记：valley 峡谷 指在峡谷里走

invade [in'veid] 武力侵略；（尤指不受欢迎地）大量涌入，蜂拥而入；侵扰侵害 invade one's privacy 侵扰隐私 词源：in 内部 + vad 走 指非法走进来

invasive [in'veisiv]（疾病）侵入的，扩散的 invasive cancer 扩散性癌症；（治疗）需开刀手术的 invasive surgery 开刀手术 词源：invade 入侵 + sive 形容词后缀（表示充满活力的 active）

invasion [in'veiʒ(ə)n] 侵害 invasion of privacy 对隐私的侵犯；（不受欢迎的人或物）涌入，蜂拥而来 the annual tourist invasion 一年一度游客的涌入；侵略 the threat of invasion 入侵的威胁 词源：invade 入侵 + sion 名词后缀

evade [i'veid] 逃税 evade tax；避责 evade one's responsibilities 词源：e 出来 + vad 走 指走出去逃避

evasive [i'veisiv] 逃避的，推脱的，含糊的 an evasive reply 含糊其词的答复 词源：evade 逃

避 + sive 形容词后缀（表示充满活力的 active）

inevitable [in'evitəb(ə)l] 不可避免的　词源：in 否定 + evade 逃避 + able 形容词后缀（表示可以……的）

pervade [pə'veid]（感觉、想法或气味）遍及弥漫 a pervading mood of sadness 普遍的悲伤情绪　词源：per 穿越 + vad 走　指味道穿越空气弥漫

pervasive [pə'veisiv] 到处存在的，弥漫的，有渗透力的 the pervasive influence of television 电视无所不在的影响　词源：pervade 弥漫 + sive 形容词后缀（表示充满活力的 active）

80. -voc-, -vok- : call　巧记：voice 人的说话声　v 开口 + o 圆形的嘴　指开口说话的声音

void [vɔid] 空虚感，孤寂感 fill the void 填补空虚；（合同或协议）无效的　词源：vo 发声 + id 形容词后缀（表示具有某种身份 identity）指嘴上说的是无效的

vogue [vəug] 时尚，流行 be in vogue　词源：vo 发声 + gue 名词后缀　指唱歌声音时尚　巧记：vo 声音 voice + gue 谐音"哥哥"指唱出好声音的哥哥是时尚达人　形近易混词：vague

vague [veig] 模糊不清的 have a vague impression / memory 印象/记忆模糊　词源：va 空 + gue 形容词后缀　指峡谷里空旷雾气模糊的

vomit ['vɔmit] 呕吐；呕吐物　词源：vo 发声（指嘴发出声音 voice）+ mit 发送　指从嘴里发声发送出呕吐物

advocate ['ædvəkeit] 提倡者，鼓吹者 an advocate for liberalism 自由主义支持者；提倡，倡导 advocate the use of violence 支持使用暴力　词源：ad 强调 + voc 发声 + ate 动词后缀　指不停发声提倡

convoke [kən'vəuk] 召集会议 convoke meetings　词源：con 共同 + vok 发声　指共同发声开会商量　同义词：convene

convocation [,kɔnvə'keiʃ(ə)n]（教会的）大型会议；（大学的）学位授予典礼，毕业典礼　词源：convoke 召集会议 + tion 名词后缀

evoke [i'vəuk] 唤起（记忆或情感）evoke sympathy 唤起同情　词源：e 出来 + vok 发声　指发声叫……出来

provoke [prə'vəuk] 煽动，挑衅 provoke sb. to do sth.；引起，激起 provoke a protest 引起抗议　词源：pro 向前 + vok 发声　指走向敌人叫喊发声挑衅

provocative [prə'vɔkətiv]（行为或话语）煽动性的 provocative comments 煽动性言论；（衣服、动作、图片）挑逗性的 provocative images of young girls 姑娘们撩人的形象　词源：provoke 挑衅 + tive 形容词后缀（表示充满活力的 active）

revoke [ri'vəuk] 废除取消（法律或决定）revoke work permit 取消工作许可证　词源：re 返回 + vok 发声　指收回发出的号令

irrevocable [i'revəkəbl] 不可撤销的 an irrevocable decision / step 最终决定/一步　词源：in 否定 + revoke 取消 + able 形容词后缀（表示可以……的）

vocation [və(u)'keiʃ(ə)n] 使命感，天职 a strong sense of vocation 强烈的使命感；（认为特别适合自己的）职业　词源：voc 发声 + tion 名词后缀　指上天发声让人有使命感

avocation [ˌævəˈkeɪʃ(ə)n] 业余爱好　词源：a 否定 + vocation 职业　指不是主职业

invocation [ˌɪnvə(u)ˈkeɪʃ(ə)n]（向神的）求助；（仪式或集会开始时的）祈祷，祷文　词源：in 内部 + voc 发声 + tion 名词后缀　指内心发声召唤神灵求助

vocal [ˈvəʊk(ə)l] 直言不讳的；声音的 the vocal organs 发声器官；声乐的 vocal music 声乐　词源：voc 发声 + cal 形容词后缀

vocalist [ˈvəʊkəlɪst]（尤指与乐队配合演唱流行歌曲的）歌手 a lead / guest / backing vocalist 领唱/特邀/伴唱歌手　词源：vocal 声乐的 + ist 名词后缀

vocabulary [və(u)ˈkæbjʊləri] 词汇；词汇量；词汇表　词源：voc 发声 + bul 建立 build + ary 名词后缀　指需要发声读出来才能建立起词汇储备

volume [ˈvɒljuːm] 音量 turn the volume up / down 把音量调大/小；容积 jars of different volumes 不同容量的罐子；一卷，一册 an encyclopedia in 20 volumes 一套 20 卷的百科全书　词源：vo 发声 + l 长时间 long + u 水 + m 山 + e 出来　指在山水间拉长声呼喊的音量

volcano [vɒlˈkeɪnəʊ] 火山 the eruption of the volcano 火山喷发　词源：源于罗马神话中的伏尔甘（Vulcan），火及锻造之神，等同于希腊神话中的赫淮斯托斯（Hephaestus）　巧记：vo 发声 + cano 加农炮 cannon 指火山喷发像加农炮开火

81. -clud-, -clus-, -clos-：close　巧记：close 关闭

conclude [kənˈkluːd] 总结；做出结论；达成协议 conclude an agreement / a treaty / a contract 达成协议/缔结条约/签订合同　词源：con 共同 + clud 关闭　指共同关闭议题

conclusive [kənˈkluːsɪv] 结论性的　词源：conclude 总结 + sive 形容词后缀（表示充满活力的 active）

conclusion [kənˈkluːʒ(ə)n] 结论；（条约贸易协定）缔结签订　词源：conclude 总结 + sion 名词后缀

disclose [dɪsˈkləʊz]（被隐瞒后）揭露，公开 disclose the identity 透露身份　词源：dis 否定 + close 关闭　指不关闭、公开　同义词：reveal

disclosure [dɪsˈkləʊʒə] 揭露，公开 the disclosure of private information 私人信息的披露　词源：disclose 揭露 + sure 名词后缀

enclose [ɪnˈkləʊz; en-]（用篱笆或围墙）圈地围地 an enclosed area 有围墙的区域；随信附上，随信装入 enclose a cheque with the order 随订单附上支票　词源：en 使动词化 + clos 关闭　指围起来关上

enclosure [ɪnˈkləʊʒə; en-] 围地围场 the bear enclosure at the zoo 动物园中的熊园；信中附件；移动硬盘外盒　词源：enclose 圈地 + sure 名词后缀

include [ɪnˈkluːd] 包含，包括　词源：in 内部 + clud 关闭　指关在内部

inclusive [ɪnˈkluːsɪv] 包含的，包括的 be inclusive of sth.；兼容并包的 an inclusive country 一个包容性很强的国家　词源：include 包含 + sive 形容词后缀（表示充满活力的 active）

inclusiveness [ɪnˈkluːsɪvnɪs] 兼容并包　词源：inclusive 包含的 + ness 名词后缀

exclude [ɪkˈskluːd; ek-]（故意）排除 a special diet that excludes dairy products 不包含奶制品的

特别食谱；不准参与 exclude sb. from doing sth. 词源：ex 出来 + clud 关闭 指撑出来后关门不让进

exclusive [ik'skluːsiv; ek-] 排外的 a racially exclusive employment policy 一项种族上排外的就业政策；独有的，专有的 an exclusive report 独家报道；高级的，昂贵的 an exclusive school 贵族学校；排斥的 be mutually exclusive 相互排斥的,互不相容的 词源：exclude 排外 + sive 形容词后缀（表示充满活力的 active）

occlude [ə'kluːd] 使闭塞，堵塞 an occluded artery / vein 闭塞的动脉/静脉 词源：oc 强调 + clud 关闭 指血液流动堵塞

preclude [pri'kluːd] 阻止，防止 preclude sb. from doing something 词源：pre 在前面 + clud 关闭 指提前关闭来阻止

preclusion [pri'kluːʒən] 阻止，防止 词源：preclude 阻止 + sion 名词后缀

recluse [ri'kluːs] 隐居者，隐士 lead the life of a recluse 过隐居的生活 词源：re 反复 + clus 关闭 指反复闭关隐居的人

seclude [si'kluːd] 隐退隐居，与世隔绝 a secluded garden / beach / spot 僻静的花园/海滩/地点 词源：se 分离 + clud 关闭 指离开世俗后闭关隐居

seclusion [si'kluːʒ(ə)n] 隐退隐居，与世隔绝 the peace and seclusion of the island 岛上的平和安静 词源：seclude 与世隔绝 + sion 名词后缀

82. -em-, -am-, -empt- : take, buy 巧记：e 出来 + m 山 指从山中获取资源

ample ['æmp(ə)l] 充足的，充裕的，绰绰有余的 ample time 充裕的时间；（房间或空间）宽敞的 ample room / space；（女性胸部）丰满的 an ample bosom 词源：am 爱 love; am 获取 take + ple 充满 指充满可以获取的爱 巧记：apple 指苹果充足的

amplify ['æmplifai] 放大（声音，音乐声或信号）an amplified guitar 带有扩音设备的电吉他；增强（某种感受）amplify the feelings of regret and fear 增加懊悔和恐惧感；详述，（进一步）阐述 amplify a statement 详述声明 词源：ample 充足的 + ify 动词后缀

amplifier ['æmplifaiə] 放大器，扩音器 词源：amplify 放大声音 + er 名词后缀

example [ig'zɑːmpl] 例子，例证；榜样 set an example to / for sb. 词源：ex 出来 + am 获取 + ple 名词后缀 指拿出来作为例子

exemplary [ig'zempləri; eg-] 模范的，榜样的 词源：example 例子 + ary 形容词后缀

exemplify [ig'zemplifai; eg-] 作为……的例子；举例说明 词源：example 例子 + fy 动词后缀 指举出例子

exempt [ig'zem(p)t; eg-] 免除，豁免 exempt sb. from sth.；免除义务的 词源：ex 出来 + empt 获取 指被挑出来可以不用履行义务

exemption [ig'zempʃn] 免除，豁免；免税 a tax exemption on the loan 贷款免税 词源：exempt 免除 + tion 名词后缀

sample ['sɑːmp(ə)l] 样本,样品,货样；试用产品 samples of new makeup 新化妆品的试用品 词

源：s 一些 some + am 获取 + ple 名词后缀　指获取的一些样本

83. -ped-, -pod- : foot　巧记：拟声词"啪嗒啪嗒"　指脚走路的声音

centipede ['sentipi:d] 蜈蚣　词源：cent 一百 + ped 脚　指有一百只脚的动物

expedition [ekspi'diʃ(ə)n] 远征探险；探险队；短途出行 a shopping expedition 购物之行　词源：ex 出去 + ped 脚 + tion 名词后缀　指出门远足探险

stampede [stæm'pi:d] 使惊慌逃跑；蜂拥，争先恐后 a cattle stampede 牛群的狂奔　词源：stamp 跺 + ped 脚　指猛兽一跺脚吓跑动物

impede [im'pi:d] 阻止，妨碍 impede the progress 阻碍进程　词源：im 否定 + ped 脚　指不让人走

pad [pæd] 护垫；鼠标垫；卫生巾；便笺本；小型停机坪；猫狗肉掌；轻声走路　词源：ped 脚　指动物脚上的肉掌垫子

podium ['pəudiəm] 讲台；乐队指挥台　词源：pod 脚 ped + ium 名词后缀（表示地点 place）　指脚踩的平台

pedal ['ped(ə)l] 踏板；油门；骑自行车　词源：ped 脚 + al 名词后缀　指长长的踏板

peddle ['ped(ə)l] 叫卖兜售（非法商品）peddle cigarettes；散布宣扬（错误观点主张）　词源：ped 脚 + dle 动词后缀（表示强调）

encyclopedia [in,saiklə'pi:diə] 百科全书　词源：en 使动词化 + cycle 圈 + ped 脚 + ia 名词后缀　指用脚绕圈走路看石柱上的文字学习百科知识

pedestrian [pə'destriən] 路人行人 a pedestrian walkway 人行通道；平淡无奇的，缺乏想象力的 a pedestrian and unimaginative painting 乏味而又缺乏想象力的画作　词源：ped 脚 + str 街道 street + ian 名词后缀　指在街道上走路的人

84. -plor- : cry　巧记：pl 恳求 please + or 嘴 oral　指嘴里发出哭喊、恳求的声音

explore [ik'splɔ:; ek-] 探索，勘探 explore (sth.) for oil / minerals / gold 勘探石油/矿物/黄金；探讨，探究 explore the possibility of a part-time job 探索兼职工作的可能性　词源：ex 出来 + plor 哭喊　指探索到资源而兴奋哭喊

exploit [ik'splɔit; ek-] 资源开采 exploit the resources；剥削压榨 exploit young people 剥削年轻人；充分利用，运用发挥 exploit the humour 运用发挥幽默；英勇行为，功绩功勋 the daring exploits of heroes 英雄英勇无畏的行为　词源：explore 探索 + it 它　指探索到它加以开采利用　词义连记：石油工人充分利用智慧开采石油的功绩让国家摆脱了外部能源压榨

deplore [di'plɔ:]（公开的）强烈谴责 deplore the invasion 强烈谴责侵略　词源：de 以不好的方式 + plor 哭喊　指哭闹叫喊大声谴责

deplorable [di'plɔ:rəbl] 让人愤慨谴责的，恶劣的 live in the most deplorable conditions 生活在最恶劣的环境里　词源：deplore 谴责 + able 形容词后缀（表示可以……的）

implore [im'plɔ:] 哀求，恳求，央求 implore sb. to do sth.　词源：im 内心 + plor 哭喊　指发自内心的哭喊，恳求帮助

5

85. -fus-：pour　巧记：f 飞落 fall + u 水 + s 路径方式　指瀑布的水下落灌注倾倒

fuse [fju:z] 引信，导火索 set the fuse to five minutes 引信设定为五分钟；（电器）保险丝 blow a fuse 烧断保险丝；（理念、特质、思想）结合，融合 fuse (sth.) with sth.；（保险丝）熔断　词源：fuse 拟声词 指引信点燃时发出的滋滋滋的声音　巧记：pour 向下倒水浇灭引信 fuse

confuse [kən'fju:z] 使迷惑；把（人、物）混淆，弄错 confuse sb. / sth. with sb. / sth.　词源：con 共同 + fus 灌倒 指把不同的液体倒在一起喝一口的迷惑口感

Confucius [kən'fju:ʃəs] 孔子　词源：confuse 使迷惑 指孔子是传道授业解惑的圣人

diffuse [di'fju:z] 分散的 a large and diffuse organization 又大又分散的机构；（光线）散播的，漫射的 diffuse light 漫射光；累赘迂回的，啰唆的 diffuse writing 冗长的文体；传播散布（观点或信息）rapidly diffused ideas and technologies 快速散播的观念和技术；平息减缓（不良情绪或局面）diffuse one's anger 平息怒气　词源：dif 分离 + fus 灌倒 指水倒在地上四散飞溅的状态

infuse [in'fju:z]（用热水）泡（茶或香草）；灌输（品质）poems infused with humour and wisdom 诗歌充满了幽默和智慧　词源：in 内部 + fus 灌倒 指向内部倒灌液体

interfuse [ˌintə'fju:z] 使（气味或风格）融合混合 perfume that interfuses herbal and woodsy scents 融合了香草和木香味道的香水　词源：inter 两者间 + fus 灌倒 指把两种液体倒在一起混合

perfuse [pə'fju:z]（向器官）灌注药品 perfuse a liver with salt solution 向肝脏灌注盐水　词源：per 穿越 + fus 灌倒 指穿过血管向器官灌注药品　巧记：per 人 person + fus 灌倒 指向人体内器官灌注药品

profuse [prə'fju:s] 众多的 profuse apologies / thanks 一再道歉/千恩万谢；大量的 profuse sweating 大量出汗；丰富的，充沛的　词源：pro 向前 + fus 灌倒 指走上前去给朋友一杯杯倒酒

profusion [prə'fju:ʒ(ə)n] 大量，丰富，充沛 a profusion of colours 五颜六色　词源：profuse 丰富的 + sion 名词后缀

refuse [ri'fju:z] 拒绝（饮酒）refuse to do sth.；垃圾，废弃物 a refuse dump 垃圾场　词源：re 向后 + fus 灌倒 指往回倒掉酒水拒绝喝掉

suffuse [sə'fju:z]（温暖颜色或液体）充满布满 a room suffused with morning light 充满晨光的房间　词源：suf 下面 + fus 灌倒 指光线或液体灌注充满下面底部　巧记：sufficient 充足的 指足够的 sufficient 就是充满 suffuse

transfuse [træns'fju:z] 输血 transfuse blood into a patient 给病人输血；灌输传达 transfuse the enthusiasm and passion for science to students 把对科学的热爱灌输给学生　词源：trans

穿越 +fus 灌倒 指穿过血管灌输血液

transfusion [træns'fju:ʒ(ə)n; trɑ:ns-; -nz-] 输血；（资金）投入注入 a transfusion of cash 现金投资　词源：transfuse 输血 +sion 名词后缀

86. -graph- : record, draw　巧记：g 土地 +r 摩擦 rub +ph 声音 指土地上石头上刻字的声音

autograph ['ɔ:təgrɑ:f]（名人的）亲笔签名　词源：auto 自己 self +graph 写 指自己写自己的名字

biography [bai'ɔgrəfi] 传记　词源：bio 生命 +graph 写 指生活经历的描写

autobiography [ɔ:təbai'ɔgrəfi] 自传　词源：auto 自己 +biography 传记 指自己写自己的传记

calligraphy [kə'ligrəfi] 书法；书法艺术　词源：calli 漂亮 beauty（源于希腊仙女凯莉丝杜 Callisto，她和宙斯 Zeus 生下阿尔卡斯 Arcas，母子俩后来变成北极上空的大小熊星座）+graph 写 指写漂亮的字

graph [grɑ:f; græf] 图表，图形　词源：graph 写　同义词：chart

graphic ['græfik] 图表的 a graphic artist 平面造型艺术家；（叙述或描写）细致的，生动的 a graphic account of unhappy childhood 对不开心童年细致入微的描述　词源：graph 写 +ic 形容词后缀

graphics ['græfiks]（计算机程序中的）制图，图形 computer graphics 计算机制图　词源：graph 写 +ics 名词后缀

photograph ['fəutəgrɑ:f] 照片；拍照；上相 sb. photograph well　词源：pho 声音 phone +to 方向 +graph 写 指发出快门声响后记录、写下图像

telegraph ['teligrɑ:f] 电报；电报机；发电报；流露意图　词源：tele 远的 far +graph 写 指写下信息发到远方

87. -gen-, -gener-, -genet- : birth　巧记：gene 基因 指基因繁殖生成

gene [dʒi:n] 基因　词源：gen 繁殖生成

genetic [dʒi'netik] 基因的；遗传学的　词源：gene 基因 +tic 形容词后缀

generic [dʒi'nerik] 一般的，普通的 generic term 通称；（产品）无商标的 generic drugs 没有商标的药物　词源：gene 基因 +ic 形容词后缀 指和普通基因基本一样的

genius ['dʒi:niəs] 天才 musical / comic / mathematical genius 音乐/喜剧/数学等天才；天赋 an architect of genius 天才建筑师　词源：gene 基因 +i 人 +us 名词后缀 指基因上有天赋的人

genesis ['dʒenisis] 开端 the genesis of the myth 神话故事的起源；世界起源；创世纪　词源：gen 繁殖生成 +sis 名词后缀 指基因生成是生命开端

genuine ['dʒenjuin] 真心实意的，真诚的 a genuine person 真诚的人；（感情或欲望）真正的 genuine interest 真正的兴趣；（物品）真的，正品的　词源：gene 基因 +ine 形容词后缀 指基因上是真的

general ['dʒen(ə)r(ə)l] 普遍的；总体的；大致的；将军　词源：gene 基因 + al 形容词后缀　指基因存在的普遍性

generous ['dʒen(ə)rəs] 慷慨的，大方的；大量的，丰富的 a generous glass of wine 一大杯葡萄酒；宽宏大量的　词源：gen 繁殖生成 + ous 形容词后缀（表示过多的）指古罗马鼓励生育，生得越多对国家越慷慨

generosity [dʒenə'rɔsəti] 慷慨大方 an act of generosity 慷慨的行为　词源：generous 慷慨的 + ity 名词后缀

generate ['dʒenəreit] 生成（电或热）；产生创造 generate revenue 创造收益　词源：gen 繁殖生成 + ate 动词后缀

generation [dʒenə'reiʃ(ə)n] 生成，产生 the generation of electricity 发电；一代人 generation gap 代沟；一代产品 the new generation of computers 新一代的计算机　词源：gen 繁殖生成 + tion 名词后缀

genre ['ʒɔnrə]（艺术、写作、音乐）体裁，流派，风格 a movie genre 电影体裁　词源：gene 基因　指基因上的不同带来风格的多样

germ [dʒɜːm] 细菌；胚胎细胞，干细胞 germ cells；萌芽 the germ of an idea / theory / feeling 观念/理论/感情的萌芽　词源：ge 繁殖生成 + r 分裂 + m 山　指细菌像山上的植物一样不停繁殖

hygiene ['haidʒiːn] 卫生，保健　词源：hy 高 high + gene 基因　指保持高水平的健康基因是讲卫生

ingenious [in'dʒiːniəs]（人）心灵手巧的；（设备）精巧的 an ingenious device　词源：in 内部 + gene 基因 + i 人 + ous 形容词后缀（表示过多的）指人内心创造性基因非常多的　形近易混词：ingenuous

ingenuous [in'dʒenjuəs] 纯真无邪的，阅历浅的 an ingenuous smile 纯真的微笑　词源：in 内部 + gene 基因 + u 水 + ous 形容词后缀（表示过多的）指人的思想像水一样单纯

ingenuity [ˌindʒi'njuːiti] 心灵手巧，足智多谋　词源：in 内部 + gene 基因 + niu 牛 + ity 名词后缀　指内心有很牛很厉害的创造性基因

organ ['ɔːg(ə)n] 器官；管风琴；政府机构 government organs　词源：or 嘴 + gene 基因　指基因生成的嘴是基本器官

organic [ɔː'gænik] 器官的；有机的，无农药的 organic food / vegetables / milk 有机食品/蔬菜/牛奶　词源：organ 器官 + ic 形容词后缀

organism ['ɔːg(ə)niz(ə)m] 有机生物；微生物；组织机构　词源：organ 器官 + ism 名词后缀

88. **-habit-** : live, dwell　巧记：habit 习惯　指习惯性的居住

cohabit [kəu'hæbit] 未婚同居 cohabit with sb.　词源：co 共同 + habit 居住　指住在一起

habitat ['hæbitæt]（动植物）栖息地 the protection of wildlife habitat 野生动植物生存环境的保护　词源：habit 居住 + at 在　指动植物栖息在某地

habitation [hæbi'teiʃ(ə)n]（人的）居住（不可数名词）signs of habitation 有人居住的迹象；居住地，住处（可数名词）the scattered habitations 分散的住处　词源：habit 居住 + tion 名词后缀

habitable ['hæbitəbl] 适宜居住的 a habitable city / planet 宜居的城市/星球　词源：habit 居住 + able 形容词后缀（表示可以……的）

habit ['hæbit] 习性；习惯；（吸毒、喝酒、抽烟的）瘾；（修道士或修女穿的）宗教长袍　词源：habit 居住

habitude ['hæbitjuːd] 民风，习俗；性情，气质 a lifelong habitude for talking too much 话多的性情　词源：habit 居住 + tude 名词后缀

inhabit [in'hæbit]（人或动物）居住 inhabited islands 有人居住的岛屿　词源：in 内部 + habit 居住　指居住到某地 live in

inhabitant [in'hæbit(ə)nt] 居民 a city of one million inhabitants 有 100 万居民的城市　词源：inhabit 居住 + ant 名词后缀

89. -her-, -hes- : stick, cling　巧记：her 她（母亲）指孩子黏着妈妈的状态

adhere [əd'hiə] 黏附，附着 adhere to sth.；坚持遵守（原则，法律，规章，信念）adhere to the principles 坚守原则　词源：ad 强调 + her 黏　指紧紧粘贴附着

adherent [əd'hiər(ə)nt]（政党、思想的）追随者，拥护者，信徒　词源：adhere 坚守 + ent 名词后缀

adhesion [əd'hiːʒ(ə)n] 黏附，黏附力 the adhesion of water drop to the leaf surface 水滴在叶子表面的黏附　词源：adhere 黏 + sion 名词后缀

adhesive [əd'hiːsiv] 黏合剂 waterproof adhesive 防水黏合剂；黏合的 adhesive tape 胶带　词源：adhere 黏 + sive 形容词后缀（表示充满活力的 active）

cohere [kə(u)'hiə]（观点、论点、信念、陈述）连贯一致 cohere with sth.；（物体）黏合　词源：co 共同 + her 黏　指黏在一起保持一致

cohesive [kəu'hiːsiv] 团结的,有凝聚力的 a cohesive force 凝聚力　词源：cohere 黏合 + sive 形容词后缀（表示充满活力的 active）

cohesion [kə(u)'hiːʒ(ə)n]（句子、文章等在语法或含义方面的）连贯一致；团结，凝聚力　词源：cohere 黏合 + sion 名词后缀

coherence [kə(u)'hiər(ə)ns; kə(u)'hiərəns] 连贯性，条理性，一致性 essay coherence 文章连贯；凝聚力　词源：cohere 黏合 + ence 名词后缀

coherent [kə(u)'hiər(ə)nt] 有条理的，一致的，连贯的 a coherent account of the event 对事件前后一致的陈述；（话语等）条理清楚的，易于理解的；（团体成员）目标一致的，有共同信念的　词源：cohere 黏合 + ent 形容词后缀（表示具有……能力的）

hesitate ['heziteit] 犹豫 hesitate about / over sth.　词源：hes 黏 + it 它 + ate 动词后缀　指粘连着藕断丝连般犹豫

hesitant ['hezit(ə)nt] 犹豫的 be hesitant to do sth.　词源：hesitate 犹豫 + ant 形容词后缀（表

示具有……能力的）

hesitation [hezi'teiʃn] 犹豫　词源：hesitate 犹豫 + tion 名词后缀

inhere [in'hiə(r)] 成为（某物）固有的一部分 the meanings which inhere in words 词语中的含义　词源：in 内部 + her 黏 指粘连在内部

inherent [in'hiər(ə)nt; -'her(ə)nt] 内在的，固有的 an inherent defect in the design 设计的内在缺陷　词源：inhere 成为（某物）固有的一部分 + ent 形容词后缀（表示具有……能力的）　同义词：intrinsic / innate

90. **-hered-, -herit-**：heir　巧记：her 她的 指她的后代

heir [eə] 男性继承人 heir to the throne 储君；（工作或传统的）继承者，承袭者，传人，接班人　词源：heir 继承人

heiress ['eəris] 女性继承人　词源：heir 继承人 + ess 名词后缀

inherit [in'herit] 继承（金钱，财产）inherit sth. from sb.；经遗传得到（父母的性格或外貌）；接手，承担（别人造成的问题）　词源：in 内部 + herit 继承人 指走到宫殿里成为继承人把东西继承拿走

inheritance [in'herit(ə)ns]（金钱，财产）家庭遗产；遗传特征 genetic inheritance 基因遗传特征　词源：inherit 继承 + ance 名词后缀

heritage ['heritidʒ]（文化）遗产，传统 cultural heritage 文化遗产　词源：herit 继承人 + age 时期 指继承人长期传承文化传统

hereditary [hi'redit(ə)ri]（疾病）遗传性的 a hereditary illness；（头衔）世袭的 a hereditary title　词源：hered 继承人 + ary 形容词后缀

91. **hemi-**：half　巧记：前缀 semi（表示一半 half）的变形 semi-final 半决赛

hemisphere ['hemisfiə] 半球 the northern hemisphere 北半球　词源：hemi 一半 + sphere 球体 指半个球体

hemicycle ['hemi,saikl] 半圆　词源：hemi 一半 + cycle 圆 指半个圆

92. **hiero-**：holy　巧记：hero 英雄 指英雄的功绩是神圣的

hieroglyph ['haiərəglif] 象形文字　词源：hiero 神圣的 + graph 写 指象形文字是神圣的描绘

hieroglyphic ['haiərəglifik] 象形文字的　词源：hieroglyph 象形文字 + ic 形容词后缀

hierarchy ['haiərɑːki] 等级，等级制度 a rigid hierarchy 严格的等级制度；统治最高层，统治集团 the church hierarchy 教会高层　词源：hier 神圣的 + arch 拱门（象征统治）指神圣统治

93. **homeo-, homo-**：the same　巧记：home 家 指一家人的是相同的

homophone ['hɔməfəun; 'həum-] 同音异义词　词源：homo 相同的 + phone 声音 指发音相

同但拼写和含义不同的词（hair 头发和 hare 兔子）

homosexual [ˌhɔmə(u)'sekʃuəl; ˌhəum-; -sjuəl] 同性恋的　词源：homo 相同的 + sex 性别 + ual 形容词后缀

homogeneous [ˌhɔmə(u)'dʒiːniəs; -'dʒen-] 同种族的，同类的 a homogeneous society 同种族人组成的社会　词源：homo 相同的 + gene 基因 + ous 形容词后缀（表示过多的）指基因上相同的人是同种族的

homogeneity [ˌhɔmədʒə'niːəti] 同种；同一性　词源：homo 相同的 + gene 基因 + ity 名词后缀　指相同基因的同一性

94. **-hospit-, -host-** : guest　巧记：hold 拿 + ost 最高级　指把人捧着当贵客

host [həust] 节目主持人 game show host 游戏节目主持人；举办 host the World Cup 举办世界杯；东道主，主办国 host city 主办城市；大量，许多 a host of sb. / sth.　词源：hold 拿 + ost 最高级　指拿在手里举起举办活动的旗帜

hostess ['həustis; -es; həu'stes] 聚会的女主人；女节目主持人；女招待女领班　词源：host 主持人 + ess 名词后缀

hospital ['hɔspit(ə)l] 医院　词源：hospit 宾客 + al 名词后缀　指医院像酒店照顾宾客一样细致入微照顾病人

hospitable [hɔ'spitəb(ə)l; 'hɔspit-] 好客的,热情友好的；（植物生长条件）适宜的 a hospitable climate 宜人的气候　词源：hospit 宾客 + able 形容词后缀（表示可以……的）指可以作为宾客对待的　巧记：hospital 医院　指医院对待病人的态度是热情友好的

hospitality [hɔspi'tæliti] 好客；（款待客人、顾客等的）食物，饮料，服务；招待，款待 corporate hospitality 公司对顾客的热情招待　词源：hospitable 好客的 + ity 名词后缀

inhospitable [ˌinhɔ'spitəbl] 不好客的；不适宜居住的　词源：in 否定 + hospitable 好客的

hotel [həu'tel; əu-] 旅馆　词源：host 宾客 + el 名词后缀　指客人休息的地方　形近易混词：motel

motel [məu'tel] 汽车旅馆　词源：motor 汽车发动机 + hotel 旅馆　指给开车旅行的人住的旅馆

hostage ['hɔstidʒ] 人质　词源：host 宾客 + age 时期　指把客人长时期当宾客扣押

hostile ['hɔstail] 敌对的,敌意的 a hostile attitude 敌意的态度；强烈反对的 be hostile to sth.；（生存环境）恶劣的 hostile environment　词源：hostage 人质 + ile 形容词后缀（表示容易……的）指人质容易对外人产生敌意的

hostility [hɔ'stiliti] 敌意,敌对 hostility towards foreign cultures 对外国文化的敌意；强烈反对 a lot of public hostility to the tax 公开反对税收　词源：hostile 敌意的 + ity 名词后缀

95. **-hum-** : ground　巧记：h 高 high + u 水 + m 山　指高山上的水土

human ['hjuːmən] 人；人的；人类；有人情味的　词源：hum 土地 + an 名词后缀　指希腊神话普罗米修斯用河水和泥土造出人类

humane [hju'mein] 人道的，仁慈的 the humane treatment of refugee 人道地对待难民　词源：human 人

humor ['hju:mə] 幽默；迁就，迎合 humor sb.　词源：human 人类 指人类会幽默搞笑、逗人开心、迎合别人

humorous ['hju:m(ə)rəs] 幽默的，诙谐的　词源：humor 幽默 + ous 形容词后缀（表示过多的）

inhume [in'hju:m] 埋葬，土葬　词源：in 内部 + hum 土地 指埋入土地

exhume [eks'(h)ju:m; ig'zju:m] 挖出遗体　词源：ex 出来 + hum 土地 指挖出土地

humble ['hʌmbl] 卑贱的 humble house 寒舍；谦虚的　词源：hum 土地 + ble 形容词后缀（表示可以……的）指像土地一样被踩踏而谦卑的

humility [hju'militi] 谦虚，谦恭　词源：humble 谦虚的 + l 长时间 long + ity 名词后缀

humid ['hju:mid]（天气）潮湿闷热的 a hot and humid summer 炎热潮湿的夏天　词源：hum 土地 + id 形容词后缀（表示具有某种身份 identity）指土地里含水多

humidity [hju'miditi]（空气）湿度；湿热　词源：humid 湿热的 + ity 名词后缀

humiliate [hju'milieit] 使蒙羞，羞辱　词源：hum 土地 + l 长时间 long + ate 动词后缀 指向人长时间扔土块羞辱对方

humiliation [,hju:mili'eiʃn] 耻辱，羞辱，丢脸　词源：humiliate 羞辱 + tion 名词后缀

humanitarian [hju,mæni'teəriən] 人道主义的 humanitarian aid 人道主义援助；人道主义者　词源：human 人类 + tarian 名词后缀

96. **hydro-** : water, hydrogen　巧记：Hydra 古希腊神话沼泽中的九头蛇海德拉 指难以根除的祸患

hydropower ['haidrə(u)pauə] 水力发电　词源：hydro 水 + power 能量

hydroplane ['haidrəplein] 水上飞机　词源：hydro 水 + plane 飞机

hydrology [hai'drɔlədʒi] 水文学　词源：hydro 水 + ology 名词后缀（表示学科）

hydrate [hai'dreit , 'haidreit] 供给水分 lotions that hydrate the skin 补水护肤液；含水化合物　词源：hydro 水 + ate 动词后缀

hydrophobia [,haidrə(u)'fəubiə] 狂犬病；恐水症　词源：hydro 水 + phobia 恐惧 fear

dehydrate [di:hai'dreit; di:'haidreit] 使脱水 the dehydrating effects of alcohol 酒精引起的脱水　词源：de 否定 + hydrate 供给水分

carbohydrate [kɑ:bə'haidreit] 碳水化合物，糖类　词源：carbon 碳 + hydro 水 + ate 名词后缀

hydrant ['haidrənt] 消防栓，消防龙头　词源：hydro 水 + ant 名词后缀

hydrogen ['haidrədʒ(ə)n] 氢　词源：hydro 水 + gen 生成 指水分解后产生的氢元素

97. **hypo-, hyp-** : below, decrease　巧记：hippo 河马 指河马在水下

hypothesis [hai'pɔθisis] 假说，猜想 confirm a hypothesis 证实假设　词源：hypo 下面 +

thesis 论点 指在下面未经证实的观点

hypocrisy [hi'pɔkrisi] 虚伪，伪善　词源：hypo 下面 + cri 批评 criticize + sy 名词后缀　指在下面暗地里批评

hypocritical [ˌhipə'kritikl] 虚伪的，伪善的，假惺惺的　词源：hypocrisy 伪善 + cal 形容词后缀　反义词：sincere

hypocrite ['hipəkrit] 伪君子，虚伪的人　词源：hypocrisy 伪善 + ite 名词后缀

hypodermic [haipə(u)'də:mik] 皮下注射器；皮下注射的 a hypodermic needle 皮下注射器针头　词源：hypo 下面 + derm 皮肤 skin 指在皮肤下面的

hypothermia [ˌhaipə'θə:miə] 体温过低　词源：hypo 下面 + therm 热 heat 指体温热度偏向下的

98. **hyper-**：extreme　巧记：hy 高 high + up 向上 + er 比较级　指越来越高的

hypersensitive [ˌhaipə'sensətiv] 过敏的 be hypersensitive to pollen 对花粉过敏；心胸狭隘的　词源：hyper 极度的 + sensitive 敏感的　同义词：allergic

hyperslow ['haipəsləu] 极慢的　词源：hyper 极度的 + slow 缓慢的

hyperactive [ˌhaipər'æktiv]（儿童）过分活跃的，多动的　词源：hyper 极度的 + active 活跃的

hypermarket ['haipəmɑ:kit] 大型超级市场　词源：hyper 极度的 + market 市场

hypertension [haipə'tenʃ(ə)n] 高血压　词源：hyper 极度的 + tension 拉力张力

hypercritical [haipə'kritik(ə)l] 挑剔苛求的，吹毛求疵　词源：hyper 极度的 + critical 批评的

hypercritic ['haipə'kritik] 苛求的人　词源：hyper 极度的 + critic 批判者

99. **-emper-, -imper-**：command　巧记：em 拿出 take + per 权力 power 指运用权力指挥命令

emperor ['emp(ə)rə] 皇帝　词源：emper 命令 + or 名词后缀

empress ['empris] 女皇；皇后　词源：emper 命令 + ess 名词后缀

empire ['empaiə] 帝国；大企业集团 a business empire　词源：emper 命令 指由权力命令支配的帝国

empirical [im'pirikl] 以实验（或经验）为依据的，经验主义的 empirical knowledge 实际经验中获得的知识　词源：empire 帝国 + cal 形容词后缀 指支配指挥帝国要以经验为依据的

imperial [im'piəriəl] 帝国的 imperial expansion 帝国的扩张　词源：imper 命令 + ial 形容词后缀

imperialism [im'piəriəliz(ə)m] 帝国主义；扩张主义 cultural / economic imperialism 文化/经济扩张　词源：imperial 帝国的 + ism 名词后缀

imperious [im'piəriəs] 专横的，飞扬跋扈的 an imperious gesture / voice / command 盛气凌人的姿势/语调/命令　词源：imper 命令 + ous 形容词后缀（表示过多的）指发布命令

过多的是专横的

imperative [im'perətiv] 强制的，必须的 it is imperative (for sb.) to do sth.；当务之急的事，紧急的事；命令语气的 an imperative sentence 祈使句；祈使语气　词源：imper 命令 + tive 形容词后缀（表示充满活力的 active）指命令的话语是必须执行的

100. **-luc-** : light　巧记：l 光 light + u 水　指水反射的光

allure [ə'luə(r)] 诱惑，魅力，吸引力 the allure of the city 城市的吸引力　词源：al 强调 + lu 光　指光亮吸引人

alluring [ə'luərɪŋ] 吸引人的 an alluring smile 迷人的微笑　词源：allure 吸引力 + ing 形容词后缀

lure [l(j)uə] 吸引力；勾引，诱惑 lure sb. into (doing) sth.；诱饵，鱼饵　词源：lu 光　指利用光亮诱惑

lust [lʌst] 强烈的欲望 lust for power 强烈的权力欲望　词源：lu 光 + ust 最高级　指最亮的　巧记：last 持续　指持续很久的强烈欲望

luxury ['lʌkʃ(ə)ri] 奢华，奢侈；奢侈品 luxury goods　词源：lux 光亮 + ury 名词后缀　指发光的奢侈品　巧记：lux 力士香皂

elucidate [i'lu:sideit] 阐明，说明　词源：e 出来 + luc 光亮 + id 身份 identity + ate 动词后缀　指让文字见光亮

illuminate [i'l(j)u:mineit] 照亮，点亮 an illuminated city 被点亮的城市；阐明，解释　词源：il 强调 + lu 光亮 + mini 小 + ate 动词后缀　指让一点点见光亮

illustrate ['iləstreit] 图例说明；做插图 an illustrated textbook 有插图的课本　词源：il 强调 + lu 光亮 + strate 直接 straight + ate 动词后缀　指让文字见光配图直接说明

illustration [ilə'streiʃ(ə)n] 示例说明；插图，图解；实例，例证　词源：illustrate 说明 + tion 名词后缀

illustrator ['iləstreitə]（图书）插图画家　词源：illustrate 说明 + or 名词后缀

illusion [i'l(j)u:ʒ(ə)n] 幻觉，错觉 an illusion of greater space 空间变大的错觉　词源：ill 生病的 + lu 光亮 + sion 名词后缀　指生病的人看到光亮出现幻觉

disillusion [ˌdisi'l(j)u:ʒ(ə)n] 使醒悟　词源：dis 否定 + illusion 幻觉　指打破幻觉

delusion [di'l(j)u:ʒ(ə)n] 错觉，妄想 the delusions of the psychos 精神病患者的妄想　词源：de 否定 + lu 光亮 + sion 名词后缀　指不正常的光亮导致妄想

lucid ['lu:sid]（文字表达）清楚的 a lucid writing style 明白易懂的写作风格；（生病或犯糊涂中偶尔）头脑神志清醒的　词源：luc 光亮 + id 形容词后缀（表示具有某种身份 identity）

lucent ['lu:snt] 发光的 a lucent orb 发光的天体；透明的，清澈的 lucent mountain streams 清澈透明的山间溪流；朗讯科技公司　词源：lu 光亮 + ent 形容词后缀（表示具有……能力的）

luminous ['lu:minəs] 发光的，夜明的，夜光的 luminous paint 发光涂料；色彩鲜艳的

luminous green 翠绿色　词源：lu 光亮 + mini 小 + ous 形容词后缀（表示过多的）指远处点点发光的

luminary ['luːmɪnəri] 名人，杰出人物 luminaries of fashion community 时尚界的名流　词源：lu 光亮 + mini 小 + ary 名词后缀　指天上发光的星星象征杰出人物

translucent [trænsˈluːsnt] 半透明的 translucent glass 半透明玻璃　词源：trans 穿越 + lucent 发光的　指穿越后有光亮的

101. -part- : divide, part　巧记：part 部分

party ['pɑːti] 政党；聚会，派对；一组；（协议的）一方；玩乐　词源：part 部分 + ty 名词后缀　指一部分人的聚集

parliament ['pɑːləm(ə)nt] 议会，国会；英国议会　词源：parlour 客厅 + ment 名词后缀　指能装下许多议员的大厅　巧记：party 政党　指政党组成议会

partisan ['pɑːtɪzæn; ˌpɑːtɪˈzæn] 党羽，党徒，铁杆分子；过分支持的，偏护的，盲目拥护的；（抗击侵略者的）游击队员　词源：party 党派 + an 名词后缀

particle ['pɑːtɪk(ə)l] 颗粒，微粒 dust particles 尘埃；粒子；微量，一点　词源：part 部分 + cle 名词后缀　指分割出来的颗粒部分

particular [pəˈtɪkjələ(r)] 特殊的；挑剔的，吹毛求疵的 be particular about / over sth.　词源：part 部分 + cular 形容词后缀　指特殊的部分

partial ['pɑːʃ(ə)l] 部分的 a partial solution to the problem 部分解决问题；偏爱的 be partial to sth.；偏袒的，不公平的 be partial to sb.　词源：part 部分 + ial 形容词后缀（表示特殊的 special）指特别喜欢某部分的

partiality [ˌpɑːʃɪˈæləti] 偏爱 a partiality for durian 偏爱榴莲；偏袒 partiality in news reporting 新闻报道中有失公正　词源：partial 偏爱的 + ity 名词后缀

impartial [ɪmˈpɑːʃ(ə)l] 公平的，公正的 an impartial inquiry 公正的调查　词源：im 否定 + partial 偏袒的　指不偏袒的　同义词：fair

impartiality [ɪmˌpɑːʃɪˈæləti] 公平，公正　词源：im 否定 + partiality 偏袒　指不偏袒

impart [ɪmˈpɑːt] 给予（某种品质）impart an Arabian flavour to the dish 给菜添加了一种阿拉伯风味；传授知识；告知消息 impart sth. to sb.　词源：im 内部 + part 部分　指把一部分信息传授到内部

impair [ɪmˈpeə] 削弱，损害　词源：im 否定 + pair 一对　指拆散一对组合削弱实力　同义词：damage

apartment [əˈpɑːtm(ə)nt] 公寓，房间　词源：a 正在 + part 部分 + ment 名词后缀　指被分成许多部分的空间是房间

compartment [kəmˈpɑːtm(ə)nt]（车厢卧铺）隔间；（厕所）隔间；（家具或塑料盒）隔层 a clear plastic storage box with 20 compartments 有 20 格的透明塑料储物盒　词源：com 共同 + part 部分 + ment 名词后缀　指整体被分为若干部分用来放置物品

department [dɪˈpɑːtm(ə)nt]（政府、学校、商场的）部门　词源：de 向下 + part 部分 + ment

名词后缀 指向下分割成不同的职能部分是部门

depart [di'pɑːt] 启程离开 depart from…for…；背离，违反常规 depart from the routine 一反常态；离职 depart one's job　词源：de 否定 + part 部分 指分离出的部分，离开整体

departure [di'pɑːtʃə] 启程出发；脱离（组织）；背离违反（惯例传统）　词源：depart 离开 + ture 名词后缀

partition [pɑː'tiʃ(ə)n] 隔墙，隔板 glass partition 玻璃隔板；硬盘分区 hard drive partition；分割国家 the post-war partition of the nation 战后对国家的分割　词源：part 部分 + it 它 + tion 名词后缀 指把空间分成若干部分的隔板

repartition [ˌriːpɑː'tiʃən] 重新分割，再分配　词源：re 反复 + partition 分割 指再次分割

participate [pɑː'tisipeit] 参与，参加 participate in sth.　词源：part 部分 + cip 拿 take + ate 动词后缀 指参与 take part in sth.

participatory [pɑːˌtisi'peitəri] 众人参与的　词源：participate 参与 + ory 形容词后缀

participation [pɑːˌtisi'peiʃn] 参与，参加　词源：participate 参与 + tion 名词后缀

partake [pɑː'teik] 参与，参加，分担 partake in sth.；吃，喝，享用 partake of some refreshment 吃些点心饮料　词源：part 部分 + take 拿 指拿起一部分食物吃喝　词义连记：参与活动的主要目的是吃喝茶点饮料

102. -cid-, -cis- : kill, cut　巧记：cut 切

accident ['æksidənt] 意外　词源：ac 强调 + cid 切杀 + ent 名词后缀 指有伤亡的意外事件

accidental [ˌæksi'dent(ə)l] 意外的 an accidental discharge of toxic gas 有毒气体的意外泄漏　词源：accident 意外 + al 形容词后缀

concise [kən'sais] 简明的，简洁的 a concise dictionary 简明词典　词源：con 共同 + cis 切杀 指一起举刀把复杂的整体切成简明的部分

decide [di'said] 决定，下决心 decide to do sth.；裁决 decide disputes 裁决争端　词源：de 向下 + cid 切杀 指下决心向下切除隐患

decision [di'siʒ(ə)n] 决定 make a decision；判决，裁决 the ultimate power of decision 最终的判决权；决断力，果断　词源：decide 下决心 + sion 名词后缀

decisive [di'saisiv] 决定性的,关键的 decisive factor 决定因素；果断的,决断的 take decisive action 采取果断行动；明确的，确定的 a decisive answer 明确的答案　词源：decide 下决心 + sive 形容词后缀（表示充满活力的 active）

excision [ik'siʒn] 切除 the excision of the tumour 肿瘤切除　词源：ex 出来 + cis 切杀 + sion 名词后缀

incident ['insid(ə)nt] 意外事件；政治事变；（两国间的）摩擦，冲突 a border / diplomatic incident 边境/外交冲突　词源：in 内部 + accident 意外 + ent 名词后缀 指给内心带来影响的重大意外事件

incidence ['insid(ə)ns]（不好的事的）发生率 a high incidence of crime 高犯罪率　词源：

incident 意外事件 + ence 名词后缀 指意外事件发生的频率

coincide [ˌkəuin'said] 同时发生，巧合 coincide with sth.；（想法观点）一致；相交，重叠，位置重合　词源：co 共同 + incide 意外事件 incident 指事件同时发生

coincident [kəu'insidənt] 同时发生的，巧合的 be coincident with sth.　词源：coincide 同时发生 + ent 形容词后缀（表示具有……能力的）

coincidence [kəu'insid(ə)ns] 巧合 What a coincidence! 真巧！；（思想观点）一致　词源：coincide 同时发生 + ence 名词后缀

incisive [in'saisiv] 切中要害的，深刻的 incisive analysis 深刻的分析　词源：in 内部 + cis 切杀 + sive 形容词后缀（表示充满活力的 active）指切入问题内部的

incision [in'siʒ(ə)n] 手术切口　词源：in 内部 + cis 切杀 + sion 名词后缀 指身体内部切口

incisor [in'saizə(r)] 门牙　词源：in 内部 + cis 切杀 + or 名词后缀 指能切食物的牙齿

insecticide [in'sektisaid] 家用杀虫剂　词源：insect 昆虫 + cid 切杀 指能杀昆虫的药剂

precise [pri'sais] 精确的 precise sales data 准确的销售数据；（人）细心的　词源：pre 在前面 + cis 切杀 指提前瞄准好精确切分

pesticide ['pestisaid] 杀害虫剂，农药　词源：pest 害虫 + cid 切杀 指消灭害虫的药剂

suicide ['s(j)uːisaid] 自杀　词源：sui 自己 self + cid 切杀　巧记：sui 谐音"隋"隋炀帝自尽

103. -flat-：blow　巧记：fl 飞行 fly + at 在……状态 指风吹起来飞行的状态

inflate [in'fleit] 使充气，膨胀 inflate the rubber dinghy 给橡皮筏充好气；吹嘘，吹捧 inflate one's self-confidence 自我膨胀；涨价，通货膨胀 inflate prices　词源：in 内部 + flat 吹气 指从内部充气

inflation [in'fleiʃ(ə)n] 充气；通货膨胀　词源：inflate 充气 + tion 名词后缀

deflation [di'fleiʃ(ə)n] 放气；通货紧缩　词源：de 否定 + inflation 充气 指不充气

deflate [di'fleit] 使放气，漏气 deflate a tyre 给轮胎放气；挫（人）傲气 deflate sb.；击破论点 deflate one's argument；通货紧缩　词源：de 否定 + flat 吹气 指不吹气

conflate [kən'fleit] 混合，合并 a city of conflated races and cultures 一座融合了多民族和多文化的城市；拼凑攒（文本或论文）　词源：con 共同 + flat 吹气 指把别人的论文放在一起吹嘘成自己的成果

conflation [kən'fleiʃən] 混合，合并；拼凑攒（文本或论文）　词源：conflate 合并 + tion 名词后缀

reflate [ˌriː'fleit] 使再通货膨胀　词源：re 反复 + inflate 通货膨胀 指再次通胀

reflation [ˌriː'fleiʃn] 再通货膨胀　词源：reflate 使再通胀 + tion 名词后缀

104. -nov-：new　巧记：nova 新星 华为 nova 系列手机

novel ['nɒv(ə)l] 长篇小说；新颖的，新奇的 a novel design 新设计　词源：nov 新的 + l 长时间 指小说精彩的内容过长时间对读者都是新颖的

novelette [ˌnɒvə'let] 中篇小说（尤指被认为写得很蹩脚的浪漫传奇小说） 词源：novel 长篇小说 + lette 小 little 指比长篇小说篇幅短一些的是中篇小说

novelty ['nɒv(ə)lti] 新颖；新奇新鲜的事物；新颖小巧而价廉的物品 词源：novel 新颖的 + ty 名词后缀

innovate ['inəveit] 创新，改革 词源：in 内部 + nov 新的 + ate 动词后缀 指内心创新

innovative ['inəvətiv] 创新的 词源：innovate 创新 + tive 形容词后缀（表示充满活力的 active）

innovation [inə'veiʃ(ə)n] 创新 词源：innovate 创新 + tion 名词后缀

innovator ['inəveitə(r)] 创新者 词源：innovate 创新 + or 名词后缀

renovate ['renəveit] 翻新整修（房子） 词源：re 反复 + nov 新的 + ate 动词后缀 指重新翻新房子

renovation [ˌrenə'veiʃn] 翻新整修（房子） 词源：renovate 翻修 + tion 名词后缀

novice ['nɒvis] 新手，初学者 novice brokers 经纪人新手；新信徒，见习修士修女 词源：nov 新的 + vice 副的 指新入行只能做副手的人

novitiate [nəu'viʃieit] 实习期，见习期 词源：novice 新手 指作为新手的见习期

105. **-hibit-**：hold 巧记：hold it a bit 的缩写形式

inhibit [in'hibit] 抑制；使羞怯 inhibit sb. from doing sth. 词源：in 内部 + hibit 拿住 指内心里拿住羞怯做某事

inhibited [in'hibitid] 拘谨的，受约束的 词源：inhibit 抑制 + ed 形容词后缀

exhibit [ig'zibit; eg-] 展出；展现（气质、情感或能力）；展览会；展品；（法庭）证物 词源：ex 出来 + hibit 拿住 指拿出来展示

exhibition [eksi'biʃ(ə)n] 展览会；展览；（某种技能、感情或行为的）展现；出洋相 make an exhibition of oneself 词源：exhibit 展出 + tion 名词后缀

prohibit [prə(u)'hibit] 禁止 prohibit sb. from doing sth. 词源：pro 向前 + hibit 拿住 指走上前拿住别人不动

6

106. **-cert-**：certain 巧记：certain 的缩写形式

ascertain [ˌæsə'tein] （警察）查出，探知 ascertain sth. from sb. / sth. 词源：as 强调 + cert 确信 指查清楚明确事实

certify ['sə:tifai] （用证书书面）证明 documents certifying they are in good health 他们的健康证明文件；（经检验）证实 certified accounts 核实过的账目；颁发（或授予）专业合格证书；正式证明（某人）有精神病 词源：cert 确信 + fy 动词后缀

certificate [sə'tifikət] 证书 birth / marriage certificate 出生 / 结婚证明书；毕业文凭 a degree

certificate 学位证书；成绩合格证书　词源：certify 证明 ＋ate 名词后缀　指用来证明资质的书面文件

certitude ['sɜːtɪtjuːd] 确信，确定，有把握 say with absolute certitude 深信不疑地说　词源：cert 确信 ＋tude 名词后缀　指确信的状态

incertitude [in'sɜːtɪtjuːd] 不确定，没把握　词源：in 否定 ＋certitude 确信　指不确信的状态

concert ['kɔnsət] 音乐会；行动一致 in concert with sb. / sth. 与……合作（或同心协力）　词源：con 共同 ＋cert 确信　指音乐家共同确信能完成的音乐会

concerted [kən'sɜːtid]（行动或努力）一致的 a concerted effort / action / attack 一致的努力/行动/攻击　词源：concert 行动一致 ＋ed 形容词后缀

concerto [kən'tʃɜːtəu] 协奏曲 a violin concerto 小提琴协奏曲　词源：concert 音乐会　指一件或几件独奏乐器与管弦乐队竞奏的器乐套曲

disconcert [ˌdɪskən'sɜːt] 使困惑不安　词源：dis 分散 ＋concert 行动一致　指行动分散没有方向使人困惑

disconcerting [ˌdɪskən'sɜːtɪŋ] 令人困惑不安的 a disconcerting question 令人困惑的问题　词源：disconcert 使困惑 ＋ing 形容词后缀

107. circum- : around　巧记：circle 圆圈 ＋u 水 ＋m 山　指水围绕着山一圈

circumscribe ['sɜːkəmskraɪb] 周围画圈，画线；限制，约束　词源：circum 围绕 ＋scribe 写　指画圆圈约束别人自由　比如孙悟空给唐僧画圈

circumspect ['sɜːkəmspekt] 小心谨慎的　词源：circum 围绕 ＋spect 看　指绕着圆圈察看周围的环境　同义词：cautious

circumfluence ['sɜːkəmfluəns] 环流，回流 circumfluence in electricity transmission 电力传输中的环流　词源：circum 围绕 ＋flu 流动 flow ＋ence 名词后缀

circumstance ['sɜːkəmst(ə)ns] 周围环境 in / under … circumstances 在某种情况下；（经济）境况　词源：circum 围绕 ＋st 站立 stand ＋ance 名词后缀　指站在原地周围的围绕的环境

circumference [sə'kʌmf(ə)r(ə)ns] 圆周；周长　词源：circum 围绕 ＋fer 带来 ＋ence 名词后缀　指围绕圆一圈带来的长度　相关词：diameter 直径　radius 半径

108. -clam-, -claim : cry, shout　巧记：cl 靠近 close ＋aim 瞄准　指靠近目标瞄准后大喊开炮

acclaim [ə'kleɪm] 为……欢呼喝彩 a widely acclaimed performance 受到广泛赞扬的演出；称赞 win international acclaim 赢得国际声誉　词源：ac 强调 ＋claim 叫喊　指大家一起叫好

acclamation [ˌæklə'meɪʃn] 欢呼喝彩；（选举以口头表决）赞成　词源：acclaim 喝彩 ＋tion 名词后缀

clamor ['klæmə] 大声喧闹声 the clamour of the market 市场的嘈杂声；大声呼吁 the public clamor for his resignation 民众要求他辞职的呼声　词源：claim 叫喊 + or 名词后缀

clamorous ['klæmərəs] 大叫大喊的，喧闹的　词源：clamor 喧闹声 + ous 形容词后缀（表示过多的）

declaim [di'kleim]（尤指在公众前）慷慨陈词 He declaimed against excessive drinking 强烈抨击酗酒　词源：de 向下 + claim 叫喊　指向下对观众大声说话

declamation [ˌdeklə'meiʃn] 慷慨陈词　词源：declaim 慷慨陈词 + tion 名词后缀

declamatory [di'klæmətəri] 慷慨激昂的 a declamatory speech style 慷慨激昂的演讲风格　词源：declaim 慷慨陈词 + ory 形容词后缀

exclaim [ik'skleim; ek-] 惊呼大叫　词源：ex 出来 + claim 叫喊　指震惊得叫喊出来

exclamation [ˌekskləˈmeiʃ(ə)n] 惊呼 exclamation mark 惊叹号；惊叹词　词源：exclaim 惊呼 + tion 名词后缀

proclaim [prə'kleim]（正式公开）宣布 proclaim a state of emergency 宣布紧急状态；表明，显示　词源：pro 向前 + claim 叫喊　指走到台前大声宣布

proclamation [prɔkləˈmeiʃn] 宣言，公告 the proclamation of independence 宣告独立　词源：proclaim 公开宣布 + tion 名词后缀

reclaim [ri'kleim] 夺回头衔 reclaim the title 夺回冠军；要求收回归还所有物 reclaim the wallet 领回钱包；回收利用（废料）reclaim battery 回收电池；开垦（荒地或沙漠）　词源：re 向后 + claim 叫喊　指大声叫喊要求收回、归还某物

reclamation [ˌrekləˈmeiʃn] 夺回头衔；要求收回归还所有物；回收利用（废料）；开垦（荒地或沙漠）　词源：reclaim 收回 + tion 名词后缀

109. **-fid-, -fess-**：faith, tell　巧记：faith 信念　指宗教对神父 father 的信任

confide [kən'faid] 相信 confide in a doctor's skill 相信医生的医术；吐露（隐私、秘密）confide sth. to sb.；（将贵重物品）托付（自己信任的人保管）　词源：con 共同 + fid 相信吐露　指相信某人并告诉他隐私

confidence ['kɔnfid(ə)ns] 信心 have confidence in sb. / sth.；知心话，秘密 share / exchange confidences 说知心话　词源：confide 相信 + ence 名词后缀

confidant ['kɔnfidænt; ˌkɔnfi'dænt; -dɑ:nt] 心腹，闺蜜，知己　词源：confide 吐露隐私 + ant 名词后缀　指相信并可以吐露隐私的朋友

confidential [kɔnfi'denʃ(ə)l] 机密的，绝密的 keep sth. confidential 保密；（言谈举止）神秘的　词源：confidence 信心 + tial 形容词后缀（表示特殊的 special）指对某物特别的有信心，需要保密的

confidentiality [ˌkɔnfiˌdenʃi'æliti] 机密，绝密 breach of confidentiality 违反保密责任　词源：confidential 机密的 + ity 名词后缀

diffident ['difidənt] 胆怯的，羞怯的 diffident manner / smile / voice 羞怯的举止/微笑/声音　词源：dif 分散 + confident 自信的　指信心分散的，不自信的

diffidence ['difidəns] 无自信心　词源：dif 分散 + confidence 自信　指信心分散，不自信

fidelity [fi'deliti]（对婚姻或原则）忠诚 fidelity to your principles 对原则的忠诚；高保真，逼真度 hi-fi (high fidelity) 高保真音响设备　词源：fid 相信 + ity 名词后缀　指相信感情，对感情忠诚

confess [kən'fes] 承认坦白 confess to (doing) sth.；（向神父）忏悔；（向警方）招供　词源：con 共同 + fess 相信吐露　指完全相信对方向对方坦白

profess [prə'fes] 公开宣称（宗教信仰）；妄称，伪称 profess to be an expert in this subject 自诩为这方面的专家；宣称，公开表明 profess his love for sb. 表示对某人的爱　词源：pro 向前 + fess 相信吐露　指向前走公开吐露

professor [prə'fesə] 教授；宣称者　词源：profess 表明 + or 名词后缀　指公开表明自己看法的人

profession [prə'feʃ(ə)n] 职业，行业；（信仰、信念、观点或感情的）宣称，公开表示，表白 a profession of faith 信仰的宣言　词源：profess 表明 + sion 名词后缀　指最早的职业是宣扬信仰的工作

professional [prə'feʃ(ə)n(ə)l] 职业的；专业的；职业；职业运动员；专业人员　词源：profession 专业 + al 形容词后缀

110. **-solv-, -solut-** : loose　巧记：sol 太阳的 solar + v 或 u 峡谷里的水　指阳光照射使水松弛

absolve [əb'zɔlv] 赦免罪责 absolve sb. from / of sth.　词源：ab 离开 + solv 松开　指离开松绑某人让他离开

absolution [ˌæbsə'luːʃn] 赦免罪责　词源：absolve 赦免 + tion 名词后缀

absolute ['æbsəluːt] 完全的，绝对的 absolute zero 绝对零度　词源：ab 离开 + solute 松开　指完全松开、放手不管的状态

dissolve [di'zɔlv]（使）溶解 sth. dissolve in sth.；解散（议会）；解除（婚姻关系）；终止（商业协议）；使消散，使变弱消失 dissolve one's anger / shyness 消除怒气/羞涩　词源：dis 分散 + solv 松开　指物质在液体中松散分离

dissolute ['disəluːt] 放荡风流的，道德沦丧的　词源：dis 分散 + solut 松开　指道德伦理观分散松散的

resolve [ri'zɔlv] 解决（问题、困难）；（使）分解 extracted and resolved DNA samples 经提取后分解的 DNA 样本；下决心（做某事）resolve to do sth.；决心；（通过投票）作决议，表决；决心，决意 strengthen one's resolve 坚定决心　词源：re 重复 + solve 松开　指重复尝试使问题解开松开

resolution [rezə'luːʃ(ə)n] 解决；坚决果断，坚定；（做某事的）决心 New Year's resolution 新年时下的决心；（经投票后的）正式决议 pass / adopt / approve a resolution 通过决议；（电视、照相机、显微镜、显示器等的）分辨率，清晰度 high / low resolution graphics 高/低清晰度的图形　词源：resolve 解决 + tion 名词后缀

resolute ['rezəlu:t] 坚决的 resolute opposition 坚决的反对；坚定的 resolute leadership 坚定的领导　词源：re 重复 + solut 松开　指重复尝试松开的想法是坚决的、坚定的

solve [sɔlv] 解决（问题）；解答（难题）solve an equation / a puzzle / a riddle 解方程/解难题/解谜　词源：solv 松开　指松开解开问题

solution [sə'lu:ʃ(ə)n] 解决，解决方案；解答，答案；溶液 saline solution 盐溶液　词源：solve 解决 + tion 名词后缀

solvent ['sɔlv(ə)nt] 溶剂；有溶解力的,可溶解的；有偿付能力的,无债务的 stay / remain / keep solvent 无债务　词源：solution 溶液 + ent 形容词后缀（表示具有……能力的）指具有溶解能力的　反义词：insolvent 无偿债能力的，破产的

111. -torqu-, -tort- : twist　巧记：t 方向 to + or 嘴 + t 方向 to　指嘴部可以向任意方向扭曲

contort [kən'tɔ:t]（肢体或面部）扭曲 a face contorted with rage 气歪了的脸　词源：con 共同 + tort 扭曲　指完全扭曲肢体

contortion [kən'tɔ:ʃn]（脸部或躯体的）扭曲，变形；扭曲的动作或姿势　词源：contort 扭曲 + tion 名词后缀

contortionist [kən'tɔ:ʃənist] 柔体杂技演员　词源：contortion 扭曲 + ist 名词后缀

distort [di'stɔ:t]（面部表情）扭曲；（图像、信号、声音）失真 a distorting mirror 哈哈镜；（真相）歪曲 a gross distortion of the fact 对事实的严重歪曲　词源：dis 分散 + tort 扭曲　指分散状态扭曲

extort [ik'stɔ:t; ek-] 敲诈，勒索（钱财）extort sth. from sb.　词源：ex 出来 + tort 扭曲　指扭曲某人拧出钱财　同义词：blackmail

retort [ri'tɔ:t] 反驳，回嘴；曲颈甑，曲颈瓶，蒸馏器　词源：re 向后 + tort 扭曲　指扭曲着嘴反着说话

torch [tɔ:tʃ] 火炬，火把；手电筒　词源：tort 扭曲 + match 火柴　指火炬是用油布扭曲缠绕做的并用火柴点燃的

torture ['tɔ:tʃə]（肉体上或精神上）折磨，煎熬；拷打，拷问　词源：tort 扭曲 + nature 性质　指外力扭曲身体的动作

torment ['tɔ:ment]（尤指精神上）痛苦，折磨；烦扰，捉弄　词源：tort 扭曲 + ment 思想 mind　指思想精神上的扭曲

tortoise ['tɔ:təs] 陆龟；龟　词源：tort 扭曲　指乌龟扭曲的身体外形　相关词：turtle 海龟 Ninja Turtle 忍者神龟

112. -tract-, -treat- : draw, pull　巧记：tr 方向 to + act 使运动　指向某个方向用力使物体运动

tractor ['træktə] 拖拉机　词源：tract 拉动 + or 名词后缀

traction ['trækʃ(ə)n]（使汽车或重物等移动的）牵引力；（医疗治疗骨折复位的）牵引

术　词源：tract 拉动 ＋tion 名词后缀

trace [treis] 仔细找寻 trace sb. / sth.；追溯源头 trace sth. (back) to sth.；迹象，踪迹，痕迹，足迹 vanish without a trace 消失得无影无踪；少量，微量 traces of poison 微量毒物；（利用特殊的电子设备）追踪电话；（大车或马车上的）挽绳，套绳　词源：tract 拉动　指拉动物体后在地面留下的痕迹

tract [trækt] 大片土地 a vast tract of woodland 一大片林地；一组器官系统 the digestive / reproductive / urinary tract 消化道/生殖道/尿道；（宣扬宗教、伦理、道德或政治的）宣传小手册 a tract on the dangers of smoking 讲吸烟危害的小册子　词源：tract 拉动　指拉着犁耕种大片土地

track [træk]（人或动物经常行走踩出来的）小路，小径；（铁路的）铁轨，轨道；（赛跑、赛车等的）跑道 track and field 田径；（唱片、录音带或激光唱片上的）歌曲，曲子；（录音磁带或计算机磁盘的）音轨，声道 soundtrack；（循着踪迹、气味等）追踪，找寻 track the lion to its lair 追踪那头狮子到它的巢穴；（人、兽、车辆等的）轨迹，足迹　词源：tract 拉动 ＋k 表示声音　指拉着东西在路上行走所发出的声音

trail [treil] 拖在后面 a plane trailing a banner 一架拖着横幅标语的飞机；（跟在他人后面）慢吞吞地走，疲惫地走，没精打采地慢走，磨蹭 trail behind sb.；（在体育比赛、竞赛比分或选举中）落后于 trail by two points 落后两分；（打猎时跟踪的）足迹，轨迹；追踪，跟踪 trail sb.；（乡间或森林里的）小路，小径 a trail through the forest 穿过森林的小路　词源：tract 拉动 ＋tail 尾巴　指拖着长长的尾巴慢吞吞地走

attract [ə'trækt] 吸引，招引　词源：at 强调 ＋tract 拉动　指事物有吸引力拉住别人关注它

attractive [ə'træktiv] 吸引人的　词源：attract 吸引 ＋tive 形容词后缀（表示充满活力的 active）

abstract ['æbstrækt] 抽象的；（画、设计等）抽象派的；（论文或书的）摘要；写……摘要　词源：ab 离开 ＋tract 拉动　指从具体中抽拉出的理念是抽象的

contract ['kɔntrækt] 合同，契约 a contract of employment 雇用合同；收缩，缩小 a contracting metal 收缩的金属；感染（疾病）contract a virus 感染病毒　词源：con 共同 ＋tract 拉动　指完全拉动事物各个部分呈现收缩状态

contractor [kən'træktə(r)] 承包人；承包商；承包公司 a building contractor 建筑承包商　词源：contract 合同 ＋or 名词后缀

detract [di'trækt]（价值、成就、快乐）降低，减损，损害 a sudden shower which detracted from enjoyment of the trip 影响旅行兴致的突然阵雨　词源：de 向下 ＋tract 拉动　指价值向下拉动

distract [di'strækt] 使分心，分散（注意力）distract sb. / sth. from sth.　词源：dis 分散 ＋tract 拉动　指把注意力拉扯到分散的状态

protracted [prə'træktid] 旷日持久的，拖延的 protracted disputes / negotiations 持久的争论/谈判　词源：pro 向前 ＋tract 拉动 ＋ed 形容词后缀　指向前拉动使时间延长

retract [ri'trækt]（动物）缩回（壳子）retract into the shell；（飞机）拉回（起落架）retract the undercarriage；收回爪子 retract the claws；收回（说过的话）retract one's statement；撤回，收回（协议、承诺等）retract an offer 撤销提议　词源：re 向后 + tract 拉动 指向后拉动

subtract [səb'trækt] 减去　词源：sub 下面 + tract 拉动 指向下拉动减少上面的数量

treat [tri:t] 请客吃饭 treat sb. to lunch 请某人吃午饭；治疗医治 treat malaria with drugs 用药物医治疟疾；对待看待 treat sb. like / as sth.；（利用化学物质或化学反应）处理 treat sewage 处理污水　词源：treat 拉动 指拉着别人请对方吃饭

treasure ['treʒə] 金银财宝 a pirate's treasure chest 海盗的财宝箱；极贵重的物品，珍宝，宝物，珍品 the priceless art treasures of the gallery 美术馆收藏的无价艺术瑰宝；很有用的人，得力帮手；珍惜，珍视 treasure one's friendship 珍视某人的友谊　词源：treat 对待 + nature 性质 指需要珍视对待的财宝

treaty ['tri:ti]（国家或政府间的）条约 a peace treaty 和平条约　词源：treat 对待 + ty 名词后缀 指国家或政府间如何对待彼此的条约

entreat [in'tri:t] 恳求，乞求 entreat sb. to do sth.　词源：en 使动词化 + treat 对待 指恳求别人善待

maltreat [ˌmæl'tri:t] 虐待（人或动物）　词源：mal 坏的 bad + treat 对待 指不好地对待

mistreat [mis'tri:t] 虐待　词源：mis 否定 + treat 对待 指不好好对待

ill-treat [ˌil 'tri:t] 虐待　词源：ill 否定 + treat 对待 指不好好对待

retreat [ri'tri:t] 军队撤退；后退避让 retreat from public life 退出公众生活；（水、雪或土地）范围缩小；（股价）下挫，下跌；（立场、想法的）改变 a retreat from hard-line policies 放弃强硬政策；静修地，静养所 a country retreat 乡村静居所　词源：re 向后 + treat 拉动 指向后拉动后退

---

113. -turb-：disorder　巧记：turn 转变 turn to be sth. 的缩写形式

disturb [di'stə:b] 打扰干扰，使事情中断；弄乱，挪动（某物）位置 disturb the papers 弄乱文件；扰乱治安　词源：dis 分散 + turb 混乱 指使分散混乱

disturbing [di'stə:biŋ] 令人不安烦扰的　词源：disturb 扰乱 + ing 形容词后缀

disturbance [di'stə:b(ə)ns] 打扰干扰；动乱骚动；精神失常　词源：disturb 扰乱 + ance 名词后缀

perturb [pə'tə:b] 使长期烦扰，焦虑　词源：per 一直 + turb 混乱 指使一直处于混乱烦恼的状态

perturbed [pə'tə:bd] 忧虑的，不安的 a perturbed young man 烦恼的年轻人　词源：perturb 长期烦扰 + ed 形容词后缀

turbine ['tə:bain; -in] 涡轮机 wind turbine 风力涡轮（发电）机　词源：turb 混乱 指涡轮机搅动使水流或气流混乱

turbulent ['tə:bjul(ə)nt] 海洋天气汹涌狂暴的，风大浪高的 turbulent sea / storm / water / air 波涛汹涌的大海/风暴/水/气；（社会、政治、地区）动荡的 the turbulent times of the revolution 革命的动荡时期　词源：turb 混乱 + l 长时期 long + ent 形容词后缀（表示具有……能力的）指长期混乱的

turbulence ['tɜːbjul(ə)ns]（空气和水的）湍流紊流，不稳定的强气流 severe turbulence during the flight 飞行中强烈的气流；社会动荡 a period of political turbulence after the war 战后的一段政治动荡时期　词源：turb 混乱 + l 长时期 long + ence 名词后缀

114. -doc-, -doct- : teach　巧记：do 做 + act 行动 指教别人做事的行为

docent ['dəusnt]（博物馆、画廊、教堂等景点）向导，讲解员　词源：doc 教导 + ent 名词后缀 指教别人知识的有能力的人

doctor ['dɒktə] 医生；博士；窜改，做手脚 doctor the figures 篡改数字；在（食物或饮料）中添加有害物质 doctored wine 做了手脚的酒；阉割动物 have the cat doctored 把猫阉割了　词源：doct 教导 + or 名词后缀

doctrine ['dɒktrin] 宗教教义 Christian doctrine 基督教教义；政策宣言 the announcement of the Monroe Doctrine 门罗主义的宣言　词源：doct 教导 + ine 名词后缀 指教导人的学说思想

doctorate ['dɒkt(ə)rət] 博士学位　词源：doctor 博士 + ate 名词后缀

docile ['dəusail] 顺从的，温顺听话的 a docile child / horse / dog 听话的孩子/驯服的马/温驯的狗　词源：doc 教导 + ile 形容词后缀（表示容易……的）指容易听从教导的

document ['dɒkjumənt] 文件，公文；（用文字或影像）记录，记载 document the crisis 记录了危机；用文献支持证明 documented evidence 有文件证明的证据　词源：doc 教导 + ment 名词后缀（表示思想 mind）指记录下思想的文件

documentary [dɒkju'ment(ə)ri] 纪录片，纪实广播（或电视）节目 make a documentary about volcanoes 拍摄关于火山的纪录片；（电影、电视、照片等）纪实的 a documentary film 纪录影片；（证据等）书面的，文件的，文献的 documentary evidence / sources / material 书面证据/文件来源/文献资料　词源：document 记录 + ary 名词形容词后缀

115. -fabul- : speak　巧记：拟声词 指说话时发出 fabfab 的声音

affable ['æfəb(ə)l] 和蔼可亲的，易交谈的　词源：af 强调 + fab 说话 指可以谈话的人是和蔼可亲的　同义词：amiable / benign / genial

confabulate [kən'fæbjuleit] 闲谈，聊天，谈话；虚构，虚谈　词源：con 共同 + fabul 说话 + ate 动词后缀 指大家一起说话

confabulation [kənˌfæbjə'leiʃn] 闲谈，聊天，谈话；虚构，虚构的故事　词源：confabulate 谈话 + tion 名词后缀

effable ['efəbəl] 可说出来的，可表达的　词源：e 出来 + fab 说出 + ble 形容词后缀（表示可以……的）指可以说出来的

ineffable [in'efəb(ə)l]（美好得）难以形容的，不可言喻的 ineffable joy 难以形容的喜悦　词源：in 否定 + effable 可表达的 指用语言形容不出来的

fable ['feib(ə)l] 寓言 Aesop's Fable 伊索寓言　词源：fab 说话　指寓言是说出来的故事

fabulous ['fæbjuləs] 寓言般的 fabulous beasts 传说中的野兽；极好的 a fabulous performance 精彩的表演；巨大的 fabulous wealth 巨额财富　词源：fable 寓言 + ous 形容词后缀（表示过多的）指像寓言般美好的让大家都说的

fab [fæb] 极好的 a fab new car 一辆极好的新车　词源：fabulous 极好的缩写形式

116. -fall-, -fals- : deceive　巧记：fall 跌落 指欺骗别人掉落陷阱

fault [fɔːlt; fɔlt] 责任过错；故障毛病 an electrical fault 电路故障；缺陷瑕疵 a design fault 设计失误；（网球）发球失误 double fault 发球双误；（地表岩石的）断层 the San Andreas fault 圣安德烈亚斯断层；找……的缺点，挑剔，指责 it is hard / difficult to fault sb. / sth. 表现得无可挑剔　词源：fall 欺骗 指被骗是犯过错

faulty ['fɔːlti; 'fɔlti]（思维方法）错误的 faulty reasoning 错误推理；（商品）有瑕疵的 faulty workmanship 不完美的做工　词源：fault 过错 + y 形容词后缀

fallacy ['fæləsi] 谬论，错误见解　词源：fall 欺骗 + cy 名词后缀 指骗人的理念

fallacious [fə'leiʃəs] 谬误的，错误的 a fallacious argument 谬误的论据　词源：fallacy 谬论 + ous 形容词后缀（表示过多的）

fallible ['fælib(ə)l] 会犯错的，易上当的 fallible humans 人孰无过　词源：fall 欺骗 + ble 形容词后缀（表示可以……的）指人可以欺骗的是容易上当的

infallible [in'fælib(ə)l] 不犯错的 an infallible memory 绝对可靠的记忆；绝对有效果的 an infallible cure 绝对灵验的良方　词源：in 否定 + fallible 易犯错的 指不容易犯错

falsify ['fɔːlsifai] 伪造，篡改（数字、记录、信息等）falsify the evidence 伪造证据　词源：fals 欺骗 + fy 动词后缀 指伪造欺骗

false [fɔːls; fɔls] 错的，不正确的 false accusations 不实的指责；伪造的 a false name and address 假名和假地址；人造的 false teeth / hair / eyelashes 假牙/假发/假睫毛；不真诚，不诚实的，装腔作势的 a false laugh 假笑　词源：fals 欺骗 指骗人的是伪造的

falter ['fɔːltə; 'fɔl-] 结巴地说，支支吾吾地说；犹豫，踌躇 falter in one's resolve 动摇决心；变弱，衰退 the faltering peace talks 一波三折的和平谈判；蹒跚，摇晃 faltering steps 摇摇晃晃的脚步　词源：fall 欺骗 + er 动词后缀（表示动作反复）指骗人时说话支支吾吾

117. -fend-, -fens- : strike　巧记：find 寻找 指猛禽寻找食物飞行 fly 时袭击猎物

fend [fend] 格挡，挡开（攻击）fend sb. / sth. off；独立生活，自强自立 fend for oneself；避开，回避（难题、批评等）fend off questions about new tax increases 避开了关于新增赋税的问题　词源：fend 攻击 指在袭击时做出的闪避格挡动作

fencing ['fensiŋ] 击剑运动；栅栏，篱笆，围栏；筑栅栏用的材料 electric fencing 电网　词源：fend 攻击 + ing 名词后缀 指击剑是袭击格挡运动

defend [di'fend] 保卫，防卫 defend sth. against / from sth.；辩护，辩解 defend sb. against /

from sb. / sth.；捍卫 defending one's title 卫冕冠军　　词源：de 向下 ＋fend 攻击　指把攻击打压下去

defence [di'fens] 防守；保护，防护 act in self-defence 出于自卫；国防 the Defense Department 国防部；辩护，辩词；防守队员，后卫　　词源：defend 防卫 ＋ence 名词后缀

defensive [di'fensiv] 防御的 take defensive measures 采取防御措施；（体育比赛）防守的 defensive play 防守型打法　　词源：defense 防卫 ＋ive 形容词后缀（表示充满活力的 active）

offend [ə'fend] 违背，违反（人情常理或道德准则）comments that offend against people's religious beliefs 有悖于人们宗教信仰的评论；犯罪，违法 young men who are likely to offend again 可能会再次犯罪的年轻人；冒犯，惹怒，得罪人 be offended by such a personal question 被私人的问题惹得很生气　　词源：of 强调 ＋fend 攻击　指违反约定强行攻击

offence [ə'fens] 进攻，攻击行为 the weapon of offence 进攻性武器；犯罪，违法行为 commit an offence 犯罪；得罪，冒犯行为 take offence (at sth.) 对（某事）介意生气　　词源：offend 违反 ＋ence 名词后缀

offensive [ə'fensiv] 进攻的 take offensive actions 采取进攻行动；（体育比赛中）进攻的，攻势的 the football team's offensive strategy 足球队的进攻策略；冒犯的，无礼的 offensive remarks 冒犯的言论；军事进攻 launch a military offensive 发起军事进攻　　词源：offense 冒犯 ＋ive 形容词后缀（表示充满活力的 active）

118. **-frag-, -fract-**：break　巧记：fr 自由 free ＋ag / act 做动作　指物体做自由运动易破碎

fraction ['frækʃ(ə)n]（数学）分数；少量，一点 hesitate for a fraction of a second 略微犹豫了一下　　词源：fract 破碎 ＋tion 名词后缀

fracture ['fræktʃə] 骨折 a fracture of the leg 腿骨骨折；（使）断裂 a fractured pipeline 破裂的管道；（使）分裂 a rumor that the party will fracture and split 党派将分崩离析的传言　　词源：fract 破碎 ＋ure 名词后缀 nature　指骨骼易碎的自然属性

fragile ['frædʒail] 易碎的 fragile china / glass / bones 易碎的瓷器/玻璃制品/骨骼；（形势）脆弱的，不牢固的 the country's fragile economy 该国脆弱的经济；虚弱无力的 be in fragile health 身体虚弱；纤巧的，精细的，纤巧美丽的 fragile beauty 纤美　　词源：frag 破碎 ＋ile 形容词后缀（表示容易……的）指非常容易破碎的

fragment ['frægm(ə)nt] 碎片，片段 glass / memory fragments 玻璃/记忆碎片；（使）碎裂，破裂，分裂 a fragmented society 一个四分五裂的社会　　词源：frag 破碎 ＋ment 名词后缀（表示分散状态）指物体碎成小片小块的形态

fragrance ['freigr(ə)ns] 香气，香味 the rich fragrance of garden flowers 庭院花卉的馥郁芳香；香水 an exciting new fragrance from Dior 迪奥推出一款令人振奋的新香水　　词源：frag 破碎 ＋grace 优雅　指香水瓶破碎后散发出的优雅香气

119. **-fil-** : thread, line 巧记：fill 充满 指向下倒满水时形成的细细水线

file [fail] 档案，文件 access / copy / create / delete / download / save a file 存取/复制/创建/删除/下载/保存文件；把（文件等）归档 documents that are filed alphabetically 按字母顺序归档的文件；提起（诉讼）file a complaint / lawsuit / petition (against sb.) 提交投诉/诉讼/请愿书；提出（申请）file for divorce 提交离婚申请；排成一行行走 file out into the theater 排队进剧院；锉刀；锉平，锉光滑 file nails 锉指甲　词源：fil 细线 指把文档排成一条线归类

filament ['filəm(ə)nt] 灯丝 an electric filament；细线 glass / metal filaments 玻璃/金属丝　词源：fil 细线 + ment 名词后缀（表示分散状态）指灯丝是细细的金属丝

defile [di'fail] 污蔑，亵渎 defile one's reputation 玷污名誉；污染 defile the river by emptying raw sewage into it 排放污水污染河流；（山中）狭路，隘路，小径 a narrow defile in the mountain　词源：de 否定 + file 文档 指用不好的文档诋毁别人

profile ['prəufail] 侧面图，侧面像；人物简介 an employee profile 雇员简介；公司概况 a company profile 公司介绍；外形，轮廓 the profile of the cathedral against the sky 天空映衬出大教堂的轮廓；（举止姿态的）高调或低调 keep a low profile / a high profile 保持低调/高调　词源：pro 向前 + file 文档 指向前提交给别人看的文档是个人简介或公司概况

120. **-fin-** : end 巧记：Finland 芬兰 指北欧神话中芬兰是世界的尽头

fin [fin] 鱼鳍，鱼翅；（飞机的）垂直尾翼 tail fins　词源：fin 终点 指鱼鳍是鱼身体的边缘终点

confine [kən'fain] 把……限制于 confine study to 100 cases 把研究限定在一百个案例以内；限制自由，拘禁，监禁 be confined to barracks 被禁闭在营房；使离不开（或受困于床、轮椅等）be confined to bed with flu 因流感卧病在床　词源：con 共同 + fin 终点 指把犯人完全拘禁直到人生终点

confinement [kən'fainmənt] 拘禁，监禁 be in solitary confinement 被单独监禁；分娩期 the expected date of confinement 预产期　词源：confine 拘禁 + ment 名词后缀

define [di'fain] 下定义 define sth. as sth.　词源：de 向下 + fin 终点 指向下给事物画出终点界限是下定义

definition [defi'niʃ(ə)n] 定义；清晰度，鲜明度 high definition television 高清电视　词源：define 下定义 + tion 名词后缀

definite ['definit] 明确的，清楚的 a definite answer 明确的答复　词源：define 下定义 + ite 形容词后缀 指定义过的是明确的

indefinite [in'definit] 不明确的，不清楚的 indefinite terminology 不明确的专门用语；无限期的 an indefinite strike 无限期罢工　词源：in 否定 + definite 明确的 指不明确的

definitely ['definitli] 明确地，肯定地　词源：definite 明确的 + ly 副词后缀

definitive [di'finitiv] 最具权威的 definitive study 最权威的研究；（协议）最终的，不可更

改的 a definitive agreement / answer / statement / version 最后的协议/答复/声明/版本；普通邮票；限定词　词源：define 下定义 + tive 形容词后缀（表示充满活力的 active）

final ['fain(ə)l] 结局；决赛 the tennis final 网球决赛；最后的　词源：fin 终点 + al 形容词后缀

finally ['fainəli] 最后　词源：final 最后的 + ly 副词后缀

finalist ['fainəlist] 决赛选手　词源：final 决赛 + ist 名词后缀

finale [fi'nɑːli; -lei]（戏剧、电影、音乐的）终场，最后一幕，高潮结尾，大结局　词源：final 最终的

finish ['finiʃ] 结束，完成　词源：fin 终点 + ish 动词后缀　形近易混词：furnish

furnish ['fəːniʃ] 为（房屋或房间）配备家具 a fully furnished flat 配备齐全的公寓套房；提供（信息）furnish sb. / sth. with sth.　词源：furniture 家具 + ish 动词后缀　指把家具放置在家中

finite ['fainait] 有限的 finite resources 有限的资源；（动词）限定的　词源：fin 终点 + ite 形容词后缀　指有终点的是有限的

finity ['fainiti] 有限，限定　词源：finite 有限的 + ty 名词后缀

infinite ['infinət]（空间或时间）无限的，无穷尽的 the infinite universe 无限的宇宙；（数量或程度上）极其多的，极其大的 an infinite variety of drinks 各种各样的饮料　词源：in 否定 + finite 有限的　指没有限度的

infinity [in'finiti] 无限 the infinity of space 太空的无限；（数学）无穷大，无穷大；无法计算的量，无限大的量 an infinity of stars 数不清的星星　词源：infinite 无限的 + ty 名词后缀

121. -flict- : strike　巧记：fly 飞行 + ct 拟声词　指飞行攻击时发出的声音

afflict [ə'flikt] 折磨，使受苦 a city afflicted by famine 一个饱受饥荒之苦的城市　词源：af 强调 + flict 袭击　指不停地遭受袭击折磨

affliction [ə'flikʃn] 痛苦，折磨；病痛 the afflictions of becoming old 人变老时的各种痛苦　词源：afflict 折磨 + tion 名词后缀

conflict ['kɔnflikt]（意见等的）矛盾 conflicts over salary settlements 对工资协议的争执；武装冲突 resolve the military conflict 解决这一武装冲突　词源：con 共同 + flict 袭击　指所有人共同袭击对方是冲突

inflict [in'flikt] 强加，施加，使（某人）遭受（不愉快的事） inflict sth. on / upon sb.　词源：in 内部 + flict 袭击　指对人内心的攻击是强加内部压力让人感到不快乐

infliction [in'flikʃn] 强加，施加 the deliberate infliction of pain on others 故意给他人造成痛苦　词源：inflict 强加 + tion 名词后缀

122. -hal- : breathe　巧记：ha 拟声词 + l 长时间 long　指长时间发出"哈哈哈"的呼吸声

hail [heil] 众人高呼万岁；冰雹；一阵 a hail of arrows / bullets 一阵乱箭/弹雨；称赞，誉

为 hail sb. / sth. as sth.　词源：hal 呼吸 + i 人　指人高呼万岁大声喘气的声音　词义连记：欢呼声像下冰雹的声音一样震撼

inhale [in'heil] 用力吸入气体 inhale deeply on another cigarette 深深地吸了一口烟　词源：in 内部 + hal 呼吸　指把气体吸入

inhaler [in'heilə(r)] 便携吸入器，（吸药用）吸入器 an asthma inhaler 哮喘呼吸器　词源：inhale 吸入气体 + er 名词后缀

inhalator ['inhə,leitə] 人工呼吸补助器　词源：inhale 吸入气体 + or 名词后缀

exhale [iks'heil; eks-] 呼出气体 exhale the smoke through one's nose 从鼻子里喷出烟雾　词源：ex 出来 + hal 呼吸　指把气体呼出

exhalation [,ekshə'leiʃn] 呼气　词源：exhale 呼出气体 + tion 名词后缀

whale [weil] 鲸鱼　词源：w 水 water + hal 呼吸　指鲸鱼在海洋浮出水面呼吸

123. -hap- : chance, luck　巧记：hope 希望　指有希望是机会运气

perhaps [pə'hæps] 可能，或许　词源：per 一直 + hap 机会运气　指一直有机会是可能

happen ['hæp(ə)n] 碰巧发生　词源：hap 机会运气 + en 动词后缀　指有机会发生

happy ['hæpi] 快乐的　词源：hap 机会运气 + y 形容词后缀　指机会运气的出现是让人幸福快乐的

haphazard [hæp'hæzəd] 无计划的，随意的 study in a haphazard manner 无计划地学习　词源：hap 机会运气 + haz 有 have + ard 形容词后缀　指没有机会运气是无计划的　同义词：unplanned

hapless ['hæpləs] 不幸运的，倒霉的 the hapless passengers who lost luggage at the airport 倒霉的乘客在机场丢了行李　词源：hap 机会运气 + less 形容词后缀（表示否定）　指没有机会运气是不幸运

mishap ['mishæp] 不幸运，倒霉事，小事故，小错误，晦气 a series of mishaps 一连串的倒霉事　词源：mis 否定 + hap 机会运气　指不好的机会运气

124. -grav- : heavy　巧记：g 厚重的土地　指希腊神话的众神之母大地女神盖亚 Gaia

grave [greiv] 坟墓 from (the) cradle to (the) grave 一辈子；严重的，严峻的 grave consequences 严重的后果；（表情）严肃的 a grave look　词源：grav 重的　词义连记：严峻的战况让站在战士坟墓边上哀悼的人表情严肃

gravity ['græviti] 重力，引力 center of gravity 重心；（局势）严重性 the gravity of the situation；（举止或言谈的态度）严肃　词源：gra 重的　指物理上的重力 G

gravitate ['græviteit]（不用被动语态）被吸引 sb. gravitate to / toward(s) sb. / sth.　词源：gravity 引力 + it 去 go + ate 动词后缀　指被引力吸引过去

agravic [ə'grævik] 失重的，无重力的　词源：a 否定 + gravity 重力 + ic 形容词后缀　指无重力的

gravid ['grævid] 怀孕的，妊娠的　词源：gra 重的 + id 形容词后缀（表示具有某种身份）

指身形重的是女性怀孕的　同义词：pregnant

gravidity [græ'vidəti] 怀孕，妊娠　词源：gravid 怀孕的 + ity 名词后缀

gravy ['greivi]（调味）肉汁；意外之财，飞来之福，非法利润，外快　词源：grav 重的 + y 名词后缀　指厚重的肉汁撒在菜肴上像得到意外之财一样

aggravate ['ægrəveit] 加重，恶化 pollution that aggravates asthma 会使气喘加重的污染；（尤指故意地）激怒，惹怒 aggravate a snake 激怒一条蛇　词源：ag 强调 + grav 重的 + ate 动词后缀　指使情况变得越来越严重

grand [grænd] 壮丽的，堂皇的，盛大的 a grand palace 壮丽堂皇的宫殿；宏大的，宏伟的 a grand design 宏伟的蓝图；一千美元或英镑；三角钢琴 a grand piano　词源：gra 重的 + and 并且　指非常重要的是宏大的　巧记：gr 伟大的 great + and 并且 + gr 伟大的 great 指越来越伟大的是宏伟的、壮丽的　词义连记：用 1 000 美元买了一个三角钢琴放在宏伟的宫殿　形近易混词：grant / grain / grind

grant [grɑːnt]（尤指正式地或法律上）同意，批准 grant sb. sth. / grant sth. to sb.；（政府）资助金 a research grant 一笔研究经费；（学校）助学金 student grants 学生助学金　词源：agree to 的简写形式　用 gr 和 t 表示同意　词义连记：政府同意批准发补助金

grain [grein] 颗粒，（粮食）谷粒 a few grains of rice 几粒大米；沙粒 a grain of sand 一粒沙子；谷物，粮食；一点点 a grain of truth in folklore and legend 民间故事和传说中的一点真实的成分　词源：gr 长 grow + rain 下雨　指在雨水下生长的粮食

grind [graind] 磨碎，磨粉 to grind coffee / corn 将咖啡/玉米粒磨成粉；磨快；磨光 a stone for grinding knives 磨刀石；苦差事 daily grind in the factory 工厂每天的繁重劳动　词源：grain 谷粒　指用磨盘磨谷粒是苦差事　相关词：millstone 磨石，磨盘

125. **-greg-**：flock　巧记：grow in a group 的简写形式

aggregate ['ægrigət] 总数，合计 in the aggregate 总体来看；总计的 aggregate demand / investment / turnover 总需求/投资/成交量；（用于制成混凝土的）粒料　词源：ag 强调 + greg 群 + ate 形容词后缀　指聚集的一群是总数

congregate ['kɔŋgrigeit] 聚集 congregate to dance in the square 聚集在大广场上跳舞　词源：con 共同 + greg 群　指群聚在一起

congregation [kɔŋgri'geiʃ(ə)n]（教堂做礼拜的）会众，教堂聚集的人群　词源：congregate 聚集 + tion 名词后缀

segregate ['segrigeit] 种族隔离 segregate sb. from sb.；使隔离 smoking areas segregated from non-smoking areas 和非吸烟区分开的吸烟区　词源：se 分离 + greg 群 + ate 动词后缀　指从人群中分离出来

segregation [ˌsegri'geiʃ(ə)n] 种族隔离；隔离（或分离）措施　词源：segregate 种族隔离 + tion 名词后缀

egregious [i'griːdʒiəs]（错误、失败、问题等）极其严重的 commit an egregious mistake 犯令人震惊的错误　词源：e 出来 + greg 群 + ious 形容词后缀（表示程度过多的）指从

一群错误里面突出的错误最严重的

gregarious [gri'geəriəs] 爱交际的，合群的；（动物）群居的　词源：greg 群 + ious 形容词后缀（表示程度过多的）　同义词：sociable

126. -dorm-, -dormit- : sleep　巧记：door 门 + room 房间　指有房门用来睡觉的房间

dormitory ['dɔːmit(ə)ri] 宿舍　词源：dorm 睡觉 + it 去 go + ory 名词后缀　指宿舍是休息睡觉的地方

dorm [dɔːm] 宿舍　词源：dorm 睡觉　指宿舍是休息睡觉的地方

dormancy ['dɔːmənsi] （火山、动植物等）休眠　词源：dorm 睡觉 + ancy 名词后缀

dormant ['dɔːm(ə)nt] 休眠状态的 a dormant volcano 一座休眠火山　词源：dorm 睡觉 + ant 形容词后缀（表示具有……能力的）　反义词：active

dormitive ['dɔːmitiv] 安眠药；安眠的　词源：dorm 睡觉 + tive 形容词后缀（表示充满活力的 active）

dose [dəus]（药物的）一剂，一服 a high / low dose 大/小剂量；给（某人）服药 dose sb. (up) with aspirin 给某人服用阿司匹林　词源：dorm 睡觉　指吃了睡觉的药　巧记：dose 谐音"豆子"指吃像豆子一样的药

7

127. -laps- : fall　巧记：lamp 灯　指灯落地摔碎的声音

lapse [læps] 疏忽，失误 a defensive lapse 防守失误；（合同、协议等）期满终止；背弃信仰 lapse from one's religion；时间流逝，匆匆过去；（两事件间的）时间间隔 a lapse of about ten seconds 约十秒钟的间隔；（逐渐）陷入，进入 lapse into unconsciousness / silence / sleep 逐渐失去知觉/陷入沉默/进入睡眠　词源：laps 跌落　指体操运动跌落下器械是失误　词义连记：运动员的失误导致陷入懊恼沉默，心里有些背弃了自己的体育信仰，但随着时间的流逝，时隔四年，又恢复了原有状态　形近易混词：lap

lap [læp] 大腿上部 sit on sb.'s lap 坐在某人大腿上；（动物）舔饮 lap up the milk 舔食牛奶；（跑道的）一圈 run three laps 跑三圈；（波浪）轻拍，冲刷 waves that lap gently against the rocks 波浪轻轻地拍打岩石　词源：l 长时间 long + p 拍打声 拟声词"来拍"　指长时间拍打大腿上部的声音　巧记：laptop 笔记本　指放在大腿上部的便携式电脑

collapse [kə'læps]（突然）倒塌；（尤指因病重而）昏倒；（尤指工作劳累后）坐下，躺下放松 collapse on the sofa to listen to music 倒在沙发上听音乐；（突然）暴跌，贬值　词义：col 共同 + laps 跌落　指全部跌落倒塌

relapse [ri'læps] 旧病复发 relapse into a coma 再次昏迷；重蹈覆辙 relapse into the bad habit of smoking 重染吸烟恶习　词源：re 反复 + laps 跌落　指再次跌落

elapse [i'læps] 时间流逝　词源：e 出来 + laps 跌落　指物体跌落时的时间流逝　形近易混

词：eclipse

eclipse [i'klips] 日月食 a total / partial eclipse 全食/偏食；(使)黯然失色 be in eclipse　词源：e 出来 + clip 夹子　指日月食是太阳月亮像回形针一样别在一起

128. **-later-**：side　巧记：late 晚的　指来晚的站在边上

lateral ['læt(ə)r(ə)l] 侧面的 do dumbbell lateral raises 做杠铃侧举；(职位、工作、关系等)平级的，同级的 lateral moves to different departments 平级调动到不同的部门　词源：later 边　指旁边的是侧面的

bilateral [bai'læt(ə)r(ə)l] 双边的 bilateral relations / agreements / trade / talks 双边关系/协议/贸易/谈判　词源：bi 两个 + later 边 + al 形容词后缀

multilateral [ˌmʌlti'lætərəl] 多边的 multilateral negotiations 多边谈判　词源：multi 多的 + later 边 + al 形容词后缀

unilateral [juːni'læt(ə)r(ə)l] 单边的 take unilateral action 采取单方面行动　词源：uni 单一的 + later 边 + al 形容词后缀

collateral [kə'læt(ə)r(ə)l] 周边的，附属的 collateral damage 附加伤害；担保品，抵押品 put up our home as collateral 抵押房子　词源：col 共同 + later 边 + al 形容词后缀　指所有边上的加在一起是周边的　词义连记：房子是周边财产，可以作为抵押品

129. **-let**：diminutive　巧记：little 的缩写形式

riverlet ['rivəlit] 小河　词源：river 河流 + let 小的
streamlet ['striːmlit] 小溪　词源：stream 小溪 + let 小的
bullet ['bulit] 子弹　词源：bull 公牛 + let 小的　指公牛的牛角尖像子弹　形近易混词：bulletin
bulletin ['bulətin] 公告，布告 bulletin board 布告栏；(电台或电视台的)新闻简报；(机构或组织的)简报　词源：bull 公牛　指股市牛市时发布的公告
bracelet ['breslit] 手镯，手链 a gold bracelet 一只金手镯　词源：brace 支架 + let 小的　指手腕上的小支架是手镯
droplet ['drɔplət] 小滴 tiny droplets of water 小滴的水　词源：drop 滴 + let 小的
diet ['daiət] 节食 go / be on a diet　词源：di 饮食 dinner + et 小的 let　指小份饮食是节食
leaflet ['liflət] 传单，单张广告 hand / pass / give / send out a leaflet on sth. 发关于某方面的传单　词源：leaf 叶子 + let 小的　指像一片叶子一样的传单
novelette [ˌnɔːvə'let] 中篇小说（尤指被认为写得很蹩脚的浪漫传奇小说）　词源：novel 长篇小说 + lette 小的　指比长篇小说篇幅短一些的是中篇小说
pamphlet ['pæmflət] 小手册 a political pamphlet 政治性的小册子　词源：palm 手掌 + let 小的　指手里拿着的小手册
booklet ['buklət] 小手册　词源：book 书 + let 小的　指一本小书
tablet ['tæblət] (刻有文字的)匾，牌；药片 vitamin tablets 维生素片；平板电脑 Tablet PC

(Tablet Personal Computer) 词源：table 桌子 + let 小的 指牌匾的形状像个小桌子

wallet ['wɔlit]（男女使用的折叠式的）钱包 词源：wall 墙 + let 小的 指钱包像一面小墙鼓鼓的 相关词：purse（英式英语）女士钱包；（美式英语）女用手提包，手袋

130. -liber- : free 巧记：Libra 天秤座 指天秤座提倡和平主义和喜欢自由随性

liberty ['libəti] 自由 The Statue of Liberty 自由女神像 词源：liber 自由的 + ty 名词后缀

liberal ['lib(ə)r(ə)l] 自由主义者，开明人士；（政治、经济、思想）开放的，自由的 a liberal attitude towards sth. 对事物开明的态度；慷慨的，大量给予的，丰富的 be liberal with money 用钱很大方；通识教育的 a liberal education 通识教育；文科的 liberal arts 文科 词源：liber 自由的 + al 形容词后缀

liberate ['libəreit] 解放，释放，使自由 liberate sb. from sth. 词源：liber 自由的 + ate 动词后缀

liberation [libə'reiʃ(ə)n] 解放 liberation from oppression / poverty 摆脱压迫/贫困 词源：liberate 使自由 + tion 名词后缀

libertine ['libəti:n] 放荡不羁的人，淫荡的人，浪荡公子 词源：liber 自由的 + ine 名词后缀

deliberate [di'lib(ə)rət] 蓄意的，故意的 a deliberate act of vandalism 故意毁坏的行为；仔细思考，深思熟虑 deliberate on / about / over sth. 词源：de 向下 + liberate 使自由 指向下使眼色故意释放给别人自由 巧记：delay 推迟 指故意地推迟进程 词义连记：故意的都是经过仔细思考过的

131. -liter- : letter 巧记：letter 文字

literature ['lit(ə)rətʃə] 文学 works of literature 文学作品；文献资料 literature review 文献综述；（推销商品或提供信息的）印刷品，宣传品 sales literature 推销宣传品 词义：liter 文字 + ture 名词后缀（表示性质 nature）

literary ['lit(ə)(rə)ri] 文学的 a literary prize 文学奖 词源：liter 文字 + ary 形容词后缀

literal ['lit(ə)r(ə)l] 字面上的，逐字的 literal meaning 字面意思 词源：liter 文字 + al 形容词后缀

literally ['lit(ə)rəli] 字面上地 take sb. / sth. literally 仅仅从字面上理解某人/某事物；实际地，确实地（= exactly） 词源：literal 字面上的 + ly 副词后缀

literate ['lit(ə)rət] 能读会写的，识字的，有文化的 computer literate / musically literate 会使用计算机的/会演奏乐器 词源：liter 文字 + ate 形容词后缀

illiterate [i'lit(ə)rət] 不识字的，文盲的 computer / musically illiterate 计算机盲/音乐盲；文盲 词源：il 否定 + literate 识字的 指不识字的

literacy ['lit(ə)rəsi] 有读写能力，有文化 promote adult literacy 提高成人文化水平 词源：literate 识字的 + cy 名词后缀

illiteracy [i'lit(ə)rəsi] 无读写能力，文盲状态 词源：il 否定 + literacy 有文化 指无文化

的状态

anti-illiteracy ['ænti:i'litərəsi] 扫除文盲　词源：anti 相反 + illiteracy 文盲状态　指扫除文盲

delete [di'li:t] 删除（文字、文件、名字）　词源：de 否定 + lete 文字（liter 的变形）指不要文字

transliterate [træns'litəreit] 音译，移译，谐音翻译（例如披萨 Pizza，歇斯底里 hysteria，咖啡 coffee）　词源：trans 穿越 + liter 文字 + ate 动词后缀　指用发音翻译

obliterate [ə'blitəreit] 擦掉（痕迹）snow that obliterates the footprints 覆盖了足迹的白雪；忘却（想法、感情、回忆）obliterate sth. from one's memory 抹去……记忆；完全毁灭 obliterate the building by the bomb 用炸弹彻底摧毁建筑物　词源：ob 否定 + liter 文字 + ate 动词后缀　指去掉文字

litter ['litə]（在公共场所乱扔的）垃圾，废弃物，杂物 drop litter 乱扔垃圾；（同时出生的）一窝（小动物）a litter of puppies 一窝小狗；猫砂（一种干物质的颗粒，放在容器中供猫在室内便溺用）cat litter；（供牲畜睡卧用的）垫草，褥草，铺栏草；使乱七八糟，使凌乱 be littered with papers 堆满报纸　词源：liter 文字　指有文字的纸质垃圾

132. **macro-** : big　巧记：m 山 mountain + acro 高　指一座高大的山

macrocosm ['mækrəukɔzəm] 宏观世界　词源：macro 大 + cosmos 宇宙　指宏大的宇宙世界

macroeconomics [ˌmækrəuˌi:kə'nɔmiks] 宏观经济学　词源：macro 大 + economics 经济学

macroworld [mækrəu'wə:ld] 宏观世界　词源：macro 大 + world 世界

macroscale ['mækrəskeil] 大规模　词源：macro 大 + scale 规模

macrobiotic [ˌmækrəubai'ɔtik] 延年益寿的，养生饮食的 a macrobiotic diet 养生饮食　词源：macro 大 + bio 生命 + tic 形容词后缀　指让生命最大化的是养生的

macro-control ['mækrəu kən'trəul] 宏观调控　词源：macro 大 + control 控制　指从大方向调整控制

133. **micro-** : small　巧记：macro 的变化　把 a 变成 i 小　指一座小山

microphone ['maikrəfəun] 麦克风　词源：micro 小 + phone 声音　指发出小声音的设备

microscope ['maikrəskəup] 显微镜　词源：micro 小 + scope 范围　指能看到小范围的设备

microworld ['maikrəuwə:ld] 微观世界　词源：micro 小 + world 世界

Microsoft ['maikrəsɔft] 微软公司　词源：micro 小 + software 软件

microprint ['maikrəprint] 缩微印刷品（比如钞票上用显微镜才能看到的小字）词源：micro 小 + print 复印　指缩小复印的文字内容

microphotograph [ˌmaikrə'fəutəgra:f] 显微图像，显微照片，缩影照片　词源：micro 小 + photograph 照片　指显微镜下拍摄的照片

microphotography ['maikrəfətəgrəfi] 微距摄影术，显微照相术　词源：micro 小 + photograph 照片 + y 名词后缀

microwave ['maikrəweiv] 微波；微波炉 heat food up in the microwave 把食物放在微波炉里热一热；用微波炉烹调（或加热） 词源：micro 小 + wave 波动 指用微小的电磁波加热食物

134. -magn-, major-, maxim- : big   巧记：m 山 moutain 指山很大

magnify ['mæɡnifai] 放大影像 a magnified image 放大了的图像；夸大 magnify the risks 夸大风险 词源：magn 大 + fy 动词后缀

magnifier ['mæɡnifaiə(r)] 放大镜 词源：magnify 放大 + ier 名词后缀

magnitude ['mæɡnitjuːd] 重大，重要性 the magnitude of the problem 问题的重要性；（恒星的）亮度；（地震）震级 词源：magn 大 + tude 名词后缀

magistrate ['mædʒistrət; -streit] 地方法官 词源：magn 大 + administrate 行政管理 指管理地方的官员大人

magnet ['mæɡnət] 磁铁，磁石，吸铁石；有吸引力的人或物 attract / draw sb. / sth. like a magnet 像吸铁石一样吸引别人 词源：magn 大 + net 网 指磁铁像一张大网一样有磁力

magnetic [mæɡ'netik] 有磁性的 magnetic materials 磁性材料；有吸引力的 a magnetic character 富有魅力的个性 词源：magnet 磁铁 + ic 形容词后缀

magnanimous [mæɡ'næniməs] 宽宏大量的 a magnanimous gesture 大度的姿态 词源：magn 大 + anim 生命 life + ous 形容词后缀（表示过多的）指对待生命非常大度宽容的 巧记：magn 大 + animal 动物 + ous 形容词后缀（表示过多的）指像大动物一样有大胸怀的

magnificent [mæɡ'nifis(ə)nt] 宏伟的，壮丽的，富丽堂皇的 词源：magni 大 + fic 做 + ent 形容词后缀（表示具有……能力的）指做得非常大的是宏伟的

magnate ['mæɡneit] 大资本家，大亨，巨头 a media / property / shipping magnate 媒体/房地产/航运业大亨 词源：magn 大 + ate 名词后缀

majority [mə'dʒɒriti] 大多数；多数票 be elected by / with a majority 多数票当选；成年，法定年龄 reach majority 达到法定年龄 词源：major 大 + ity 名词后缀

major ['meidʒə] 主要的,重大的 major problem 主要问题；（大学的）主修专业；少校 a major in the army 陆军少校；大调 a symphony in C major C 大调交响乐 词源：major 大

majesty ['mædʒisti] 陛下 Your / Her / His Majesty；雄伟壮丽，庄严崇高 the majesty of the palace 宫殿的雄伟壮丽 词源：major 大 + est 最高级 + ty 名词后缀

maximum ['mæksiməm] 最大值 a maximum of 20 children in a class 每班至多 20 名学生；最大的 the maximum speed / temperature / volume 最快速度/最高气温/最大体积 词源：maxim 大 + um 名词后缀

maximize ['mæksimaiz] 使最大化 maximize profit 利润最大化；使（计算机视窗）最大化；充分利用 maximize the space 充分利用空间 词源：maxim 大 + ize 动词后缀

135. mal-, pessim- : bad 巧记：male 男人 指男人不坏女人不爱

malice ['mælis] 恶意恶毒，害人之心 do it out of sheer malice 纯粹出于恶意这么做 词源：mal 坏的 + ice 冰 指又坏又冰冷的心

malicious [mə'liʃəs] 恶毒的 malicious gossip / lies / rumours 恶毒的流言蜚语/谎言/谣言 词源：malice 恶毒 + ous 形容词后缀（表示过多的）

malign [mə'lain]（公开地）诽谤，诬蔑，中伤 a much maligned hero 一个深受诽谤的英雄；有害的 a malign influence 有害的影响 词源：mal 坏的 + lign 说谎 lie 指说谎话污蔑别人

malignant [mə'lignənt] 恶毒的 a malignant look 凶狠的目光；（癌、疾病等）恶性的，致命的 malign 诽谤 + ant 形容词后缀（表示具有……能力的）

maltreat [ˌmæl'triːt] 虐待 词源：mal 坏的 + treat 对待 指不好地对待

malcontent ['mælkəntent] 不满意的人，牢骚满腹的人 词源：mal 坏的 + content 满意的 指不满意的人

malpractice [ˌmæl'præktis] 医疗渎职 medical malpractice 医疗失误；玩忽职守 a malpractice suit 渎职诉讼 词源：mal 坏的 + practice 指不好好做事

malnutrition [mælnju'triʃ(ə)n] 营养不良 词源：mal 坏的 + nutrition 营养 指不好的营养

malfunction [mæl'fʌŋ(k)ʃ(ə)n]（机械或人体器官的）故障，失灵 a malfunction in one of the engines 其中一个引擎的失灵 词源：mal 坏的 + function 功能 指功能不好使

pessimism ['pesimiz(ə)m] 悲观 a mood of pessimism about the future 一种对于未来的悲观情绪；悲观主义 词源：pessim 坏的 + ism 名词后缀表示（某种学说主义）

pessimist ['pesimist] 悲观主义者 词源：pessimism 悲观主义 + ist 名词后缀

pessimistic [ˌpesi'mistik] 悲观的 be pessimistic about sth.；悲观主义的 词源：pessimist 悲观主义者 + ic 形容词后缀

136. -man- : stay, dwell 巧记：m 山 指像山一样坚韧不动

maintain [mein'tein; mən'tein] 维持关系；养家养车；坚持说，坚持认为 词源：main 停留 stay + tain 拿着 指停留并保持拿着不动的状态是维持 巧记：mountain 指像山一样维持不动

maintenance ['meint(ə)nəns; -tin-] 保持维持；维持养护 car maintenance 汽车保养；（付给前妻或前夫的）赡养费,生活费 pay maintenance to sb. 付给某人生活费 词源：maintain 维持 + ance 名词后缀

mainstream ['meinstriːm] 主流行为，主流思想；主流群体；主流的 词源：main 停留 + stream 溪流 指停留在大众心中的是主流的

remain [ri'mein] 保持原状，仍然是 remain silent / standing / seated / motionless 依然沉默/站着/坐着/一动不动 词源：re 反复 + main 停留 指一直停留在原地保持原状

remainder [ri'meində] 剩余物，剩余部分，剩余时间 the remainder of one's political career 某人政治生涯剩余的时间；其他人员；（数学除法的）差数，余数；廉价出售的图书，

滞销图书　词源：remain 仍然是 + er 名词后缀

remnant ['remnənt] 剩余物，残余物 the remnants of a meal 剩饭剩菜；（织物的）零头零料，布头　词源：remain + ant 名词后缀

mansion ['mænʃ(ə)n] 宅第，公馆，大官邸（指庄园大房子）A Dream of Red Mansions《红楼梦》；（常复数）用于公寓楼名 10 Tom Mansions, Jerry Road 杰瑞路汤姆公寓 10 号　词源：man 停留 + sion 名词后缀　指居住停留的大房子

manor ['mænə(r)]（封建领主的）领地；庄园大宅（指庄园大房子和它周边的土地）a manor house；（警察）管辖区　词源：man 停留 + or 名词后缀

menace ['menəs] 威胁，恐吓；危险的事物或人 be a menace to security 对安全的威胁　词源：men 停留 man + ace 一流的　指停留下来一流的人是对其他人的威胁

immanent ['imənənt]（特质）内在固有的，无所不在的 immanent power of love 无处不在的爱的力量　词源：im 内部 + man 停留 + ent 形容词后缀（表示具有……能力的）指停留在内心的　形近易混词：imminent

imminent ['iminənt] 即将来临的，逼近的 the imminent menace of invasion 迫在眉睫的入侵威胁　词源：im 内部 + min 一点点 mini + ent 形容词后缀（表示具有……能力的）指危险即将进入内部的

permanent ['pəːm(ə)nənt] 永久的，永恒的 a permanent job 固定工作；烫发（= perm = permanent wave）　词源：per 一直 + man 停留 + ent 形容词后缀（表示具有……能力的）指一直存在停留的

permanence ['pəːmənəns] 永久，永恒 the permanence of parental love 父母永恒的爱　词源：permanent 永恒的 + ence 名词后缀

137. **-mand-, -mandat-**：command　巧记：manu 手 + d 做动作 do 指指挥官用手势命令士兵做出战术动作

command [kə'mɑːnd] 指挥命令；赢得博得 command sympathy / support / respect 获得同情/支持/尊重；俯瞰眺望 the tower that commands the city 俯瞰城市的塔楼；（操纵计算机程序的）计算机的指令 command language；（尤指对语言的）掌握运用能力 have a good command of English 精通英语　词源：com 共同 + mand 命令　指命令所有人共同行动　词义连记：精通外语和计算机指令的指挥官在高处俯瞰军队下命令赢得了士兵的尊敬

commander [kə'mɑːndə] 指挥官，长官 commander in chief 总司令，最高统帅　词源：command 指挥命令 + er 名词后缀

commando [kə'mɑːndəu] 突击队员 a commando raid 突击队员的偷袭　词源：command 指挥命令 + do 做　指执行命令做特别任务的士兵

demand [di'mɑːnd] 强烈坚决要求 demand that… / to do sth. / sth. of sb.；市场需求 supply and demand 供求关系　词源：de 向下 + mand 命令　指向下说话以命令的语气强烈要求

demanding [di'mɑːndiŋ] 苛求的 a demanding boss 苛刻的老板　词源：demand 强烈要求 + ing 形容词后缀　指过分要求的　同义词：exacting

mandate ['mændeit] 授权令 had a mandate to honour the cheque 授权兑现支票；（授予某国对别国或地区的）托管领土令，委任统治权，托管权；授权（委员会或机构）做某事 mandate the UN assembly to draft a constitution 授权联合国大会起草一份章程；下命令，指示 mandate that... 词源：mand 命令 + ate 名词后缀

mandatory ['mændət(ə)ri] 依法强制的（指从事某些工作需要穿着佩戴的防护装备是必须的） 词源：mandate 命令指示 + ory 形容词后缀 指像命令指示一样必须执行的

countermand [ˌkauntə'mɑːnd] 撤销命令 countermand the order to attack 撤销进攻的命令 词源：counter 相反 + mand 命令 指不要原有命令

reprimand ['reprimɑːnd] 训斥，谴责，责备 reprimand sb. for (doing) sth. 词源：re 重复 + pri 在前面 pre + mand 命令 指在前面反复强调命令斥责没有执行的人

Mandarin ['mændərin] （中国）官话，普通话 词源：mand 命令 + darin 谐音"大人"古代对官员的称谓 指（中国帝制时代的）高级官吏说的命令语气的话

mandarin ['mændərin] 橘子，柑橘；（政府行政部门的）高级官员，政界要员；（中国帝制时代的）高级官吏 词源：mand 命令 + darin 谐音"大人"古代对官员的称谓 指说命令话语的高级官员边说话边吃橘子

138. **mani-, manu-**: hand 巧记：man 人 + i 小 mini 指人的小手

manage ['mænidʒ] 驾驭控制（人或动物的行为）manage a big and vicious horse 驾驭一匹脾气暴烈的大马；合理安排，有效使用（时间、金钱等）manage time and money 合理利用时间和金钱；管理运营（某企业或部门）manage a football team 管理一支足球队；努力完成（困难的事），应对 manage to do sth. 词源：mani 手 + age 时间 指用手长时间驾驭控制

management ['mænidʒm(ə)nt] 经营管理 a lack of management experience 缺乏管理经验；（公司或组织的）管理层 management decisions 管理层的决定 词源：manage 应对 + ment 名词后缀

manuscript ['mænjuskript] 手稿，原稿 an unpublished / original manuscript 未经发表的/原始的手稿 词源：manu 手 + script 写 指手写的原稿

manual ['mænju(ə)l] （机器的）使用手册，指南 a user manual 用户指南；手动的，手工的 a manual gearbox 手动变速箱 词源：manu 手 + al 形容词后缀

manufacture [mænju'fæktʃə] （用机器大量）生产制造；（用机器大批量制造的）商品；编造（虚假情况、借口）manufacture stories 编故事 词源：manu 手 + fact 做 + ture 名词后缀（表示性质 nature）指在工厂手工制作商品

manufacturing [ˌmænju'fæktʃəriŋ] 制造，制造业 词源：manufacture 制造 + ing 名词后缀

manipulate [mə'nipjuleit] 推拿正骨，推拿治疗；（暗中）操纵，控制（某人的思想和行为）manipulate children into seeking fame 操纵孩子追求名望；熟练巧妙地操控（信息或系统）manipulate knobs and levers 操纵旋钮和控制杆 词源：mani 手 + pul 推动 + ate 动词后缀 指用手推动身体的部位进行推拿按摩

manacle ['mænəkl] 手铐，脚镣；给……戴上镣铐　词源：mani 手 + cle 名词后缀　指犯人手上带的东西

manicure ['mænikjuə] 修指甲，指甲护理 have a manicure　词源：mani 手 + care 照顾　指好好照顾手指甲　相关词：pedicure 足部护理

maneuver [mə'nuvə] 熟练谨慎的动作，机动动作 a complicated maneuver of the tank 坦克复杂的机动；策略手段，花招伎俩 diplomatic maneuvers 外交策略；军事演习（常复数）be on maneuvers in the desert 在沙漠军事演习；改变事态的机会，回旋余地 have room for maneuver 有回旋余地；精心策划，使花招 maneuver sb. into the management 使花招让某人进入了管理层；巧妙操控移动 maneuver the car into the parking space 熟练地把车停进了车位　词源：mani 手 + over 在上面　指手在操纵杆上面巧妙控制

manifest ['mænifest]（船、飞机、火车的）载货清单 the ship's cargo manifest 船的货物清单；（船、飞机、火车的）乘客名单；显而易见的，明显的 a manifest error 明显的错误；表明，显示（感情、态度等）manifest one's intention 表明意图　词源：mani 手 + est 最高级　指手里面拿的单据是显而易见的

139. **-mar-, -mer-** : sea　巧记：Mercury 墨丘利神；水星　他是罗马神话中众神的使者，形象是头戴一顶插有双翅的帽子，脚穿飞行鞋，手握魔杖，行走如飞的人。他也是医药、旅行者、偷盗贼、商业和小偷的守护神。此外，水星在天上运行的速度很快，所以用他的名字来命名

marine [mə'ri:n] 海洋的，海上的 marine life 海洋生物；（美国或英国皇家）海军陆战队士兵　词源：mar 大海 + ine 形容词后缀

mariner ['mærinə] 海员水手　词源：marine 海洋的 + er 名词后缀　同义词：sailor

maritime ['mæritaim] 海洋的，海事的 maritime industry 海运业；近海的，沿海的 maritime provinces 沿海省份　词源：mar 大海 + time 时间　指长时间在海洋上的

submarine ['sʌbməri:n; sʌbmə'ri:n] 潜艇；海底的 submarine cables 海底电缆　词源：sub 下面 + marine 海洋的　指在海洋下面的

commerce ['kɔmə:s] 商业 chamber of commerce 商会　词源：com 共同 + mer 大海　指各国共同在海洋上进行商业往来

commercial [kə'mə:ʃ(ə)l] 商业的，贸易的 commercial center 商业中心；电视广告 a toy commercial 玩具广告　词源：commerce 商业 + cial 形容词后缀（表示特殊的 special）

mercy ['mə:si] 仁慈，怜悯 show mercy to sb. 对某人仁慈宽恕　词源：mer 大海 + cy 名词后缀　指大海的包容仁慈

merciful ['mə:siful; -f(ə)l] 仁慈的，怜悯的　词源：mercy 仁慈 + ful 形容词后缀（表示充满的）

merciless ['mə:siləs] 冷酷的，无情的　词源：mercy 仁慈 + less 形容词后缀（表示否定）

merchant ['mə:tʃ(ə)nt] 商人 wine / coal / timber merchant 葡萄酒商/煤炭商/木材商　词源：mer 大海 + change 交换 + ant 名词后缀　指在海上交换商品的商人

merchandise ['mɜːtʃ(ə)ndais; -z] 商品，货品 a range of official Disney merchandise 一系列的正版迪士尼商品；（利用广告等进行）推销　词源：merchant 商人 + ise 名词后缀　指商人交易的商品

mercury ['mɜːkjəri] 水银　词源：mer 大海　指水银流动起来像大海

mermaid ['mɜːmeid]（传说中的）美人鱼　词源：mer 大海 + maid 少女　指传说中的美人鱼像海里的少女

meridian [mə'ridiən] 子午线，经线；（从地球表面某一点观测到的太阳或其他星体达到的）最高点　词源：mer 大海 + dia 天 day　指经过海洋的子午线

antemeridian [æntimə'ridiən] 上午的　词源：ante 在前面 + meridian 子午线　指中午前的

postmeridian ['pəustmə'ridiən] 下午的　词源：post 在后面 + meridian 子午线　指中午后的

140. -mater-, -matr- : mother　巧记：mother 的词形变化

maternal [mə'tɜːn(ə)l] 母亲的，母性的 maternal love 母爱；慈母似的　词源：mater 母亲 + al 形容词后缀

maternity [mə'tɜːniti] 母性，母亲身份；孕妇的，产妇的 be on maternity leave 休产假　词源：maternal 母性的 + ity 名词后缀

matrimony ['mætriməni] 结婚，婚姻 join together in holy matrimony 携手走进神圣的婚姻　词源：matri 母亲 + mony 名词后缀（表示和钱 money 相关）指妈妈给的钱作为彩礼或嫁妆用来结婚　同义词：marriage

matron ['meitr(ə)n] 上年纪的已婚妇女，主妇；女护士长（现常称为 senior nursing officer）；（学校的）女舍监；（监狱的）女看守　词源：matr 母亲 + on 正在（表示正在进行的状态）指像妈妈一样正在看着别人的女性

maid [meid] 未婚少女，姑娘 old maid（不结婚的）老姑娘；（大户人家或宾馆的）女仆 a kitchen maid 厨房女佣人　词源：ma 母亲 mama + id 身份　指可以有母亲身份的少女

mermaid ['mɜːmeid]（传说中的）美人鱼　词源：mer 大海 + maid 少女　指传说中的美人鱼像海里的少女

maiden ['meid(ə)n] 未婚少女，姑娘；（飞机或船）首次飞行的/航行的 maiden flight / voyage 初次飞行/首航　词源：maid 少女 + en 名词后缀

matriarchy ['meitriɑːki] 母权制，母系制；母系社会　词源：matr 母亲 + arch 拱门（表示统治 rule）+ y 名词后缀　指母性统治的社会　反义词：patriarchy

mature [mə'tʃuə] 成熟的 mature market 成熟的市场；（债券或保单）票据到期应付的　词源：ma 母亲 mama + ture 名词后缀（表示性质 nature）指像妈妈一样成熟的

immature [ˌimə'tjuə; ˌimə'tjɔː] 不成熟的 immature behaviour 幼稚行为　词源：im 否定 + mature 成熟的　指不成熟的

premature ['premətjuə] 不成熟的；（婴儿）早产的 a premature birth 早产；仓促的，过早的 make a premature decision 做草率的决定　词源：pre 在前面 + mature 成熟的　指提前成熟的是过早成熟的

mammal ['mæm(ə)l] 哺乳动物　词源：ma 母亲 + ma 母亲 + al 名词后缀　指哺乳动物是母亲胎生的

madam ['mædəm] 女士，夫人；对身居要职的妇女的称呼　词源：ma 母亲　指像母亲一样有担当能照顾别人的女性

mistress ['mistris] 情妇；（私立学校的）女教师；（仆人的或狗、马等动物的）女主人；（有权势的女子，女能人，女强人）控制着某事物，是某事的能手 be (a / the) mistress of sth.　词源：Miss 未婚的小姐姐（ma 母亲的词形变化）+ stress 压力　指带来压力的小姐姐

141. **-medi-**：middle　巧记：middle 的词形变化

meddle ['med(ə)l] 干涉，管闲事 meddle in / with sth.；胡乱摆弄 meddling with one's things 弄乱某人的东西　词源：medi 中间　指来到中间干涉　同义词：interfere / intervene

meadow ['medəu] 草地；牧场　词源：medi 中间 + low 低的　指山下低处的草地牧场　形近易混词：mellow

mellow ['meləu]（水果或酒）醇香甘美的 mellow flavour 芳醇的味道；（声音）圆润悦耳的 mellow voice 悦耳的嗓音；（颜色或光线）柔和的，不耀眼的 the mellow golden light of dusk 傍晚柔和的金色光线　词源：smell 味道 + low 低的　指味道浓厚香醇的

mediate ['mi:dieit] 调停，调解，斡旋 mediate between A and B；减轻……的影响 mediate the effects of malnutrition 减轻营养不良造成的影响　词源：medi 中间 + ate 动词后缀　指走到冲突中间调停

mediator ['mi:dieitə(r)] 调停人（或机构）　词源：mediate 调停 + or 名词后缀

meditate ['mediteit]（宗教上）冥想，打坐；沉思 meditate on / upon sth.；策划（不好的事）meditate revenge 计划复仇　词源：medi 中间 + t 思考 think + ate 动词后缀　指坐在中间思考进退　同义词：contemplate

medicate ['medikeit] 用药物治疗　词源：medi 中间 + c 治疗 cure + ate 动词后缀　指用药物进行治疗达到身体健康的中间平衡状态

medication [medi'keiʃ(ə)n] 药物，药剂 be on medication for high blood pressure 服用药物治疗高血压　词源：medicate 药物治疗 + tion 名词后缀

medicine ['meds(ə)n; 'medisin] 药品；医疗；医学 traditional Chinese medicine 传统的中国医学　词源：medi 中间 + ine 名词后缀　指治疗疾病使人体健康达到平衡的学科　相关词：pharmacy

medical ['medik(ə)l] 医疗的 medical staff 医务人员；医学的；（身体）体格检查　词源：medicine 医学 + al 形容词后缀　相关词：pharmaceutical

pharmacy ['fɑ:məsi] 药店；药剂学，制药学　词源：farm 农场 + cy 名词后缀　指在农场里种植各种草药供药学制药研究

pharmaceutical [,fɑ:mə'su:tik(ə)l; -'sju:-] 制药的 the pharmaceutical industry 制药业　词源：pharmacy 制药学 + al 形容词后缀

medium ['mi:diəm] 媒质，媒介物，传导体 magnetic media（计算机储存信息的介质，例

如软盘或磁带）；（传播信息的）媒介，（报纸或电视等）传播媒介 the medium of radio / television 广播/电视媒介；手段，方法 a good medium for learning English 一种学习英语的好方法；五分熟的 medium steak 半熟的牛排；中号的 a medium-size dress 一件中号连衣裙；通灵的人，灵媒，巫师　词源：medi 中间 + ium 名词后缀

media ['miːdiə] 媒体，大众传媒 media hype 媒体炒作　词源：medi 中间 + ia 名词后缀

immediate [i'miːdiət] 立即的；当下的 the most immediate problem 最急迫的问题；（关系或级别）最接近的，直系的 immediate family 直系亲属（如父母、儿女、兄弟姐妹等）　词源：im 否定 + medi 中间 + ate 形容词后缀　指不在中间停留的是立即的　同义词：prompt

intermediate [ˌintə'miːdiət]（时间进程）中期的，中间的 an intermediate stage 中间阶段；（班级或课程）中级的 an intermediate textbook 中级课本；（学生或运动员）中等水平的 intermediate learners of Mandarin 中等程度普通话学习者；中级学生或运动员 a ski resort for beginners and intermediates 适合滑雪初学者和中级水平者的度假胜地　词源：inter 两者间 + medi 中间 + ate 形容词后缀　指在初级高级之间的等级是中级的

medieval [ˌmedi'iːvl] 中世纪的 a medieval castle 一座中世纪城堡；古老的，旧式的　词源：medi 中间 + evening 黑夜 + al 形容词后缀　指中世纪的黑暗

Mediterranean [ˌmeditə'reiniən] 地中海 the Mediterranean；地中海地区；地中海的，地中海地区的，地中海地区特有的 Mediterranean climate 地中海气候　词源：medi 中间 + terr 土地 + ocean 大海　指在土地的中间有个大海是地中海

timid ['timid] 胆小的，胆怯的 a timid voice 羞怯的声音　词源：t 方向 to + i 人 + mid 中间　指站在中间不敢动的人是胆小的

intimidate [in'timideit] 使胆怯，恐吓，威胁 intimidate sb. into doing sth.　词源：in 内部 + timid 胆小的 + ate 动词后缀　指使人内心胆小

142. **-memor-** : mindful　巧记：希腊神话中的记忆女神莫涅莫绪涅（Mnemosyne），她是宙斯的第五个妻子，生下了九位缪斯女神。作为主管艺术与科学的缪斯女神的母亲，记忆女神在许多神话和传说中是口头叙事诗人的庇护者，因为诗人需要借助她的神奇力量来复述前人流传下来的诗歌。在冥界中，记忆女神掌管着一眼泉水，该泉水的作用与"遗忘之河"（Lethe）相反，喝下后可以永保记忆

memory ['mem(ə)ri] 记忆，记忆力；计算机存储器，存储量，内存 RAM (random access memory)　词源：memor 思想记忆 + y 名词后缀

memorize ['meməraiz] 死记硬背，熟记，记住 memorize a poem 记住一首诗　词源：memor 思想记忆 + ize 动词后缀

remember [ri'membə] 记起，记得；纪念 be remembered for / as sth. 因某事而成名（或名留青史）　词源：re 反复 + mem 思想记忆 + er 动词后缀（表示动作反复性）

commemorate [kə'meməreit] 纪念 commemorate the wedding anniversary 纪念结婚纪念日　词源：com 共同 + memor 思想记忆 + ate 动词后缀　指大家一起回忆

memorial [mə'mɔːriəl] 纪念馆，纪念堂 Lincoln Memorial 林肯纪念堂；纪念碑 a war memorial 阵亡将士纪念碑；纪念的 a memorial statue 纪念雕像；纪念物 a watch which is a memorial to a hero 对英雄表达纪念的手表　词源：memor 思想记忆 ＋ial 名词后缀（表示特殊的 special）指有特殊纪念意义的

immemorial [imi'mɔːriəl] 年代久远没人记得的，无法追忆的 an immemorial convention 古老的传统；史前的，远古的　词源：im 否定 ＋memorial 纪念的 指无人纪念的

memorandum [memə'rændəm] 备忘录　词源：memor 思想记忆 ＋random 随机的 指随机通过记忆写下的文件记录

memo ['meməu] 备忘录 write / send / circulate a memo 写/发送/传阅备忘录　词源：memorandum 的简写形式

memoir ['memwɑː]（名人）回忆录，自传；实录，传略，地方志，大事记　词源：memor 思想记忆 ＋i 人 ＋r 成长 rise 指回忆名人成长之路的书

143. **-ment-**：mind　巧记：Mentor 门特　门特（Mentor）是古希腊神话里的人物，他是奥德修斯（Odysseus）的好朋友。奥德修斯在出征特洛伊前，将自己的儿子忒勒玛克斯托付给了门特。门特把忒勒玛克斯培养成了一个有思想的人，他的名字也被赋予了良师益友的含义

mentor ['mentɔː（r)] 良师益友；导师　词源：ment 思想 ＋or 名词后缀 指思想上的导师

mental ['ment(ə)l] 心智的，思想的 mental health 精神健康　词源：ment 思想 ＋al 形容词后缀

mentality [men'tæliti]（尤指被视为错误或愚蠢的）心态 a get-rich-quick mentality 一夜暴富的心态　词源：mental 思想的 ＋ity 名词后缀

mention ['menʃ(ə)n]（作名词）提及，说起 make no mention of sth. 没有提及某事；（作动词）提及，说起 mention sth. to sb.　词源：ment 思想 ＋tion 名词后缀 指思想上想到某人或某事

mend [mend] 修补（衣物的破洞裂口）mend our shoes 修补鞋子；修理（破损物件）mend the bike 修自行车；（断骨）愈合；改正不良行为 mend one's ways；消释前嫌，重修旧好 mend fences with sb.　词源：ment 思想 指思想上的修正

amend [ə'mend]（法律文件、声明文稿或讲演稿）修改，修订 amend evidence 修改证词　词源：a 正在 on ＋mend 思想 指思想修正

amendment [ə'mendmənt]（法律、文件的）改动，修正案，修改，修订 constitutional amendments 宪法修正案　词源：amend 修订 ＋ment 名词后缀

comment ['kɔment] 评论，意见（可作名词或动词）comment on sth.　词源：com 共同 ＋ment 思想 指大家共同发表自己的意见

commentary ['kɔmənt(ə)ri]（在电视或电台上进行的）现场解说 give a full commentary on the game 对比赛全程实况报道；评注性著作，评论文 political commentary 政论　词源：comment 评论 ＋ary 名词后缀 指体育评论员的解说

commentate ['kɔmənteit] 体育比赛作解说 commentate on the game　词源：comment 评

论 + ate 动词后缀

commentator ['kɔmənteitə] 实况解说员 a sports commentator 体育解说员；评论员 political commentators 政治评论员　词源：commentate 体育评论 + or 名词后缀

commend [kə'mend] 公开称赞 commend sb. for sth.；推荐，推崇 command sb. / sth. (to sb.)　词源：com 共同 + mend 思想　指有共同思想获得称赞

recommend [rekə'mend] 推荐 recommend sb. / sth. (to sb.)；劝告，建议 a recommended price of $100 建议售价 100 美元　词源：re 反复 + commend 称赞　指不停称赞是推荐

recommendation [ˌrekəmen'deiʃ(ə)n] 推荐；推荐信（= letter of recommendation）；正式建议，提议 make a recommendation to do sth.　词源：recommend 推荐 + tion 名词后缀

Mencius [menʃiəs] 孟子　词源：men 思想　指孟子是伟大的思想家

commence [kə'mens] 开始 commence with sth. 以……开始　词源：com 共同 + mence 思想　指人开始有自己的思想　巧记：谐音"可慢死"指抱怨节目开始得可慢死了

commencement [kə'mensm(ə)nt] 开始，开端 the commencement of building work 建筑工程的破土动工；（授予学位的）毕业典礼　词源：commence 开始 + ment 名词后缀　指毕业典礼是人生新阶段的开始

dementia [di'menʃə] 痴呆 senile dementia 老年性痴呆　词源：de 否定 + ment 思想 + ia 名词后缀（表示疾病）指思想不正常

demented [di'mentid] 发疯的；痴呆的　词源：de 否定 + ment 思想 + ed 形容词后缀

documentary [dɔkju'ment(ə)ri] 纪录片，纪实广播（或电视）节目 make a documentary about volcanoes 拍摄关于火山的纪录片；（电影、电视、照片等）纪实的 a documentary film 纪录影片；（证据等）书面的，文件的，文献的 documentary evidence / sources / material 书面证据/文件来源/文献资料　词源：doc 教导 + ment 思想 + ary 名词后缀　指记录行为思想的纪录片

remind [ri'maind] 提醒，使想起 remind sb. of sth.　词源：re 重复 + mind 思想　指使思想上重复想起

reminder [ri'maində] 提醒物 a constant reminder of investment risks 投资风险的时刻提醒；（提醒做某事的）提示信，通知单 a reminder from the physician for a physical examination 医生寄来的叫去作体检的提示信　词源：remind 使想起 + er 名词后缀

reminiscent [ˌremi'nisnt] 使人想起的 be reminiscent of sb. / sth.；回忆往事的，怀旧的 a reminiscent smile 回忆往事时露出的微笑　词源：remind 使想起 + scent 味道　指味道使人想起的

reminiscence [ˌremi'nis(ə)ns]（可数名词，常复数）回忆往事的谈话，回忆录 reminiscences of the childhood experiences 儿时经历回忆录；（不可数名词）回忆，追忆；（可数名词，常复数）使人想起类似事物的东西，引起联想的相似事物 music that is full of reminiscences of Arabic rhythms 充满让人想起阿拉伯韵律的音乐　词源：reminiscent 回忆往事的 + ence 名词后缀

144. -milit- : army 巧记：mili-表示一千 指成千上万的士兵组成军队

militant ['milit(ə)nt] 好战的，好斗的 militant groups 好战团体；激进的 militant attitudes 激进态度；激进分子，好斗分子；斗士，富有战斗精神的人 词源：milit 军队 + ant 形容词后缀（表示具有……能力的）指军队是好斗的

military ['milit(ə)ri] 军队的，军事的，军用的 a military coup 军事政变；军队，军方 词源：milit 军队 + ary 形容词后缀

militate ['militeit] 阻止，妨碍 militate against building the nuclear power station 阻止建核电站 词源：milit 军队 + ate 动词后缀 指动用军队的军事力量阻止

militia [mi'liʃə] 民兵，民兵组织 a right-wing militia group 右翼民兵团体 词源：milit 军队 + ia 名词后缀

militarism ['militərizəm] 军国主义 词源：milit 军队 + ism 名词后缀（表示学说主义）

militarize ['militəraiz] 使军事化 a militarized zone 军事化地区 词源：milit 军队 + ize 动词后缀

145. -minent- : hang 巧记：mini 小 + ent 名词后缀 指悬挂着的小物品

eminent ['eminənt]（在某专业中）杰出的，显赫的 an eminent architect 著名的建筑师 词源：e 出来 + minent 悬挂 指悬挂出来的照片或奖杯证明是杰出的

imminent ['iminənt] 即将来临的，逼近的 the imminent menace of invasion 迫在眉睫的入侵威胁 词源：im 内部 + min 一点点 mini + ent 形容词后缀（表示具有……能力的）指危险即将进入内部的 形近易混词：immanent

immanent ['imənənt]（特质）内在固有的，无所不在的 immanent power of love 无处不在的爱的力量 词源：im 内部 + man 停留 + ent 形容词后缀（表示具有……能力的）指停留在内心的

preeminent [pri'eminənt] 杰出的，卓越的 the poet's preeminent position in society 诗人在社会上的显要地位 词源：pre 在前面 + eminent 杰出的 指在别人前面更加杰出的

prominent ['prɔminənt] 杰出的，卓越的 a prominent artist 杰出的艺术家；凸起的 a prominent nose 高鼻子；位置突出的，明显的 the prominent position on the cover 封面的显著位置 词源：pro 向前 + minent 悬挂 指悬挂在墙上向前突出的奖状表示杰出的

146. mini- : small 巧记：m 山 + i 小 + n 水 + i 小 指小山小河

minibus ['minibʌs] 小型客车，面包车 词源：mini 小 + bus 公交车

miniskirt ['miniskə:t] 迷你裙，超短裙 词源：mini 小 + skirt 裙子

minister ['ministə] 部长，大臣 cabinet ministers 内阁部长；牧师 词源：mini 小 + st 站立 stand + er 名词 指站在下面听君主命令的谨小慎微的大臣

ministry ['ministri] 政府部门 the Ministry of Defense 国防部；牧师职位 词源：minister 部长 + y 名词后缀

administer [əd'ministə] 行政管理 administer a charity 管理慈善机构；执行实施 administer the law 执法；用药治疗 administer aspirins to sb. 给某人服用阿司匹林　词源：ad 强调 + minister 部长　指部长对部门进行行政管理

administrative [əd'ministrətiv] 行政的，管理的 an administrative job 行政管理工作　词源：administer 行政管理 + tive 形容词后缀（表示充满活力的 active）

administrator [əd'ministreitə]（公司、机构的）行政管理人员 a library administrator 图书馆行政管理人员　词源：administer 行政管理 + or 名词后缀

administration [ədmini'streiʃ(ə)n] 行政管理 Master of Business Administration（简称 MBA）工商管理硕士；（尤指美国）政府 the Bush administration 布什政府；（药物的）施用 the administration of antibiotics 抗生素的施用；执行实施 the administration of justice 司法　词源：administer 行政管理 + tion 名词后缀

minify ['minifai] 缩小 minify the code 缩减代码　词源：mini 小 + fy 动词后缀

minimize ['minimaiz] 使程度最小化 minimize the investment risk 最小化投资风险；轻视，使显得不重要 minimize the problem of discrimination 轻视歧视问题；将（计算机文件或程序）最小化　词源：mini 小 + ize 动词后缀

minimum ['miniməm] 最低限度的，最小的 the minimum age for retirement 退休的最低年龄；最少量　词源：mini 小 + um 名词后缀

minor ['mainə]（大学中的）辅修专业；未成年人 films suitable for minors 适合未成年人看的电影；次要的 minor changes 小改变；小调 the key of C minor C 小调　词源：min 小 + or 名词后缀

minority [mai'nɔriti; mi-] 少数；少数派；少数民族 students from minority groups 来自少数族裔的学生　词源：min 小 + ity 名词后缀

minus ['mainəs] 减号；减去；负号（= minus sign）；负数的 a minus figure/ number 负数；零下的 minus ten 零下十度；负面的，使显得有欠缺的 minus points 毛病缺点；不利条件，不足 pluses and minuses 利弊；成绩略低于 A（或 B 等）A minus A 减的成绩　词源：min 小 + us 名词后缀

miniature ['minitʃə] 微缩模型；微型画，小画像；微缩的，微型的 a miniature city 微缩城市　词源：mini 小 + ture 名词后缀（表示性质 nature）

diminish [di'miniʃ] 减少降低；贬低轻视（重要性或价值）diminish the importance of discoveries 贬低发现的重要性　词源：di 分散 dis + mini 小 + ish 动词后缀　指分散变小　同义词：decrease / reduce

illuminate [i'l(j)u:mineit] 照亮，点亮 illuminate the stadium 照亮体育场；阐明，解释 illuminate the philosopher's thinking 阐明哲学家的思想　词源：il 强调 + lu 光亮 + min 小 + ate 动词后缀　指光线一点点点亮

seminar ['seminɑ:] 研讨会 a teaching seminar 教学研讨班　词源：se 分离 + min 小 + ar 名词后缀　指分开的小会　巧记：谐音"塞满了"指研讨会上塞满了人

luminary ['lu:minəri] 发光天体；发光体；名人，杰出人物 luminaries of the society 社会的

名流　词源：lu 光亮＋min 小＋ary 名词后缀　指天上小又亮的发光天体　词义连记：杰出人物是天上的星宿下凡人间

147. -mir-：wonderful, strange　巧记：m 山＋i 小＋r 河 river 指山倒映在水中的小巧精美的景色

mirror ['mirə] 镜子；反映出（相似的情况）music that mirrors the optimism in the country 反映出这个国家的乐观精神的音乐　词源：mir 奇妙的＋or 名词后缀　指镜子反射影响是很奇妙的

miracle ['mirək(ə)l] 奇迹 an economic miracle 经济奇迹　词源：mir 奇妙的＋cle 名词后缀　指镜子里出现的奇观

miraculous [mi'rækjuləs] 奇迹般的，不可思议的 make a miraculous recovery 奇迹般地康复　词源：miracle 奇迹＋ous 形容词后缀（表示过多的）

mirage ['mirɑːʒ; mi'rɑːʒ] 海市蜃楼；妄想，幻想 chase a mirage 追一个虚幻的梦　词源：mir 奇妙的＋age 名词后缀（表示长时间）指长时间出现的由镜面反射产生的美妙景色

admire [əd'maiə] 羡慕，钦佩 admire sb. for (doing) sth.；欣赏，观赏 admire the view 欣赏风景　词源：ad 强调＋mir 奇妙的　指人们看到镜子里的自己时钦佩自己的外表

admiring [əd'maiəriŋ] 羡慕的，钦佩的 admiring eyes 钦佩的目光　词源：admire 钦佩＋ing 形容词后缀

admiration [ædmə'reiʃ(ə)n] 羡慕，钦佩 gaze at sb. in admiration 钦佩地凝视着某人；爱慕　词源：admire 钦佩＋tion 名词后缀

admiral ['ædmərəl] 海军上将　词源：admire 钦佩＋al 名词后缀　指让人钦佩的海军上将

148. -mob-, -mot-, -mov-：move　巧记：move 移动 m 山＋o 太阳＋v 峡谷＋e 出来　指太阳在山和峡谷中运动一天的轨迹

mobile ['məubail] 易移动的 a mobile library / shop / clinic 流动图书馆/商店/诊所；（劳动力或社会阶层）流动的；行动方便的，腿脚灵便的 a lavatory designed for those who are less mobile 专门为行动不便的人设计的厕所；手机　词源：mob 移动＋ile 形容词后缀（表示容易……的）

immobile [i'məubail] 不移动的，固定的 sit immobile 坐着一动不动；不能正常走动的 the illness that leaves sb. completely immobile 使某人完全丧失活动能力的疾病　词源：im 否定＋mobile 易动的　指不容易移动的

emotion [i'məuʃ(ə)n] 强烈情感 lose control of one's emotions 情绪失控　词源：e 出来＋mot 移动＋tion 名词后缀　指内心出来的情感

emotional [i'məuʃ(ə)n(ə)l] 情感的，情绪的 emotional stress 情绪紧张；有感染力的，激动人心的 emotional music 有感染力的音乐；感情用事的 get emotional on these occasions 在这些场合容易感情冲动　词源：emotion 情感＋al 形容词后缀

motion ['məuʃ(ə)n] 运动 Newton's laws of motion 牛顿的运动定律；（做手势或头部动作）示意 motion to sb. to do sth.；（会议）动议，提议 put forward a motion 提出一项动议　词源：mot 移动 ＋ tion 名词后缀

commotion [kə'məuʃ(ə)n]（突然的）混乱，喧闹 the commotion caused by the superstar's visit 超级明星来访带来的喧闹　词源：com 共同 ＋ mot 移动 ＋ tion 名词后缀　指共同移动带来的混乱

movement ['mu:vm(ə)nt]（身体部位的）运动，动作 the dancer's elegant movements 舞蹈演员优美的动作；社会运动 the women's movement 妇女运动；军队调动 troop movements；乐章 the first movement of the symphony 交响乐的第一乐章　词源：mov 移动 ＋ ment 名词后缀

remote [ri'məut] 遥远的 a remote village 一个偏远的小村庄；（机会）渺茫的 remote chance；遥控器（＝ remote control）　词源：re 反复 ＋ mot 移动　指反复移动变得越来越远的

remove [ri'mu:v] 移走（车辆）；开除（学校）；解除（职务）；卸载（软件）；清除（污渍） remove stains；脱掉（衣物）　词源：re 向后 ＋ mov 移动　指步骤向后移动是移除卸载

mobilize ['məubəlaiz] 动员（军队或运动员）；帮助（某物更轻松）移动 the physiotherapist who mobilizes the patient's elbow 帮助病人活动肘部的物理治疗师　词源：mob 移动 ＋ l 长时间 long ＋ ize 动词后缀　指长时间做人们的动员

demobilize [di'məubəlaiz] 使军人复员 help demobilized soldiers adapt to civilian life 帮助复员军人适应平民生活　词源：de 否定 ＋ mobilize 动员　指不动员继续参军

demote [ˌdi:'məut] 使降职　词源：de 向下 ＋ mot 移动　指职位向下移动　反义词：promote

promote [prə'məut] 升职 promote sb. to manager 提升某人为经理；促销推销 promote a new book 推销新书；促进推动 promote economic growth 促进经济增长；倡议提倡 promote the idea of energy conservation 提倡能源节约；（体育运动队）升级　词源：pro 向前 ＋ mot 指进程向前移动

promotion [prə'məuʃn] 升职提拔；产品促销；促进推广；提倡倡导；（体育运动队的）升级　词源：promote 促进 ＋ tion 名词后缀

prompt [prɔm(p)t] 促使激励 prompt sb. to do sth.；给（演员）提词提醒；（计算机上输入信息的）提示提醒；立即的 take prompt action 采取立即行动　词源：promote 的词形变化

motivate ['məutiveit] 激励，鼓励 motivate sb. to do sth.；成为……的动机　词源：mot 移动 ＋ i 小 ＋ ate 动词后缀　指一点点移动

motive ['məutiv]（隐藏的）动机 a motive for (doing) sth.；（文艺作品或音乐作品的）主题，主旋律（＝ motif）　词源：mot 移动 ＋ tive 名词后缀

motivation [məuti'veiʃ(ə)n]（外部明显的）动力，原因 a motivation for (doing) sth.；积极性 improve students' motivation 提高学生的积极性　词源：mot 移动 ＋ tion 名词后缀

motor ['məutə] 引擎，发动机 motor vehicle 机动车辆　词源：mot 移动 ＋ or 名词后缀

motorcycle ['məutəsaik(ə)l] 摩托车　词源：motor 发动机 ＋ cycle 圈　指有发动机带轮子的

摩托车

motorboat ['məutəbəut] 摩托艇　词源：motor 发动机 + boat 船

motorway ['məutəwei] 高速公路　词源：motor 发动机 + way 路 指机动车行驶的路

mob [mɔb]（成群的）暴民；（同类的）一群人 an excited mob of football fans 一群激动的球迷；帮派团伙；团团围住（明星）；（鸟群或兽群）围攻，成群袭击　词源：mob 移动 move + battle 指具有攻击性的移动的一群人　形近易混词：mop

motel [məu'tel] 汽车旅馆（附有停车设施）　词源：mot 移动 + el 名词后缀 指给开车的人住的旅馆

mop [mɔp] 拖把；乱蓬蓬的头发 a mop of curly blonde hair 乱蓬蓬的金色卷发；拖地擦地 mop the floor；擦干抹去（液体）mop the sweat from the face 擦去脸上的汗水；消灭肃清 mop up any remaining rebellion 肃清残余反叛　词源：mo 移动 + p 向前 pro 指拖把向前移动拖地

mow [məu] 割草 mow the lawn 修草坪　词源：mo 移动 + w 水 指移动割草时溅出的草水味道

mower ['məuə] 割草机　词源：mow 割草 + er 名词后缀

149. **-mon-, -monit-**：warn　巧记：Juno Moneta 在罗马神话中，天后叫作朱诺（Juno），等同于希腊神话中的赫拉（Hera）。她是掌管人类婚姻的婚姻女神。罗马人喜欢选择在气候宜人、百花盛开的六月份结婚，用掌管婚姻的天后朱诺（Juno）为六月命名，称作 June。天后朱诺曾多次警告罗马人会遇到的危险，帮助他们化险为夷。一次，高卢人试图偷袭，这时朱诺神庙的鹅嘎嘎大叫，惊醒了罗马人，敌人被击退。罗马人认为鹅是朱诺的化身，为罗马人示警，称其为 Juno Moneta（警告者朱诺），moneta 的含义是"警戒者、警告者"。后来，罗马人建了一座 Juno Moneta 神庙，又把第一个造币厂设在了神庙里，希望女神能守护他们的财富。在 Juno Moneta 神庙里铸造出来了最早的货币，所以罗马人用 moneta 表示货币，英语中的 money（钱）和 mint（造币厂）都是源自 moneta 这个单词，而单词 monetary（货币的）也保留了 moneta 的拼写形式

monitor ['mɔnitə] 监控，监视，监听；监视器，显示器 computer monitor 计算机显示屏；检测仪，监视仪，监护仪 a heart monitor 心脏监护仪；监督员，核查员 send UN peace monitors to the area 派遣联合国和平监督员到该地区；班长　词源：monit 警告 + or 名词后缀 指给别人提出警告是监控

admonish [əd'mɔniʃ] 严厉警告，告诫 admonish sb. for chewing gum in class 因上课嚼口香糖告诫某人　词源：ad 强调 + mon 警告 + ish 动词后缀

admonition [,ædmə'niʃ(ə)n] 告诫，责备　词源：admonish 告诫 + tion 名词后缀

admonitor [əd'mɔnitə] 劝告者，劝诫者　词源：admonish 告诫 + or 名词后缀

premonish [pri:'mɔniʃ] 预警，预感到　词源：pre 在前面 + mon 告诫 + ish 动词后缀 指提前警告

premonition [ˌpriːməˈniʃn]（不好的）预感 a premonition of failure 失败的预感　词源：premonish 预警 + tion 名词后缀

monument [ˈmɔnjum(ə)nt] 纪念碑 a monument to heroes 英雄纪念碑；纪念塔；纪念馆；名胜古迹　词源：monu 警告 + ment 名词后缀

monumental [mɔnjuˈment(ə)l] 丰碑式的，伟大的 a monumental contribution to charity 对慈善的重大贡献；极大的，非常大 a monumental task 艰巨的任务；纪念性的 a monumental arch 纪念拱门　词源：monument 纪念碑 + al 形容词后缀

monster [ˈmɔnstə] 怪物，怪兽 a prehistoric monster with nine heads 史前九头怪兽；庞然大物；异常大的，庞大的，巨大的 monster mushrooms 巨大的蘑菇　词源：mon 警告 + er 名词后缀　指罗马人相信出现一些怪异变态的生物是神灵被激怒后发出的警告，预示着将有大灾大难发生

monstrous [ˈmɔnstrəs] 道德败坏的，骇人的 monstrous injustice 骇人听闻的不公平；巨大的 a monstrous wave 巨浪　词源：monster 怪物 + ous 形容词后缀（表示过多的）　指像怪物一样做了过多的骇人的破坏活动

150. **mono-, mon-**：single　巧记：moon 月亮 指只有一个月亮或每个月（大概29.5 天）都有一个月相盈亏周期的变化（新月→蛾眉月→上弦月→凸月→满月→凸月→下弦月→蛾眉月→新月）

month [mʌnθ] 月份　词源：mon 单一 + th 名词后缀　指每个月都有一个月相盈亏周期

monarch [ˈmɔnək] 君主　词源：mon 单一 + arch 统治　指一个人统治

monarchy [ˈmɔnəki] 君主政体，君主制 abolish the monarchy 废除君主政体；君主国　词源：monarch 君主 + y 名词后缀

monk [mʌŋk] 修道士，僧侣　词源：mon 单一　指自己修行的人

monastery [ˈmɔnəst(ə)ri] 修道院，寺院　词源：monk 修道士 + ast 最高级 + ery 名词后缀　指修道士修行最多的地方

monotone [ˈmɔnətəun] 单调，单调的声音 answer the question in a dull monotone 用单调的语气回答问题　词源：mono 单一 + tone 语气　指语气单一没有抑扬顿挫

monotonous [məˈnɔt(ə)nəs] 单调的，乏味的 monotonous work 单调乏味的工作　词源：monotone 单调 + ous 形容词后缀（表示过多的）

monopoly [məˈnɔp(ə)li] 垄断，独占，专营 have a monopoly on energy 对能源实行垄断；垄断者，垄断企业，专卖者；大富翁（棋类游戏，游戏者以玩具钞票买卖房地产）　词源：mono 单一 + pol 政治 politics + y 名词后缀　指一个政治团体说了算

monologue [ˈmɔn(ə)lɔg]（戏剧或电影的）独白；独角戏；滔滔不绝的讲话，个人的长篇大论　词源：mono 单一 + log 话语　指一个人在说话

monogamy [məˈnɔɡəmi] 一夫一妻制 a monogamous marriage 一夫一妻制的婚姻　词源：mono 单一 + gam 结婚 + y 名词后缀　指与一人结婚

montage [ˌmɔnˈtɑːʒ] 蒙太奇（一种剪辑理论，它是影像制作、音乐制作或写作的一种手法，

即把不同的影像等有趣而奇特地剪辑和组合在一起）；蒙太奇作品，综合（组合）式作品，剪辑组合物　词源：mon 单一 + age 名词后缀（表示长时间）指花长时间把不同影像部分剪辑和组合在一起

151. **multi-** : many　巧记：m 山 + u 水 指山多水多

multiply ['mʌltiplai] 乘 multiply A by B；成倍增加 multiply the risk of health problems 大大增加有健康问题的风险；繁殖 rabbits that multiply rapidly 迅速繁殖的兔子　词源：multi 多的 + ply 折叠 指成倍折叠

multiple ['mʌltipl] 许多的 multiple versions of the same song 一首歌曲的多种版本；（数学的）倍数　词源：multi 多的 + ple 充满 ful 指又多又满的

multitude ['mʌltitju:d] 大量，众多 a multitude of stars 这么多的星星；群众，民众 enlighten the multitude 启发群众；人群 clamoring multitudes 闹哄哄的人群　词源：multi 多的 + tude 名词后缀 指众多的状态

multidirectional [mʌltidi'rekʃənl] 多方向的　词源：multi 多的 + direction 方向 + al 形容词后缀

multinational [mʌlti'næʃ(ə)n(ə)l] 多国的，跨国的；跨国公司　词源：multi 多的 + nation 国家 + al 形容词后缀

multiracial [ˌmʌlti'reiʃl] 多种族的 a multiracial society 多种族的社会　词源：multi 多的 + race 种族 + cial 形容词后缀（表示特殊的 special）

multiparty [ˌmʌlti'pɑ:ti] 多党派的　词源：multi 多的 + party 党派

multilateral [ˌmʌlti'lætərəl] 多边的 multilateral negotiations 多边谈判　词源：multi 多的 + later 边 + al 形容词后缀

multilingual [mʌlti'liŋgw(ə)l] 多语言的 a multilingual classroom 多语课堂　词源：multi 多的 + lingua 舌头（指语言 language）+ al 形容词后缀

multimedia ['mʌltimi:diə] 多媒体的 a multimedia teaching approach 多媒体教学方法　词源：multi 多的 + media 媒体

152. **-mony** : event or state　巧记：money 钱 指有钱的状态

acrimony ['ækriməni]（态度或言辞）尖刻，讥讽 settle the dispute without acrimony 没有唇枪舌战解决纠纷　词源：acri 尖锐 sharp + mony 名词后缀 指有钱人的尖酸刻薄

ceremony ['seriməni] 典礼仪式 an awards / opening ceremony 颁奖/开幕仪式；礼节礼仪　词源：cere 谷类（来自希腊神话掌管谷类的女神 Ceres）+ mony 名词后缀 指花许多钱举办庆祝谷物丰收的仪式

harmony ['hɑ:məni]（音乐）和弦；（合唱）和声 sing in harmony 用和声唱歌；和谐 be in harmony with sth.　词源：harp 竖琴 + mony 名词后缀 指昂贵的竖琴发出的声音和谐

hegemony [hi'dʒeməni; -'ge-]（一国对其他国的）霸权　词源：hege 谐音"黑哥"黑社会大哥 + mony 名词后缀 指黑社会大哥有钱搞霸权

matrimony ['mætriməni] 结婚，婚姻 join together in holy matrimony 携手走进神圣的婚姻生活　词源：matri 母亲 ＋ mony 名词后缀　指妈妈给的钱作为彩礼或嫁妆用来结婚

patrimony ['pætriməni] 祖传财产，遗产　词源：patri 父亲 ＋ mony 名词后缀　指爸爸留下的钱是遗产　同义词：inheritance

153. -nomy：a field of study　巧记：not my study field 指一般人不擅长的学科领域

astronomy [ə'strɔnəmi] 天文学　词源：astro 星星 ＋ nomy 名词后缀（表示学科）　形近易混词：astrology

astrology [ə'strɔlədʒi] 占星术（指研究星体位置和运动对人的运势和事件的影响）　词源：astro 星星 ＋ ology 名词后缀（表示学科）指观察星星算运势

astronomer [ə'strɔnəmə] 天文学家　词源：astronomy 天文学 ＋ er 名词后缀

economy [i'kɔnəmi] 经济；经济体；节约，节俭 an economy fare 经济舱票价　词源：eco 生态或经济 ＋ nomy 名词后缀

economics [i:kə'nɔmiks; ek-] 经济学　词源：economy 经济 ＋ ics 名词后缀（表示学科）

economic [,i:kə'nɔmik; ek-] 经济的 economic growth 经济增长　词源：economy 经济 ＋ ic 形容词后缀　形近易混词：economical

economical [i:kə'nɔmik(ə)l; ek-] 节约的 an economical car 经济节油型汽车　词源：economy 经济 ＋ ical 形容词后缀　巧记：cal 谐音"抠"指抠门的是节约的

autonomy [ɔ:'tɔnəmi]（地方或机构）自治，自治权；自主能力，自主权 give teachers considerable autonomy 给予教师相当大的自主权　词源：auto 自己 self ＋ nomy 名词后缀　指自己管理自己

autonomous [ɔ:'tɔnəməs]（地方或机构）自治的 an autonomous region 自治区；有自主能力的，自主的　词源：autonomy 自治 ＋ ous 形容词后缀（表示过多的）

agronomy [ə'grɔnəmi] 农学，农艺学　词源：agro 田地 ＋ nomy 名词后缀　指研究农作物生长的学科

154. -nomin-：name　巧记：name 名字 ＋ mini 小　指名气小的名字

nominate ['nɔmineit] 提名 nominate sb. for (as) sth.；任命指派 nominate sb. to the legislative council 任命某人为立法委员会委员　词源：nomin 名字 ＋ ate 动词后缀

nomination [nɔmi'neiʃ(ə)n] 提名 the nominations for the Academy Awards 奥斯卡金像奖提名；任命 sb.'s nomination as chief executive officer 任命某人为首席执行官　词源：nominate 提名 ＋ tion 名词后缀

nominal ['nɔmin(ə)l] 名义上的，有名无实的 the nominal leader of the country 国家的名义领袖；象征性的 pay a nominal rent 付一点象征性的租金　词源：nomin 名字 ＋ al 形容词后缀

nominee [nɔmi'ni:] 被提名者 a presidential nominee 被提名为总统候选人的人　词源：nomin 名字 ＋ ee 名词后缀

anonymous [ə'nɒniməs] 匿名的 an anonymous letter 匿名信；无特色的 live a dull and anonymous countryside life 过枯燥平淡无特色的乡村生活　词源：an 否定 + onym 名字 name + ous 形容词后缀（表示过多的）

antonym ['æntənim] 反义词　词源：ant 相反 + onym 名字 name

synonym ['sinənim] 同义词　词源：syn 相同 + onym 名字 name

155. -nunc-, -nounc- : announce　巧记：noun 名词 指大声读一个个名词是宣布 最早指信使大声说话

noun [naun] 名词　词源：noun 大声说 指大声说出一个个名词

pronoun ['prəunaun] 代词　词源：pro 代替 in place of + noun 名词 指代替名词的词

announce [ə'nauns] 郑重宣布（决定或计划）announce one's engagement 宣布订婚；（机场或火车站的）广播通知；大声而肯定地说　词源：an 强调 + nounc 大声说 强调正式大声说出

announcement [ə'naunsm(ə)nt]（重要或正式的）声明，公告 make an announcement of a peace agreement 发表和平协议公告；（报纸上的）通告　词源：announce 宣布 + ment 名词后缀

enunciate [i'nʌnsieit]（清晰地）念字发音 enunciate each word slowly and carefully 每个字都念得又慢又仔细；（清晰地）阐明 enunciate the vision of the company 阐明对公司未来的看法　词源：e 出来 + nunc 大声说 + i 一点 + ate 动词后缀 指一点点清楚地大声说出来

enunciation [i,nʌnsi'eiʃn] 清晰发音；清晰阐明　词源：enunciate 清晰说明 + tion 名词后缀

pronounce [prə'nauns] 正确发音；（正式）宣布，宣告 pronounce you man and wife 宣布你们结为夫妻　词源：pro 向前 + nounc 大声说 指走上前正式大声说出

pronunciation [prə,nʌnsi'eiʃ(ə)n]（语言或词的）发音　词源：pronounce 宣布 + tion 名词后缀

denounce [di'nauns] 公开谴责 denounce a political scandal 谴责政治丑闻；告发举报 denounce sb. to the police 向警方告发某人　词源：de 以不好的方式 + nounc 大声说 指以语气不好的方式大声说话

denunciation [di,nʌnsi'eiʃ(ə)n] 谴责，斥责 a denunciation of the government's economic policies 对政府经济政策的谴责　词源：denounce 公开谴责 + tion 名词后缀

renounce [ri'nauns] 公开声明放弃（要求/头衔/特权/权利等）renounce one's claim to the throne 宣布放弃继承王位的权利；公开宣布放弃（理想/原则/信仰/暴力等）renounce the use of violence 声明放弃使用暴力；公开宣布断绝与某人的关系 renounce former business associates 公开宣布和以前的生意伙伴散伙　词源：re 向后 + nounc 大声说 指大声说出退出的话

renunciation [ri,nʌnsi'eiʃn]（对信仰或生活方式等）摒弃放弃；弃绝物质享受，克己禁欲　词源：renounce 放弃 + tion 名词后缀

8

156. -par-：1）equal　巧记：partner 伙伴 指伙伴关系的平等

separate ['sep(ə)reit] 分开的 separate bedrooms 独立卧室；使分开；分居分手　词源：se 分离 + par 相等的 + ate 动词后缀 指从同等地位中分离

separated ['sepəreitid] 夫妻分居的　词源：separate 使分开 + ed 形容词后缀

disparate ['disp(ə)rət] 迥然不同的，不相干的，全异的，悬殊的 disparate groups of people 不同群体的人　词源：dis 分离 + par 相等的 + ate 形容词后缀 指不相同的

disparity [di'spæriti]（由不公正对待引起的）完全不同，差异，悬殊 the disparity between rich and poor 贫富悬殊　词源：disparate 迥然不同的 + ity 名词后缀

parity ['pæriti]（薪金、权利或权力的）相同，等同 demand pay parity 要求同工同酬；（两国货币的）平价　词源：par 相等的 + ity 名词后缀

imparity [im'pæriti] 不平等，差异 the imparity of higher education opportunity 高等教育机会不平等　词源：im 否定 + parity 等同

compare [kəm'peə] 比较对比 beyond / without compare 无与伦比；把……比作，与……相似　词源：com 共同 + par 相等的 指把两个相同的事物进行比较

comparable ['kɔmp(ə)rəb(ə)l] 可比较的，可相提并论的 comparable figures at the same period of time last year 去年同期的可比数据　词源：compare 比较 + able 形容词后缀（表示可以……的）

comparison [kəm'pæris(ə)n] 比较 make / draw a comparison between sb. / sth.　词源：compare 比较 + on 名词后缀

comparative [kəm'pærətiv] 比较的 comparative study / analysis 比较研究/分析；相对的 comparative comfort / freedom / wealth 相对的舒适/自由/富裕；（形容词或副词的）比较级形式　词源：compare 比较 + tive 形容词后缀（表示充满活力的 active）

2）show　巧记：partner 伙伴 指向伙伴展示

apparent [ə'pær(ə)nt]（常作表语）明显的 it is apparent to sb. that…　词源：ap 强调 + par 展示 + ent 形容词后缀（表示具有……能力的）　巧记：appear 的形容词形式

transparent [træn'spær(ə)nt; trɑːn-; -'speə-] 透明的 transparent glass 透明的玻璃　词源：trans 穿越 + par 展示 + ent 形容词后缀（表示具有……能力的）指被光线穿过后能显示光线的　巧记：trans 穿越 + parent 父母 指父母能看透孩子的一切，在父母面前孩子的行为是透明的

3）bring forth　巧记：partner 伴侣 指夫妻或伴侣生育子女

parent ['peər(ə)nt] 父母 foster parents 养父母　词源：par 生育 + ent 名词后缀

parental [pə'rentl] 父母的，双亲的 parental consent 父母同意　词源：parent 父母 + al 形容词后缀

parenthesis [pə'renθisis] 圆括号　词源：parent 父母 + thesis 主题　指括号像父母保护孩子一样把主题保护好

multiparous [mʌl'tipərəs] 一胎多子的　词源：multi 多的 + par 生育 + ous 形容词后缀（表示过多的）

157. **para-**：1) by the side of, past, to one side, aside from　巧记：p 向上 + r 植物分裂生长　指植物枝叶在彼此旁边向上生长

paraphrase ['pærəfreiz]（用更容易理解的文字）意译，改述　词源：para 旁边 + phrase（以某种方式）措辞表达　指用旁边的另一种方式说明

parallel ['pærəlel] 平行的 parallel tracks 平行的小路；相似之处，相似特征 draw parallels between brains and computers 比较人脑和计算机；与……相匹敌 an achievement that has never been paralleled 难以匹敌的成就　词源：para 旁边 + ll 两条线 + e 出来 + l 一条线　指在彼此旁边的三条平行线

parasite ['pærəsait] 食客，依赖他人过活者；寄生虫　词源：para 旁边 + site 位置　指在旁边一起生活的食客

parameter [pə'ræmitə] 限定因素，界限范围，参数 set the parameters of the inquiry 设定调查范围　词源：para 旁边 + meter 测量 measure　指把周边需要测量的边界划出来

paragraph ['pærəgrɑ:f] 文章段落　词源：para 旁边 + graph 写　指在一段文字旁边写下一段文字

parade [pə'reid] 游行 a victory parade 胜利游行；阅兵 a military parade 军事检阅；炫耀展示 parade the trophy 炫耀奖杯；一连串没完没了的人或事件 a parade of visitors 没完没了的访客　词源：para 旁边 + ade 名词后缀（表示强调）指在彼此旁边列队前进

paralyze ['pærəlaiz] 使瘫痪；使停顿，不能正常运作 paralyze the economy 使经济陷入瘫痪　词源：para 旁边 + ly 躺着 lie + ze 动词后缀　指躺在旁边起不来

2) beyond　巧记：p 向上 + r 植物分裂生长　指植物向上生长的顶端优势超越侧枝生长

paramount ['pærəmaunt] 极重要的　词源：para 超越主茎 + mount 山 mountain　指超越山峰高度的

paranormal [ˌpærə'nɔ:ml] 超正常的　词源：para 超越 + normal 正常的

paradise ['pærədais] 天堂；伊甸园；乐土，乐园（指美好的环境）a tropical paradise 一个热带的人间乐园　词源：para 超越 + dise 死亡 die　指超越死亡的地方是天堂

paranoid ['pærənɔid] 多疑的，疑神疑鬼的 be paranoid about one's personal security 对某人的人身安全疑神疑鬼；偏执狂的，有妄想狂的　词源：para 超越 + noise 噪声 + id 名词后缀（表示具有某种身份）指弄出很多噪声的人思想是妄想的、偏执的

parapsychology [ˌpærəsai'kɔlədʒi] 超心理学（研究某些人声称具有的思维上超感知能力的学科，比如预测未来）　词源：para 超越 + psychology 心理学

3) subsidiary to　巧记：p 向上 + r 植物分裂生长　指植物枝叶附属于彼此

paralegal [ˌpærə'li:gl] 律师助手，助理　词源：para 附属的 + legal 法律的　指律师的助理

paramilitary [ˌpærə'milətri] 准军事的　词源：para 附属的 + military 军事的　指随时可转化成军事用途的

4）protection of or against　巧记：p 向上 + r 植物分裂生长　指植物长成伞状可以遮风挡雨

paradox ['pærədɔks] 自相矛盾的人、事物或情况；悖论　词源：para 保护抵制 + dox 名词后缀（表示观点想法 opinion）

parapet ['pærəpit]（屋顶、桥梁、城墙等边上的）矮墙，护墙　词源：para 保护抵制 + pet 宠物　指防止宠物袭击的矮墙

parasol ['pærəsɔl]（海滩上或餐馆外等处的）大遮阳伞　词源：para 保护抵制 + sol 太阳的 solar　指防晒的大遮阳伞

parachute ['pærəʃuːt] 降落伞　词源：para 保护抵制 + chute 自由下落时发出的声音　指起到保护作用、抵制自由下落的装置是降落伞

paratroops ['pærətruːps] 伞兵部队　词源：para 降落伞 parachute + troops 军队　指装备降落伞的部队

158. -pater-, -patr- : father　巧记：papa 爸爸

paternity [pə'təːniti] 父亲身份　词源：pater 父亲 + ity 名词后缀

paternal [pə'təːn(ə)l] 父亲般的 paternal love 父爱　词源：paternity 父亲身份 + al 形容词后缀

patriot ['pætriət; 'peit-] 爱国者　词源：patr 父亲 + ot 名词后缀　指爱祖国就像爱父亲一样的人

patriotic [ˌpeitri'ɔtik] 爱国的 patriotic songs 爱国歌曲　词源：patriot 爱国者 + ic 形容词后缀

patriotism ['peitriətiz(ə)m] 爱国主义　词源：patriot 爱国者 + ism 名词后缀（表示学说主义）

compatriot [kəm'pætriət; -'peit-] 同胞　词源：com 共同 + patriot 爱国者　指所有的爱国者都是同胞

patriarchy ['peitriɑːki] 父系社会；男权至上的社会制度　词源：patri 父亲 + arch 拱门（表示统治 rule）+ y 名词后缀　指男性统治的社会

patrimony ['pætriməni] 祖传财产，遗产　词源：patri 父亲 + mony 名词后缀　指爸爸留下的钱是遗产　同义词：inheritance

patron ['peitr(ə)n] 赞助者，资助人 a patron of the artists 艺术家的赞助者；（商店、餐馆或酒店）老顾客 recreation facilities for patrons 为顾客准备的娱乐设施　词源：patr 父亲 + on 正在　指像父亲一样资助钱财的资助者

patronize ['pætrəˌnaiz] 资助（机构或活动）；光顾（商店或餐馆）；高傲地对待他人　词源：patron 资助者 + ize 动词后缀　指资助别人时用高傲的态度对待他们

expatriate [ˌeks'pætriət] 居住国外的人，侨民；居住在国外的 expatriate workers 在国外工作的人　词源：ex 出去 + compatriot 同胞 + ate 动词后缀　指出国移居的同胞

repatriate [ˌriːˈpætrieit] 遣返某人回国 repatriated refugees 被强制遣送回国的难民；把钱或利润汇回国内　词源：re 向后＋compatriot 同胞＋ate 动词后缀　指让同胞返回国家

159. **-pet-, -peat, -petit-** : seek　巧记：pet 宠物　指宠物寻觅食物

appetite [ˈæpitait] 食欲，胃口 spoil one's appetite 影响某人的食欲；欲望，爱好 have an appetite for knowledge 有求知欲　词源：ap 强调＋pet 寻求＋ite 名词后缀　指寻求美食的胃口

appetizer [ˈæpitaizə]（餐前的）开胃小吃或开胃饮料　词源：appetite 胃口＋er 名词后缀

compete [kəmˈpiːt] 比赛，竞争 compete (with / against sb.) for sth.　词源：com 共同＋pet 寻求　指大家共同出发争先恐后寻求到达终点

competition [ˌkɔmpiˈtiʃ(ə)n] 比赛，竞赛　词源：compete 竞争＋tion 名词后缀

competitor [kəmˈpetitə] 比赛者，竞争者　词源：compete 竞争＋or 名词后缀

competent [ˈkɔmpit(ə)nt] 有能力的，能胜任的 be competent to do sth.　词源：compete 竞争＋ent 形容词后缀（表示具有……能力的）

competitive [kəmˈpetitiv] 竞争的；（产品或价格）有竞争力的 competitive prices 有竞争力的价格　词源：compete 竞争＋tive 形容词后缀（表示充满活力的 active）

impetus [ˈimpitəs] 刺激，促进，推动力 provide impetus for further reform 提供改革的推动力　词源：im 内部＋pet 寻求＋us 名词后缀　指向内部发力寻求推动力

petition [piˈtiʃ(ə)n] 请愿书 a petition against the new shopping mall 反对修建新购物中心的请愿书；（向政府或组织）请愿 petition sb. to do sth.　词源：pet 寻求＋tion 名词后缀　指寻求帮助的书信

perpetual [pəˈpetʃuəl; -tjuəl] 连续不断的，无休止的 the perpetual noise of the traffic 连续不断的交通噪声；（令人讨厌地）一再重复的 perpetual nagging 没完没了的唠叨；永久的，永恒的 perpetual motion machine 永动机　词源：per 一直＋pet 寻求＋al 形容词后缀　指不停寻求的

repeat [riˈpiːt] 重复　词源：re 重复＋peat 寻求　指通过重复来寻求真知温故而知新

repeated [riˈpiːtid] 反复的 repeated absences from class 一再旷课　词源：repeat 重复＋ed 形容词后缀

repetition [ˌrepiˈtiʃ(ə)n] 重复 learn by repetition 通过重复来学习　词源：repeat 重复＋tion 名词后缀

repertoire [ˈrepətwɑː]（某个表演者或团体的）全部剧目，常备节目，保留节目；全部技能 the excellent repertoire of a football player 足球运动员的出色球技　词源：repeat 重复　指可以重复演出的节目是保留节目

160. **-phil-** : love　巧记：Philip 菲利普　指爱马的人，源于希腊名字腓力（Philippos），含义是马的好朋友

philosophy [fiˈlɔsəfi] 哲学　词源：phil 爱＋soph 智慧＋y 名词后缀　指哲学是研究爱和智慧的学科

philosopher [fi'lɔsəfə] 哲学家；思想深刻的人　词源：philosophy 哲学 + er 名词后缀

philology [fi'lɔlədʒi] 文字学，语文学　词源：phil 爱 + log 圆木 + ology 名词后缀（表示学科）指喜爱研究圆木上刻的文字的学科

philharmonic [ˌfilhɑː'mɔnik]（用于管弦乐队或音乐团体的名称中）爱好音乐的，爱乐的 the Berlin Philharmonic 柏林爱乐乐团　词源：phil 爱 + harmony 和声 + ic 形容词后缀 指热爱音乐旋律和声的

philanthropy [fi'lænθrəpi] 慈善行为　词源：phil 爱 + anthropo 人 指爱所有的人，对他们乐善好施　形近易混词：anthropology

philanthropist [fi'lænθrəpist] 慈善家　词源：philanthropy 慈善行为 + ist 名词后缀　形近易混词：anthropologist

anthropology [ˌænθrə'pɔlədʒi] 人类学　词源：anthropo 人 + ology 名词后缀（表示学科）

anthropologist [ˌænθrə'pɔlədʒist] 人类学家　词源：anthropology 人类学 + ist 名词后缀

161. **-phon-**: sound　巧记：phone 声音 指发出的 ff 声

phone [fəun] 电话机；打电话　词源：phon 声音

phonetic [fə'netik] 语音的；音标的 phonetic symbols 音标符号　词源：phone 声音 + tic 形容词后缀 指标识发音的符号

phonetics [fə'netiks] 语音学　词源：phonetic 语音的 + cs 名词后缀（表示学科）

phenomenon [fi'nɔminən] 现象 cultural phenomenon 文化现象；非凡的人或事物　词源：phen 声音 + omen 预示 + on 名词后缀 指某种声音预示着某种现象

phenomenal [fə'nɔminl] 了不起的，非凡的 a phenomenal success 极大的成功　词源：phenomenon 现象 + al 形容词后缀 指现象级的

emphasize ['emfəsaiz] 着重强调 emphasize the importance of temperance 强调自我克制的重要性；重读单词或短语　词源：em 使动词化 + pha 声音 + ize 动词后缀 指放大声音来强调　同义词：stress

emphasis ['emfəsis] 强调，重点 put / place emphasis on sth.；（单词或短语的）重读，重音　词源：em 使动词化 + pha 声音 + is 名词后缀

euphony ['juːfəni] 和谐的声音，悦耳之音；（英语语音的修辞手法）语音和谐　词源：eu 好的 + phon 声音 + y 名词后缀 指发出和谐好听的声音

euphonious [juː'fəuniəs] 悦耳的，动听的，和谐的 euphonious door chimes 动听的门铃声　词源：euphony 悦耳声 + ious 形容词后缀（表示过多的）指有非常多悦耳声音的

homophone ['hɔməfəun; 'həum-] 同音异形异义词　词源：homo 相同的 same + phone 声音 指发音相同的单词，例如 hair / hare

gramophone ['græməfəun] 留声机，唱机　词源：gram 写 + phone 声音 指可以记录下声音的设备

microphone ['maikrəfəun] 麦克风　词源：micro 小 + phone 声音 指发出小声音的设备

stereophone ['stiəriəfəun] 头戴式立体声耳机　词源：stereo 立体的 stand + phone 声音

symphony ['simf(ə)ni] 交响乐　词源：sym 共同 + phon 声音 + y 名词后缀　指 orchestra 交响乐队共同发出乐器演奏的声音

symphonic [sim'fɔnik] 交响乐的　词源：symphony 交响乐 + ic 形容词后缀

telephone ['telifəun] 电话机；打电话　词源：tele 远的 + phone 声音　指能听到远方声音的设备

videophone ['vidiə(u)fəun] 可视电话　词源：video 视频 + phone 电话

162. **physio-** : nature　巧记：phone 声音 指自然界物质发出的特有声音代表了它们各自不同的天然属性

physiology [ˌfizi'ɔlədʒi] 生理学；（人或动植物的）生理机能 plant physiology 植物的生理机能　词源：physio 天性 + ology 名词后缀（表示学科）

physician [fi'ziʃ(ə)n] 内科医生　词源：physic 天性 + ian 名词后缀　指内科医生负责调理病人的生理属性

physics ['fiziks] 物理学 the laws of physics 物理定律　词源：physic 天性 + cs 名词后缀（表示学科）　指物理学是研究物质属性的学科

physicist ['fizisist] 物理学家　词源：physics 物理学 + ist 名词后缀

physical ['fizik(ə)l] 身体的 physical examination 体检；物理学的 physical laws 物理定律；物质的 the physical properties of gold 金子的物理性质；自然的，符合自然规律的 a physical explanation for this phenomenon 对这一现象合乎自然规律的解释　词源：physic 天性 + al 形容词后缀　指人或物质本身天然属性的

physique [fi'ziːk]（人的）体格，体形 the powerful physique of a rugby player 橄榄球运动员健壮的体形　词源：physic 天性 + ique 名词后缀

163. **-pict-** : paint　巧记：pi 作画 paint + ct 拟声词 指绘画时喷颜色的声音

depict [di'pikt] 描绘，描写 depict sb. / sth. as sth.　词源：de 向下 + pict 作画　指向下用颜料作画

picture ['piktʃə] 图画；照片；（电视或电影的）图像，画面；电影 the year's best picture 年度最佳影片；（常复数）电影院 go to the pictures 去看电影；情况，局面 the overall picture 总体形势；想象，设想 picture sb. / sth. as sth.　词源：pict 作画 + ture 名词后缀（表示性质 nature）

picturesque [ˌpiktʃə'resk] 风景如画的 a picturesque university 风景如画的大学；语言生动的 a picturesque account of life at sea 对海上生活生动的描述　词源：picture 图画 + esque 形容词后缀（表示如……似的）

pictorial [pik'tɔːriəl] 画报，画刊 Warship Pictorial 舰艇画报；有插图的，用图片的 a pictorial record of the shopping excursion 购物游的照片记录　词源：pict 作画 + ial 形容词后缀（表示特殊的 special）指特别配上图片的

164. -polis-, -polit-：city　巧记：people 人们　指人们组成了城市

Acropolis [ə'krɔpəlis] 古希腊雅典卫城　词源：acro 高 + polis 城市　指卫城是建在高处的城市，用于防范外敌入侵的要塞

polis ['pəulis] 希腊城邦　词源：polis 城市

poll [pəul] 民意测验 conduct a poll 进行民意测验；投票 go to the polls 参加投票　词源：polis 城市　指城市的民意　巧记：pol 人们 people 的缩写形式　指人民的意愿

politics ['pɔlitiks] 政治 party politics 党派政治　词源：polit 城市　指想法获得城市居民的支持得到权力就是政治

political [pə'litik(ə)l] 政治的 political party 政党　词源：politics 政治 + al 形容词后缀

politician [pɔli'tiʃ(ə)n] 政治家；善于玩弄权术者，见风使舵者，投机钻营者　词源：politics 政治 + ian 名词后缀

policy ['pɔləsi] 政策，方针 foreign policy 外交政策；保险单 an insurance policy 保险单；（处事）原则，为人之道 it is sb.'s policy to do sth.　词源：politics 政治 + y 名词后缀　指政治上制定的策略

cosmopolis [kɔz'mɔpəlis] 国际都市，大都会　词源：cosmos 宇宙 + polis 城市　指像宇宙一样特别大的城市

cosmopolitan [ˌkɔzmə'pɔlit(ə)n] 全世界的，世界性的 a cosmopolitan resort 国际性的度假胜地；见多识广的 cosmopolitan young people 见多识广的年轻人；四海为家的人，周游世界的人　词源：cosmos 宇宙 + polit 城市 + an 形容词后缀

metropolis [mi'trɔp(ə)lis] 大都会 a bustling metropolis 一个繁忙的大都市　词源：metro 地铁 + polis 城市　指有地铁的城市是大都会

metropolitan [metrə'pɔlit(ə)n] 大都会的 the Metropolitan Police 都市警队（负责伦敦地区的警察部队）　词源：metropolis 大都会 + an 形容词后缀

monopoly [mə'nɔp(ə)li] 垄断，独占，专营 have a monopoly on energy 对能源实行垄断；垄断者，垄断企业，专卖者；大富翁（棋类游戏，游戏者以玩具钞票买卖房地产）　词源：mono 单一 + pol 政治 politics + y 名词后缀　指一个政治团体说了算

165. -port-：carry　巧记：Portuguese 葡萄牙的　指葡萄牙海运发达，港口携带运输大量货物；也可理解为由 per（引导，穿越）变化而来，表示城市大门或入口

port [pɔːt]（葡萄牙盛产的）波尔图葡萄酒 a glass of port 一杯波尔图葡萄酒；港口 vessels in port 进港停泊的船只；（计算机与其他设备连接的）接口，端口 computer ports （指机箱后面的各种接口，如电源、鼠标、键盘、网线、麦克风、音频输出输入、USB、显示器、打印机等接口）；（船或飞机的）左舷 on the port side 在左舷　词源：port 携带　指携带货物的港口

porter ['pɔːtə]（火车站、机场或旅馆）行李搬运工　词源：port 港口 + er 名词后缀

portable ['pɔːtəb(ə)l] 便携的，手提的 portable mobile charger 便携式手机充电宝　词源：port 携带 + able 形容词后缀（表示可以……的）指可以便于携带的

portfolio [pɔːt'fəuliəu] 公文包 a portfolio bag；文件夹 a handmade iPad leather portfolio 手工制作苹果平板电脑皮夹；（艺术家或摄影师的）作品选集；（求职时用以证明资历的）作品或整套照片；（个人或机构公司的）有价证券组合，投资组合 a share / investment portfolio 股份/投资组合；（部长或大臣的）职责 the defence portfolio 国防部长职责　词源：port 携带 + folio 折叠 fold 指易携带可折叠的文件夹

deport [di'pɔːt]（将违法者或无合法居留权的人）驱逐出境　词源：de 否定 + port 携带 指不让携带物品进港口

deportee [ˌdiːpɔː'tiː] 被驱逐者　词源：deport 驱逐出境 + ee 名词后缀

export [ik'spɔːt; ek-; 'ek-] 出口的商品 a fall in the number of exports 出口产品量的下跌；出口 export agricultural commodities 出口农产品　词源：ex 出去 + port 携带 指携带货物出去

import [im'pɔːt; 'im-] 进口的商品 a ban on oil imports 禁止石油进口；进口 import raw materials 进口原材料；（新鲜事物）引进 import exotic rhythms to traditional music 把异国风情的韵律引入传统音乐　词源：im 内部 + port 携带 指携带货物进入

importation [ˌimpɔː'teiʃən] 进口 a law prohibiting the importation of crabs 禁止进口螃蟹的法令；（新鲜事物）引进 restrictions on the importation of movies 对引进电影的限制

report [ri'pɔːt] 报告，汇报　词源：re 向后 + port 携带 指携带数据资料返回做汇报

support [sə'pɔːt] 支持；供养抚养 supports one's family 养家；支撑承受（物体的重量） support the weight of sth.；证实证明 support the hypothesis 证实假设　词源：sup 下面 sub + port 携带 指在下面用头顶着行李携带它们前行

supportive [sə'pɔːtiv] 支持的，给予帮助的 a supportive family 支持自己的家庭　词源：support 支持 + tive 形容词后缀（表示充满活力的 active）

supporter [sə'pɔːtə] 支持者，拥护者 supporters of refugee deportation 支持驱逐难民的人；（运动队的）球迷　词源：support 支持 + er 名词后缀

transport [træn'spɔːt; trɑːn-] 运输　词源：trans 穿越 + port 携带 指携带货物穿山越岭

transportation [ˌtrænspɔː'teiʃ(ə)n; trɑːns-] 运输　词源：transport 运输 + tion 名词后缀

166. **-poss-, -pot-**：power　巧记：power 力量的词形变化

possible ['pɔsib(ə)l] 可能的　词源：poss 力量 + ible 形容词后缀（表示可以……的）指用力量可以达成的

impossible [im'pɔsib(ə)l] 不可能的　词源：im 否定 + possible 可能的

potent ['pəut(ə)nt]（药）有效力的；（酒）有劲的；（武器）强有力的，有威力的；（男性）有性功能的　词源：pot 力量 + ent 形容词后缀（表示具有……能力的）

impotent ['impət(ə)nt] 无能为力的 an impotent monarch 无能为力的君主；（男性）阳痿的　词源：im 否定 + potent 有威力的

potency ['pəutnsi]（药物的）效力，效能；威力，影响力 the potency of lust for power 权力欲望的影响力；（男性的）性功能　词源：potent 有效力的 + cy 名词后缀

potential [pə'tenʃl] 潜在的 potential customers 潜在的客户；潜力 achieve / fulfill / realize one's (full) potential 发挥某人的（全部）潜力　词源：potent 有威力的 + ial 形容词后缀（表示特殊的 special）指以后有特殊威力的

pot [pɒt] 锅 pots and pans 锅碗瓢盆；壶 make a pot of coffee 煮一壶咖啡；罐 jam / paint / yoghurt pot 果酱罐/油漆罐/酸奶瓶；花盆 herbs growing in pots 盆栽的草本植物　词源：pot 力量 指有提供热能力量的容器

pottery ['pɒt(ə)ri] 陶器 a piece of pottery 一件陶制品；陶艺　词源：pot 锅 + er 比较级（强调动作反复）+ y 名词后缀 指砂锅是陶器的代表

poultry ['pəʊltri] 家禽；家禽肉　词源：pou 小的 pau + let 小的 指小小的家禽　巧记：pot 锅 + l 长时间 + ry 名词后缀 指长时间放在锅里烹饪的家禽肉

possess [pə'zes] 拥有（物品或财产）possess a work permit 有国外就业工作许可证；具有（某种品质或能力）possess a supernatural ability 有超能力；（感觉或情绪）支配影响某人 sth. possess sb. (to do sth.)　词源：poss 力量 power + ss 钱$$ 指拥有权力和金钱就可以掌控支配一切

possession [pə'zeʃ(ə)n] 拥有 take possession of the property 获得房产的所有权；个人财产 personal possessions 私人物品；控球 win / get / lose possession of the ball 赢得/得到/失去对球的控制　词源：possess 拥有 + sion 名词后缀

possessive [pə'zesiv]（爱情或友情上）占有欲强的 be possessive of / about sb. / sth.；（语法中的）所有格的　词源：possess 拥有 + ive 形容词后缀（表示充满活力的 active）

167. post- : after, behind　巧记：p 放置 put + ost 最高级 指放置到最后

post-war [,pəʊst'wɔː] 战后的 food rationing in the post-war period 战后食物配给的时期　词源：post 向后 + war 战争

postgraduate [pəʊs(t)'grædjuət] 研究生　词源：post 向后 + graduate 大学毕业生 指大学毕业后继续学习的学生

postscript ['pəʊs(t)skript]（信件）附言；（书籍）后记　词源：post 向后 + script 写 指写在信件后面的补充内容　缩写为 PS

postulate ['pɒstjuleit] 假定，假设 a postulate that water exists on the planet 行星上有水的假设；提出理论性假设，认为……为实 postulate a 100-year lifespan for the concrete bridge 假定混凝土桥的寿命为 100 年　词源：post 向后 + late 后面的 指认为后面发生的事情为真实的　同义词：hypothesis / assumption / presumption

postpone [pəʊs(t)'pəʊn; pə'spəʊn] 推迟，延迟 postpone doing sth.　词源：post 向后 + pon 放置 指向后放置安排

168. -proof : resistant to　巧记：p 上面 up + roof 屋顶 指高高的屋顶可以抵挡风雨

waterproof ['wɔːtəpruːf] 防水的　词源：water 水 + proof 抵抗的

bulletproof ['bulitpruːf] 防弹的　词源：bullet 子弹 + proof 抵抗的

lightproof ['laitpru:f] 防光的，不透光的　词源：light 光 + proof 抵抗的
dustproof ['dʌstpru:f] 防尘的　词源：dust 尘土 + proof 抵抗的
shockproof ['ʃɔkpru:f] 防震的　词源：shock 震动 + proof 抵抗的

169. **psycho-, psych-** : spirit, soul, mind　巧记：在希腊神话中，普塞克（Psyche）是一位国王的第三个女儿，拥有绝世美貌，人们对她的仰慕甚至超过了女神维纳斯（Venus）。然而她的美貌并不能带给她一个如意郎君，在她的父亲向阿波罗求签之后，得知自己丈夫将是可怕的毒蛇，而且将被送到高山岩石上。正当普塞克独自在高山上绝望哭泣时，维纳斯的爱子丘比特（Cupid）却要让她成为自己的妻子，只是丘比特一直隐身，并不告知自己的真实身份。后来普塞克的两个姐姐出于嫉妒，唆使普塞克在晚上点灯看看她的丈夫的真实面貌，导致丘比特被烛油烫伤。维纳斯知道了这件事后，非常气愤，加上之前对于普塞克的嫉妒，几乎要将普塞克置于死地。普塞克对于自己的行为后悔不已，主动来到维纳斯面前认罪，并希望能见到自己的丈夫，请求他的原谅。维纳斯自然不会轻易答应，想出了种种刁难的办法。在众神的帮助下，这些难题都一一解决了。但还有最后一个难题，就是维纳斯让她到地狱里去向那里的王后索要一些"美容"，就在普塞克成功地获取装有美容的盒子往回走时，她实在克制不住自己的好奇心，打开了盒子。盒子里并没有什么"美容"，却只有一个地狱的睡眠鬼。当睡眠鬼被放出盒外时，立即侵入了普塞克的身体，让她毫无知觉地倒在路上，如同死去一般。这时丘比特的伤已经治愈，他也非常想念普塞克，赶紧飞到了她的身边。丘比特轻轻拂去普塞克脸上的睡眠鬼，深情地将爱妻吻醒了。后来，普赛克的名字就用来指心灵灵魂

psychic ['saikik] 有超自然力量的 psychic phenomena 超自然现象；（人）有特异功能的，能知未来的；通灵的人，有特异功能的人，能预知未来的人　词源：psych 心灵 + ic 形容词后缀
psychiatry [sai'kaiətri] 精神病学　词源：psych 心灵 + i 人 + t 治疗 treat + ry 名词后缀　指治疗人精神疾病的学科
psychiatrist [sai'kaiətrist] 精神科医生　词源：psychiatry 精神病学 + ist 名词后缀
psychopath ['saikəpæθ] 精神病患者　词源：psych 心灵 + path 疼痛 pain 指精神上疼痛的人
psychology [sai'kɔlədʒi] 心理；心理学 child psychology 儿童心理学　词源：psych 心灵 + ology 名词后缀（表示学科）
psychological [saikə'lɔdʒik(ə)l] 心理的 psychological state 心理状态；心理学的　词源：psychology 心理学 + al 形容词后缀

170. **-punct-** : point　巧记：pun 击打声 + ct 拟声词　指击打某个点发出的声音
punch [pʌntʃ] 打孔 punch the ticket 票上打孔；打卡上下班 punch in / out；用拳头重击 punch sb. in the face 打脸　词源：pun 点 + ch 拟声词　指在某个点上砰唿的打孔声

puncture ['pʌŋ(k)tʃə]（轮胎上刺破的）小孔；（皮肤上被刺破的）扎孔，刺伤；刺破，扎破 puncture a tyre 扎破轮胎　词源：punct 点 + ture 名词后缀（表示性质 nature）指打出一点点的小孔

acupuncture ['ækjupʌŋktʃə(r)] 针灸，针刺疗法　词源：acu 尖锐的 acute + puncture 刺破　指针灸治疗刺破皮肤

punctuate ['pʌŋ(k)tʃueit; -tju-] 给……加标点符号；不时打断 the speech punctuated by bursts of applause 不时被阵阵掌声打断的讲演　词源：punct 点 + ate 动词后缀　指不时地点击打断

punctuation [pʌŋ(k)tʃu'eiʃ(ə)n; -tju-] 标点符号　词源：punctuate 不时打断 + tion 名词后缀　指标点符号是用来打断间隔文字的

punctual ['pʌŋ(k)tʃuəl; -tjuəl] 准时的，按时的 be punctual for appointments 准时赴约　词源：punct 点 + al 形容词后缀　指按点到达的

punctuality [,pʌŋktju'æliti] 准时，按时　词源：punctual 准时的 + ity 名词后缀

171. **-pur-**：pure　巧记：p 上面 up + u 水　指山上的水是清澈纯净的

pure [pjuə] 纯的，纯净的 pure cotton 纯棉；完全的，纯粹的 meet sb. by pure chance 遇见某人纯属偶然；纯洁的，无邪的 pure and innocent children 纯洁天真的孩子；纯种的 the purest breed of horses 最纯种的马　词源：pur 纯的

purity ['pjuəriti] 纯洁；纯度 the purity of tap water 自来水的纯度　词源：pure 纯的 + ity 名词后缀

impure [im'pjuə(r)] 不纯的，掺杂质的 impure gold 不纯的金子；道德败坏的，淫乱的　词源：im 否定 + pure 纯的

purify ['pjuərifai] 使（物质）纯净 purified water 纯净水；（灵魂、心灵或思想）净化　词源：pur 纯的 + fy 使动词化

purge [pə:dʒ] 清除异己 purge extremists from the party 把极端分子清除出党；消除不良风气 purge the minds of prejudice 消除头脑中的偏见；泻药　词源：pur 纯的 + ge 大哥　指清洗党派里的大哥

172. **-put-**：think　巧记：put 放置　指放置算卦的工具估算前途命运

dispute [di'spju:t; 'dispju:t] 争端，分歧 settle a territorial dispute 解决领土纠纷　词源：dis 分散 + put 思考　指想不到一起有分歧

impute [im'pju:t]（常指不公正地把责任等）归因于 impute the silence to shyness 把沉默归因于害羞　词源：im 内部 + put 思考　指内心思考找内因

compute [kəm'pju:t] 计算 compute the losses 计算损失　词源：com 共同 + put 思考　指把数据放在一起计算思考

computer [kəm'pju:tə] 计算机，电脑 a computer programmer 程序员　词源：compute 计算 + er 名词后缀　指能够计算数据的机器

putative ['pjuːtətiv] 公认的，被普遍认可的 the putative father of her children 被认为是她孩子们父亲的那个人　词源：put 思考 + tive 形容词后缀（表示充满活力的 active）指经过众人充分思考后的

repute [ri'pjuːt] 名誉，名声 a pianist of international repute 一位享有国际声誉的钢琴家　词源：re 重复 + put 思考　指让人反复思考想起的是名誉声望

reputation [repju'teiʃ(ə)n] 名誉，名望 a museum that lives up to its reputation 名副其实的博物馆　词源：repute 名声 + tion 名词后缀

173. **-quir-, -quisit-, -quest** : seek　巧记：q 树上的猴子　指猴子的好奇心驱使它寻求探索新事物，源于腓尼基字母 qoph 猴子

acquire [ə'kwaiə] 养成（习惯）acquire a habit of gambling 养成赌博的习惯；（通过努力、能力、行为表现）获得，得到 acquire a reputation for honesty 获得了诚实的名声；学到，习得（知识或技能）acquire skills as a surgeon 习得外科医生的技能；购得 acquire new premises 购得新办公楼　词源：ac 强调 + quir 寻求　指强烈寻求知识

acquisitive [ə'kwizitiv]（对钱财）贪得无厌的，贪婪的，渴求获取财物的 acquisitive real estate developers 贪婪的房地产开发商　词源：acquire 获得 + tive 形容词后缀（表示充满活力的 active）　同义词：greedy

acquired [ə'kwaiəd] 已习得的，获得的 acquired knowledge and wealth 通过努力获得的知识和财富　词源：acquire 习得 + ed 形容词后缀

acquisition [ˌækwi'ziʃ(ə)n]（知识、技能等的）获得，习得 the acquisition of language 语言的习得；（土地、权力、金钱等的）获得，得到 the acquisition of new land for development 获得新的土地用于开发；（多指贵重的）购置物 hold an exhibition of new acquisitions 为新购得的艺术品举办展览　词源：acquire 获得 + tion 名词后缀

query ['kwiəri] 疑问，质问 have a query about sth.　词源：que 寻求 + er 比较级（强调动作反复）+ y 名词后缀　指不停地重复寻求答案

quest [kwest]（长期的）寻求，追求 the long quest for peace 对和平的长期寻求　词源：que 寻求 + est 最高级　指时间最长、最耐心的寻求

inquire [in'kwaiə] 询问打听 inquire sth. of sb.；调查探究 inquire into sth.　词源：in 内部 + quir 寻求　指向内部打听消息

enquire [in'kwaiə] 询问打听 enquire sth. of sb.；调查探究 enquire into sth.　词源：en 使动词化 + quir 寻求

inquiry [in'kwairi] 询问打听，质询（比如体育比赛质询分数）；调查探究 a fraud inquiry 诈骗案调查　词源：inquire 询问 + ry 名词后缀

enquiry [in'kwairi] 询问打听，质询（比如体育比赛质询分数）；调查探究 a fraud enquiry 诈骗案调查　词源：enquire 询问 + ry 名词后缀

inquisition [ˌinkwi'ziʃn]（昔日罗马天主教惩罚异教徒的）宗教法庭，异端裁判所；（威胁性的或令人不快的）审查盘问 conduct an inquisition into the details of the politician's personal life 盘问政客的个人生活细节　词源：in 内部 + quisit 寻求 + tion 名词后缀　指寻求改变异教徒内心异端信仰的地方

inquisitive [in'kwizitiv] 好奇的，爱刨根问底的，过分打听别人私事的；勤学好问的，爱钻研的 an inquisitive mind 勤学好问的精神　词源：in 内部 + quisit 寻求 + tive 形容词后缀（表示充满活力的 active）　同义词：curious

question ['kwestʃ(ə)n] 问题；怀疑；询问质问　词源：quest 寻求 + tion 名词后缀

questionable ['kwestʃ(ə)nəb(ə)l] 有问题的；（品德等）值得怀疑的，可能不诚实（或不道德）的，别有用心的 a man of questionable character 人品有问题的人　词源：question 问题 + able 形容词后缀（表示可以……的）

questionnaire [ˌkwestʃə'neə; ˌkestjə-] 问卷 fill in a questionnaire 填调查表　词源：question 问题 + naire 名词后缀

conquest ['kɒŋkwest] 征服，克服 the conquest of space 征服太空；占领（或征服）的土地；爱情上被俘虏的人，爱情的俘虏 boast about many conquests 吹嘘获得了许多女孩的芳心　词源：con 共同 + que 寻求 + est 最高级　指共同寻求财富的最高级形式是征服

conquer ['kɒŋkə] 征服 conquered territories 被征服的领土；克服 conquer one's nerves and fear 克服紧张和恐惧　词源：con 共同 + que 寻求 + er 比较级（强调动作反复）指反复不停地寻求财富

request [ri'kwest]（下级对上级正式或礼貌的）主观要求，请求 make an urgent request for medical aid 紧急要求医疗援助　词源：re 重复 + quest 寻求　指反复寻求帮助

require [ri'kwaiə]（上级对下级）客观要求，需要 require downsizing 需要裁员紧缩；（法律或规章制度）规定，客观要求　词源：re 重复 + quir 寻求　指反复寻求帮助

requisite ['rekwizit] 必需品 toilet requisites 洗漱用品；必须的 lack the requisite qualifications 缺少必要的资历　词源：require 要求 + ite 名词后缀　指要求必须有的物品

exquisite ['ekskwizit; ik'skwizit; ek-] 精致的，精美的 the most exquisite craftsmanship 最精美的工艺；(疼痛或快乐)感觉强烈的　词源：ex 出来 + quisit 寻求 + ite 形容词后缀　指经过努力寻求出来的是最精美的　同义词：delicate / dainty

174. -rad-, -ras- : scrape　巧记：r 植物分裂生长　指植物生长时刮擦土壤

erase [i'reiz] 擦去抹掉（文字）；抹去（磁带录音）；清除（记忆）；消除消灭 erase poverty and injustice 消灭贫困和不公正　词源：e 出去 + ras 刮擦

eraser [i'reizə] 橡皮　词源：erase 擦去 + er 名词后缀

erasable [i'reisəbl] 可消除的，可擦去的 erasable markers 可擦除笔迹的记号笔　词源：erase 擦去 + able 形容词后缀（表示可以……的）

abrade [ə'breid]（与岩石等硬物相互作用而）磨损 ropes abraded by the rocks 被岩石磨损的绳子；擦伤（皮肤）　词源：ab 离开 + rad 刮擦　指一点点打磨刮擦

abrasive [ə'breisiv] 有研磨作用的 abrasive paper 砂纸；（用来擦洗表面或使表面光滑的）

磨料；粗鲁的，生硬的 an abrasive manner 粗鲁的举止　词源：abrade 磨损 + sive 形容词后缀（表示充满活力的 active）

raze [reiz] 夷为平地，把（城镇或建筑物）彻底破坏 raze the city to the ground 把城市彻底摧毁　词源：raz 刮擦 指不停刮擦彻底破坏

razor ['reizə] 剃须刀 an electric razor 电动剃须刀　词源：raz 刮擦 + or 名词后缀 指刮擦胡须的工具

175. -radic- : root　巧记：red 红色 指红色的萝卜扎根在土里生长

radish ['rædiʃ] 萝卜 a bunch of radishes 一捆萝卜　词源：radi 根 + ish 名词后缀　巧记：red 红色的 + dish 菜肴 指红色的菜肴是萝卜　相关词：daikon 白萝卜（＝ white radish）谐音"大根"指大白萝卜是很长很大的一根

radical ['rædik(ə)l] 重大的，根本的 propose radical changes 建议进行根本改革；激进的 radical views 激进的观点；（主张社会和政治作彻底变革的）激进分子　词源：radic 根 + al 形容词后缀 指动了根基的

eradicate [i'rædikeit] 根除，消灭 eradicate racism from sport 杜绝体育中的种族歧视　词源：e 出来 + radic 根 + ate 动词后缀 指连根拔起

176. -rid-, -ris- : laugh　巧记：ride 骑马 指骑马的有钱人嘲笑别人

deride [di'raid] 嘲笑，讥讽 deride one's opponents 嘲讽对手　词源：de 向下 + rid 笑 指向下嘲笑别人

derisive [di'raisiv; -z-] 嘲弄的，讥讽的 derisive laughter 讥笑　词源：deride 嘲笑 + sive 形容词后缀（表示充满活力的 active）

derision [di'riʒn] 嘲笑，讥讽 become an object of universal derision 成了众人嘲弄的对象　词源：deride 嘲笑 + sion 名词后缀

ridicule ['ridikjuːl] 嘲笑，奚落 ridicule one's peers 奚落同龄人　词源：rid 嘲笑 + l 长时间 指长时间嘲笑　同义词：mock / tease / taunt / sneer

ridiculous [ri'dikjuləs]（带鄙视别人的）荒唐的，可笑的，傻的　词源：ridicule 嘲笑 + ous 形容词后缀（表示过多的）同义词：absurd（不带鄙视别人的客观上）荒唐的 / ludicrous

177. -rog- : ask　巧记：roar 吼叫 + g 哥哥 gege 指吼叫着的哥哥大声询问

arrogant ['ærəg(ə)nt] 高傲的，自大的 an arrogant attitude 傲慢的态度　词源：ar 强调 + rog 询问 + ant 形容词后缀（表示具有……能力的）指说话大声趾高气扬的

abrogate ['æbrəgeit] 废除，取消（法律或协议）abrogate the treaty 废除条约　词源：ab 离开 + rog 询问 + ate 动词后缀 指问都不问就离开

derogate ['derəgeit] 贬低，贬损 derogate one's achievements 贬低某人的成就　词源：de 向下 + rog 询问 + ate 动词后缀 指向下语气不好的询问

interrogate [in'terəgeit]（长时间）审问，讯问 interrogate the suspect 审讯嫌疑犯　词源：

inter 两者间 ＋rog 询问 ＋ate 动词后缀　指在嫌疑犯间来回询问

interrogation [ɪnˌterəˈɡeɪʃ(ə)n] 审问，讯问　词源：interrogate 审问 ＋tion 名词后缀

surrogate [ˈsʌrəɡət] 替代的，代理的 a surrogate mother 代孕母亲；替代品，替代者 an official surrogate for the president's re-election campaign 总统连任选举官方代理人　词源：sur 上面 ＋rog 询问 ＋ate 名词后缀　指在台上代理别人发出询问的人

178. **-rot-** : wheel　巧记：r 跑 run ＋o 圆 ＋t 方向 to　指向某个方向滚动；也可谐音记忆"绕它"指绕着它转动

rotate [rə(ʊ)ˈteɪt] 使旋转，使转动 rotate the steering wheel 转动方向盘；（天体）旋转；（人员）轮换，（工作）轮值；轮换队员；（庄稼）轮作，轮种　词源：rot 转动 ＋ate 动词后缀

rotation [rə(ʊ)ˈteɪʃ(ə)n] 旋转，转动 the daily rotation of the Mercury on its axis 水星每天的自转；轮班，换班 job rotation 工作的轮换；（庄稼）轮作，轮种 crop rotation　词源：rotate 使转动 ＋tion 名词后缀

rotary [ˈrəʊt(ə)ri] 旋转的，转动的 rotary gears 旋转的齿轮；环形路口（＝roundabout）　词源：rotate 使转动 ＋ry 形容词后缀

roll [rəʊl]（纸、胶卷、钱等的）卷，卷轴 a roll of film 一卷胶卷；（食物）卷 a spring / chicken roll 春卷/鸡肉卷；名单，名册 call / take the roll 点名；卷起（衣袖或裤腿）roll up sleeves 卷起袖子；使滚动；（打雷或敲鼓的）隆隆声或咚咚声 a drum roll 鼓的咚咚声；掷骰子 roll the dice；左右摇晃 rolling of a ship 船的摇晃；（人）打滚翻身；卷烟　词源：ro 转动 ＋ll 两个长棍　指两个长棍滚动　巧记：the Easter Egg Roll 复活节滚彩蛋比赛　每年的复活节美国总统都要邀请孩子和他们的父母，到白宫的草坪举行滚彩蛋的游戏，孩子们使用一个长柄勺子推动一颗鸡蛋在草地上滚动，谁跑得最快，谁就能得到丰厚的奖励，活动会通过电视向全球转播　形近易混词：reel

reel [riːl]（胶布或电影胶片）一卷，卷轴，卷盘 a fishing rod and reel 钓竿和钓线轴；迷惑震惊 reel from the defeat 因失败而晕头转向；蹒跚跟跄 reel away from the bar 跌跌撞撞地离开酒吧　词源：roll 滚动 ＋ee 眼睛　指眼球转动，感到天旋地转，走路踉跄

roller [ˈrəʊlə]（把东西弄平等的）碾子，滚筒 a paint roller 刷漆滚筒；（用于移动无轮重物的）滚棒，滚杆，滚柱 move the boat on rollers 用滚子来移动船；卷发夹；卷浪，巨浪　词源：roll 滚动 ＋er 名词后缀

roast [rəʊst] 烘烤 roast a hog 烤一只乳猪；烤好的 roast chicken 烧鸡　词源：ro 滚动 ＋ast 最高级　指烘烤食物需要不停滚动防止烤焦

enroll [ɪnˈrəʊl] 使入伍，入学，入会；报班，登记，注册（课程）enroll in the special aerobics course 报名参加专门的有氧运动课程　词源：en 使动词化 ＋roll 卷轴　指让名字登记在名单卷轴上

9

179. -san- : health　巧记：son 太阳　指阳光可以杀菌有利于健康，在希腊神话里太阳神阿波罗是掌管光明、预言、音乐、艺术、畜牧和医药之神，也是消灾解难之神，精通弓箭射术，同时也是人类文明、迁徙和航海者的保护神

sanitation [ˌsæni'teiʃ(ə)n] 公共卫生，环境卫生 disease resulting from poor sanitation 公共卫生条件差导致的疾病　词源：san 健康 + it 它 + nation 国家　指国家层面的公共卫生

sanitary ['sænit(ə)ri] 卫生的，清洁的 sanitary facilities 卫生设施　词源：san 健康 + it 它 + ary 形容词后缀　指让它健康的是卫生的

sane [sein]（人）神志清醒的，头脑清楚的；明智的，清醒的（方法）a sane way to settle the problem 解决问题的明智方法　词源：san 健康

insane [in'sein] 精神错乱的 a hospital for the insane 精神病院　词源：in 否定 + sane 神志清醒的

sanity ['sæniti] 心智健全，神志正常 keep / lose one's sanity 保持/失去头脑清醒　词源：sane 神志清醒的 + ity 名词后缀

sanitarium [ˌsænə'teəriəm] 疗养院，疗养所 a hysterical patient transferred to the sanitarium 被转到疗养院的歇斯底里的病人　词源：sanitary 卫生的 + ium 名词后缀（表示地点 place）　指干净卫生的地方

sanguine ['sæŋgwin] 乐观的，充满自信的 be sanguine about the prospects 对前景保持乐观　词源：san 健康 + gu 变得 go + ine 形容词后缀　指态度变得阳光健康的是乐观的　同义词：optimistic

180. -sat-, -satis-, -satur- : enough　巧记：罗马神话的萨图恩（Saturnus 或 Saturn），掌管大地丰饶的农业保护神，寓意丰收富足，也可指土星

satisfy ['sætisfai] 使满意；满足需求　词源：satis 充足 + fy 动词后缀

satisfaction [ˌsætis'fækʃ(ə)n] 满意　词源：satisfy 使满足 + tion 名词后缀

satisfactory [ˌsætis'fækt(ə)ri] 令人满意的　词源：satisfy 使满足 + ory 形容词后缀

satiate ['seiʃieit] 使（需求）充分满足，使（欲望）过饱 satiate people's growing appetite for a healthier bite 满足人们日益增长的健康一餐的胃口需求　词源：sat 充足 + i 人 + ate 动词后缀　指满足人的需求或欲望

satiation [ˌseiʃi'eiʃn] 知足，满足　词源：satiate 使满足 + tion 名词后缀

satiable ['seiʃiəbl] 可满足的 satiable curiosity 满足了的好奇心　词源：satiate 使满足 + able 形容词后缀（表示可以……的）

insatiable [in'seiʃəbl] 不知足的，贪得无厌的 have an insatiable desire for wealth 对财富有不知足的欲望　词源：in 否定 + satiable 不满足的

satire ['sætaiə] 讽刺；讽刺作品 a stinging satire on American politics 一部对美国政治的尖锐讽刺的作品　词源：sat 充足 + ire 名词后缀　指由满满的各种混合水果组成的菜肴　后指诗歌中多种主题的混合使用会起到讽刺的效果

satirize ['sætəraiz] 讽刺 a play satirizing the entertainment industry 一部讽刺娱乐业的戏剧　词源：satire 讽刺 + ize 动词后缀

saturate ['sætʃəreit] 使湿透 the saturated carpet 浸湿了的地毯；使市场饱和 saturate the market；使充满 be saturated with commercials 充斥着广告　词源：satur 充足 + ate 动词后缀

saturated ['sætʃəreitid] 湿透的，浸透的 a shirt saturated with sweat 被汗水湿透的衬衫；饱和的 a saturated solution 饱和的溶液　词源：saturate 使湿透 + ed 形容词后缀

unsaturated [ʌn'sætʃureitid; -tjur-] 未饱和的　词源：un 否定 + saturated 饱和的

saturation [sætʃə'reiʃ(ə)n] （化学）饱和度；饱和，饱和状态 market saturation 市场饱和；饱和报道，连篇累牍的报道 give sth. / sb. saturation coverage

181. **-sci-**：know　巧记：scientia 拉丁语　指知识

science ['saiəns] 科学 the laws of science 科学定律；理科 science students / courses 理科学生/课程　词源：sci 知道 + ence 名词后缀

pseudoscience [ˌsjuːdəu'saiəns] 伪科学　词源：pseudo 假的 false + science 科学

conscience ['kɒnʃ(ə)ns] 良心 have a clear / guilty conscience 问心无愧/有愧　词源：con 共同 + science 科学　指做科学需要有良心不能弄虚作假

conscientious [ˌkɒnʃi'enʃəs] 凭良心做事的，认认真真的 a conscientious student / teacher / employee 勤勉认真的学生/一丝不苟的老师/认真负责的员工　词源：conscience 良心 + scientist 科学家 + ious 形容词后缀（表示过多的）指科学家做科学研究的态度是勤勤恳恳的

conscious ['kɒnʃəs] 有意识的，清醒的，有知觉的；注意到，意识到 be conscious of sth.；特别关注的 health-conscious consumers 有健康意识的消费者　词源：con 共同 + sci 知道 + ious 形容词后缀（表示过多的）指完全知道来龙去脉是有意识的　同义词：aware

unconscious [ʌn'kɒnʃəs] 无意识的，昏迷的，失去知觉的；未意识到的 be unconscious of sth.　词源：un 否定 + conscious 有意识的　指人睡眠或昏迷的状态

consciousness ['kɒnʃəsnis] 神志清醒；思想意识 class-consciousness 阶级意识　词源：conscious 有意识的 + ness 名词后缀

subconscious [sʌb'kɒnʃəs] 下意识的，潜意识的 a subconscious reaction 潜意识的反应　词源：sub 下面 + conscious 有意识的　指下意识的

subconsciousness [ˌsʌb'kɒnʃəsnis] 下意识，潜意识　词源：subconscious 下意识的 + ness 名词后缀

omniscient [ɒm'nisiənt] 无所不知的，全知的 omniscient parents in children's eyes 孩子眼里无所不知的父母　词源：omni 全部 all + sci 知道 + ent 形容词后缀（表示具有……能

力的）

nescient ['neʃiənt] 无知的，无学问的 be nescient of contemporary art 对当代艺术无知的　词源：ne 否定 no + sci 知道 + ent 形容词后缀（表示具有……能力的）指不知道的

prescient ['presiənt] 有预知能力的，能预知未来的 give a prescient warning 预先警告　词源：pre 在前面 + sci 知道 + ent 形容词后缀（表示具有……能力的）指能够提前知道的

prescience ['presiəns] 预知，先见之明 the prescience of the price fluctuation 价格波动的先见之明　词源：prescient 有预知能力的 + ence 名词后缀

182. **se-**：away from, apart from, without　巧记：s 牙齿（腓尼基字母含义）+ e 出来 指上下牙齿彼此分离；也可发音记忆为拟声词 si "撕" 指撕开分离发出的声音

secular ['sekjulə] 世俗的，非宗教的 secular music 世俗音乐　词源：se 种子 seed 指每天过播种耕地的世俗生活　巧记：se 分离 + particular 特殊的 指和特殊的宗教事务分离的是世俗的

seclude [si'kluːd] 隐退隐居，与世隔绝 live a secluded life 过与世隔绝的生活　词源：se 分离 + clude 关闭 close 指离开世俗后闭关隐居

seclusion [si'kluːʒ(ə)n] 隐退隐居，与世隔绝 enjoy peace and seclusion 享受太平和清静　词源：seclude 与世隔绝 + sion 名词后缀

secure [si'kjuə; si'kjɔː] 固定的，牢靠的 a secure aerial 牢固的电线；可靠的，稳定的 a secure job / income 稳定的工作/收入；安全的；有安全感的；保证安全；为（债务或贷款）作抵押 use the house to secure the loan 用房子作抵押贷款　词源：se 分离 + cure 照顾 care 指在离开时陪着照顾

insecure [ˌinsi'kjuə; ˌinsi'kjɔː] 不安全的；无自信的；没有把握的；不牢靠的　词源：in 否定 + secure 安全的

security [si'kjuərəti] 安全；安保措施；保障；抵押品 use the car as security for the loan 用车作为抵押品得到贷款　词源：secure 安全的 + ity 名词后缀

securities [si'kjuəritis] 证券　词源：security 指保证价值安全的东西是证券

seduce [si'djuːs] 诱奸，勾引；诱惑，引诱，诱使 seduce sb. into doing sth.　词源：se 离开 + duc 引导 lead 指引导某人离开去做某事

select [si'lekt] 精选；精选的；奢华的，一流的　词源：se 分离 + lect 选择 choose 指分离出其他后精选出的

selective [si'lektiv] 择优的　词源：select 精选 + tive 形容词后缀（表示充满活力的 active）

selection [si'lekʃ(ə)n] 精挑细选；精品；挑选，选择，选拔 natural selection 自然选择　词源：select 精选 + tion 名词后缀

sell [sel] 销售　词源：se 分离 + ll 长时间 指长时间与物品分离是卖掉它

sale [seil] 出售；大减价　词源：sell 的名词形式

salesman ['seilzmən] 男售货员　词源：sale 卖 + man 人 指卖货的人

segregate ['segrigeit] 种族隔离 segregate sb. from sb.；使隔离 smoking areas segregated from non-smoking areas 和非吸烟区分开的吸烟区　词源：se 分离＋greg 群 flock＋ate 动词后缀　指从人群中分离出来

seminar ['seminɑː] 研讨会 a teaching seminar 教学研讨班　词源：se 分离＋min 小＋ar 名词后缀　指分成小组开会　巧记：谐音"塞满了"指研讨会上塞满了人

separate ['sep(ə)reit] 分开的 separate bedrooms 独立卧室；使分开；分居分手　词源：se 分离＋par 相等的＋ate 动词后缀　指从同等地位中分离

183. **-sed-, -sid-, -sess-**：sit　巧记：可能源于意大利南部方言 sede 椅子 chair；也可记忆为 Sedan 色当，法国东北部一个城镇，欧洲人的轿车称为 sedan，据说轿子最初出现在法国的色当，色当也坐落着欧洲最大的军事城堡色当城堡；还可看作 sit down 的缩写形式

sedan [si'dæn] 轿车 a sedan chair 轿子　词源：sed 坐 指轿子 后指轿车

sedentary ['sed(ə)nt(ə)ri] 久坐不动的 health problems posed by our sedentary lifestyles 久坐不动的生活方式引起的健康问题；（人或动物）不迁移的，定居的 sedentary people living in the virgin forest 长期居住在原始森林的人们　词源：sedan 轿车＋ary 形容词后缀　指在开车坐着不动的状态

saddle ['sæd(ə)l] 马鞍；自行车车座；使承担（苦差事）be saddled with debts 负担上债务　词源：sad 坐＋dle 名词后缀（表示强调程度）指一直坐的位置是马鞍或车座

preside [pri'zaid] 主持（活动、会议、仪式等）preside at the committee meeting 主持委员会会议；负责（重要局面）；掌管领导 preside over the company 领导公司　词源：pre 在前面＋sid 坐　指坐在前面主持工作

president ['prezid(ə)nt] 总统；校长；（公司）董事长；（银行）行长　词源：preside 主持＋ent 名词后缀　形近易混词：precedent

precedent ['presid(ə)nt] 先例 set a precedent for sth. 创造先例；惯例 break with precedent 打破惯例　词源：precede 在……前面＋ent 名词后缀

unprecedented [ʌn'presidentid] 空前的，前所未有的 an event that is unprecedented in recent history 近代历史上没有先例的事件　词源：un 否定＋precedent 先例　指没有先例的

reside [ri'zaid] 居住定居 reside abroad 定居国外；（问题）存在于 reside in sth. / sb.；（权力或权利等）隶属于 reside in sth. / sb.　词源：re 重复＋sid 坐　指坐在一个地方很长时间是居住

resident ['rezid(ə)nt] 居民；（美国的）高级专科住院实习医生；居住的,居留的 the resident population of sanitarium 疗养院的住院人数　词源：reside 居住＋ent 名词后缀

residence ['rezid(ə)ns] 住宅，住所 the ambassador's official residence 大使官邸；（在某国的）居住权,居留许可 a residence permit 居留许可证；居住,定居 take up residence in the new house 住进了新家　词源：reside 居住＋ence 名词后缀

obsess [əb'ses] 使痴迷 be obsessed by computers 迷上了电脑　词源：ob 强调＋sess 坐　指

坐在王座或豪车里舍不得离开被迷惑住

obsessive [əb'sesiv] 痴迷的，迷恋的，难以释怀的 be obsessive about luxury goods 对奢侈品痴迷；强迫症患者　词源：obsess 使痴迷 + sive 形容词后缀（表示充满活力的 active）

obsession [əb'seʃ(ə)n] 痴迷，着魔 an unhealthy obsession with losing weight 对减肥的病态迷恋　词源：obsess 使痴迷 + sion 名词后缀

session ['seʃ(ə)n]（议会等的）一次正式会议 a session of the UN General Assembly 一届联合国大会；（法庭的）一次开庭；一段时间 a photo / recording / training session 拍照/录音/训练时段　词源：sess 坐 + sion 名词后缀　指坐着开会

seminar ['seminɑ:] 研讨会 a teaching seminar 教学研讨班　词源：se 坐（或 se 分离）+ min 小 + ar 名词后缀　指分成小组坐着开会　巧记：谐音"塞满了"指研讨会上塞满了人

subside [səb'said]（情绪或疼痛）逐渐平复；（建筑物）沉降；地陷；风平；浪静；水退　词源：sub 下面 + sid 坐　指坐下后使表面下沉下陷

subsidize ['sʌbsidaiz]（政府）资助，补贴 subsidize agricultural exports 补贴出口农产品　词源：sub 下面 + sid 坐 + ize 动词后缀　指坐下开会商讨发资助或补贴　巧记：sub + sidize 谐音"塞袋子"指把补助塞到袋子里分发

subsidy ['sʌbsidi]（政府的）资助金，补贴 trade subsidies 贸易补贴　词源：subsidize 资助 + y 名词后缀　形近易混词：subsidiary

subsidiary [səb'sidiəri] 附属的 a subsidiary issue 附带问题；子公司，附属公司　词源：sub 下面 + side 边 + ary 名词后缀　指下面分支机构

dissident ['disid(ə)nt] 持不同政见者 a political dissident　词源：dis 分散 + sid 坐 + ent 名词后缀　指不坐在一起的人是不同意见者

assiduous [ə'sidjuəs] 勤奋的，刻苦的 an assiduous insurance salesman 勤勤恳恳的保险销售人员　词源：as 强调 + sid 坐 + u 水 + ous 形容词后缀（表示过多的）指坐着读书流汗的　同义词：diligent / conscientious

184. **-seg-, -sect-**：cut　巧记：se 分离 + g 球体 globe（ct 拟声词）指把球体切开发出的声音

section ['sekʃ(ə)n] 部分；报纸版面 the sports section of the newspaper 报纸的体育栏；（建筑的）横切面，剖面图；（数学中的）截面；（在显微镜下观察的）切片　词源：sect 切 + tion 名词后缀

bisect [bai'sekt] 切两半 bisect an apple 苹果一切两半　词源：bi 两个 + sect 切　指切成两个部分

sector ['sektə] 扇形；（商业、贸易等的）部门，行业 banking sector 银行业；（军事管制的）区域，地带　词源：sect 切 + or 名词后缀　指扇形区域

segment ['segm(ə)nt]（水果或花）瓣；片，段，部分 diverse segments of the population 人口中多样的组成部分；分割，划分　词源：seg 切 + ment 名词后缀（表示细碎）

insect ['insekt] 昆虫　词源：in 内部 + sect 切　指身体切分成一段一段的动物是昆虫

insecticide [in'sektisaid] 家用杀虫剂　词源：insect 昆虫 + cid 切杀 cut 指能杀昆虫的药剂

intersection [intə'sekʃ(ə)n] 十字路口　词源：inter 两者间 + sect 切 + tion 名词后缀　指两条路交叉相切

185. -sembl- : together　巧记：same 的词形变化　指把相似的东西放在一起

assemble [ə'semb(ə)l] 集合；召集 assemble a world-class team 召集了一个世界一流水平的团队；装配 assemble a bookshelf 组装书架　词源：as 强调 + sembl 聚集　指聚集相似的零件组装机器　巧记：Avengers Assemble 复仇者联盟

assembly [ə'sembli] 立法机构，会议，议会 the UN General Assembly 联合国大会；集会 a public assembly 公共集会；组装 an auto assembly plant 汽车装配厂　词源：assemble 集合 + y 名词后缀

ensemble [ɔn'sɔmb(ə)l]（经常在一起演出的小型）乐团，剧团，舞剧团 a wind / string / brass ensemble 木管器乐/弦乐器/铜管乐器演奏组；成套东西；全套衣服　词源：en 使动词化 + sembl 聚集　指使演员聚集在一起的演出团体

resemble [ri'zemb(ə)l] 长得像某人或某物　词源：re 重复 + sembl 聚集　指情侣或朋友重复相聚会发现彼此长得越来越像

186. -sen- : old　巧记：se 离开（或坐 sed）+ n 门　指出家门坐在门口的老人

senate ['senit]（古罗马的）元老院；参议院　词源：sen 老的 + ate 名词后缀

senator ['senətə]（古罗马元老院的）元老；参议员　词源：senate 参议院 + or 名词后缀

senior ['si:niə; 'si:njə] 老年人 a senior center 老年活动中心；（地位或职位）较高的 a senior officer 高级军官；（体育运动或比赛）成人的，高级水平的 participate in senior competitions 参加成人比赛；上级，上司；高水平运动员；（中学或大学）最高年级的学生，毕业班学生，大四学生　词源：sen 老的 + i 人 + or 名词后缀　反义词：junior

senile ['si:nail] 年老糊涂的，老迈的 a senile old man 一个年老糊涂的老人　词源：sen 老的 + ile 形容词后缀（表示容易……的）指容易老糊涂的

187. -simil-, -simul- : similar　巧记：same 的词形变化

assimilate [ə'simileit] 吸收，理解，掌握 assimilate new concepts 理解接受新观念；使融入，使同化 assimilate refugees into the community 让难民融入社区　词源：as 强调 + simil 相似的 + ate 动词后缀　指把相似的事物吸收在一起

similar ['similə] 相似的 have similar tastes in dancing 有相似的舞蹈品味　词源：simil 相似的 + ar 形容词后缀

similarity [simə'lærəti] 相似处 the similarities and differences of their designs 他们设计的相似处和不同处　词源：similar 相似的 + ity 名词后缀

simile ['siməli] 明喻　词源：simil 相似的　指句子中用 as 或 like 进行比喻　相关词：metaphor 暗喻

simultaneous [ˌsim(ə)l'teiniəs] 同时发生的, 同步的 simultaneous translation / interpreting 同声传译　词源：simul 相似的 + tan 十个 ten + ous 形容词后缀（表示过多的）　指同时出现十个以上的

simulate ['simjuleit]（用计算机或模型等）模拟, 模仿 simulate interviews 模拟面试；冒充, 假装, 伪装 simulate grief 装出悲伤　词源：simul 相似的 + ate 动词后缀　形近易混词：emulate

simulation [ˌsimju'leiʃən] 模拟, 仿真 a simulation model 仿真模型；冒充, 假装 the simulation of genuine concern 假装真诚关心　词源：simulate 模拟 + tion 名词后缀　巧记：电脑游戏 The Sims 模拟人生 / SimCity 模拟城市

emulate ['emjuleit]（因仰慕）效仿, 模仿 emulate the success of software companies 效仿软件公司的成功　词源：e 出来 + simulate 模拟　指模仿出来

188. **-sol-**：1）alone　巧记：solo 意大利语 指独唱或独奏

sole [səul] 唯一的, 仅有的 the sole purpose 唯一的目的；脚掌；鞋底 leather soles 皮鞋底　词源：sol 单独　指每个人鞋底纹路是唯一的

solo ['səuləu] 独唱, 独奏；独唱的, 独奏的；独自的 a solo voyage across the sea 独自横跨大洋的航行　词源：sol 单独

soloist ['səuləuist] 独唱者；独奏者　词源：solo 独唱独奏 + ist 名词后缀

solitary ['sɔlit(ə)ri] 单个的, 唯一的 a solitary goal 唯一入球；孤独无伴的 take a solitary walk 独自散步；喜欢独处的 solitary tigers 独居的老虎；隐士, 隐居者（= hermit）　词源：soli 单独 + ary 形容词后缀 指喜欢一个人待着的

solid ['sɔlid] 固体；固体的 solid fuel 固体燃料；结实的, 牢固的 a solid piece of furniture 一件结实的家具；可靠的, 靠得住的 solid evidence 可靠的证据　词源：sol 单独 + id 名词后缀（表示具有某种身份 identity）指固体是单独的一个整体

solidarity [ˌsɔli'dæriti] 团结一致 make an appeal for solidarity 呼吁团结　词源：solid 固体 + ity 名词后缀　指像固体一样紧密团结在一起

solitude ['sɔlitjuːd] 独处, 独居 write a novel in solitude 清静地写小说　词源：soli 单独 + tude 名词后缀

soliloquy [sə'liləkwi]（戏剧）独白　词源：soli 单独的 solo + loqu 说 + y 名词后缀　指一个人独自说话

isolate ['aisəleit] 使孤立, 隔离 isolate sb. from sb.　词源：i 人 + sol 单独 + ate 动词后缀　指让一个人单独自己待着　形近易混词：insulate

insulate ['insjuleit] 使绝缘；使隔热 an insulated house 隔热隔音的房子；使隔音；使免受（不良影响）insulate sb. from sth.　词源：isolate 的词形变化

solicit [sə'lisit] 恳求 solicit aid from the government 向政府求助；拉皮条　词源：soli 单独 + cit 召唤 call 指一个人召唤别人

2）sun　巧记：s 发光 shine + o 圆圆的太阳 + l 长长的光线 指太阳在天上发光

desolate ['des(ə)lət] 荒凉的，无人烟的 a bleak and desolate landscape 一片荒凉的景色　词源：de 否定 ＋sol 太阳 ＋ate 形容词后缀　指没有太阳光照的地方是荒凉的

solar ['səulə] 太阳的 a solar eclipse 日食；太阳能的 solar energy 太阳能　词源：sol 太阳 ＋ar 形容词后缀　反义词：lunar

solemn ['sɔləm]（仪式）庄严的，隆重的 a solemn ritual；（誓言）郑重的 a solemn vow；（表情）严肃的　词源：sol 太阳　指像太阳一样庄严庄重的

parasol ['pærəsɔl]（海滩上或餐馆外等处的）大遮阳伞　词源：para 保护抵制 ＋sol 太阳的 solar　指防晒的大遮阳伞

solace ['sɔləs] 安慰，慰藉 seek solace in music 在音乐中找到安慰；给以安慰的人（或事物）be a solace to sb.　词源：sol 太阳　指用太阳般的温暖安慰别人

console [kən'səul] 安慰，慰藉 console oneself with sth.；（机器、电子设备或计算机等的）操纵控制台　词源：con 共同 ＋sol 太阳　指一起给某人阳光般的温暖　词义连记：游戏机的控制台可以缓解压力、带来安慰

189. **-son-**：sound　巧记：sound 的缩写形式

sonic ['sɔnik] 声音的；声速的；声波的 sonic waves 声波　词源：son 声音 ＋ic 形容词后缀

supersonic [suːpə'sɔnik; sjuː-] 超音速的 a supersonic aircraft 超音速飞机　词源：super 上面 ＋son 声音 ＋ic 形容词后缀　指速度在声速之上的

subsonic [ˌsʌb'sɔnik] 亚音速的 subsonic flight 亚声速飞行　词源：sub 下面 ＋son 声音 ＋ic 形容词后缀　指速度在声速之下的

sonorous ['sɔn(ə)rəs; sə'nɔːrəs]（声音）洪亮浑厚的 a sonorous voice of the bass 男低音饱满浑厚的嗓音　词源：son 声音 ＋ous 形容词后缀（表示过多的）

sonar ['səunɑː] 声呐　词源：son 声音 ＋ar 名词后缀　指船只或潜艇上利用声波探测水下目标位置的仪器

sonata [sə'nɑːtə] 奏鸣曲 a piano sonata 钢琴奏鸣曲　词源：son 声音　指突出某个乐器声音特色的乐曲形式，通常为一个乐器和一个钢琴，钢琴作为伴奏，比如长笛奏鸣曲；也可只有一个钢琴，叫钢琴奏鸣曲

dissonant ['disənənt] 声音不协和的，不悦耳的 dissonant notes 不协和音符　词源：dis 分散 ＋son 声音 ＋ant 形容词后缀（表示具有……能力的）

dissonance ['disənəns] 不协和音；不一致 the dissonance between what we are told and what we see 我们被告知的和所见的不一致　词源：dissonant 不和谐的 ＋ance 名词后缀

resonate ['rez(ə)neit] 使共鸣，使回响 a resonating chamber 产生回音的房间；引起（想法或观念的）共鸣 a petition that resonates with voters 引起投票者共鸣的请愿；充满（某种含义或特性）a poem that resonates with complex emotions 一首充满了复杂情感的诗　词源：re 重复 ＋son 声音 ＋ate 动词后缀　指让声音重复是使共鸣

resonant ['rezənənt]（声音）洪亮的，回荡的 the violin's resonant tone 小提琴回荡优美的

音色；共鸣的，共振的；充满着某物的，洋溢着某物的 paintings resonant with traditions of folk art 洋溢着民间艺术传统的画作　词源：resonate 使共鸣 + ant 形容词后缀（表示具有……能力的）

unison ['ju:nɪs(ə)n] 齐唱，齐奏，齐声 recite in unison 齐声背诵；共同，一致 act in unison to compete with foreign businesses 一致行动与外国企业竞争　词源：uni 一 + son 声音　指众人发出同一个声音是齐唱

190. **-soph-** : wise, wisdom　巧记：Sophia 索菲亚 指女性人名，代表女性的智慧。索菲亚的形象神圣而俊美，有天使的翅膀。在希腊语里，圣索菲亚指 Holy Wisdom（上帝的智慧），世界上许多教堂都用 Saint Sophia（圣索菲亚）来命名，土耳其的伊斯坦布尔、乌克兰的基辅、俄罗斯的诺夫哥罗德、中国的哈尔滨都建有圣索菲亚教堂。

philosophy [fɪ'lɔsəfɪ] 哲学　词源：phil 爱 + soph 智慧 + y 名词后缀　指哲学是研究爱和智慧的学科

philosopher [fɪ'lɔsəfə] 哲学家；思想深刻的人　词源：philosophy 哲学 + er 名词后缀

sophomore ['sɔfəmɔ:]（大学或高中的）二年级学生　词源：soph 智慧 + more 更多的　指大二的学生比大一的学生更聪明

sophist ['sɔfɪst] 诡辩家，诡辩者；（指怀疑态度的）哲人，智者；（古希腊的）哲学教师　词源：soph 聪明 + ist 名词后缀　指特别有智慧、聪明的人善于诡辩

sophistry ['sɔfɪstrɪ] 诡辩术；诡辩　词源：sophist 诡辩家 + ry 名词后缀

sophisticate [sə'fɪstɪkeɪt] 老于世故的人　词源：soph 聪明 + histic 历史 history + ate 名词后缀　指又聪明又懂历史的人

sophisticated [sə'fɪstɪkeɪtɪd] 精于世故的 a sophisticated witty man 一个见多识广、说话风趣的人；（机器、系统、方法等）精妙复杂的 a highly sophisticated sonar system 非常精密的声呐系统　词源：sophisticate 老于世故的人 + ed 形容词后缀

sophistication [sə,fɪstɪ'keɪʃn] 精于世故；精妙复杂　词源：sophisticate 老于世故的人 + tion 名词后缀　巧记："Simplicity is the ultimate sophistication." — Leonardo da Vinci 达·芬奇名言

191. **-sort-** : select　巧记：拉丁语 sortiri 拟声词 指抽选物品时发出的声音 嗖的一声把所需的物品种类抽选出来

sort [sɔ:t] 种类，类型 all sorts of candies 各种各样的糖果；分类，整理 sort rubbish into plastics, glass and paper 把垃圾分为塑料、玻璃和纸三类　词源：sort 选择　指抽选的物品是不同类别的

assort [ə'sɔ:t] 分类，归类 assort the samples 分类样本　词源：as 强调 + sort 选择　指抽选同类物品归类　形近易混词：assert

assert [ə'sə:t] 固执己见，坚决主张　词源：as 强调 + sert 连接　指紧紧连接自己的观点

assorted [ə'sɔ:tɪd] 类别混杂的, 什锦的 assorted chocolates 什锦巧克力　词源：assort 分类 + ed

形容词后缀

consort ['kɔnsɔːt , kən'sɔːt]（统治者的）配偶；（与名声不好的人）结交，厮混 consort with criminals 与罪犯厮混；一组演奏古音乐的乐师；一组演奏古音乐的乐器；一群，一组 a consort of specialists 一群专家；伙伴，同伙 the fraud and his consorts 骗子和他的同伙 词源：con 共同 + sort 选择 指抽选出在一起的同类人

escort ['eskɔːt] 护送，护卫 escort the gold by guards 由守卫护送黄金；陪同游览 escort buyers around the property 陪同买主看房；受雇陪同 词源：esc 逃跑 escape + sort 选择 指抽选护卫协助逃跑

resort [ri'zɔːt] 度假胜地 a seaside / ski resort 海滨/滑雪度假胜地；最后手段 a last resort；诉诸某种手段 resort to law 诉诸法律 词源：re 重复 + sort 选择 指反复抽选去度假的同一个地方 词义连记：指不停去度假胜地思考最后的大招来使用

192. **-sper-** : hope 巧记：spring 的词形变化 指春天带来希望

desperate ['desp(ə)rət] 绝望的；极度渴望的 be desperate for sth. 词源：de 否定 + sper 希望 + ate 形容词后缀 指没有希望的时候会极度渴望 巧记：美剧 Desperate Housewives 绝望的主妇 相关词：despair

despair [di'speə] 绝望 strive for success in despair 在绝望中奋斗争取成功；失望 despair of sb. / (doing) sth. 词源：des 分散 dis + pair 组 指拆散一对组合让人失望

despairing [di'speəriŋ] 绝望的 a despairing look / sigh 绝望的神情/叹气 词源：despair 失望 + ing 形容词后缀

prosper ['prɔspə] 繁荣，兴旺 词源：pro 向前 + sper 希望 指前方有希望 同义词：thrive 繁荣 the + river 指有河流经过的地方会繁荣

prosperous ['prɔsp(ə)rəs] 繁荣的，兴旺的 a prosperous port 繁荣的港口 词源：prosper 繁荣 + ous 形容词后缀（表示过多的）

prosperity [prɔ'speriti] 繁荣，兴旺 a period of cultural prosperity 文化繁荣时期 词源：prosper 繁荣 + ity 名词后缀

193. **-stitut-** : set up 巧记：st 站立 stand + it 它 + ut 在 at 指让它站立起来

constitute ['kɔnstitjuːt] 形成，构成 constitute a threat to the society 对社会构成一种威胁；（合法或正式地）成立，设立 constitute a committee 设立委员会 词源：con 共同 + stitut 建立 指多个部分共同形成构成

constituent [kən'stitjuənt]（选区的）选民；成分，构成要素 the constituents of sugar 糖的成分；构成的 the WTO and its constituent members 世界贸易组织及其成员国 词源：constitute 形成 + ent 名词后缀

constitution [kɔnsti'tjuːʃ(ə)n] 宪法，章程 propose a new amendment to the constitution 对宪法提出一项新的修正案；建立，形成 the constitution of an auditing committee 设立审计委员会；组成，构成 the chemical constitution of the dye 染料的成分；体质，体格 have a strong / weak constitution 体格强壮/虚弱　词源：constitute 形成 + tion 名词后缀

constitutional [ˌkɔnstiˈtjuːʃ(ə)n(ə)l] 宪法的 constitutional rights 宪法规定的权利；体质的，体格的 constitutional weakness 体质虚弱；保健散步　词源：constitution 宪法 + al 形容词后缀

institute [ˈinstitjuːt] 制定（规定或制度）；提出诉讼；研究所 a research institute；大学，学院 institutes of higher education 高等学校　词源：in 内部 + stitute 建立 指建在山林或沙漠内部隐藏起来的研究所　词义连记：研究所里需要制定制度保密研究成果

institution [ˌinstiˈtjuːʃ(ə)n]（大学、银行等规模大的）公共机构 a financial institution 金融机构；（由来已久的）风俗习惯，制度 the institution of marriage 婚姻制度　词源：institute 研究所 + nation 国家 指国家层次上的公共机构　词义连记：大型公共机构都有一套由来已久的制度

destitute [ˈdestitjuːt] 极度贫困的，一无所有的；缺乏 be destitute of sth.　词源：de 否定 + stitut 建立 指建不起来房子的是极度贫困的　同义词：impoverished / deprived / poor

restitute [ˈrestitjuːt]（环境或生态）复原，恢复 restitute the geographical environment and ecosystem 复原地理环境和生态系统；（失物或被窃之物的）归还　词源：re 重复 + stitut 建立 指再次建成原有建筑恢复原状归还

restitution [ˌrestiˈtjuːʃn]（失物或被窃之物的）归还 the restitution of art treasures to the owner 艺术珍品的物归原主；（对毁坏之物的）赔偿　词源：restitute 归还 + tion 名词后缀

superstition [ˌsuːpəˈstiʃ(ə)n; ˌsjuː-] 迷信　词源：super 上面 + stitut 建立 + tion 名词后缀 指在上面凭空建立的没有科学基础的伪科学学说

substitute [ˈsʌbstitjuːt] 替补队员 a substitute goalkeeper 替补守门员；代课老师 a substitute teacher；替代品 a salt substitute 盐的代用品；替代，替换 substitute A for B　词源：sub 下面 + stitut 建立 指在球队下面建起另一个备用的预备队

194. **-string-, -strict-, -strain, -straint, -stress**：draw tight　巧记：straight 直的 指绷直的绳子是拉紧的

strict [strikt] 严厉的，严格的　词源：strict 拉紧

stretch [stretʃ] 伸展（肢体）；变松拉长 stretch the shoes 撑大鞋；（山水）延伸绵延；（长而窄的）一片地域或水域，一段路 a beautiful stretch of countryside road 一段美丽的乡村道路；连续一段时间 a stretch of two months 一连两个月　词源：stret 拉紧 + ch 伸手 reach 指拉伸展开身体去触摸

strain [strein] 焦虑紧张 the stresses and strains of unemployment life 失业生活的紧张和压力；（缆绳的）拉力张力；拉紧绷紧（绳子）strain against the rope；全力以赴 strain every nerve to do sth.；（肌肉）拉伤扭伤 strain a muscle；（动植物的）品种 different strains of herbs 不同品种的草药；（疾病的）类型 a new strain of the flu virus 一种新型的流感病毒　词源：strain 拉紧 指拉紧身体部位是扭伤　词义连记：运动员的焦虑紧张使全身绷紧，在全力以赴比赛后，导致肌肉拉伤，不得不用不同种类的植物药物来治疗不同种类的

伤病　形近易混词：stain

stain [stein] 玷污，弄脏 stain the carpet 弄脏地毯；（给木制品）染色，着色 stain the wood carvings 给木雕刻上色；（液体形成的）污点，污渍 remove a coffee stain 除去咖啡污迹　词源：stay 待着 指待着擦不掉的污渍

stringent ['strin(d)ʒ(ə)nt]（法律、规章、标准等）严格的，严厉的 stringent pollution regulations 严格的污染管理条例；（经济状况）紧缩的 stringent economic policies 紧缩的经济政策　词源：string 拉紧 + ent 形容词后缀（表示具有……能力的）

string [striŋ]（拴气球的）细绳；一串 a string of pearls 一串珍珠；一系列 a string of political scandals 一系列政治丑闻；（计算机程序中的）字符串；（弦乐器的）琴弦　词源：string 拉紧 指可以拉紧的细绳

constrict [kən'strikt]（喉咙或血管）收缩收紧；限制约束（行动上的自由）　词源：con 共同 + strict 拉紧 指一起拉紧绳子是限制束缚

constriction [kən'strikʃn] 收缩收紧 ease the tie's constriction of the neck 缓解领带对脖子的压迫；限制约束　词源：constrict 限制 + tion 名词后缀

restrict [ri'strikt] 限制，控制 restrict the number of job candidates to five 限制应聘者数量为五人　词源：re 重复 + strict 拉紧 指反复拉紧是限制

restriction [ri'strikʃ(ə)n] 限制，控制 impose a restriction on sth. 对某事实行限制　词源：restrict 限制 + tion 名词后缀

constrain [kən'strein] 抑制，限制，约束 constrain sb. from doing sth.　词源：con 共同 + strain 拉紧 指共同拉紧绳子是约束

constraint [kən'streint] 抑制，限制，约束 the constraints of family life 家庭生活的约束　词源：constrain 的名词形式

restrain [ri'strein]（武力）阻止 restrain sb. from doing sth.；克制（情绪或行为）restrain one's ambitions 压制野心　词源：re 重复 + strain 拉紧 指反复拉紧是抑制　形近易混词：refrain

restraint [ri'streint] 克制约束 show / exercise restraint 保持克制；管制措施 impose restraints on some imports 对一些进口产品实行了管制控制　词源：restrain 的名词形式

refrain [ri'frein] 克制，抑制，忍住 refrain from (doing) sth.；经常重复的评价（或抱怨）；叠句，副歌　词源：re 重复 + frain 冻雨 freezing rain 指被冻雨反复冰冻是抑制　词义连记：反复说要克制的话（比如说不能喝酒，不能喝酒，不能喝酒）是叠句

stress [stres] 压力；精神压力，心理紧张；强调；重音　词源：stress 拉紧

mistress ['mistris] 情妇；（私立学校的）女教师；（仆人的或狗、马等动物的）女主人；（有权势的女子、女能人、女强人）控制着某事物，是某事的能手 be (a / the) mistress of sth.　词源：Miss 未婚的小姐姐（ma 母亲的词形变化）+ stress 压力 指带来压力的小姐姐

distress [di'stres]（船或飞机）遇险 a distress signal 求救信号；忧虑悲伤 sb. be in distress；贫困困苦 economic / financial distress 经济/财务困难；使不安，使忧虑　词源：dis 分散 + stress 压力 指水压或气压使船只或飞机逐渐分解是遇险

195. **-sult-** : leap　巧记：sail 航行　指船在海上跳跃航行发出的嗖嗖声

assault [ə'sɔːlt; ə'sɔlt]（军事）攻击，袭击 an assault rifle 突击步枪；（口头或书面）抨击，严厉批评；人身袭击，侵犯他人身体；（向困难或危险事物发起的）闯关，冲击难关 mount an assault on unemployment 向失业发起攻势；攻克解决难题 assault the problems　词源：as 强调 + sault 跳跃 sult 指跳出来攻击

consult [kən'sʌlt] 请教，咨询 consult sb. about sth.；查阅 consult a dictionary 查词典　词源：con 共同 + sult 跳跃　指孩子们一起跳到老师面前请教

consultant [kən'sʌlt(ə)nt] 顾问；高级顾问医师，会诊医生　词源：consult 咨询 + ant 名词后缀　指被咨询的人

consul ['kɒns(ə)l] 领事；古罗马执政官　词源：consult 的变形　指领事是帮助解决在国外的本国国民咨询问题的人

consulate ['kɒnsjələt] 领事馆　词源：consul 领事 + ate 名词后缀　相关词：embassy 大使馆

desultory ['des(ə)lt(ə)ri; -z-] 语无伦次的，漫无目的的 a desultory talk 漫无边际的谈话　词源：de 否定 + sult 跳跃 + ory 形容词后缀　指话语跳来跳去

exult [ig'zʌlt; eg-] 欢欣鼓舞，扬扬得意，兴高采烈 exult at / in / over sth.　词源：ex 出去 + sult 跳跃　指开心得跳出门口

insult [in'sʌlt] 侮辱 insult sb. by doing sth.　词源：in 内部 + sult 跳跃　指跳到敌人内部用语言侮辱对方

result [ri'zʌlt] 结果；源于 result from sth.；导致 result in sth.　词源：re 向后 + sult 跳跃　指反弹弹回的结果　同义词：outcome / consequence

196. **syn-, sym-** : with, together, at the same time　巧记：same 的变化　指相似的物品放在一起

system ['sistəm] 系统，体制　词源：sys 相同 + item 一件物品　指把相似的物品放在一起组成体系

systematic [sistə'mætik] 系统的，有序的 a systematic reform 系统性改革　词源：system 体系 + tic 形容词后缀

symbol ['simb(ə)l] 象征 a symbol of peace 和平的象征；符号 the chemical symbol for iron 铁的化学符号　词源：sym 相同 + bol 球 ball　指像七龙珠一样把七个相似的球放在一起召唤神龙，象征实现一个愿望

symbolize ['simbəlaiz] 象征　词源：symbol 象征 + ize 动词后缀　同义词：represent

syllable ['siləb(ə)l] 音节　词源：syl 相同 + label 标签　指用标签标注相似药品的方法标注音节

syllabus ['siləbəs] 教学大纲　词源：syl 相同 + label 标签 + us 名词后缀　指用相似的标签共同标注说明一门课程，教学大纲的标签包括课程教学目标、课程教学要求、课程教学内容、课程教学对象、课程日程安排、课程使用教材、课程考核方式、课程分数构

成等方面

sympathy ['simpəθi] 同情 have sympathy for sb. / sth.；（尤指政治方面的）赞同，支持 be in sympathy with sth.；（与某人的）同感，共鸣　词源：sym 相同（same 衍生出来的前缀）+ path 疼痛　指感到相同的痛是同情　同义词：compassion

sympathetic [simpə'θetik] 有同情心的；赞成的，支持的 be sympathetic to sth.；合意的，合适的（环境）；招人喜欢的（人或人物角色）　词源：sympathy 同情 + tic 形容词后缀

symmetry ['simitri] 对称；相似　词源：sym 相同 + metr 测量 measure + ry 名词后缀　指测量出相同的距离是对称

symphony ['simf(ə)ni] 交响乐　词源：sym 相同 + phon 声音 + y 名词后缀　指 orchestra 交响乐队共同发出乐器演奏的声音

symphonic [sim'fɔnik] 交响乐的　词源：symphony 交响乐 + ic 形容词后缀

synchronize ['siŋkrənaiz] 使时间同步 synchronized swimming 花样游泳　词源：syn 相同 + chron 时间 + ize 动词后缀　指使时间节点相同

synthesis ['sinθisis] 综合，合成 the synthesis of art and life 艺术与生活的结合；（物质在动植物体内的）合成 the synthesis of proteins 蛋白质的合成；（人工）合成 the synthesis of penicillin 青霉素的合成；（用电子手段对声音、语音或音乐的）合成 speech synthesis software 语音合成软件　词源：syn 相同 + thesis 主题　指把相似的主题放在一起合成

synonym ['sinənim] 同义词　词源：syn 相同 + onym 名字 name

symposium [sim'pəuziəm] 古希腊酒会；专题研讨会 an international symposium on sanitation 公共卫生国际研讨会；专题论文集　词源：sym 相同 + pos 摆姿势 pose + ium 名词后缀（表示地点 place）指古希腊学者拿着酒杯摆个姿势在一个地方讨论问题

symptom ['sim(p)təm] 症状；（存在严重问题的）征兆 a symptom of inflation 通货膨胀的征兆　词源：sym 相同 + atom 原子　指相同的发病症状表现出有相同的致病原子

197. **-tect-**：cover　巧记：t 树 tree 指树像伞一样的遮盖作用

detect [di'tekt] 发现，察觉 detect the enemy aircraft by radar 用雷达侦测敌机　词源：de 否定 + tect 覆盖　指揭开遮盖

detective [di'tektiv] 侦探，警探 a detective story / novel 侦探故事/小说；私人侦探　词源：detect 发现 + tive 名词后缀　指能察觉异常的人

detector [di'tektə] 探测器，检测器 a metal detector 金属探测器　词源：detect 发现 + or 名词后缀　指能察觉异常的仪器

protect [prə'tekt] 保护 protect sb. / sth. from sth.　词源：pro 向前 + tect 覆盖　指向前覆盖住不让别人看到是保护

architecture ['ɑːkitektʃə] 建筑；建筑风格，建筑式样；建筑学　词源：arch 拱门 + tect 覆盖 + natrue 名词后缀　指覆盖着拱门的建筑

architect ['ɑːkitekt] 建筑师　词源：architecture 建筑　指设计建筑的人

198. **tele-** : far or relating to television　巧记：t 方向 to + l 长 long 指 to be long 的缩写　表示时间长距离远

telecommunications ['telikə,mjuːni'keiʃənz] 电信，电讯　词源：tele 远 + communiction 交流　指远处的沟通

telegram ['teligræm] 电报　词源：tele 远的 + gram 写 graph 指写下信息发到远方　同义词：telegraph

telecommuter [,telikə'mjuːtə(r)]（在家通过电话和电脑与共事者联系的）远程工作者　词源：tele 远的 + commuter（远距离）上下班往返的人

telepathy [tə'lepəθi]（双胞胎的）心灵感应，传心术　词源：tele 远 + path 疼痛　指能感受到远方别人的疼痛

telephone ['telifəun] 电话机；打电话　词源：tele 远的 + phone 声音　指能听到远方声音的设备

teleconference ['telikɔnf(ə)r(ə)ns] 远程会议，电视（电话）会议　词源：tele 远的 + conference 会议

telescope ['teliskəup] 单筒望远镜　词源：tele 远的 + scope 范围　指能看到远处范围的观察设备　相关词：microscope 显微镜 / a pair of binoculars 一副双筒望远镜

televise ['telivaiz] 电视转播，直播 televise the debate live 直播辩论　词源：tele 远的 + vis 看　指远方能看见是电视转播

teleplay ['teləplei] 电视剧　词源：tele 电视 television + play 戏剧　指电视上播的戏剧

199. **-tempor-** : time　巧记：time 的词形变化；也可理解为寺庙 temple 的词形变化，指寺庙的功能之一是敲钟报时

tempo ['tempəu]（音乐演奏的）速度；（生活的）节奏步调 the busy tempo of city life 城市生活的繁忙节奏　词源：tempor 时间 指用多长时间演奏完音乐是速度

temporal ['temp(ə)r(ə)l] 时间的 spatial and temporal dimensions 时空维度；（与宗教相对应的）世俗的，尘世的 spiritual and temporal joys 精神和世俗快乐　词源：tempor 时间 + al 形容词后缀

temporary ['temp(ə)rəri] 暂时的，临时的 temporary relief from pain 疼痛的短暂缓解　词源：tempor 时间 + ary 形容词后缀　反义词：permanent

contemporary [kən'temp(ə)r(ər)i] 当代的,同时代的 contemporary art / music / dance 当代艺术/音乐/舞蹈；同时代的人　词源：con 共同 + temporary 暂时的 指把所有临时出现的加起来是当代的

extemporize [ik'stempəraiz] 即兴演说或即兴表演　词源：ex 出来 + tempor 时间 + ize 动词后缀　指短时间出来的演说或表演　同义词：improvise

temper ['tempə] 脾气 lose one's temper 发脾气；使缓和，使温和 temper the summer heat with / by cool sea breezes 用清凉的海风消暑；使（金属）回火锻炼 tempered steel 经过回火的钢材　词源：tempor 时间 指长时间形成的脾气

temperance ['temp(ə)r(ə)ns]（因道德或宗教信仰的）戒酒禁酒；（自我）节制克制　词源：temper 脾气 + ance 名词后缀　指脾气要抑制　巧记：temper 脾气 + rance 谐音"忍死"指脾气忍死是节制克制　巧记：古希腊的哲学家柏拉图 Plato 在《理想国》The Republic 里提出了四大基本美德 The Four Cardinal Virtues，即 Prudence 谨慎精明，Justice 正义公正，Fortitude 坚韧毅力，Temperance 自我克制

temperament ['temp(ə)rəm(ə)nt] 气质，性情，性格，禀性 have an artistic temperament 有艺术家的气质　词源：temper 脾气 + ment 思想 mind　指脾气加思想是气质

temperature ['temp(ə)rətʃə] 温度；体温；气氛　词源：temper 脾气 + nature 自然　指大自然的脾气体现在温度变化上

temperate ['temp(ə)rət] 气候温和的，温带的 temperate climate / zone / region 温和的气候/温带/温带地区；心平气和的，（语言或行为）不过激的 have a temperate conversation 心平气和的谈话　词源：temper 脾气 + ate 形容词后缀　指大自然脾气温和的地带是温带的　同义词：mild / moderate

temporize ['tempəraiz]（为争取时间而）拖延，不迅速做决定　词源：tempor 时间 + ize 动词后缀　指使时间延长

200. **-text-**：weave　巧记：t 树 tree　指树的纹路像编织出来的一样

text [tekst] 正文，文本；课本教材（= textbook）；（用手机给某人）发短信 text sb.　词源：text 编织　指编课本像编织衣物

textual ['tekstʃuəl]（书或杂志等）原文的 a textual analysis of the fiction 小说文本分析　词源：text 文本 + ual 形容词后缀

textile ['tekstail]（丝绸、棉布或羊毛等）纺织品 import silk textiles from China 从中国进口丝织品；（常复数）纺织业　词源：text 编织 + ile 名词后缀

texture ['tekstʃə]（指光滑或粗糙的）质地，（纹理）手感 the soft texture of velvet 天鹅绒柔软的质地；（食物）口感；（音乐或文学的）谐和统一感，艺术神韵　词源：text 编织 + ture 名词后缀（表示性质 nature）指织物的质地手感

context ['kɔntekst] 上下文，语境（比如单词的词义会因上下文语境的不同而改变）；环境，背景 political / social / historical context 政治/社会/历史背景　词源：con 共同 + text 文本　指全部文本组成上下文的语言情境

subtext ['sʌbtekst] 潜台词，字面下意思　词源：sub 下面 + text 文本　指下面隐藏的文本含义

pretext ['pri:tekst] 托词，借口 leave the company early on the pretext of visiting the clients 借口见客户而早早离开了公司　词源：pre 在前面 + text 文本　指提前说的文本话语是借口

201. **-tox-**：poison　巧记：to 去 + x 没有　指去下毒使中毒消失

toxin ['tɔksin] 毒素（生物体自然产生的毒物）　词源：tox 毒 + in 内部　指内部产生的有毒物质

toxic ['tɔksik] 有毒的 toxic gas 毒气　词源：tox 毒＋ic 形容词后缀　同义词：poisonous

poisonous ['pɔizənəs] 有毒的；（人）恶毒的，以挑拨是非而取乐的；充满敌意的，令人极不愉快的 the poisonous atmosphere of the office 办公室的敌对气氛　词源：poison 毒＋ous 形容词后缀（表示过多的）　形近易混词：poignant

poignant ['pɔinjənt] 令人伤心的，心酸的 a poignant memory 心酸的回忆；（讽刺或话语）尖刻的，尖锐的 poignant satire / remarks　词源：poign 尖端 point＋ant 形容词后缀（表示具有……能力的）指内心被刺痛的感觉

toxicity [tɔk'sisəti] 毒性 the minor toxicity of the drug 药的轻微毒性　词源：toxic 有毒的＋ity 名词后缀

intoxicate [in'tɔksikeit] 使中毒；使喝醉；使欣喜若狂　词源：in 内部＋tox 毒＋ate 动词后缀　指喝酒过多导致酒精中毒或极度兴奋的状态

intoxicated [in'tɔksikeitid] 喝醉的；（因爱情、成功、权力等）极为兴奋的，得意忘形的　词源：intoxicate 使醉酒欣喜＋ed 形容词后缀

toxicide ['tɔksisaid] 解毒药　词源：tox 毒＋cid 切杀 指消毒杀毒的药剂

detoxify [ˌdiː'tɔksifai] 解毒；戒酒；戒毒　词源：de 否定＋tox 毒＋fy 动词后缀

toxicology [ˌtɔksi'kɔlədʒi] 毒物学，毒理学　词源：tox 毒＋ology 名词后缀（表示学科）

antitoxic [ænti'tɔksik] 抗毒素的，抗毒的 antitoxic serum 抗毒血清　词源：anti 相反＋toxic 有毒的 指抵抗毒性的　形近易混词：antibiotic

antibiotic [ˌæntibai'ɔtik] 抗生素（比如青霉素、盘尼西林 Penicillin）；抗生素的　词源：anti 相反＋bio 生命＋tic 形容词后缀 指抵抗细菌生长的药品

202. **trans-**：across, beyond, change into another form　巧记：train 的词形变化 指火车穿山越岭

translucent [træns'luːsnt] 半透明的 translucent glass 半透明玻璃　词源：trans 穿越＋lucent 发光的 指穿越后有光亮的

transact [træn'zækt; trɑːn-; -'sækt] 交易，交换；业务办理　词源：trans 穿越＋act 做动作 指做以物易物的交易动作

transaction [træn'zækʃ(ə)n; trɑːn-; -'sæk-] 交易，交换；业务办理　词源：transact 交易＋tion 名词后缀

transparent [træn'spær(ə)nt; trɑːn-; -'speə-] 透明的 transparent glass 透明的玻璃　词源：trans 穿越＋par 展示＋ent 形容词后缀（表示具有……能力的）指被光线穿过后能显示光线的　巧记：trans 穿越＋parent 父母 指父母能看透孩子的一切，在父母面前孩子的行为是透明的

transcend [træn'send; trɑːn-] 超越，胜过　词源：trans 穿越＋scend 攀爬 指翻山越岭的功绩超越他人

transcendence [træn'sendəns] 卓越　词源：transcend 超越＋ence 名词后缀

transcendent [træn'send(ə)nt; trɑːn-] 卓越的　词源：transcend 超越＋ent 形容词后缀（表

示具有……能力的）

transform [træns'fɔːm; trɑːns-; -nz-] 使改变；使变形 Transformers 变形金刚　词源：trans 穿越 + form 形式　指穿越过一个过程后改变形态

transit ['trænsit; 'trɑːns-; -nz-] 运输 goods damaged in transit 在运输中损坏的货物；交通运输系统 the city's public transit system 城市的公共交通运输系统　词源：trans 穿越 + it 走　指人或货物穿越城市移动

transition [træn'ziʃ(ə)n; trɑːn-; -'siʃ-] 过渡，转变，变迁 the transition from school to work 从学校到工作的过渡　词源：trans 穿越 + it 走 + tion 名词后缀

transitional [træn'ziʃ(ə)n(ə)l; -'siʃ-] 过渡的 a transitional period / government 过渡时期/政府　词源：transition 过渡 + al 形容词后缀

transient ['trænziənt] 短暂的，一时的 transient fashions 短暂的时尚；（逗留时间）很短的　词源：trans 穿越 + ent 形容词后缀（表示具有……能力的）

transliterate [træns'litəreit] 音译，移译，谐音翻译（例如披萨 Pizza，歇斯底里 hysteria，咖啡 coffee）　词源：trans 穿越 + liter 文字 + ate 动词后缀　指用发音翻译

transfer [træns'fəː; trɑːns-; -nz-] 调动工作；学生转学；地点转移，搬运迁移；运动员转会；账户转账；转移感情；电话转接；交通工具换乘；传染疾病　词源：trans 穿越 + fer 带来　指带着物品转移

transmit [trænz'mit; trɑːnz-; -ns-] 传送信号；传授知识；传承文化；传染疾病；传播（声、热或光）　词源：trans 穿越 + mit 发送　指穿越时间空间发送信息

transport [træn'spɔːt; trɑːn-] 运输　词源：trans 穿越 + port 携带　指携带货物穿山越岭

transportation [trænspɔː'teiʃ(ə)n; trɑːns-] 运输　词源：transport 运输 + tion 名词后缀

transpose [træn'spəuz] 调换（顺序或位置）transpose letters to change the spelling 调换字母顺序改变拼写形式；使（乐曲）变调　词源：trans 穿越 + pos 放置 put　指调整穿过原有位置重新摆放

transfuse [træns'fjuːz] 输血 transfuse blood into a patient 给病人输血；灌输传达 transfuse the enthusiasm and passion for science to students 把对科学的热爱灌输给学生　词源：trans 穿越 + fus 灌倒　指穿过血管灌输血液

transplant [træns'plɑːnt; trɑːns-; -nz-] 移植（器官或皮肤）；移栽（植物）；使搬迁　词源：trans 穿越 + plant 种植　指让植物穿山越岭移种到别的地方

traverse ['trævəs; trə'vəːs] 跋涉，横跨，横穿 traverse the national park 横穿国家公园　词源：travel 旅行 + vers 转向　指像马可波罗一样在欧亚大陆旅行，转向经过不同的国家

203. **-tut-, -tuit-**：watch　巧记：tour 旅行（to 去 + u 水 + r 跑 ruan）　指老师带着学生在海上旅行观察世界学习知识

tuition [tjuː'iʃ(ə)n] 学费（= tuition fees）；（对个人或小组的）教学，讲课，指导　词源：tuit 看 + tion 名词后缀　指学费是交给老师看孩子和学技能的钱　形近易混词：intuition

intuition [intju'iʃ(ə)n] 直觉（= a gut feeling）feminine intuition 女性的直觉　词源：in 内部 +

tuit 看 + tion 名词后缀　指内心里能看到的是直觉

tutor ['tjuːtə]（英国大学）导师；家教，私人教师；教，指导，辅导 tutor sb. in sth.　词源：tut 看 + or 名词后缀　指看着学生做练习的人

tutorial [tjuː'tɔːriəl]（大学导师的）个别或小组辅导；教程，辅导材料（比如游戏界面 menu 中的选项 tutorial 可以教玩家游戏操作）；大学导师的，辅导的　词源：tutor 辅导 + ial 形容词后缀（表示特殊的 special）指教师给予特殊个别辅导时用的辅导教程

tutelary ['tjuːtiləri] 守护的 a tutelary goddess 守护女神；守护神　词源：tut 看 + l 长时间 long + ary 形容词后缀　指长时间看着别人是守护的

10

204. uni- : one　巧记：u 水 + n 水 + i 一　指水汇集在一起成为一体

universe ['juːnivəːs] 宇宙　词源：uni 一 + vers 转向 turn 指万事万物最终都转向同一主体融入宇宙　同义词：cosmos

universal [juːni'vəːs(ə)l] 普遍的，全世界的，全体的，共同的 reckon music as a universal language 认为音乐是全世界的语言　词源：universe 宇宙 + al 形容词后缀

university [juːni'vəːsiti] 大学　词源：universe 宇宙 + ity 名词后缀　指大学的知识像宇宙般浩瀚

uniform ['juːnifɔːm] 制服 a nurse's uniform 护士服；全部相同的，一致的 uniform procedures 相同的步骤　词源：uni 一 + form 形式　指统一形式的衣服

unify ['juːnifai] 使（国家）统一，使成一体 unify the nation 统一国家　词源：uni 一 + fy 动词后缀　指使成为一个整体

unification [juːnifi'keiʃ(ə)n] 国家统一　词源：unify 使统一 + tion 名词后缀

unit ['juːnit]（计量用的）单位（比如瓦特是电力的单位）；（单独的事物、人或群体）单位，单元（比如家庭是社会的单位）；（教科书的）单元；（军队的）小队 a medical unit 医疗小组；一件商品 the unit cost 一件商品的成本；（机器的）部件，元件 central processing unit 中央处理器（CPU）；（成套家具中的）一件，组合件 kitchen units 成套厨房的组件；（楼的）一套住房；（医院的）科，室，部门 intensive care unit 特护病房（ICU）　词源：uni 一　指一个物件

unite [juː'nait] 团结，联合 unite the opposition parties 联合各反对党　词源：uni 一 + it 走 go　指一起走是团结

united [ju'naitid]（人或群体）团结的，共同的，一致的 a united effort 共同努力；（国家）联合的，统一的 build a united Europe 建立统一的欧洲；用于团队和公司名称 Manchester United 曼彻斯特联队　词源：unite 团结 + ed 形容词后缀

unity ['juːnəti] 团结，统一 economic unity 经济统一；（艺术）整体性　词源：unite 团结 + y 名词后缀

unique [juː'niːk] 独特的，独一无二的 a unique opportunity 难得的机会　词源：uni 一 + ique 形容词后缀（表示如……似的）指单一的是独特的　形近易混词：antique 古董；古老的　同义词：distinctive

union ['juːnjən; -iən] 工会 trade union；协会，俱乐部 the golf union 高尔夫球协会；联盟，联邦 the European Union 欧洲联盟；结合，联合 the perfect union of craftsmanship and design 工艺和设计的完美结合；结为夫妻，结婚，婚姻　词源：uni 一 + on 正在 指联盟是正在存在的一个整体

unilateralism [ˌjuːni'lætrəlizəm] 单边主义　词源：uni 一 + later 边 + ism 名词后缀（表示主义学说）

unison ['juːnis(ə)n] 齐唱，齐奏，齐声 recite in unison 齐声背诵；共同，一致 act in unison to compete with foreign businesses 一致行动与外国企业竞争　词源：uni 一 + son 声音　指众人发出同一个声音是齐唱

unicorn ['juːnikɔːn] 独角兽　词源：uni 一 + corn 玉米　指独角兽唯一的角像玉米的形状

205. **-urb-**：city　巧记：u 水 + r 分裂生长 rise + b 两间房子 B　指大江大河旁边树立起一排排房子形成城市

urban ['əːb(ə)n] 城市的 urban life 城市生活　词源：urb 城市 + an 形容词后缀　反义词：rural 乡村的

urbane [əː'bein]（男子）温文尔雅的，彬彬有礼的　词源：urban 城市的 + e 出来　指城市的人是彬彬有礼的

urbanize ['əːbənaiz] 使城市化 urbanize rural areas 让农村地区城市化　词源：urban 城市的 + ize 动词后缀

urbanization [ˌəːbənai'zeiʃən] 城市化　词源：urbanize 城市化 + tion 名词后缀

suburb ['sʌbəːb] 郊区 live in the suburbs 住在郊区　词源：sub 下面 + urb 城市　指城市下面的附属的部分是郊区

suburban [sə'bəːb(ə)n] 郊区的 a noisy suburban street 一条吵闹的郊区街道；（生活或态度）平淡乏味的，呆板保守的　词源：suburb 郊区 + an 形容词后缀　词义连记：指住郊区的人思想是呆板的

206. **-vag-**：wander　巧记：v 峡谷 + a 正在 + g 走 go 指正在峡谷里游荡

vagrant ['veigr(ə)nt] 流浪者，（尤指）乞丐　词源：vag 漫步 + ant 名词后缀 指漫步街头无家可归的人　同义词：beggar / tramp

vague [veig] 模糊的 a vague outline of plan 模糊的计划概述　词源：vag 漫步 + gue 哥哥 gege 指哥哥漫步时目的地是模糊的　巧记：va 空空的峡谷 指峡谷里的景色是模糊的

extravagance [ik'strævəgəns] 奢华 the extravagance of the palace 宫殿的富丽堂皇　词源：extra 额外的 + vag 漫步 + ance 名词后缀 指能够世界各地漫步旅游的是奢华　同义词：luxury / lavishness

extravagant [ik'strævəg(ə)nt; ek-] 奢华的 extravagant celebrations 奢华的庆祝活动；不切实际的 the extravagant claims / promises 夸大其词/不切实际的承诺　词源：extra 额外的 + vag 漫步 + ant 形容词后缀（表示具有……能力的）指能够在世界各地漫步旅游是奢华的　同义词：luxurious / lavish

divagate ['daivə‚geit]（文章或谈话）跑题，离题 divagate from the subject 偏离主题　词源：di 分散 + vag 漫步 + ate 动词后缀 指文章主题走散了

207. **-vari-**：change　巧记：v 峡谷 + a 正在 + ri 河流 river 指峡谷里的河流是多变的

vary ['veəri]（根据情况）改变 vary the rhythm of the music 改变音乐韵律；（大小或形状等）不同 vary considerably 大相径庭　词源：vari 改变

various ['veəriəs] 多样的 various people 形形色色的人　词源：vary 改变 + ous 形容词后缀（表示过多的）　同义词：diverse

varied ['veərid] 多样的 varied art forms 多样的艺术形式　词源：vary 改变 + ed 形容词后缀

variety [və'raiəti] 种类 a variety of food 多种食物　词源：vary 改变 + ty 名词后缀

variable ['veəriəb(ə)l] 可变的 variable temperatures 变化不定的气温；（实验）变量，可变因素　词源：vary 改变 + able 形容词后缀（表示可以……的）　反义词：constant 常量

invariable [in'veəriəb(ə)l] 不变的，永恒的 an invariable principle 一贯的原则　词源：in 否定 + variable 可变的

variant ['veəriənt] 变体，变化形式；变体的，变形的 a variant form of the word 单词的不同拼写形式　词源：vary 改变 + ant 名词后缀

variation [veəri'eiʃ(ə)n]（数量或水平等的）改变，变化 air pressure variations 气压变化；（音乐）变奏，变奏曲 theme and variations 主题与变奏曲　词源：vary 改变 + tion 名词后缀

208. **-vir-**：man　巧记：Virgo 处女座 指处女座的人性格很 man，大方无私，稳重可靠，严格要求自我，像男人一样意志坚强，坚持自己的理念；也可记为 Virginia 美国弗吉尼亚州，这个名字是为了纪念一生未婚的英国伊丽莎白女王一世"童真女王"（The Virgin Queen）。伊丽莎白女王一世一生坎坷，性格比男人还坚毅，是一位女中豪杰。她成为英格兰女王后，宗教上采取了新教与天主教兼容的政策，成功稳定了国内的局势。政治上加强王权，确立议会作为专制统治工具的作用。经济上实行重商主义政策及"圈地运动"，鼓励创办工商业，刺激资本主义经济发展。军事上则对外实行海外扩张，亲率大军打败了西班牙的"无敌舰队"。伊丽莎白一世当政时期的诗歌、散文、戏剧等艺术创作空前繁荣，出现了威廉·莎士比亚、弗朗西斯·培根等著名的文学家

virile ['virail]（男性机能）强的，精力充沛的；有男性气概的 a virile performance 雄壮的演奏　词源：vir 男性 + ile 形容词后缀（表示容易……的）指容易具有男性气概的

virtue ['vəːtjuː; -tʃuː] 美德；优点 the virtues of free trade 自由贸易的好处　词源：vir 男性 + tue 真的 true 指有成就的真正男人散发出的个性美德　巧记：天主教的七美德 The Seven Holy Virtues 包括 Faith 忠诚、希望 Hope、慷慨 Charity、正义 Justice、坚韧 Fortitude、节制 Temperance、谨慎 Prudence　反义词：vice

virtuoso [ˌvəːtʃuˈəusəu] 音乐大师，大演奏家　词源：virtue 美德 指品德高尚的音乐大师

virtual ['vəːtjuəl] 虚拟的 Virtual Reality (VR) 虚拟现实技术　词源：virtue 美德 + al 形容词后缀 指美德被认为比较虚无缥缈的东西

virtually ['vəːtjuəli] 实际上的　词源：virtual 的副词 但与 virtual 的意思正好相反

virgin ['vəːdʒin] 处女；童男；未开发的，原始状态的，天然的 virgin forest 原始森林　词源：Virgo 处女座

209. **-viv-, -vit-, -vig-**：live　巧记：viv 拟声词 拉丁语 指在古罗马元老院前罗马公民抛鲜花向恺撒、屋大维的功绩表达敬意时情不自禁发出的 vivo 欢呼声，后来 vivo 欢呼声也用于表达对意大利歌剧艺术的惊叹和赞美；中国古代升堂喊的威武声和 vivo 发音也很相似；也可记为 vivo 手机，指 vivo 的产品充满活力

vivid ['vivid]（记忆、梦境或描述等）生动的，活泼的，清晰的，逼真的 vivid illustrations 生动的图解说明　词源：viv 活 + id 名词后缀（表示身份 identity）　同义词：picturesque / graphic

vivace [viˈvɑːtʃei]（音乐）活泼的，轻快的　词源：viv 活 + ac 活跃的 active 指音乐演奏积极、活跃、速度快

vivacious [viˈveiʃəs; vai-]（女性或城市）活泼的，生气勃勃的 a vivacious disposition 活泼外向的个性　词源：viv 活 + ac 活跃的 active + ious 形容词后缀（表示过多的）

vivacity [viˈvæsəti]（女性或城市）活力，活泼 beauty and vivacity 美丽与活泼　词源：viv 活 + city 城市 指城市的职场女性充满活力

survive [səˈvaiv] 生存；艰难度日　词源：sur 上面 + viv 活 指在水面上活下来

survival [səˈvaiv(ə)l] 生存　词源：survive 生存 + al 名词后缀

vitamin ['vitəmin; 'vait-] 维他命 vitamin deficiency 维生素缺乏　词源：vit 活 + min 小 mini 指食物中含有的让人或动物生长和活得好的微小营养元素

vital ['vait(ə)l] 极其重要的，必不可少的 a vital clue 重要线索；生命的，维持生命所必需的 vital signs 生命体征（比如呼吸和体温）；生气勃勃的，充满活力的　词源：vit 活 + al 形容词后缀 指对生命存活极其重要的

devitalize [diːˈvaitəlaiz] 使（生命、活力或效果）衰弱 devitalized tissue 失活组织　词源：de 否定 + vital 生命的 + ize 动词后缀 指使活力消失

revive [riˈvaiv] 使（经济、产业或传统）复兴，振兴 revive the economy 让经济复苏；（使人或动植物）恢复精力，苏醒；（使旧戏剧）重新上演　词源：re 重复 + viv 活 指再次活跃起来

revival [riˈvaiv(ə)l] 复兴，振兴 a revival of the timber industry 木材产业的复兴；再流行 a revival of medieval music 中世纪音乐的再次流行；(旧戏剧) 重新上演　词源：revive 使复兴 + al 名词后缀

vigour ['vigə] 活力，精力，热情　词源：vi 活 + gour 哥哥 指有活力的哥哥　巧记：谐音"伟哥"指男性壮阳药　形近易混词：rigour

rigour ['rigə]（学术、思想、研究或科学的）严密，严谨 academic and scientific rigour 学术和科学的严谨；严酷，艰苦 withstand the rigours of a harsh winter 经受住严冬的严酷考验；严格，严厉　词源：ri 站立 rise + gour 哥哥 指站得笔直的兵哥哥很严厉

vigorous ['vig(ə)rəs] 强健的，精力旺盛的；强有力的，积极的 take vigorous exercise 做剧烈运动　词源：vigor 活力 + ous 形容词后缀（表示过多的）　形近易混词：rigorous

rigorous ['rig(ə)rəs] 谨慎的 a rigorous analysis 严谨的分析；严格的，严厉的 rigorous army training 严苛的军训　词源：rigour 严格 + ous 形容词后缀（表示过多的）

210. **-vict-, -vinc-**：conquer or overcome　巧记：v 胜利的手势 + ct 声音 指征服后发出的胜利欢呼声；古罗马恺撒的名言"我来，我看见，我征服。"中的三个拉丁语词根就是 veni，vidi，vici，指恺撒来到的世界的任何地方，看到的土地都可以被他征服

convict [kən'vikt] 宣判……有罪 convict sb. of shoplifting 判某人犯有偷窃商店货物罪；罪犯 an escaped convict 越狱犯　词源：con 共同 + vict 征服 指完全征服别人的途径之一是通过判对方有罪进行改造

conviction [kən'vikʃ(ə)n] 判罪，定罪 have no previous convictions 没有犯罪前科；深信，坚信；坚定的主张（或信念）strong political convictions 坚定不移的政治信念　词源：convict 定罪 + tion 名词后缀　词义连记：指罪犯定罪后还大声叫喊坚信自己无罪

convince [kən'vins] 使信服，说服 convince sb. of sth.　词源：con 共同 + vinc 征服 指征服别人的想法

convincing [kən'vinsiŋ] 令人信服的，有说服力的 convincing evidence of the guilt 证明有罪的有说服力的证据　词源：convince 使信服 + ing 形容词后缀

invincible [in'vinsib(ə)l] 不可战胜的 an invincible air force 无敌的空军　词源：in 否定 + vinc 征服 + ible 形容词后缀（表示可以……的）

evict [i'vikt]（依法从房屋或土地）驱逐，赶走 evict sb. from sth.　词源：e 出去 + vict 征服 指征服别人把他赶走

eviction [i'vikʃn]（依法从房屋或土地）驱逐，赶走 face eviction from one's home 面临着被赶出家门　词源：evcit 驱逐 + tion 名词后缀

victor ['viktə]（战斗或比赛的）胜利者　词源：vict 征服 + or 名词后缀 指征服者是胜利者

victim ['viktim] 受害者 famine victims 饥荒的灾民　词源：victor 胜利者 + im 否定 指没有胜利的人是受害者

victory ['vikt(ə)ri] 胜利 narrow victory 险胜　词源：victor 胜利者 + ry 名词后缀

victorious [vik'tɔːriəs] 得胜的，胜利的 the victorious army / team 胜利之师/获胜的球队　词

源：victor 胜利者 + ious 形容词后缀（表示过多的）

211. **-vol-, -volunt-** : will　巧记：vo 发声 voice + l 长时间 long 指嘴里长时间嘟囔的事儿是自己的意愿

volition [və'liʃn] 自愿 of one's own volition 出于自愿　词源：vol 意愿 + tion 名词后缀

volunteer [ˌvɔlən'tiə] 志愿者；志愿兵；自愿做事 volunteer to do sth.　词源：volunt 意愿 + er 名词后缀

voluntary ['vɔlənt(ə)ri] 自愿的 voluntary donations 自愿捐赠　词源：volunt 意愿 + ary 形容词后缀

benevolent [bi'nev(ə)l(ə)nt]（人）慈善的，乐善好施的；（笑容或态度）和蔼的 a benevolent smile / attitude　词源：bene 好 + vol 意愿 + ent 形容词后缀（表示具有……能力的）指有好的意愿的　同义词：charitable　反义词：malevolent

malevolent [mə'lev(ə)l(ə)nt] 恶毒的 malevolent gaze 恶毒的注视　词源：mal 坏的 + vol 意愿 + ent 形容词后缀（表示具有……能力的）指意愿不好的是恶毒的　同义词：malignant / malicious / vicious

volatile ['vɔlətail]（液体或物质）易挥发的；（人或情绪）易激动的，易怒的；（情况或局势）易变的，动荡 a volatile political situation 动荡的政治局势　词源：vol 意愿 + at 正在 + ile 形容词后缀（表示容易……的）指意愿容易变来变去的　巧记：volcano 火山 指火山是易变的

212. **-volv-, -volut-** : turn over　巧记：volv 拟声词 指"喔呜"的翻转声；也可记为 volve 沃尔沃汽车 指沃尔沃汽车的安全性能高经得住翻滚旋转

valve [vælv]（暖气管子上的）阀门；（心脏或血管的）瓣膜；（铜管乐器的）阀键，活塞　词源：volv 旋转 指阀门是旋转的开关

velocity [və'lɔsəti] 转速，速度，高速 the velocity of light 光速　词源：volv 旋转 + ity 名词后缀 指发动机的转速

evolve [i'vɔlv] 进化 evolve from sth.；逐步发展 evolve into sth.　词源：e 出来 + volv 旋转 指旋转出来的过程是进化

evolution [ˌiːvə'luːʃ(ə)n; 'ev-] 进化 the evolution of mammals 哺乳动物的进化；进化论 the theory of evolution 进化论；逐步发展 the evolution of the computer 计算机的发展　词源：evolve 进化 + tion 名词后缀

involve [in'vɔlv]（使）参与 involve sb. in (doing) sth.；包含，包括　词源：in 内部 + volv 旋转 指旋转进入是参与包括

involvement [in'vɔlvm(ə)nt] 参与，插手 involvement in the fraud 参与诈骗；和（某人）恋爱，有染 involvement with sb.　词源：involve 参与 + ment 名词后缀

involving [in'vɔlviŋ] 包括，涉及（= including）　词源：involve 包括 + ing 介词后缀

revolve [ri'vɔlv]（使）围绕……旋转（例如地球、卫星、风扇或回转炮塔）revolve around sth.；以……为中心，以……为主题 revolve around increasing income 以提高收入为中心　词源：re 重复 + volve 旋转

revolving [ri'vɔlviŋ] 旋转的 perform on a revolving stage 在旋转舞台上表演　词源：revolve 旋转 + ing 形容词后缀

revolver [ri'vɔlvə] 左轮手枪　词源：revolve 旋转 + er 名词后缀

revolt [ri'vəult] 反叛，造反 revolt against the military dictatorship 反抗军事独裁；违抗，拒绝服从（权威、规定或法律）revolt against parental discipline 不遵从父母管束；使作呕，使反感 a revolting smell 让人作呕的气味　词源：re 向后 + volt 旋转 volut 指向后旋转是反转反抗

revolution [revə'luːʃ(ə)n]（天体）旋转 the revolution of the earth around the sun 地球环绕太阳的公转；（发动机或车轮）旋转一周 a speed of 300 revolutions per minute 每分钟 300 转的转速；革命 the French Revolution 法国大革命；巨变，大变革 a cultural revolution 文化上的大变革　词源：re 重复 + volut 旋转 + tion 名词后缀　指翻转天地是革命

revolutionary [revə'luːʃ(ə)n(ə)ri] 革命的 a revolutionary uprising 革命起义；革命性的，突破性的，创新的 a revolutionary new drug 一种革命性的新药；革命者，革命家　词源：revolution 革命 + ary 形容词后缀

213. -tempt- : test　巧记：time 次数　指参与测试的次数

tempt [tem(p)t] 勾引，诱惑 tempt sb. into doing sth.　词源：tempt 测试　指一次次测试别人是勾引

tempting ['tem(p)tiŋ] 诱惑人的 a tempting offer 诱人的提议　词源：tempt 勾引 + ing 形容词后缀

temptation [tem(p)'teiʃ(ə)n] 诱惑 resist the temptation 抵挡诱惑；诱惑物　词源：tempt 勾引 + tion 名词后缀

attempt [ə'tem(p)t] 尝试，企图 attempt to do sth.　词源：at 强调 + tempt 测试　指多几次测试是尝试

contempt [kən'tem(p)t] 蔑视，轻视 show contempt for sb. / sth.；藐视法庭 be jailed for contempt of court 因藐视法庭被关押　词源：con 共同 + tempt 测试　指大家都能参加的测试会让人觉得简单而对它产生蔑视

214. -tend-, -tens-, -tent- : stretch　巧记：t 方向 to + end 终点　指延伸至终点

attend [ə'tend] 注意，关注 attend to the warning signs 注意警示牌；参加，出席 attend the meeting 参会；看护，照料 patients attended by doctors 医生照顾的病人；陪同 ministers who attend the king 陪同国王的大臣；处理，料理（生意或个人事务）attend to clients' needs and demands 处理客户需求　词源：at 强调 + tend 延伸　指思维的延伸是关注某活动并想参加出席

attendance [ə'tend(ə)ns] 出席 take attendance 点名 / attendance rate 出勤率；出席人数 a decline / drop in attendances 出席人数下降；(保镖或助手)陪侍照顾 be in attendance (on sb.)　词源：attend 出席 + ance 名词后缀

attendant [ə'tend(ə)nt] 服务员 flight attendant（客机的）乘务员；（重要政治人物的）侍从，随从；伴随的，随之而来的，附带的 attendant problems / risks 随之而来的问题/风险　词源：attend 照料 + ant 名词后缀

attention [ə'tenʃ(ə)n] 注意，注意力，关注 divert / distract / draw attention from sth. 转移注意力；（军队口令）立正；特别照料（或维修保养）be in need of medical attention 需要治疗　词源：attend 关注 + tion 名词后缀

attentive [ə'tentiv] 专注的，专心的 attentive audience 专注的观众；照顾周到的 be attentive to sb. / sth.　词源：attend 关注 + tive 形容词后缀（表示充满活力的 active）

contend [kən'tend] 竞争，争夺 contend for power 夺权；主张，声称 contend that...　词源：con 共同 + tend 延伸 指大家一起伸手去争夺目标

contention [kən'tenʃ(ə)n] 争论，争端，口角 a source of contention 纷争的根源；（争论时的）论点，主张 reject the contention 拒绝这种观点　词源：contend 争夺 + tion 名词后缀 指争夺时爆发的口角　形近易混词：content

content [kən'tent]（书、讲话、节目或网站等的）内容；目录 a table of contents 目录；含量 protein content 蛋白质含量；心满意足的 be content with sth.　词源：contain 的名词形式 指包含了很多内容　词义连记：书的目录内容丰富、信息含量高，让人十分满意的　反义词：discontent

discontent [diskən'tent] 不满意的 be discontent with sth.　词源：dis 否定 + content 心满意足的 指不满意的

distend [di'stend]（内部压力导致）膨胀，肿胀 a distended belly / abdomen 肿胀的肚子　词源：dis 分散 + tend 延伸

distension [di'stenʃn]（内部）膨胀，肿胀 distension of the stomach 胃胀　词源：distend 膨胀 + sion 名词后缀

extend [ik'stend; ek-]（路或房子）延长延伸；延长（期限）extend a visa 延长签证期限；伸展（手或腿）；提供给予 extend a warm welcome to sb. 热烈欢迎某人　词源：ex 出去 + tend 延伸 指延伸到外面

extent [ik'stent; ek-] 程度 to a certain extent / to some extent 在某种程度上　词源：extend 的名词形式

extensive [ik'stensiv; ek-]（庭院）宽敞的；（面积）广阔的；（研究）广泛的；（知识）全面的　词源：extend 延伸 + sive 形容词后缀（表示充满活力的 active）

intensive [in'tensiv] 强化的,密集的 intensive training 强化训练；集约的 intensive agriculture 集约农业　词源：in 内部 + ten 延伸 + sive 形容词后缀（表示充满活力的 active）指内部像太阳一样特别活跃的是强化的

intense [in'tens]（疼痛/压力/兴趣/寒冷/炽热/光亮）强烈的；（战斗或比赛）激烈的；（人在感情或意见上）极为强烈的，极为严肃的，较真的（贬义）an intense young man 一

个较真的年轻人　词源：in 内部＋tens 延伸（可理解为 ten 十倍＋s 谐音"死"）指身体内延伸十倍快要痛死的感觉　词义连记：较真的运动员忍着强烈的疼痛参加激烈的比赛

tense [tens]（动词的）时态；（肌肉）拉紧的，绷紧的；（形势或神经）紧张的 feel tense 感到紧张的　词源：tens 延伸　巧记：tense 谐音"疼死"指肌肉拉紧时疼死了　词义连记：使用不同时态造句时舌头肌肉是绷紧的，内心感觉是紧张的

tension ['tenʃ(ə)n] 拉力张力 tension on the bridge 桥受到的拉力；（电线、绳子或肌肉等的）拉紧绷紧；（情绪）紧张焦虑；（局势或关系）紧张；（作家或电影导演制造的）紧张气氛　词源：tense 拉紧的＋sion 名词后缀

intensify [in'tensifai]（使）加强，（使）加剧 intensify the close combat training 加强近身格斗训练　词源：intensive 强化的＋fy 动词后缀

intensity [in'tensiti]（光/声音/色彩/风暴/感情/观点）强度，强烈，激烈　词源：intense 强烈的＋ity 名词后缀

intend [in'tend] 意图，打算 intend to do sth.　词源：in 内部＋tend 延伸 指内心意愿的延伸

intent [in'tent] 意图，目的 with good intent 出于一片好意；专注的，专心致志的 an intent gaze / look 专注的目光/神情；决定执意（做）某事 be intent on / upon (doing) sth.　词源：intend 的名词形式

intention [in'tenʃ(ə)n] 意图，意向 have no intention of doing sth. 无意做某事　词源：intend 打算＋tion 名词后缀

pretend [pri'tend] 假装 pretend to do sth.；（用于否定句和疑问句）自诩妄称 sb. can't pretend that... 某人不能妄称或不敢说……　词源：pre 在前面＋tend 延伸 指在众人前手舞足蹈延伸四肢做动作假装有本领

pretentious [pri'tenʃəs] 自命不凡的，矫情能装的 a pretentious fraud 自命不凡的骗子　词源：pretend＋ious 形容词后缀（表示过多的）

tent [tent] 帐篷 pitch / put up a tent 搭帐篷　词源：tent 延伸 指军队帐篷延伸数里远

tentative ['tentətiv] 不确定的，临时的 tentative plans 临时计划；踌躇不决的，犹豫的 a tentative greeting 犹豫羞怯的问候　词源：tent 帐篷＋tive 形容词后缀（表示充满活力的 active）指搭帐篷是临时的

tenant ['tenənt] 房客，租户　词源：tent 帐篷＋ant 名词后缀 指帐篷里住的人是租户　反义词：landlord 房主

tend [tend]（经常）趋向于 tend to do sth.；（对羊群、病人或花园等）照顾，照料 tend (to) sb. / sth.　词源：tend 延伸 指习惯性动作的延伸是趋向于

tendency ['tend(ə)nsi] 趋势，趋向 a tendency toward inflation 通胀趋势；（性情）倾向 aggressive / suicidal / criminal / artistic tendencies 暴力倾向/自杀倾向/犯罪倾向/艺术气质　词源：tend 趋向于＋ency 名词后缀　同义词：trend

trend [trend] 趋势 current trends in education 教育的目前动向　词源：t 方向 to＋r 跑 run＋

end 终点 指跑向终点的趋势

tentacle ['tentək(ə)l]（海洋动物如章鱼等的）触手，触角，触须；（大地方、大公司或系统产生的难以避免的不好的）影响（常复数）the corruption that spreads its tentacles 影响越来越大的腐败　词源：tent 延伸 + a 正在 + cle 名词后缀 指动物正在延伸的触手　区分：antenna

antenna [æn'tenə]（昆虫和甲壳类动物的）触角，触须；天线 television / radio antennas 电视机/收音机天线　词源：ante 在前面 + na 谐音"拿"指昆虫头前拿捏方向探路的触角　同义词：aerial 天线；空中的；从飞机上的；（滑雪的）空中技巧（常复数）

215. **-termin-**：border　巧记：Terminus 罗马神话中的边界之神。它具有石身人像的外貌，没有手和脚，象征无法移动，是罗马领土、私人领地、帝国道路的官方分界线（ter 土地 earth + min 小 mini 指把土地分成小块的界碑）

terminal ['tɜːmin(ə)l]（飞机、公共汽车、轮船或货物运输的）终点站，集散站 Terminal 2 机场 2 号航站楼；（计算机）终端设备（至少包括键盘和屏幕）；（疾病）晚期的　词源：termin 边界 + al 形容词后缀

determine [di'tɜːmin] 决定，左右，直接影响 a determining factor 决定性因素；决心做某事 determine to do sth.；查明，确定 determine the cause of the corruption 查明腐败原因　词源：de 向下 + termin 边界 指向下划清界限需要下决心

determined [di'tɜːmind]（努力或反对）坚决的，坚定的 a determined effort to quit smoking 坚决戒烟的努力；决意做某事 be determined to do sth.　词源：determine 决定 + ed 形容词后缀

terminate ['tɜːmineit]（使）停止，（使）终止，（使）结束 terminate a marriage by divorce 通过离婚结束婚姻；解雇 workers terminated because of slacking and missing work 因为懒散和误工而被解雇的工人；（公共汽车、火车或船）到达终点站　词源：termin 边界 + ate 动词后缀 指到边界为止

terminator ['tɜːmineitə]（月球或行星表面的）明暗界线；（阿诺德·施瓦辛格主演的系列电影）终结者　词源：terminate 结束 + or 名词后缀

termite ['tɜːmait] 白蚁　词源：terminate 结束 + ite 名词后缀 指白蚁啃食终结一切

exterminate [ik'stɜːmineit; ek-]（把人或动物彻底）消灭，根除 exterminate termites and cockroaches 消灭白蚁和蟑螂　词源：ex 出去 + terminate 结束 指赶出去使终结

exterminator [eks'tɜːmi,neitə]（背着杀虫剂药瓶、拿着喷管、戴着面具消灭害虫或有害动物的）扑灭者 a mosquito and locust exterminator 灭蚊和灭蝗者　词源：exterminate 消灭 + or 名词后缀

216. **-terr-**：1) earth, land　巧记：t 方向 to + e 出来 + r 植物向上分裂生长 指植物生长的土地

territory ['terit(ə)ri] 领土，版图，领地 disputed / foreign territory 有争议的领土；（鸟兽）

地盘；（经验或知识的）领域；（销售员，工作所负责的）地区　词源：terr 土地 + it 走 go + ory 名词后缀　指可以自由行走的自己的土地

terrestrial [tə'restriəl] 地球的 terrestrial life 地球上的生物；（动植物）陆地上的，陆生的；（电视/广播/频道）地面的（而不是卫星的）terrestrial TV / broadcasting / channels　词源：terr 土地 + rest 休息 + ial 形容词后缀（表示特殊的 special）指在陆地上休息的特殊的

extraterrestrial [,ekstrətə'restriəl] 外星生物，外星人；地外的 extraterrestrial beings / life 外星人/生命　词源：extra 超出 + terrestrial 地球的　指地球之外的

terrace ['terəs]（坡地上的）梯田；（足球场的）阶梯看台；（房屋或餐馆外的）露天平台 a roof terrace 屋顶平台；（相互连接的）一排房屋，排屋　词源：terr 土地 + ace 扑克牌里的 Ace　指类似 Ace 形状的梯形

terrain [tə'rein] 地形 rugged mountain terrain 崎岖的山区地形　词源：terr 土地 + rain 雨　指土地受雨水影响形成不同的地形

Terran ['terən] 地球人　词源：terr 土地 + r 跑 run + an 名词后缀　指电脑游戏《星际争霸》中地球上跑的人族

subterranean [,sʌbtə'reiniən] 地下的，地表下的 a subterranean river / bunker 地下河/掩体　词源：sub 下面 + terr 土地 + eous 形容词后缀（表示过多的）

Mediterranean [,meditə'reiniən] 地中海 the Mediterranean；地中海地区；地中海的，地中海地区的,地中海地区特有的 Mediterranean climate 地中海气候　词源：medi 中间 + terr 土地 + ocean 大海　指在土地的中间有个大海是地中海

turf [tə:f] 草皮，人工草皮 newly laid turf 新铺的草皮；赛马（运动）或赛马跑道 the turf；地盘，势力范围 sb.'s own / home turf 某人的主场；赶走（某人）turf sb. out (of sth.) / turf sb. off (sth.)　词源：tur 土地 terr + f 飞 fly 指在土地草皮上飞跑　巧记：谐音"特舒服"指在草皮上跑起来特别舒服

2）frighten　巧记：terr 土地　指地震让人恐惧害怕

terrify ['terifai] 使害怕，使恐惧　词源：terr 使害怕 + fy 动词后缀

terror ['terə] 恐惧，恐怖 scream in terror 害怕得尖叫；可怕的人或恐惧的事；（捣乱难管的小朋友）讨厌鬼，小捣蛋　词源：terr 使害怕 + or 名词后缀

terrorize ['terəraiz] 恐吓，恫吓，威胁 terrorize sb. into doing sth.　词源：terror 害怕 + ize 动词后缀

terrorist ['terərist] 恐怖分子　词源：terror 害怕 + ist 名词后缀

deter [di'tə:]（通过让对方意识到做某事会有困难或坏结果）制止，威慑阻止，使不敢 deter sb. from (doing) sth.　词源：de 以不好的方式 + ter 使害怕 terr　指以不好的语气或方式威慑、阻止、使害怕

deterrent [di'ter(ə)nt] 威慑物，威慑力量 nuclear deterrent 核威慑力量　词源：deter 阻止 + ent 名词后缀

deteriorate [di'tiəriəreit] 恶化,变坏 deteriorate into a war 演变成战争　词源：de 向下 + terr

可怕的 terrible + i 小 + or 比较级 er + ate 动词后缀 指一点点变得越来越可怕的糟糕的

detergent [di'tə:dʒ(ə)nt] 洗涤剂，洗衣粉，洗洁精，去污剂　词源：deter 阻止 + gent 生成 generate 指阻止细菌生成的洗衣粉

217. **-test-**：witness　巧记：test 测试可以见证能力水平

attest [ə'test]（作不及物动词）证明，是……的证据 A attest to B（比如奢侈品能证明某人的财富）；（作及物动词）给……作见证（以现场签字作为证人的方式）attest a will 给遗嘱作见证　词源：at 强调 + test 见证 指通过让大家见证来证明

protest ['prəutest]（公开）抗议，反对 protest against the new legislation 抗议新法规；坚持说，力言申辩 protest one's innocence 坚称无罪　词源：pro 向前 + test 见证 指游行时举牌子向前走让人见证自己的反对观点

Protestant ['prɔtistənt]（16 世纪脱离罗马天主教的基督教教派成员）新教徒；新教徒的　词源：protest 抗议 + ant 名词后缀 指抗议反对原有教派的人

contest ['kɔntest] 竞赛 a beauty contest 选美比赛；（比赛或选举）争夺角逐 contest the leadership 角逐领导权；质疑抗辩，提出异议 contest a will 对遗嘱提出质疑　词源：con 共同 + test 见证 指大家共同见证的比赛

contestant [kən'testənt] 竞争者，参赛者，选手　词源：contest 比赛 + ant 名词后缀

detest [di'test] 厌恶，憎恨 detest politics 厌恶政治　词源：de 否定 + test 见证 指不想见证是厌恶　巧记：de 否定 + test 考试 指不喜欢考试是厌恶

testify ['testifai]（在法庭上）出庭作证 testify against sb. 出庭作证指控某人；证明，证实 A testify to B　词源：test 见证 + fy 动词后缀

testimony ['testiməni] 证词 contradictions in one's testimony 证词里面的矛盾；证明 a testimony to the phenomenal engineering skills 对非凡工程技术的证明　词源：test 见证 + mony 名词后缀

218. **-onym-**：name　巧记：name 的词形变化

anonymous [ə'nɔniməs] 匿名的 an anonymous letter 匿名信；无特色的 live a dull and anonymous countryside life 过枯燥平淡无特色的乡村生活　词源：an 否定 + onym 名字 name + ous 形容词后缀（表示过多的）

anonymity [ænə'nimiti] 匿名；无特色 the anonymity of the restaurant decoration 餐厅毫无特色的装饰风格　词源：anonymous 匿名的 + ity 名词后缀

acronym ['ækrənim] 首写字母缩略词（例如北约 NATO = North Atlantic Treaty Organization；雷达 RADAR = Radio Detection and Ranging；激光 LASER = Light Amplification by Stimulated Emission of Radiation）　词源：acro 高 + onym 名字 name 指把词组里单词的第一个字母抽出来大写加高后组成的词　形近易混词：acrimony

acrimony ['ækriməni]（态度或言辞）尖刻，讥讽 settle the dispute without acrimony 没有唇枪舌战解决纠纷　词源：acri 尖锐 sharp + mony 名词后缀 指有钱人的尖酸刻薄

antonym ['æntənim] 反义词　词源：ant 相反 ＋ onym 名字 name
synonym ['sinənim] 同义词　词源：syn 相同 ＋ onym 名字 name
pseudonym ['suːdənim] 假名，笔名　词源：pseudo 假的 false ＋ onym 名字 name　巧记：美国著名作家马克•吐温 Mark Twain，原名是萨缪尔•兰亨•克莱门 Samuel Langhorne Clemens，他取笔名马克•吐温，是为了怀念青少年时期在密西西比河上做水手和领航员的一段生活经历，在测量水深时测水员会经常叫道 "Mark Twain !"，意思是"两个标记"，指水深两英寻（1 英寻约 1.8288 米），这是轮船安全航行的必要条件

219. -opt- : 1) choose　巧记：o 眼睛；太阳 ＋ pt 拟声词　指在阳光下用眼睛选择挑选物品
opt [ɔpt] 选择 opt for sth. / to do sth.　词源：opt 选择
option ['ɔpʃ(ə)n] 选择；（使用计算机程序时的）选项（比如复制、粘贴或剪切）；选修课 advice on choosing options 对选择选修课的建议；（未来的）买卖选择权 share options 股票期权（让员工可按固定价格购买所属公司的股票）　词源：opt 选择 ＋ tion 名词后缀
optional ['ɔpʃ(ə)n(ə)l] 可选择的 an optional extra 可选配件（比如汽车的真皮座椅）；选修的 compulsory and optional courses 必修和选修课程　词源：option 选择 ＋ al 形容词后缀
optimal ['ɔptim(ə)l] 最佳的，最适宜的 the optimal use of class time 对课上时间的充分利用　词源：opt 选择 ＋ m 大 max ＋ al 形容词后缀　指选择后好处会最大化的　同义词：optimum
optimum ['ɔptiməm] 最优的，最适宜的 the optimum conditions for effective teaching 保证教学效果的最佳条件　词源：opt 选择 ＋ m 大 max ＋ um 地点 place　指选择出来的最佳场所
optimist ['ɔptimist] 乐观者，乐观主义者　词源：opt 选择 ＋ ist 名词后缀　指认为自己总有选择的人是乐观主义者　反义词：pessimist
optimistic [ɔpti'mistik] 乐观的 be optimistic about the outcome of the test 对测试结果乐观；乐观主义的　词源：optimist 乐观主义者 ＋ ic 形容词后缀　指乐观主义者的想法是乐观的　反义词：pessimistic
optimism ['ɔptimiz(ə)m] 乐观 cautious optimism 谨慎的乐观；乐观主义　词源：optimistic 乐观的 ＋ ism 名词后缀（表示主义学说）　反义词：pessimism
adopt [ə'dɔpt] 采纳（建议或政策）adopt the one-child policy 采用独生子女政策；收养（孩子或宠物）adopt a pet 收养宠物；提名（某人）为候选人 adopt sb. as a parliamentary candidate 提名某人作为议员候选人　词源：ad 强调 ＋ opt 选择　指反复选择后才确定使用　形近易混词：adapt / adept
adapt [ə'dæpt] （使）适应 adapt to new environments 适应新环境；（为适应不同人群）改造，改装（汽车配置/设备功能/食物口味/教学大纲等）an adapted car 改装车；（把小说或书变成影视剧的）改编，改写 adapt a novel for television 把小说改编成电视剧　词源：

ad 强调 ＋ apt 合适的 appropriate 指反复改变以适应

adept [ə'dept; 'ædept] 内行的，熟练的 be adept at / in sth.；内行，老手　　词源：ad 强调 ＋ ept 专家 expert 指是某方面的专家

adoption [ə'dɒpʃ(ə)n] 采用，采纳 the adoption of new technology 新技术的采用；收养，领养；（候选人的）提名　　词源：adopt 采纳 ＋ tion 名词后缀

2）eye　巧记：o 眼睛；太阳 ＋ pt 拟声词 指腓尼基字母 o 表示眼睛

optical ['ɒptɪk(ə)l] 视力的 an optical defect 视力缺陷；光学的 an optical instrument 光学仪器；光存贮的 an optical disk 光盘　　词源：opt 眼睛 ＋ cal 形容词后缀　　巧记：an optical shop 眼镜店

optics ['ɒptɪks] 光学 fibre optics 光纤　　词源：opt 眼睛 ＋ ics 名词后缀（表示学科）

optician [ɒp'tɪʃ(ə)n] 验光配镜技师　　词源：opt 眼睛 ＋ cian 名词后缀

220. -ori-, -ort- : rise　巧记：o 太阳 ＋ ri 升起 rise 指太阳的升起

abort [ə'bɔːt]（使）流产堕胎；（因困难或危险使活动）中止 abort the mission 中止任务　　词源：ab 离开 ＋ ort 升起 指不让生命诞生

abortion [ə'bɔːʃ(ə)n] 人工流产，堕胎　　词源：abort 堕胎 ＋ tion 名词后缀

orient ['ɔːrɪənt; 'ɒr-] 东方 the Orient；确定方位 orient oneself in the mist 在薄雾里确定方向；熟悉新环境 orientate oneself to college life 适应大学生活；针对 an organization orientated to profits 以盈利为目的的机构　　词源：ori 升起 ＋ ent 名词后缀 指太阳升起的东方　　反义词：Occident 西方

oriental [ɔːrɪ'ent(ə)l; ɒr-]（中国和日本）东方的 a beautiful exquisite oriental rug 精美的东方地毯；（中国人或日本人）东方人　　词源：orient 东方 ＋ al 形容词后缀　　反义词：occidental 西方人

orientation [ˌɔːrɪən'teɪʃ(ə)n; ˌɒr-] 目标方向 an orientation towards marketing more products 营销更多商品的目标；（个人的政治或宗教信仰等方面的）态度观点，取向倾向 sexual orientation 性取向；（任职等前的）培训训练，迎新会 the orientation week for new students 全体新生熟悉情况的迎新周

disoriented [dɪ'sɔːrɪəntɪd] 失去方向的，迷失方向的 become disoriented in the sea 海上迷失方向的；迷惑的，头脑混乱的 feel shocked and disoriented 震惊而茫然不知所措的　　词源：dis 分散 ＋ orient 确定方向 ＋ ed 形容词后缀 指确定不了方向的

organ ['ɔːg(ə)n]（人体或动植物的）器官 an organ transplant 器官移植；（教堂内的）管风琴；（官方的）机构 the parliament and other decision-making organs 议会和其他决策机构；机关报刊（宣传某个团体的报纸或杂志）　　词源：or 升起 ＋ gan 基因 gene 指基因生成组成器官

origin ['ɒrɪdʒɪn] 起源；（常复数）出身，血统 humble origins 卑微的出身　　词源：ori 升起 ＋ gin 基因 gene 指基因的诞生源头

original [ə'rɪdʒɪn(ə)l; ɒ-] 起初的，最早的 the original meaning of the word 单词的原意；新

颖的，独创的 original ideas and designs 独创的见解和设计；原作的，真迹的，非复制的 original documents 文件正本；（艺术作品或文件的）原作，原件　词源：origin 起源 + al 形容词后缀

originally [ə'ridʒin(ə)li] 起初地，最早地　词源：original 起初的 + ly 副词后缀　同义词：initially

originality [ə,ridʒi'næliti] 独创性 lack originality 缺乏创意　词源：original 起初的 + ity 名词后缀

originate [ə'ridʒineit; ɔ-]（不及物动词）起源；（及物动词）创立，发起 originate new songs for the musicals 给音乐剧写新歌　词源：origin 起源 + ate 动词后缀

221. **-ot** : person　巧记：or 的变形　指人

patriot ['pætriət; 'peit-] 爱国者　词源：patr 父亲 + ot 名词后缀　指爱祖国就像爱父亲一样的人

compatriot [kəm'pætriət; -'peit-] 同胞　词源：com 共同 + patriot 爱国者　指所有的爱国者都是同胞

pilot ['pailət]（船的）领航员，领港员；（飞机或宇宙飞船上的）飞行员 automatic pilot（飞机的）自动驾驶仪；（电视的）试播节目 a pilot for a new sitcom 新情景喜剧的试播；驾驶（飞行器）；领航（船只）；试验性的，试点的 a pilot project 试点项目　词源：pil 脚 ped + ot 名词后缀　指在驾驶室里领航员脚步频繁地走来走去观察船的前进方向　词义连记：领航员对航线的领航是试验性的

zealot ['zelət]（宗教或政治信仰方面的）狂热者 religious zealots 宗教狂热分子　词源：zeal 热情 + ot 名词后缀　指非常有热情、激情的人　巧记：Z 指热情的佐罗留下他的象征符号 Z　同义词：fanatic

idiot ['idiət] 白痴　词源：idea 观念 + ot 名词后缀　指想法呆傻的人

222. **pre-** : before, in front of, in advance　巧记：p 向前 + r 升起 rise + e 出来　指向前走看见前方升起的太阳或烟雾

previous ['pri:viəs] 以前的；返回上级菜单　词源：pre 在前面 + vi 路 + ous 形容词后缀（表示过多的）　指以前走过的路

preview ['pri:vju:]（戏剧或电影）预演预映；（电影、电视节目）预告片；预审；预习　词源：pre 在前面 + view 看　指提前看一遍

prediction [pri'dikʃ(ə)n] 预言，预测　词源：pre 在前面 + dict 说 + tion 名词后缀　指提前说出

prepay ['pri:'pei] 预先支付　词源：pre 在前面 + pay 支付　指提前支付

preoccupy [pri:'ɔkjupai] 使全神贯注，占据某人思想 sth. preoccupy sb.　词源：pre 在前面 + occupy 占用　指先入为主提前占用了全部大脑思维空间

preoccupied [pri:'ɔkjupaid] 全神贯注的，入神的 be preoccupied with sth.　词源：preoccupy

使全神贯注 +ed 形容词后缀

preoccupation [pri,ɔkju'peiʃ(ə)n] 全神贯注，入神 the management's preoccupation with costs and profits 管理层对于成本和利润的全心关注　词源：preoccupy 使全神贯注 +tion 名词后缀

prescient ['presiənt] 有预知能力的，能预知未来的 give a prescient warning 预先警告　词源：pre 在前面 + sci 知道 + ent 形容词后缀（表示具有……能力的）指能够提前知道的

prescience ['presiəns] 预知，先见之明 the prescience of the price fluctuation 价格波动的先见之明　词源：prescient 有预知能力的 + ence 名词后缀

prevision [pri:'viʒən] 预知，先见　词源：pre 在前面 + vision 视野　指提前看见未来

precognition [,pri:kɔg'niʃn] 预知，预感　词源：pre 在前面 + cogn 知道 + tion 名词后缀　指提前知道

providence ['prɔvid(ə)ns] 天意，天命 divine providence 天意　词源：pro 向前 + vid 看 + ence 名词后缀　指人要学会向前看明白过去的一切都是天意　巧记：providence 天意就是上天 provide 提供的 provision 规定

premonish [pri:'mɔniʃ] 预警，预感到　词源：pre 在前面 + mon 告诫 + ish 动词后缀　指提前警告

premonition [,pri:mə'niʃn]（不好的）预感 a premonition of failure 失败的预感　词源：premonish 预警 + tion 名词后缀

prehistory [,pri:'histri] 史前时期　词源：pre 在前面 + history 历史

preliterate [pri:'litərit] 无文字的 a preliterate tribe 无文字的部落；不会写字的 preliterate children 还不会写字的孩子们　词源：pre 在前面 + liter 文字 + ate 形容词后缀　指在文字出现前的

premature ['premətjuə] 不成熟的；（婴儿）早产的 a premature birth 早产；仓促的，过早的 make a premature decision 做草率的决定　词源：pre 在前面 + mature 成熟的　指提前成熟的是过早成熟的

prejudice ['predʒudis] 偏见 a cultural prejudice against fat people 传统上对胖人的偏见；损害，不利于 the slackness that prejudices the chances of getting a promotion 不利于获得升职机会的懒散　词源：pre 在前面 + jud 判断 judge + ice 名词后缀　指提前的主观性判断是偏见　巧记：Pride and Prejudice 傲慢与偏见

223. **-preci-**：price　巧记：price 的词形变化

appreciate [ə'pri:ʃieit; -si-] 理解，明白（重要性或价值）；欣赏，鉴赏，赏识 appreciate sb. 赏识某人；感激；增值，升值　词源：ap 强调 + preci 价格 + ate 动词后缀　指价格上升是增值　词义连记：感激有机会欣赏增值的艺术品，理解明白它们艺术上的重要性

appreciative [ə'pri:ʃətiv] 有欣赏力的，表示赞赏的 appreciative audience / applause 表示赞赏的观众/赞赏的掌声；感激 be appreciative of one's support 感激某人的支持　词源：

appreciate 感激 + tive 形容词后缀（表示充满活力的 active）

appreciation [əpriːʃi'eiʃ(ə)n; -si-] 理解；欣赏；感激；增值　词源：appreciate 感激 + tion 名词后缀

appreciable [ə'priːʃəbl] 明显的，可察觉的 have an appreciable effect on sth. 对某事有明显的效果　词源：appreciate 理解明白 + able 形容词后缀（表示可以……的）指可以理解明白的是明显的

praise [preiz]（公开地）称赞，赞扬，表扬；（在教堂唱赞美诗）颂扬，赞颂（上帝）　词源：preci 价格　指因价值大价格高而赞扬

appraise [ə'preiz] 评估，鉴定（艺术品、房产或珠宝等价值）；上下打量 appraise the young girl 打量着年轻女孩　词源：ap 强调 + praise 赞美　指反复赞美物品好是鉴定

appraisal [ə'preiz(ə)l] 评估，鉴定 an accurate appraisal of the situation 对形势准确的评估；（上司对雇员的）工作表现评估　词源：appraise 鉴定 + al 名词后缀

depreciate [di'priːʃieit; -si-] 贬低，轻视（重要性）depreciate the importance of aesthetic education 贬低美学教育的重要性；贬值，跌价；使折旧 depreciate the computers 使计算机折旧　词源：de 否定 + preci 价格 + ate 动词后缀　指价格变得不高

depreciation [di,priːʃi'eiʃ(ə)n; -si'ei-] 贬值，跌价 currency depreciation 货币贬值　词源：depreciate 贬值 + tion 名词后缀

precious ['preʃəs] 宝贵的，珍贵的 precious possessions 贵重物品　词源：preci 价格 + ous 形容词后缀（表示过多的）指价格过高的是宝贵的

224. **-prim-, prior-**：first　巧记：pre 的变化　指在前面的是首要的

prime [praim] 最重要的，首要的 the prime objective 首要目标；质量一流的 prime beef 优质牛肉；盛年，年富力强的时期，壮年时期 a leader in the prime of life 一位正当盛年的领袖；使准备好（应付某个情况）prime sb. with / for sth.；在（金属、木材等上）涂底漆　词源：prim 首先　巧记：Optimus Prime 变形金刚的擎天柱

primacy ['praiməsi] 首位，第一位 the primacy of the family 家庭至上　词源：prime 首要的 + cy 名词后缀

premier ['premiə; 'priː-] 最好的，最重要的 The FA Premier League 英格兰足球超级联赛；首相，总理　词源：prem 首先 + er 比较级

primary ['praim(ə)ri] 首要的，主要的 the primary purpose / aim / objective 主要目标；小学教育的 primary education 小学教育；最初的，最早的 a primary therapy for depression 抑郁症的基础治疗　词源：prim 首先 + ary 形容词后缀

primeval [prai'miːvl] 远古的，原始的 primeval forests 原始森林；本能的 primeval urges 本能的冲动　词源：prim 首先 + ev 夜晚 evening + al 形容词后缀　指最初的黑暗时期

primitive ['primitiv] 原始的 a primitive society 原始社会；老式的，简陋的 primitive facilities 简陋的设施；（动物或植物）原始的，低等的；本能的 the primitive instinct of survival 求生的本能　词源：prim 首先 + tive 形容词后缀（表示充满活力的 active）

supreme [suː'priːm]（级别、地位、权力或影响力）至高无上的 the Supreme Commander 最高统帅/the Supreme Court 最高法院；（程度）最大的，极度的 a supreme effort 最大的努力　词源：supper 上面 + prem 首先　指高高在上起首要作用的

prior ['praiə] 先前的 require prior experience in advertising 要求有从事广告行业的先前经验；先于……，在……之前 prior to sth.（= before）；犯罪前科　词源：prior 首先

priority [prai'ɔriti] 当务之急,优先处理的事项 a top priority；优先,优先权 take priority over sth. 优先考虑某事　词源：prior 首先 + ty 名词后缀

prioritize [prai'ɔrətaiz] 按优先顺序列出 prioritize one's learning tasks 按照轻重缓急安排学习任务；优先考虑处理 prioritize the needs of seniors 优先满足老年人的需要　词源：priority 优先 + ize 动词后缀

225. -spire-：breathe　巧记：sp 喷射（拟声词）+ ire 空气　指喷射出气体是呼吸

aspire [ə'spaiə] 追求，渴望，有志于 aspire to (do) sth.　词源：a 正在 + spire 呼吸　指人正在气喘吁吁地向目标奔跑

conspire [kən'spaiə] 密谋 conspire (with sb.) to do sth. / conspire against sb. / sth.　词源：con 共同 + spire 呼吸　指同一鼻孔出气

conspiracy [kən'spirəsi] 密谋　词源：conspire 密谋 + cy 名词后缀

expire [ik'spaiə; ek-]（签证、护照或租约等正式文件）到期,过期,失效；（任期）届满；逝世,故去　词源：ex 出去 + spire 呼吸　指不再呼吸

inspire [in'spaiə] 激励,鼓舞 inspire sb. to do sth.；激起,唤起（某种感情或反应）inspire great respect 使人敬佩；启发思考,引起联想,赋予（某人）创作灵感 exquisite designs inspired by wildlife 从野生动物中得到灵感的精美设计　词源：in 内部 + spire 呼吸　指在大自然里深吸一口气获得灵感

inspiration [inspi'reiʃ(ə)n] 灵感 draw inspiration from sb. / sth. 获取灵感；给人灵感的人（或事物）；鼓舞人心的人（或事物）；（突然想到的）好主意,妙计　词源：inspire 激励 + tion 名词后缀

perspire [pə'spaiə(r)] 出汗，流汗　词源：per 一直 + spire 呼吸　指皮肤一直呼吸是出汗　巧记：per 人 person + spire 呼吸　指人做运动呼吸出汗

perspiration [pəːspi'reiʃ(ə)n] 汗,汗水　词源：pespire 呼吸 + tion 名词后缀　巧记：Genius is one per cent inspiration and ninety-nine per cent perspiration. 爱迪生名言：天才是百分之一的灵感加上百分之九十九的汗水　同义词：sweat

respire [ri'spaiə(r)] 呼吸　词源：re 重复 + spire 呼吸　指正常的反复呼吸状态

respiration [respi'reiʃ(ə)n] 呼吸 artificial respiration 人工呼吸　词源：respire 呼吸 + tion 名词后缀

226. -tribut-：give　巧记：tribe 部落　指部落间给予贡品

tribute ['tribjuːt]（一国向他国交纳的）贡品,贡赋,贡金；（对逝者的）致敬,赞美,颂

词 pay tribute to the heroes 向英雄致敬　词源：tribut 给予　指给予赞美歌颂

attribute [ə'tribju:t]（人的职业）特性，属性 have leadership attributes 有成为领导的素质；归因于 attribute sth. to sb. / sth.；认为……是某人所说、所写或所画 a saying attributed to Confucius 认为是孔子说的一句格言　词源：at 强调＋tribute 贡品　指贡品是谁献出的就是归因于谁的功劳

attributive [ə'tribjətiv] 定语的　词源：attribute 属性＋tive 形容词后缀（表示充满活力的 active）指有某种属性限定的

contribute [kən'tribju:t; 'kɔntribju:t] 贡献，捐献，捐助（款或物）contribute sth. to / towards sth.；（为报纸、杂志、电台或电视节目）撰稿, 投稿 contribute a number of articles to the magazine 给这家杂志撰写了一些稿件；导致，促使 a contributing factor 一个起作用的因素　词源：con 共同＋tribut 给予　指大家一起给予帮助是贡献

contributive [kən'tribjutiv] 有贡献的 be contributive to the world trade 对世界贸易有贡献；有促进作用的 a contributive factor 一个起作用的因素　词源：contribute 贡献＋tive 形容词后缀（表示充满活力的 active）

contributor [kən'tribjutə] 捐助人，做出贡献的人 important contributors to the economy 为发展经济做出了重要贡献的人；撰稿人，投稿人 a regular contributor to the magazine 杂志的定期投稿人；起作用的人或因素 the principal contributor to air pollution 空气污染的主要因素　词源：contribute 贡献＋or 名词后缀

contribution [kɔntri'bju:ʃ(ə)n] 贡献 make a contribution to sth. 做出贡献；捐款 contributions to charities 慈善捐款；（给雇主或政府用作医疗保险、养老金等津贴的）定期缴款 income tax and national insurance contributions 收入税和国家保险金的定期缴款；（书、报纸、杂志、广播、录音、讨论等的）稿件　词源：contribute 贡献＋tion 名词后缀

contributory [kən'tribjətəri] 起促进作用的 a contributory factor 一个起作用的因素；（退休金计划或保险金计划）由雇主与雇员共缴的 a contributory pension plan 由雇主与雇员共同出资的养老金计划　词源：contribute 导致＋ory 形容词后缀

distribute [di'stribju:t; 'distribju:t]（有计划地）分配，分发 distribute leaflets to passers-by 向路人派发传单；（人、动植物或财富等）分布；配送（货物），分销 distribute milk to the local shops 给当地商店配送牛奶　词源：dis 分散＋tribut 给予　指分散贡品给大家

distributor [di'stribjutə] 批发商，分销商 the largest software distributor 最大的软件批发商；（发动机的）配电器，配电盘　词源：distribute 分发＋or 名词后缀

distribution [distri'bju:ʃ(ə)n] 分配，分发 the distribution of food and medicines to the refugees 向难民分发食品和药物；分布 the distribution of world wealth 世界财富的分布；（商品）配货，分销 worldwide distribution systems 全球经销系统　词源：distribute 分发＋tion 名词后缀

227. **-prob-, -prov-**：prove　巧记：prove 的词形变化

probable ['prɔbəb(ə)l] 可能的；可能入选的人或可能获胜的人　词源：prob 证明＋able

形容词后缀（表示可以……的）指可以证明是对的

probability [ˌprɔbə'biliti] 可能性　词源：probable 可能的 + ity 名词后缀

approbate ['æprəuˌbeit]（官方）认可或赞许 approbate the nominees to the Supreme Court 批准最高法院提名人　词源：ap 强调 + prob 证明 + ate 动词后缀　指证明是对的会给予批准

approbation [ˌæprə'beiʃ(ə)n]（官方）认可或赞许 win the approbation of the school board 获得校董会批准　词源：approbate 认可 + tion 名词后缀

probation [prə'beiʃ(ə)n]（留职）察看期；缓刑；（新工作）试用期，见习期；（为表现不理想的学生而设的）试读期　词源：prob 证明 + tion 名词后缀　指一段证明的时期

approve [ə'pruːv]（官方机构）批准，通过（计划或要求）approve a proposal 批准提议；（某人）赞成，同意（想法或行为）approve of sth.　词源：ap 强调 + prov 证明　指证明是对的会给予批准　反义词：disapprove

approval [ə'pruːv(ə)l] 批准 appointments requiring parliamentary approval 需要议会批准的任命；同意 nod in approval 点头表示同意　词源：approve 批准 + al 名词后缀

disapprove [disə'pruːv]（官方机构）不批准，不同意 disapprove the sale of the corporation 不批准出售公司；（某人）不赞同，反对（想法或行为）disapprove of the rude behaviour 反对无礼的行为　词源：dis 否定 + approve 批准　指不批准　形近易混词：disprove

disprove [dis'pruːv] 证明……是错误（或虚假）的 disprove the theory 证明理论是错误的　词源：dis 否定 + prov 证明　指证明是假的　反义词：prove

improve [im'pruːv] 改善，改进　词源：im 内部 + prov 证明　指内部证明有进步是改善　同义词：ameliorate / refine

reprove [ri'pruːv] 责备，指责 reprove customers for smoking in the restaurants 指责顾客在饭店抽烟　词源：re 重复 + prov 证明　指上级反复让下级证明计划的可行性是指责　同义词：reprimand / reproach / rebuke

228. -proxim-：near　巧记：pro 向前 + x 否定 + im 内部　指向前走还没有到达内部是靠近

proximity [prɔk'simiti]（时间或距离的）接近，临近，邻近 an apartment in the proximity of the university 靠近大学的公寓　词源：proxim 靠近 + ity 名词后缀　同义词：vicinity

approximate [ə'prɔksimət] 大约的，大致的 an approximate cost 大致的成本；类似，近似 A approximates to B　词源：ap 强调 + proxim 靠近 + ate 形容词后缀　指靠得非常近是近似的

approximately [ə'prɔksimətli] 大概地，大约地　词源：approximate 大约的 + ly 副词后缀

approximation [əˌprɔksi'meiʃn] 近似值 a rough approximation of sales 粗略估算的销售量；类似事物 a close approximation to an economic crisis 和一场经济危机类似　词源：approximate 大约的 + tion 名词后缀

6

词汇练习题

Group 1

1. If you want this painkiller, you'll have to ask the doctor for a _____.
   A. transaction   B. permit   C. settlement   D. prescription
2. The _____ from childhood to adulthood is always critical time for everybody.
   A. conversion   B. transition   C. turnover   D. transformation
3. It is hard to tell whether we are going to have a boom in the economy or a _____.
   A. concession   B. recession   C. submission   D. transmission
4. His use of color, light and form quickly departed from the conventional style of his _____ as he developed his own technique.
   A. descendants   B. predecessors   C. successors   D. ancestors
5. Failure in a required subject may result in the _____ of a diploma.
   A. refusal   B. betrayal   C. denial   D. burial
6. To help students understand how we see, teachers often draw an _____ between an eye and a camera.
   A. image   B. analogy   C. imitation   D. axis
7. A 1994 World Bank report concluded that _____ girls in school was probably the single most effective anti-poverty policy in the developing world today.
   A. assigning   B. admitting   C. involving   D. enrolling
8. The author of this report is well _____ with the problems in the hospital because he has been working there for many years.
   A. acquainted   B. informed   C. accustomed   D. known

9. When the farmers visited the city the first time, they were _____ by its complicated traffic system.

   A. evoked   B. bewildered   C. diverted   D. undermined

10. If Japan _____ its relation with that country, it will have to find another supplier of raw materials.

    A. precludes   B. terminates   C. partitions   D. expires

11. They were _____ in their scientific research, not knowing what happened just outside their lab.

    A. submerged   B. drowned   C. immersed   D. dipped

12. You should _____ to one or more weekly magazines such as *Time*, or *Newsweek*.

    A. ascribe   B. order   C. reclaim   D. subscribe

13. The automatic doors in supermarkets _____ the entry and exit of customers with shopping carts.

    A. furnish   B. induce   C. facilitate   D. allocate

14. Each workday, the workers followed the same schedules and rarely _____ from this routine.

    A. deviated   B. disconnected   C. detached   D. distorted

15. The little girl was _____ by the death of her dog since her affection for the pet had been real and deep.

    A. grieved   B. suppressed   C. oppressed   D. sustained

16. A visitor to a museum today would notice _____ changes in the way museums are operated.

    A. cognitive   B. rigorous   C. conspicuous   D. exclusive

17. Most people tend to think they are so efficient at their job that they are _____.

    A. inaccessible B. irreversible   C. immovable   D. irreplaceable

18. Being impatient is _____ with being a good teacher.

    A. intrinsic   B. ingenious   C. incompatible   D. inherent

19. For a particular reason, he wanted the information to be treated as _____.

    A. assured   B. reserved   C. intimate   D. confidential

20. Fortune-tellers are good at making _____ statements such as "Your sorrows will change."

    A. philosophical B. ambiguous   C. literal   D. invalid

Group 1　Detailed Answers (1–20)

1. D　参考译文：如果你想买这个止痛药，就必须有医生开的处方。

   A. transaction 交易　　　　　　　　B. permit 允许

   C. settlement 解决　　　　　　　　 D. prescription 处方

2. B 参考译文：由童年到成年的过渡阶段对每个人来说往往都是很重要的一段时期。
   A. conversion 转变信仰　　　　　　　B. transition 过渡
   C. turnover 成交量　　　　　　　　　D. transformation 变化
3. B 参考译文：很难判断我们的经济是要经历繁荣还是衰退。
   A. concession 妥协　　　　　　　　　B. recession 衰退
   C. submission 屈服　　　　　　　　　D. transmission 传播
4. B 参考译文：当他形成自己的技艺后，在使用色彩、光线和图形方面很快摆脱了前辈们的那些传统风格。
   A. descendant 后代　　　　　　　　　B. predecessor 前人
   C. successor 继任者　　　　　　　　　D. ancestor 祖先
5. C 参考译文：必修科目考试不及格可能会导致得不到毕业证。
   A. refusal 拒绝　　B. betrayal 背叛　　C. denial 否认　　D. burial 埋葬
6. B 参考译文：为了帮助学生更好地理解我们是如何看见东西的，老师们经常把眼睛和照相机作类比。
   A. image 意象　　B. analogy 类比　　C. imitation 模仿　　D. axis 轴
7. D 参考译文：世界银行1994年的一份报告得出这样的结论：学校招收女生可能是发展中国家消除贫困的唯一最为有效的途径。
   A. assign 指派　　B. admit 承认　　C. involve 包含　　D. enroll 招收
8. A 参考译文：这篇报道的作者对医院的问题非常熟悉，因为他已经在那里工作许多年了。
   A. acquaint 熟悉　　B. inform 告知　　C. accustom 习惯　　D. know 知道
9. B 参考译文：当这些农民第一次来到城里时他们被复杂的交通系统搞得晕头转向。
   A. evoke 恳求　　B. bewilder 迷惑　　C. divert 转移　　D. undermine 颠覆
10. B 参考译文：如果日本终止与那个国家的关系，它就不得不另寻找原材料供应者。
    A. preclude 防止　　B. terminate 终止　　C. partition 分割　　D. expire 过期
11. C 参考译文：他们沉浸于科学研究，对实验室外发生的事浑然不知。
    A. submerge 淹没　　　　　　　　　B. drown 溺水
    C. immerse 沉浸　　　　　　　　　 D. dip 浸入
12. D 参考译文：你应该订一两种周刊，比如《时代周刊》或《新闻周刊》。
    A. ascribe 归因于　　　　　　　　　B. order 命令
    C. reclaim 重新要求　　　　　　　　D. subscribe 订阅
13. C 参考译文：超市的自动门给推着购物车的消费者出入提供了方便。
    A. furnish 配备　　　　　　　　　　B. induce 引起
    C. facilitate 使便利　　　　　　　　　D. allocate 分配
14. A 参考译文：每天这些工人都按照同样的日程表工作，很少有变动。
    A. deviate 避开，偏离　　　　　　　B. disconnect 割断
    C. detach 分开　　　　　　　　　　D. distort 扭曲

15. A 参考译文：这个小女孩对狗的死感到悲痛，因为她对宠物怀有真挚、深厚的感情。
    A. grieve 悲伤   B. suppress 压抑   C. oppress 镇压   D. sustain 维持

16. C 参考译文：今天到博物馆参观的人会注意到博物馆的运作方式发生了显著的变化。
    A. cognitive 认知的   B. rigorous 严格的
    C. conspicuous 明显的   D. exclusive 独特的

17. D 参考译文：大多数人认为非常胜任自己的工作，以至于他们是不可替代的。
    A. inaccessible 不可获得的   B. irreversible 不可逆转的
    C. immovable 不为所动的   D. irreplaceable 不可替代的

18. C 参考译文：没有耐心和做一名好老师是矛盾的。
    A. intrinsic 内在的   B. ingenious 聪明的
    C. incompatible 矛盾的   D. inherent 固有的

19. D 参考译文：由于某种特殊原因，他希望将这个消息保密。
    A. assured 确信的   B. reserved 保守的
    C. intimate 亲密的   D. confidential 机密的

20. B 参考译文：算命者擅长说模棱两可的话，比如："你会时来运转"。
    A. philosophical 复杂的   B. ambiguous 模糊的
    C. literal 字面的   D. invalid 无效的

Group 2

21. The tenant must be prepared to decorate the house _____ the terms of the contract.
    A. in the vicinity of   B. in quest of
    C. in accordance with   D. in collaboration with

22. The winners of the football championship ran off the field carrying the silver cup _____.
    A. turbulently   B. tremendously   C. triumphantly   D. tentatively

23. He said that they had been _____ obliged to give up the scheme for lack of support.
    A. gravely   B. regrettably   C. forcibly   D. graciously

24. The law on drinking and driving is _____ stated.
    A. extravagantly B. empirically   C. exceptionally   D. explicitly

25. Their claims to damages have been convincingly _____.
    A. refuted   B. overwhelmed   C. repressed   D. intimidated

26. Please don't _____ too much on the painful memories. Everything will be all right.
    A. hesitate   B. linger   C. retain   D. dwell

27. The jobs of wildlife technicians and biologists seemed _____ to him, but one day he discovered their difference.
    A. identical   B. vertical   C. parallel   D. specific

28. Mary became _____ homesick and critical of the United States, so she flew from her home in West Bloomfield to her hometown in Austria.

   A. completely   B. sincerely   C. absolutely   D. increasingly

29. Despite almost universal _____ of the vital importance of women's literacy, education remains a dream for many women in some countries of the world.

   A. identification   B. compliment   C. confession   D. acknowledgement

30. In today's medical community, little agreement exists on the _____ for defining mental illness.

   A. legislation   B. requirement   C. criteria   D. measures

31. The lady in this strange tale very obviously suffers from a serious mental illness. Her plot against a completely innocent old man is a clear sign of _____.

   A. impulse   B. insanity   C. inspiration   D. disposition

32. The Prime Minister was followed by five or six _____ when he got off the plane.

   A. laymen   B. servants   C. directors   D. attendants

33. There is no doubt that the _____ of these goods to the others is easy to see.

   A. prestige   B. superiority   C. priority   D. publicity

34. All the guests were invited to attend the wedding _____ and had a very good time.

   A. feast   B. congratulations   C. festival   D. recreation

35. The price of the coal will vary according to how far it has to be transported and how expensive the freight _____ are.

   A. payments   B. charges   C. funds   D. prices

36. The manager gave her his _____ that her complaint would be investigated.

   A. assurance   B. assumption   C. sanction   D. insurance

37. Although the model looks good on the surface, it will not bear close _____.

   A. temperament   B. contamination   C. scrutiny   D. symmetry

38. We are doing this work in the _____ of reforms in the economic, social and cultural spheres.

   A. context   B. contest   C. pretext   D. texture

39. While a full understanding of what causes the disease may be several years away, _____ leading to a successful treatment could come much sooner.

   A. a distinction   B. a breakthrough
   C. an identification   D. an interpretation

40. Doctors are often caught in a _____ because they have to decide whether they should tell their patients the truth or not.

   A. puzzle   B. perplexity   C. dilemma   D. bewilderment

Group 2　Detailed Answers (21–40)

21. C　参考译文：房客必须按照合同条款对房子进行装修。
    A. in the vicinity of 附近　　　　　　B. in quest of 寻找……，追求……
    C. in accordance with 根据　　　　　D. in collaboration with 与……合作

22. C　参考译文：足球锦标赛的冠军举着银质奖杯得意地绕场一周。
    A. turbulently 动荡地
    B. tremendously 相当地，非常多地
    C. triumphantly 成功地，耀武扬威地
    D. tentatively 暂时地，短暂地

23. B　参考译文：他说因为缺乏支持，他们不得不遗憾地放弃这个主题。
    A. gravely 严重地　　　　　　　　　B. regrettably 遗憾地，后悔地
    C. forcibly 强制地　　　　　　　　　D. graciously 优雅地

24. D　参考译文：关于饮酒和驾驶的法律已经制定得很清楚了。
    A. extravagantly 奢侈地，过度地　　B. empirically 经验主义地
    C. exceptionally 例外地　　　　　　D. explicitly 明晰地，直率地

25. A　参考译文：他们的赔偿损害要求被有说服力地驳倒了。
    A. refuted 驳斥，反驳，驳倒的　　　B. overwhelmed 压倒性的，不知所措的
    C. repressed 被抑制的，被压抑的　　D. intimidated 恐吓的，恐怖的

26. D　参考译文：请不要太多地回想痛苦的记忆，一切都将会好起来的。
    A. hesitate 犹豫，踌躇
    B. linger 逗留，闲荡，拖延（常与 on 连用，表示人苟延残喘或事物继续存留）
    C. retain 保留，保持
    D. dwell 居住，踌躇（常与 on 连用，表示细想，详述；dwell in 表示居住于某地）

27. A　参考译文：野生动物技术专家和生物学家的工作对他来说没什么区别，但是有一天他发现了他们两者的不同。
    A. identical 相同的　　　　　　　　B. vertical 垂直的
    C. parallel 平行的　　　　　　　　　D. specific 特别的

28. D　参考译文：玛丽日渐思乡，同时也对美国感到不满，于是她从她西布卢姆菲尔德的家回到了奥地利家乡。
    A. completely 完全地，彻底地　　　B. sincerely 真诚地
    C. absolutely 完全地，绝对地　　　　D. increasingly 日益增加地

29. D　参考译文：尽管在妇女受教育的至关重要性上（人们）有统一的共识，在世界上的一些国家，接受教育对妇女仍然是一个梦。
    A. identification 鉴定；身份证　　　B. compliment 赞美
    C. confession 坦白，供认　　　　　　D. acknowledgement 承认，感谢

30. C　参考译文：当今医学上，在定义精神病的标准时很少有相同意见。

A. legislation 立法，法规　　　　　B. requirement 要求
   C. criteria 标准　　　　　　　　　D. measures 度量，措施

31. B 参考译文：这本奇异小说里的女士有严重的精神疾病，她对完全无辜的老人实施的阴谋体现了她的疯狂。
   A. impulse 冲动　　　　　　　　　B. insanity 疯狂，愚昧
   C. inspiration 激动，鼓舞，灵感　　D. disposition 性情，气质

32. D 参考译文：首相走下飞机，后面跟着五六个随从。
   A. laymen 外行，门外汉
   B. servants 仆人
   C. directors 主任，主管，董事，导演
   D. attendants 侍者，护理人员

33. B 参考译文：毫无疑问，很容易看出来这批货物比其他货物更好。
   A. prestige 威望
   B. superiority 优势 have superiority to 表示比……优越
   C. priority 优先，重点
   D. publicity 宣传

34. A 参考译文：所有的客人都被邀请参加婚宴，并且度过了愉快的一段时间。
   A. feast 宴会，表示婚礼宴会等用 feast
   B. congratulations 祝贺
   C. festival 节日
   D. recreation 消遣，娱乐活动

35. B 参考译文：煤价会根据它如何被运输和运费的价格是否昂贵改变。
   A. payments 支付　　　　　　　　B. charges 费用
   C. funds 基金　　　　　　　　　　D. prices 价格

36. A 参考译文：经理向她保证会对她的投诉进行调查。
   A. assurance 承诺，保证　　　　　B. assumption 设想，承担
   C. sanction 批准，制裁　　　　　　D. insurance 保险

37. C 参考译文：尽管模型的表面看起来挺好，却经不起仔细检查。
   A. temperament 气质　　　　　　　B. contamination 污染
   C. scrutiny 仔细检查　　　　　　　D. symmetry 对称

38. A 参考译文：我们正在做的这项工作是在经济、社会和文化领域改革的背景下进行的。
   A. context 背景，语境　　　　　　B. contest 比赛
   C. pretext 借口，理由　　　　　　D. texture 质地，神韵

39. B 参考译文：尽管还需要几年才能全面了解什么是导致疾病的原因，但在治疗方面的突破会来得快些。
   A. a distinction 不同，杰出　　　　B. a breakthrough 突破
   C. an identification 识别　　　　　D. an interpretation 口译，说明

40. C 参考译文：医生经常处于一种进退两难的状态，他们必须决定是否应该告诉病人真相。

    A. puzzle 拼图游戏，难题   B. perplexity 困惑，茫然

    C. dilemma 进退两难   D. bewilderment 迷惑，迷茫

Group 3

41. To _____ important dates in history, countries create special holidays.

    A. commend   B. memorize   C. propagate   D. commemorate

42. His successful negotiations with the Americans helped him to _____ his position in the government.

    A. contrive   B. consolidate   C. heave   D. intensify

43. Please do not be _____ by his offensive remarks since he is merely trying to attract attention.

    A. distracted   B. disregarded   C. irritated   D. intervened

44. Once you get to know your mistakes, you should _____ them as soon as possible.

    A. rectify   B. reclaim   C. refrain   D. reckon

45. He wouldn't answer the reporters' questions, nor would he _____ for a photograph.

    A. summon   B. highlight   C. pose   D. marshal

46. The club will _____ new members the first week in September.

    A. enroll   B. subscribe   C. absorb   D. register

47. If you don't _____ the children properly, they'll just run riot.

    A. mobilize   B. warrant   C. manipulate   D. supervise

48. The players are _____ about who their coach will be.

    A. foreseeing   B. speculating   C. fabricating   D. contemplating

49. We should _____ our energy and youth to the development of our country.

    A. dedicate   B. cater   C. ascribe   D. cling

50. Just because I'm _____ to him, my boss thinks he can order me around without showing me any respect.

    A. redundant   B. trivial   C. versatile   D. subordinate

51. Many scientists remain _____ about the value of this research program.

    A. sceptical   B. stationary   C. spacious   D. specific

52. Depression is often caused by the _____ effects of stress and overwork.

    A. total   B. increased   C. terrific   D. cumulative

53. A human's eyesight is not as _____ as that of an eagle.

    A. eccentric   B. acute   C. sensible   D. sensitive

54. It is _____ that women should be paid less than men for doing the same kind of work.
    A. abrupt   B. absurd   C. adverse   D. addictive
55. Shoes of this kind are _____ to slip on wet ground.
    A. feasible   B. appropriate   C. apt   D. fitting
56. We'll be very careful and keep what you've told us strictly _____.
    A. rigorous   B. confidential   C. private   D. mysterious
57. The members of Parliament were _____ that the government had not consulted them.
    A. impatient   B. tolerant   C. crude   D. indignant
58. Some American colleges are state-supported, others are privately _____, and still others are supported by religious organizations.
    A. ensured   B. attributed   C. authorized   D. endowed
59. The prison guards were armed and ready to shoot if _____ in any way.
    A. intervened   B. incurred   C. provoked   D. poked
60. Many pure metals have little use because they are too soft, rust too easily, or have some other _____.
    A. drawbacks   B. handicaps   C. bruises   D. blunders

Group 3   Detailed Answers (41–60)

41. D 参考译文：为了纪念历史上的重大日子，国家创造了特别的节日。
    A. commend 称赞，推崇   B. memorize 记住，背下
    C. propagate 宣传，繁殖   D. commemorate 庆祝，纪念

42. B 参考译文：他和美国人成功的磋商帮助他巩固了他在政府中的地位。
    A. contrive 设法做到，谋划   B. consolidate 加强，巩固
    C. heave 举起，抬起   D. intensify 强化，加剧

43. C 参考译文：他仅仅是想引起注意，请不要为他的无礼行为感到生气。既然对方只是试图引起人们的注意，就不应该对对方的行为愤慨，所以答案 C，irritate 表示气愤与 offensive remarks 构成同现关系。
    A. distracted 心烦意乱的   B. disregarded 忽视的，蔑视的
    C. irritated 激怒的，气愤的   D. intervened 干涉的，介入的

44. A 参考译文：一旦你知道你犯错误了，就应该尽快改正它们。本题为词汇同现题，与 mistakes 同现的应该是改正，即 rectify，其他单词 refrain, reclaim, reckon 与 mistakes 不构成搭配关系。
    A. rectify 更正，修改   B. reclaim 收回，要求归还
    C. refrain 节制，避免   D. reckon 估计，猜想

45. C 参考译文：他不会回答记者的问题，也不会接受拍照。本题表示摆姿势拍照，应该用动词 pose。
    A. summon 召集，召唤

B. highlight 突出，使显著

C. pose 摆姿势，装腔作势，提出问题，导致造成

D. marshal 整理想法，调集军队，引导人群，元帅，司礼官，主事官，治安官

46. A 参考译文：俱乐部在九月的第一个星期招纳新会员。本题表示招纳新会员，表示吸收的为 absorb。

A. enroll（新生报到）注册　　　　B. subscribe 订购，订阅

C. absorb 吸收　　　　　　　　　D. register 登记注册

47. D 参考译文：如果你不正确监督孩子们，他们将会变得调皮捣蛋。本题为假设关系同现题，想要孩子们不胡作非为，就要适当监控，答案为 supervise。

A. mobilize 动员　　　　　　　　B. warrant 保证，担保，批准

C. manipulate 操作，操纵，巧妙处理　D. supervise 监督

48. B 参考译文：运动员正在猜测他们的教练是谁。本题为词汇固定搭配题，speculate about 表示推测，猜测，其他选项没有此搭配用法。

A. foreseeing 预见，预知

B. speculating 推测，投机

C. fabricating 制造，生产，编造，捏造，伪造

D. contemplating 考虑，打算，沉思，细想，凝视，注视

49. A 参考译文：我们应该把青春和力量献给我们国家的发展。本题为词汇固定搭配题，dedicate...to... 表示献身于……。

A. dedicate 献身，致力，题献（一部著作给某人），举行建筑物落成典礼

B. cater 迎合，满足需求，提供饮食，承办酒席

C. ascribe 归因于，认为是……所写，认为……具有……的特点

D. cling 抓紧，抱紧，粘着，附着，依恋，依附，坚持，坚守

50. D 参考译文：仅仅因为我是他的下属，我的老板就认为他可以随意指使我而不给我一点尊重。本题为同现题，自己与老板显然是从属关系，所以答案为 subordinate。

A. redundant 多余的　　　　　　B. trivial 琐细的，微不足道的

C. versatile 多才多艺的　　　　　D. subordinate 从属的，上级对下级的

51. A 参考译文：许多科学家仍然对这个研究项目的价值持怀疑态度。本题为词汇固定搭配题，be sceptical about 表示对……持怀疑态度。

A. sceptical 怀疑的　　　　　　　B. stationary 静止的

C. spacious 宽敞的　　　　　　　D. specific 具体的

52. D 参考译文：一个人的压抑是长时间的紧张和过度工作所致的。

A. total 总计　　　　　　　　　　B. increased 增加的

C. terrific 极好的　　　　　　　　D. cumulative 积累的

53. B 参考译文：人的视力不像鹰的眼睛一样敏锐。

A. eccentric 古怪的　　　　　　　B. acute 敏锐的

C. sensible 可感觉到的，明智的　　D. sensitive 敏感的

54. B 参考译文：即使干同样的活，女人得到的待遇却比男人的低，这的确很荒谬。从结构上来讲，absurd 后从句中一般应该用 should + 原形动词。
    A. abrupt 突然的，陡峭的	B. absurd 荒谬的，可笑的
    C. adverse 不利的，相反的	D. addictive 上瘾的
55. C 参考译文：穿这种鞋在潮湿的地板上很容易滑倒。本题为词汇固定搭配题，be apt to do sth. 表示易于做某事。
    A. feasible 可行的，切实可行的
    B. appropriate 合适的，得体的
    C. apt 易于……的，有……倾向的，适当的，聪明的
    D. fitting 适合的，相称的
56. B 参考译文：我们会很小心，把你告诉我们的话严格保密。
    A. rigorous 严格的，严厉的	B. confidential 保密的
    C. private 私人的，私有的	D. mysterious 神秘的
57. D 参考译文：国会会员对于政府没有征求他们的意见感到很气愤。
    A. impatient 不耐烦	B. tolerant 宽容的
    C. crude 粗鲁的	D. indignant 气愤的
58. D 参考译文：一些美国大学是州立的，其他是私人捐助的，还有一些是宗教组织支持的。本题为信息复现题，所填单词表达的是 support 的含义。四个选项中与 support 意思相近的为 endow，即大学由私人出资。
    A. ensured 确保，保证	B. attributed 归结于
    C. authorized 批准	D. endowed 捐赠，赋予
59. C 参考译文：监狱守卫全副武装，随时准备射击以任何方式挑衅的人。
    A. intervened 干涉，干预，插入	B. incurred 招致，发生
    C. provoked 激怒，挑拨，煽动	D. poked 刺，戳
60. A 参考译文：许多纯金属没有什么用处，因为它们太软，太容易锈蚀，或者有其他的缺点。
    A. drawbacks 缺点，退税（指进口原料加工成产品后再出口时退还其进口时的关税）
    B. handicaps 障碍，阻碍
    C. bruises 瘀伤，擦伤
    D. blunders 跌跌撞撞地走，犯大错

Group 4

61. It was _____ that the restaurant discriminated against black customers.
    A. addicted	B. alleged	C. assaulted	D. ascribed
62. The medicine _____ his pain but did not cure his illness.

A. activated   B. alleviated   C. mediated   D. deteriorated

63. He is the only person who can _____ in this case, because the other witnesses were detained mysteriously.

A. testify   B. charge   C. accuse   D. rectify

64. Professor Hawking is _____ as one of the world's greatest living physicists.

A. dignified   B. clarified   C. acknowledged   D. illustrated

65. The financial problem of this company is further _____ by the rise in interest rates.

A. increased   B. strengthened   C. reinforced   D. aggravated

66. We shall probably never be able to _____ the exact nature of these sub-atomic particles.

A. assert   B. impart   C. ascertain   D. notify

67. All the people in the stadium cheered up when they saw hundreds of colorful balloons _____ slowly into the sky.

A. ascending   B. elevating   C. escalating   D. lingering

68. Many years had _____ before they returned to their original urban areas.

A. floated   B. elapsed   C. skipped   D. proceeded

69. What you say now is not _____ with what you said last week.

A. consistent   B. persistent   C. permanent   D. insistent

70. Military orders are _____ and cannot be disobeyed.

A. defective   B. conservative   C. alternative   D. imperative

71. Some educators try to put students of similar abilities into the same class because they believe this kind of _____ grouping is advisable.

A. homogeneous   B. instantaneous   C. spontaneous   D. anonymous

72. Even sensible men do _____ things sometimes.

A. abrupt   B. absurd   C. acute   D. apt

73. The commission would find itself _____ at every turn if its members couldn't reach an agreement.

A. collided   B. savaged   C. crumbled   D. hampered

74. Grain production in the world is _____, but still millions go hungry.

A. staggering   B. shrinking   C. soaring   D. suspending

75. He developed a _____ attitude after years of frustration in his career.

A. sneaking   B. disgusted   C. drastic   D. cynical

76. They believed that this was not the _____ of their campaign for equality but merely the beginning.

A. climax   B. summit   C. pitch   D. maximum

77. Several guests were waiting in the _____ for the front door to open.

A. porch   B. vent   C. inlet   D. entry

78. As the mountains were covered with a _____ of cloud, we couldn't see their tops.

A. coating   B. film   C. veil   D. shade

79. We couldn't really afford to buy a house so we got it on hire purchase and paid monthly _____.

    A. investments   B. requirements   C. arrangements   D. installments

80. The magician made us think he cut the girl into pieces, but it was merely an _____.

    A. illusion   B. impression   C. image   D. illumination

Group 4　Detailed Answers (61–80)

61. B　参考译文：据称这家餐厅歧视黑人顾客。
    A. addicted 使沉溺，使上瘾　　B. alleged 宣称，断言
    C. assaulted 攻击，袭击　　D. ascribed 归因于，归咎于

62. B　参考译文：药物减轻了他的疼痛但是没有治愈他的病。
    A. activated 激活　　B. alleviated 使痛苦等减轻
    C. mediated 居间调停　　D. deteriorated 恶化

63. A　参考译文：他是唯一一个能给这案子作证的人，因为其他的目击者们都被神秘拘押起来了。
    A. testify 证明，证实，作证　　B. charge 控诉，责令，告诫，收费
    C. accuse 控告，谴责，非难　　D. rectify 矫正，调整

64. C　参考译文：霍金教授是世界上公认仍健在的最伟大的物理学家之一。
    A. dignified 有威严的，有品格的　　B. clarified 澄清了的
    C. acknowledged 公认的　　D. illustrated 有插图的，说明的

65. D　参考译文：这家公司的经济状况由于利率的上升而更加恶化。
    A. increased 增加的　　B. strengthened 加强的
    C. reinforced 加固的　　D. aggravated 恶化的

66. C　参考译文：我们可能将永远不会确定这些亚原子颗粒的真正性质。
    A. assert 声称，固执己见
    B. impart 给予（某种品质），传授（知识、智慧），告知，透露（信息）
    C. ascertain 确定，查明
    D. notify 通告，通知

67. A　参考译文：当体育馆里的所有人看到上百个彩色气球慢慢升上天空的时候都欢呼了起来。
    A. ascending 攀登，上升　　B. elevating 提高，抬高
    C. escalating 战争升级　　D. lingering 逗留，徘徊，拖延

68. B　参考译文：许多年过去了，他们才回到他们原来居住的城区。
    A. floated 浮动，漂浮　　B. elapsed 时间过去，流逝
    C. skipped 跳过，蹦　　D. proceeded 继续进行

69. A　参考译文：你现在所说的和你上周所说的不一致。

A. consistent 一致的 B. persistent 坚持的，固执的
C. permanent 永久的 D. insistent 坚持的，坚决要求的

70. D 参考译文：军事命令是强制性的而且是不能违背的。
A. defective 有缺陷的
B. conservative 保守的
C. alternative 替换物，两者选其一的
D. imperative 强制的，命令性的

71. A 参考译文：一些教育家试图把有着共同能力的学生放在一个班级，因为他们相信这种同性质的分类是明智的。
A. homogeneous 同类的，同性质的 B. instantaneous 瞬间的，即刻的
C. spontaneous 自发的，本能的 D. anonymous 匿名的

72. B 参考译文：即使理智的人有时也会做荒谬的事情。
A. abrupt 突然的 B. absurd 荒谬的，不合理的
C. acute 尖的，敏锐的 D. apt 恰当的

73. D 参考译文：这个委员会将发现他们举步维艰，假如委员们不能够达成一致的意见。
A. collided 碰撞 B. savaged 野蛮的
C. crumbled 粉碎，崩溃 D. hampered 妨碍

74. C 参考译文：全球谷物产量已经有很大的上升，但是仍然有数以万计的人在挨饿。
A. staggering 摇晃，蹒跚 B. shrinking 收缩，皱缩
C. soaring 高飞，滑翔，剧增 D. suspending 吊，悬；暂停

75. D 参考译文：由于多年来在事业上的挫折，他变得玩世不恭。
A. sneaking 鬼鬼祟祟 B. disgusted 厌恶的
C. drastic 剧烈的 D. cynical 愤世嫉俗的

76. A 参考译文：他认为这不是他们争取平等运动的高潮，而只是开端而已。
A. climax 高潮 B. summit 高峰 C. pitch 音高 D. maximum 最大值

77. A 参考译文：几个客人在门廊里等待前门开。
A. porch 门廊 B. vent 通风口 C. inlet 进水口 D. entry 入口

78. C 参考译文：因为云雾笼罩着群山，所以我们看不到它的山顶。
A. coating 涂层 B. film 薄膜
C. veil 面纱，一层 D. shade 阴影

79. D 参考译文：我们买不起房子，所以我们只有买分期付款的房子，按月付钱。
A. investments 投资 B. requirements 要求
C. arrangements 安排 D. installments 分期付款的一期付款

80. A 参考译文：魔术师让我们相信他把那个女孩切成了碎片，但实际上只是一个幻觉而已。
A. illusion 幻觉 B. impression 印象
C. image 意象 D. illumination 照明

Group 5

81. A good education is an _____ you can fall back on for the rest of your life.
    A. asset   B. ethic   C. inventory   D. obligation
82. Giving a gift can convey a wealth of meaning about your appreciation of their _____ and the importance you place upon the relationship.
    A. solidarity   B. priority   C. superiority   D. hospitality
83. The designer has applied for a _____ for his new invention.
    A. tariff   B. discount   C. version   D. patent
84. The toy maker produces a _____ copy of the space station, exact in every detail.
    A. minimal   B. minimum   C. miniature   D. minor
85. An energy tax would curb ordinary air pollution, limit oil imports and cut the budget _____.
    A. disposition   B. discrepancy   C. defect   D. deficit
86. They have decided to _____ physical punishment in all local schools.
    A. put away   B. break away from
    C. do away with   D. pass away
87. Astronauts are _____ all kinds of tests before they are actually sent up in a spacecraft.
    A. inclined to   B. subjected to   C. prone to   D. bound to
88. Individual sports are run by over 370 independent governing bodies whose functions usually include _____ rules, holding events, selecting national teams and promoting international links.
    A. drawing on   B. drawing in   C. drawing up   D. drawing down
89. Up until that time, his interest had focused almost _____ on fully mastering the skills and techniques of his craft.
    A. restrictively B. radically   C. inclusively   D. exclusively
90. All the ceremonies at the 2000 Olympic Games had a unique Australian flavor, _____ of their multicultural communities.
    A. noticeable   B. indicative   C. conspicuous   D. implicit
91. I have had my eyes tested and the report says that my _____ is perfect.
    A. outlook   B. vision   C. horizon   D. perspective
92. He was looking admiringly at the photograph published by Collins in _____ with the Imperial Museum.
    A. collection   B. connection   C. collaboration   D. combination
93. In those days, executives expected to spend most of their lives in the same firm and, unless

they were dismissed for _____, to retire at the age of 65.

    A. integrity   B. denial   C. incompetence   D. deduction

94. Others viewed the findings with _____, noting that a cause-and-effect relationship between passive smoking and cancer remains to be shown.

    A. optimism   B. passion   C. caution   D. deliberation

95. The 1986 Challenger space-shuttle _____ was caused by unusually low temperatures immediately before the launch.

    A. expedition   B. controversy   C. dismay   D. disaster

96. When supply exceeds demand for any product, prices are _____ to fall.

    A. timely   B. simultaneous   C. subject   D. liable

97. The music aroused an _____ feeling of homesickness in him.

    A. intentional   B. intermittent   C. intense   D. intrinsic

98. I bought an alarm clock with a(n) _____ dial, which can be seen clearly in the dark.

    A. supersonic   B. luminous   C. audible   D. amplified

99. The results are hardly _____; therefore, he cannot believe they are accurate.

    A. credible   B. contrary   C. critical   D. crucial

100. This new laser printer is _____ with all leading software.

    A. comparable   B. competitive   C. compatible   D. cooperative

Group 5   Detailed Answers (81–100)

81. A 参考译文：良好的教育是一生都能让你受益的财富。fall back on 依靠，有助于。

    A. asset 财富   B. ethic 道德，伦理

    C. inventory 库存清单，详细目录   D. obligation 义务

82. D 参考译文：赠送礼物能表达你对别人盛情款待的感激之情和你对别人的重视。

    A. solidarity 团结   B. priority 优先

    C. superiority 优越   D. hospitality 热情好客

83. D 参考译文：设计师已为他的新发明申请了专利。

    A. tariff 关税   B. discount 折价   C. version 版本   D. patent 专利

84. C 参考译文：玩具商制造了一个空间站的模型，与实物完全一致。

    A. minimal 最少的   B. minimum 最少

    C. miniature 微小的，微型的   D. minor 少数的

85. D 参考译文：能源税可以抑制空气污染，限制石油进口并减少财政赤字。

    A. disposition 处理

    B. discrepancy 差异

    C. defect 缺陷

    D. deficit 赤字 budget deficit 是固定搭配，表示财政赤字

86. C 参考译文：他们决定在所有地方学校中消除体罚现象。

A. put away 使用完毕将某物收起或放入箱子、抽屉等，省钱

B. break away from 脱离，挣脱

C. do away with 废除，消除

D. pass away 去世

87. B 参考译文：宇航员在进入航天器之前需经过各种各样的测试。

A. inclined to 倾向于，后面接动词

B. subjected to 使某人遭受、经历某事

C. prone to 有……的可能，易于……，表示易产生某种不好的结果

D. bound to 将要，一定，表示必定要发生某事，后面接动词

88. C 参考译文：单项体育运动由 370 多个独立的管理机构掌管，他们的责任是起草规章制度，举办赛事，选拔国家队，加强国际联系。

A. drawing on 利用，一段时间或某事件临近结束

B. drawing in（白昼）渐短，使某人参与某事，吸引某人

C. drawing up 起草，拟订

D. drawing down 引来，招致

89. D 参考译文：在那之前，他的兴趣几乎全部集中在全面掌握手艺的技巧上。

A. restrictively 严格地   B. radically 极端地，激进地

C. inclusively 包含地，在内地   D. exclusively 唯一地

90. B 参考译文：2000 年奥运会所有的仪式都带有一种独特的澳大利亚风情，这表明他们是多元文化的社会。

A. noticeable 明显的，易见的

B. indicative 表明的，表示的，常与 of 连用，表示表明或暗示某事物

C. conspicuous 明显的，惹人注目的，常与 for 连用，表示因某事而引人注目

D. implicit 含蓄的，不明确的，常与 in 连用，表示某事不言而喻 sth. be implicit in sth.

91. B 参考译文：我检查了我的眼睛，检查报告说视力是完好的。

A. outlook 景色，风光，观点，见解，展望

B. vision 视力，视觉，眼力

C. horizon 地平线，视野，范围

D. perspective 远景，前途，观点，看法

92. C 参考译文：他非常赞叹地观赏着科林斯和皇家博物馆联合出版的图片。

A. collection 收集，收藏

B. connection 连接，联系

C. collaboration 协作，合作,尤指合作出版和合著 be in collaboration with 与……合作，合著

D. combination 连接，联合，合并

93. C 参考译文：那时，除了因为不称职而被解雇外，执行官要终生待在同一家公司直到 65 岁退休。

241

A. integrity 正直，完整　　　　　　B. denial 否认，拒绝
   C. incompetence 无能力　　　　　　D. deduction 扣除，推理

94. C 参考译文：其他人以谨慎的态度看待这个研究结果，他们注意到癌症和被动吸烟之间的因果关系还有待被发现。
   A. optimism 乐观，乐观主义　　　　B. passion 激情，热情
   C. caution 小心，警告，谨慎　　　　D. deliberation 熟思，从容，考虑

95. D 参考译文：1986年挑战者宇宙飞船事故是由于发射前的异常低温引起的。
   A. expedition 探险队，远征，短途出行
   B. controversy 争议，辩论
   C. dismay 沮丧，惊慌
   D. disaster 灾难

96. D 参考译文：任何产品供大于求时，价格都会下跌。
   A. timely 及时的，适时的
   B. simultaneous 同时的，同时发生的
   C. be subject to sth. 受限于……，易受……影响
   D. liable 有做某事的倾向，有可能做某事

97. C 参考译文：音乐使他产生了强烈的思乡情绪。
   A. intentional 有意图的，故意的
   B. intermittent 间歇的，断断续续的
   C. intense 强烈的，剧烈的
   D. intrinsic 内在的，本质的

98. B 参考译文：我买了一只带发光表盘的闹钟，这样可以在黑暗中看清楚。
   A. supersonic 超音速的
   B. luminous 发光的，明亮的
   C. audible 听得见的
   D. amplified 放大的，增强的

99. A 参考译文：这些结果很难令人相信，因此他认为它们不精确。
   A. credible 可信的
   B. contrary 相反的，结果不精确不一定就是相反的
   C. critical 评论的，批评的，危急的
   D. crucial 至关紧要的

100. C 参考译文：这台新激光打印机与所有的主要软件都兼容。
   A. comparable 可比较的
   B. competitive 竞争的
   C. compatible 可兼顾的，可协调的，和谐的
   D. cooperative 合作的

Group 6

101. The ball _____ two or three times before rolling down the slope.
   A. swayed   B. bounced   C. hopped   D. darted
102. He raised his eyebrows and stuck his head forward and _____ it in a single nod, a gesture that boys used then for OK when they were pleased.
   A. shrugged   B. tugged   C. jerked   D. twisted
103. Many types of rock are _____ from volcanoes as solid, fragmentary material.
   A. flung   B. propelled   C. ejected   D. injected
104. With prices _____ so much, it is difficult for the school to plan a budget.
   A. vibration   B. fluctuating   C. fluttering   D. swinging
105. The person who _____ this type of approach for doing research deserves our praise.
   A. originated   B. speculated   C. generated   D. manufactured
106. _____ that the demand for power continues to rise at the current rate, it will not be long before traditional sources become inadequate.
   A. Concerning   B. Ascertaining   C. Assuming   D. Regarding
107. Connie was told that if she worked too hard, her health would _____.
   A. deteriorate   B. degrade   C. descend   D. decay
108. We find that some birds _____ twice a year between hot and cold countries.
   A. transfer   B. commute   C. migrate   D. emigrate
109. As visiting scholars, they willingly _____ to the customs of the country they live in.
   A. submit   B. conform   C. subject   D. commit
110. More than 85 percent of French Canada's population speaks French as a mother tongue and _____ to the Roman Catholic faith.
   A. caters   B. adheres   C. ascribes   D. subscribes
111. The professor found himself constantly _____ the question: "How could anyone do these things?"
   A. presiding   B. poring   C. pondering   D. presuming
112. Weeks _____ before anyone was arrested in connection with the bank robbery.
   A. terminated   B. elapsed   C. overlapped   D. expired
113. In order to prevent stress from being added in the metal, expansion joints are fitted which _____ the stress by allowing the pipe to expand or contract freely.
   A. relieve   B. reconcile   C. reclaim   D. rectify
114. How much of your country's electrical supply is _____ from water power?
   A. deduced   B. detached   C. derived   D. declined

115. She had recently left a job and had helped herself to the copies of the company's client data, which she intended to _____ in starting her own business.

    A. dwell on   B. come upon   C. base on   D. draw upon

116. The glass vessels should be handled most carefully since they are _____.

    A. intricate   B. fragile   C. subtle   D. crisp

117. Hill slopes are cleared of forests to make way for crops, but this only _____ the crisis.

    A. accelerates   B. prevails   C. ascends   D. precedes

118. He blew out the candle and _____ his way to the door.

    A. converged   B. groped   C. strove   D. wrenched

119. Often such arguments have the effect of _____ rather than clarifying the issues involved.

    A. obscuring   B. prejudicing   C. tackling   D. blocking

120. I found it difficult to _____ my career ambitions with the need to bring up my children.

    A. consolidate   B. intensify   C. amend   D. reconcile

Group 6　Detailed Answers (101–120)

101. B　参考译文：球在滚下坡以前弹起了两三次。

    A. swayed 摇摆

    B. bounced 反弹，弹跳，尤指撞击物体或物体表面后弹回

    C. hopped 单脚跳，（鸟、蛙等）跳跃，指人和动物的跳跃动作

    D. darted 飞奔，投掷

102. C　参考译文：他挑起眉毛，头往前一探，猛地点了一下，这是当时男孩子们在高兴时摆出的姿势，表示 OK。

    A. shrugged 耸肩

    B. tugged 拖，拉（一个物体）

    C. jerked 猛拉，急推，只有它能与 head 连用，例如 He jerked his head back.（他猛地回过头来）

    D. twisted 扭曲，扭弯，身体和表情都可以扭曲，但是头不能

103. C　参考译文：许多种岩石是以固体碎片形式从火山中喷发出来的。

    A. flung 猛投，掷，抛

    B. propelled 推进，驱使

    C. ejected 逐出，喷射 eject from 表示从内部喷射出来、弹出，强调由于内部的压力或推力而向外的喷射

    D. injected 注射（药液）

104. B　参考译文：由于价格波动太大，学校很难做财政预算。

    A. vibration 振动，摇摆

B. fluctuating 变动，波动，（价格）涨落，多指价格和情绪波动，例如 Prices fluctuate from year to year.（价格年年波动）

C. fluttering 鼓翼，飘动，悸动，乱跳，烦扰，例如 My heart fluttered wildly.（我的心猛烈跳动着）

D. swinging 摇摆，摆动，回转，旋转，例如 swing his arms（挥动他的手臂）

105. A 参考译文：发明这种研究方法的人值得我们赞扬。

   A. originated 起源，发明，创立，英文解释为 have the idea for something and start it，例如 originate the practice of monthly reports（开创了每月报告的惯例）

   B. speculated 推测，思索，做投机买卖

   C. generated 产生，创造，英文解释为 cause sth. to happen，例如 generate a discussion（造成一场争论）

   D. manufactured 制造，加工

106. C 参考译文：假设对电的需求以当前的速度继续增长，不久这些传统的资源就不够了。

   A. Concerning 涉及，关于   B. Ascertaining 确定，探知
   C. Assuming 假定，假设   D. Regarding 关于

107. A 参考译文：Connie 被告知如果工作太努力，她的健康就会越来越糟。

   A. deteriorate 恶化

   B. degrade 使堕落，使受屈辱，降低品格（身价、价值等），例如 You degrade yourself when you tell a lie.（当你说谎时会贬低你自己的身份）

   C. descend 下降，下来

   D. decay 使腐朽，使腐烂，使衰退

108. C 参考译文：我们发现一些鸟一年之中在天寒和天暖的国家之间迁徙两次。

   A. transfer 移交，转移，调任

   B. commute 往来，指经常乘车往来于工作地点和住所之间

   C. migrate 迁徙，指鸟类随季节而定期迁移以及鱼类的洄游

   D. emigrate 主要指人移居国外，英文解释为 to leave one's own country in order to go and live in another country

109. B 参考译文：作为访问学者，他们愿意遵守所在国的传统习俗。

   A. submit 常与 to 连用，服从，顺从，使降服，例如 refuse to submit to an unjust decision（拒绝服从不公正的决定），还表示提出，提交，例如 I submitted my papers to the examiner.（我把试卷交给主考官）

   B. conform 常与 to 或 with 连用，从众，随大流，符合，遵守，例如 conform to the customs of society（遵守社会习俗）

   C. subject 常与 to 连用，受限制，受制约 be subject to sth.

   D. commit 常与 to 连用，致力于，承诺保证，犯罪犯错，例如 They were committed to follow orders.（他们对命令全力以赴）

110. B 参考译文：85%以上的法裔加拿大人以法语作为他们的母语，并信奉罗马天主教。
    A. caters 常与 to 或 for 连用，迎合，投合，例如 cater for the need of the customers（迎合顾客的需求）
    B. adheres 常与 to 连用，坚持，拥护，追随
    C. ascribes 常与 to 连用，归纳于某一具体原因、来源或根源，例如 ascribe the poor harvest to drought（把歉收归咎于干旱）
    D. subscribes 常与 to 连用，捐款，例如 subscribe to a charity（为慈善事业捐款），另外也可表示同意，例如 I subscribe to your opinion.（我赞成你的意见）

111. C 参考译文：教授发现自己总是思考这个问题，"怎么会有人做这些事呢？"。
    A. presiding 主持
    B. poring 不及物动词，常与 over 连用，仔细阅读，凝视 pore over sth.
    C. pondering 考虑，深思，例如 He pondered the words thoroughly.（他说每一句话都要仔细掂量）
    D. presuming 假定，假设，认为

112. B 参考译文：几个星期过去了，涉嫌银行抢劫案的人仍然一个也没被逮捕。
    A. terminated 停止，结束，终止，我们可以说一件事结束了，但不能说一段时间结束了
    B. elapsed 时间过去，消逝，流逝
    C. overlapped 重叠
    D. expired 期满，届满，终止，表示任期或有效期终止

113. A 参考译文：为了防止金属受到增加的压力，人们安装了膨胀接点，可以使管子自由胀缩，从而缓解压力。
    A. relieve 减轻，解除，援救，救济   B. reconcile 使和解，使和谐，使顺从
    C. reclaim 要求归还，收回，开垦   D. rectify 纠正，调整

114. C 参考译文：你们国家的电力供应中，水力发电占多大比例？
    A. deduced 推论，演绎   B. detached 分开，分离
    C. derived 获得，源于   D. declined 下降

115. D 参考译文：她最近辞去了一份工作，并擅自取走该公司的客户资料，打算自己开公司时使用。
    A. dwell on 细想，详述   B. come upon 偶然发现，某种感觉袭来
    C. base on 基于   D. draw upon 利用

116. B 参考译文：玻璃器皿要小心使用，因为它们易碎。
    A. intricate 复杂的，错综的
    B. fragile 易碎的，脆的
    C. subtle 敏感的，微妙的
    D. crisp 脆的，（天气）干冷的，多用来表示食物

117. A 参考译文：山坡上的树木被砍光了，种上了庄稼，但这只会激化危机。

A. accelerates 加速，促进　　　　　B. prevails 流行
C. ascends 攀登，上升　　　　　　D. precedes 领先

118. B 参考译文：他吹灭了蜡烛，摸索着走到门口。
A. converged 汇合，集中　　　　　B. groped 摸索
C. strove 努力，奋斗　　　　　　D. wrenched 猛扭

119. A 参考译文：这些争论的效果往往是使问题更加模糊，而不是澄清涉及的问题。
A. obscuring 使暗，使模糊　　　　B. prejudicing 存在偏见
C. tackling 解决，处理　　　　　　D. blocking 妨碍，阻碍

120. D 参考译文：我觉得很难将自己的事业雄心和带孩子的需求统一起来。
A. consolidate 巩固　　　　　　　B. intensify 加强
C. amend 修正　　　　　　　　　　D. reconcile 使一致

Group 7

121. It is fortunate for the old couple that their son's career goals and their wishes for him _____.
   A. coincide　　B. collaborate　　C. comply　　D. conform

122. As the trial went on, the story behind the murder slowly _____ itself.
   A. convicted　　B. haunted　　C. unfolded　　D. released

123. Mutual respect for territorial _____ is one of the bases upon which our two countries develop relationships.
   A. reliability　　B. unity　　C. entirety　　D. integrity

124. The design of this auditorium shows a great deal of _____. We have never seen such a building before.
   A. orientation　　B. originality　　C. illusion　　D. invention

125. The damage to my car was _____ in the accident, but I have a lingering fear even today.
   A. insufficient　　B. ambiguous　　C. negligible　　D. ignorant

126. Many countries have adopted systems of _____ education in order to promote the average level of education.
   A. constrained　　B. compulsory　　C. cardinal　　D. conventional

127. In addition to the rising birthrate and immigration, the _____ death rate contributed to the population growth.
   A. declining　　B. inclining　　C. descending　　D. increasing

128. Don't let such a _____ matter as this come between us, so that we can concentrate on the major issue.

A. trivial   B. partial   C. slight   D. minimal

129. The cut in her hand has healed completely, without leaving a _____.
A. defect   B. wound   C. sign   D. scar

130. Over the past ten years, natural gas production has remained steady, but _____ has risen steadily.
A. consumption   B. dissipation   C. disposal   D. expenditure

131. In November 1987 the government _____ a public debate on the future direction of the official sports policy.
A. induced   B. initiated   C. promoted   D. designated

132. Europe's earlier industrial growth was _____ by the availability of key resources, such as abundant and cheap labor, coal, and iron ore.
A. constrained   B. remained   C. sustained   D. detained

133. We've just installed a fan to _____ cooking smells from the kitchen.
A. eject   B. expel   C. exclude   D. exile

134. We work to make money, but it's a _____ that people who work hard and long often do not make the most money.
A. dilemma   B. conflict   C. prejudice   D. paradox

135. Very few people could understand the lecture the professor delivered because its subject was very _____.
A. intriguing   B. indefinite   C. obscure   D. dubious

136. I had eaten Chinese food often, but I could not have imagined how _____ and extravagant a real Chinese banquet could be.
A. fabulous   B. gracious   C. handsome   D. prominent

137. Because of the _____ noise of traffic I couldn't get to sleep last night.
A. progressive   B. provocative   C. perpetual   D. prevalent

138. If you go to the park every day in the morning, you will _____ find him doing physical exercise there.
A. logically   B. ordinarily   C. invariably   D. persistently

139. Although she's an _____ talented dancer, she still practices several hours every day.
A. rationally   B. additionally   C. traditionally   D. exceptionally

140. The idea is to _____ the frequent incidents of collision to test the strength of the windshields.
A. simulate   B. accumulate   C. forge   D. assemble

Group 7   Detailed Answers (121–140)

121. A 参考译文：老两口感到庆幸的是，儿子自己的事业目标和他们对儿子的期望一致。
A. coincide 一致   B. collaborate 合作

C. comply 顺从　　　　　　　　D. conform 符合

122. C　参考译文：随着审判的继续，谋杀案背后的故事慢慢地展现开来。

　　A. convicted 宣判，convict sb. (of sth.) 表示（陪审团或法官）宣判某人有某罪

　　B. haunted 萦绕，缠绕，常出现，主语为思绪或鬼魂

　　C. unfolded 展现，显露，常与反身代词连用，表示事物自身显示出来，unfold oneself 表示故事、情节等展开、呈现，unfold a map 表示展开地图

　　D. released 释放，松开，发布，上映，release sb. / sth. from sth. 表示从……释放某人或某物，release sth. to sb. 表示向某人发布某事，句中主语是 story, story released itself 不符合语法逻辑

123. D　参考译文：相互尊重领土完整是我们两国关系得以发展的基础。

　　A. reliability 可靠性

　　B. unity 团结，民族的统一

　　C. entirety 整体、全部

　　D. integrity 完整，完全，诚实正直，territorial integrity 领土完整

124. B　参考译文：礼堂的设计体现了很大的独创性，我们以前从未见过这样的建筑物。

　　A. orientation 方位，方向　　　　B. originality 创意，独创性

　　C. illusion 幻觉，幻象　　　　　D. invention 发明

125. C　参考译文：事故中我车子的损伤并不严重，但至今我还心有余悸。

　　A. insufficient 不足的，不等的，通常指数量上不充足

　　B. ambiguous 模棱两可的，有歧义的

　　C. negligible 无关紧要的，可忽略的

　　D. ignorant 无知的，不知道的，通常指人

126. B　参考译文：许多国家采用了义务教育制度，以提高教育的平均水平。

　　A. constrained 被强迫的，通常指声音、态度，例如 a constrained smile 苦笑

　　B. compulsory 义务的，强制性的

　　C. cardinal 最主要的，最基本的，而基础教育正确的表达应该为 elementary education

　　D. conventional 惯例的，传统的

127. A　参考译文：除了出生率的上升和移民人数的增加，死亡率的下降也是人口增长的一个因素。

　　A. declining 逐渐减小、衰退或变小　　B. inclining 倾向性的，倾斜的

　　C. descending 空间、位置的下降　　　D. increasing 增加的

128. A　参考译文：别让这样的小事来妨碍我们，以便我们可以全神贯注地来处理重要问题。

　　A. trivial 不重要的，琐碎的，指平凡而常见的事物，没有特殊的价值和重要性

　　B. partial 部分的，偏袒的

　　C. slight 程度轻微而不重要的

　　D. minimal 量或程度最小的，最低的

129. D 参考译文：她手掌上的伤口完全愈合了，没有留下疤痕。

    A. defect 过失，缺点

    B. wound 创伤，伤口，相当于 cut

    C. sign 记号，迹象，常指一般的痕迹，而不指伤疤

    D. scar 结疤，使留下疤痕，创伤

130. A 参考译文：在过去的十年里，天然气生产量始终保持不变，但消费量却在稳步上升。

    A. consumption 消费，消费量，消耗

    B. dissipation 浪费，挥霍，消散，指时间、金钱方面

    C. disposal 处理，清理，布置，指处理废弃物

    D. expenditure 花费，消耗，费用，强调时间、金钱、劳力等方面，反义词 revenue

131. B 参考译文：1987 年 11 月，政府就官方体育运动方针政策的未来走向发起了一场公开辩论。

    A. induced 引起，注意所填词的主语是 government，只能说它的某种行为引起争论，而不是它本身

    B. initiated 发起，initiate a debate 发起一场辩论

    C. promoted 促进，提拔，推销

    D. designated 指派，选派

132. C 参考译文：欧洲早期的工业发展由于关键资源，充裕而廉价的劳动力，煤、铁矿石等原材料供应的源源不断而得到维系。

    A. constrained 限制，克制

    B. remained 保持，不及物动词，不用于被动语态

    C. sustained 支持，维持

    D. detained 留住，耽搁，拘留

133. B 参考译文：我们刚安装了一台电扇以将厨房中的烹调味排走。

    A. eject 将人逐出，将液体等从内部排出，突然喷出

    B. expel 排走，排出，指用力排出或驱除

    C. exclude 指范畴上把某物排除在外

    D. exile 将人逐出本土，放逐，使流亡

134. D 参考译文：我们靠工作挣钱，但一个看似矛盾的事实是，那些长时间努力工作的人往往又不是挣钱最多的人。

    A. dilemma 必须在两种行为或事物之间进行选择时的进退两难的情况

    B. conflict 矛盾，抵触，指意见或欲望等的不和

    C. prejudice 偏见

    D. paradox 似是而非的说法、观点或现象

135. C 参考译文：很少有人能听懂这位教授的讲座，因为讲座的主题太晦涩。

    A. intriguing 迷人的，引起兴趣的

B. indefinite（答复、观点等）不明确的，含糊的，并没有难以理解的意思

C. obscure 晦涩的，费解的，含糊的

D. dubious 可疑的，靠不住的

136. A 参考译文：我以前经常吃中餐，但从未想象过一场正式的中式宴会有那么丰盛奢侈。

    A. fabulous 极好的，极妙的

    B. gracious 亲切的，优美雅致的，雍容华贵的，通常指人或对人的态度

    C. handsome 漂亮的，慷慨的

    D. prominent 突出的，杰出的

137. C 参考译文：由于没完没了的交通噪声，昨晚我一夜没法入睡。

    A. progressive 进步的，先进的

    B. provocative 挑衅的，刺激的，多用来修饰言行，例如 a provocative argument 挑衅的言论

    C. perpetual 无休止的，永恒的，永久的

    D. prevalent 流行的，普遍的

138. C 参考译文：如果你每天早晨去公园，总是会发现他在那儿锻炼身体。

    A. logically 合乎逻辑地，逻辑上

    B. ordinarily 平常地，普通地

    C. invariably 总是，不变地

    D. persistently 坚持不懈地，执意地

139. D 参考译文：尽管她是一位非常杰出的舞者，她每天还要练习好几个小时。

    A. rationally 讲道理地，理性地

    B. additionally 附加地，又

    C. traditionally 传统地

    D. exceptionally 格外地，异常地

140. A 参考译文：这种理论是模拟经常发生的碰撞事故，以测试挡风玻璃的强度。

    A. simulate 模拟，模仿（某环境以用于研究、训练等）

    B. accumulate 积累，积聚

    C. forge 锻造，伪造

    D. assemble 召集，装配

Group 8

141. I told him that I would _____ him to act for me while I was away from office.

    A. identify   B. authorize   C. rationalize   D. justify

142. We all enjoy our freedom of choice and do not like to see it _____ when it is within the

legal and moral boundaries of society.

  A. compacted B. dispersed C. delayed D. restricted

143. Allen will soon find out that real life is seldom as simple as it is _____ in commercials.

  A. drafted B. depicted C. alleged D. permeated

144. Diamonds have little _____ value and their price depends almost entirely on their scarcity.

  A. subtle B. eternal C. inherent D. intrinsic

145. Retirement is obviously a very complex period of _____ and the earlier you start planning for it, the better.

  A. transition B. transaction C. transmission D. transformation

146. As one of the youngest professors in the university, Mr. Brown is certainly on the _____ of a brilliant career.

  A. porch B. threshold C. edge D. course

147. They are _____ investors who always make thorough investigations both on local and international markets before making an investment.

  A. indecisive B. implicit C. cautious D. conscious

148. Most people in the modern world _____ freedom and independence more than anything else.

  A. illuminate B. fascinate C. cherish D. embody

149. Doctors are interested in using lasers as a surgical tool in operations on people who are _____ to heart attack.

  A. prone B. disposed C. infectious D. accessible

150. These were stubborn men, not easily _____ to change their mind.

  A. tilted B. converted C. persuaded D. suppressed

151. The circus has always been very popular because it _____ both the old and the young.

  A. facilitates B. fascinates C. immerses D. indulges

152. By patient questioning the lawyer managed to _____ enough information from the witnesses.

  A. evacuate B. withdraw C. impart D. elicit

153. George enjoys talking about people's private affairs. He is a _____.

  A. solicitor B. coward C. gossip D. rebel

154. The new secretary has written a remarkably _____ report within a few hundred words but with all the important details included.

  A. concise B. brisk C. precise D. elaborate

155. His face _____ as he came in after running all the way from school.

  A. flared B. fluctuated C. fluttered D. flushed

156. Steel is not as _____ as cast iron; it does not break as easily.

A. elastic B. brittle C. adaptable D. flexible

157. A big problem in learning English as a foreign language is lack of opportunities for _____ interaction with proficient speakers of English.

A. instantaneous B. provocative C. verbal D. dual

158. Within ten years they have tamed the _____ hill into green woods.

A. vacant B. barren C. weird D. wasteful

159. The _____ of our trip to London was the visit to Buckingham Palace.

A. summit B. height C. peak D. highlight

160. Harold claimed that he was a serious and well-known artist, but in fact he was a(n) _____.

A. alien B. client C. counterpart D. fraud

Group 8 Detailed Answers (141–160)

141. B 参考译文：我告诉他当我不在办公室时，我会授权他替我行使职权。

    A. identify 识别，鉴别 　　　　B. authorize 批准，授权
    C. rationalize 合理化 　　　　　D. justify 证明……是正当的

142. D 参考译文：我们都享有选择的自由，并且不希望看到这一自由在社会法律和道德的范围内受到限制。

    A. compacted 使坚实，压实 　　B. dispersed 分散，驱散，消散
    C. delayed 耽搁，延误 　　　　　D. restricted 限制

143. B 参考译文：艾伦很快会发现现实生活很少能像商业广告中所描述的那么简单。

    A. drafted 起草，设计 　　　　　B. depicted 描述，描写
    C. alleged 宣称，断言 　　　　　D. permeated 弥漫，渗透

144. D 参考译文：钻石本身不具有什么内在价值，其价格几乎完全取决于其稀缺程度。

    A. subtle 微妙的，难以捉摸的
    B. eternal 永恒的，不朽的
    C. inherent 虽然也有内在固有的意思，通常指事物与生俱来的特性、成分等，不能修饰价值
    D. intrinsic 价值或性质方面所固有的，内在的

145. A 参考译文：退休显然是一个非常复杂的转变阶段，他越早有所准备就越好。

    A. transition 转变，过渡
    B. transaction 交易，事务
    C. transmission 传送，传输，转播
    D. transformation 转变，转化，一般指形体上或性格上的完全改变或全面的彻底的社会变革 a character / social transformation

146. B 参考译文：作为大学最年轻的教授之一，布朗先生正处于辉煌事业的开始阶段。

    A. porch 门廊

B. threshold 门槛，开端 on the threshold of 指刚刚开始，在……的开始，快要……

C. edge 边缘，刀刃 on the edge of 指在……的边上

D. course 过程，航线 in the course of 表示在……的过程中，on course 表示航线或航向正确，但没有 on the course of 这种表达方式

147. C 参考译文：他们是谨慎的投资者，在做出每笔投资前，总是要对当地和国际市场进行彻底调查。

  A. indecisive 优柔寡断的，非决定性的

  B. implicit 暗示的，含蓄的

  C. cautious 谨慎的，小心的

  D. conscious 有意识的，清醒的

148. C 参考译文：当今世界的绝大多数人珍视自由和独立胜于其他任何事物。

  A. illuminate 阐明，照亮   B. fascinate 吸引，迷住

  C. cherish 珍视，珍惜   D. embody 体现，包括

149. A 参考译文：医生们很乐意为容易受到心脏病侵袭的病人实施激光外科手术。

  A. prone 易于……的，倾向于……的 be prone to 是固定搭配

  B. disposed 倾向于，乐意 be disposed for sth. / be disposed to do sth. 愿意做某事，而句中结构是 be...to sth.

  C. infectious 感染的

  D. accessible 能接近的，能得到的

150. C 参考译文：他们很固执，不容易被说服改变主意。

  A. tilted 使倾斜   B. converted 使转变

  C. persuaded 说服   D. suppressed 抑制

151. B 参考译文：马戏团总是很受欢迎，因为它吸引老人也吸引年轻人。

  A. facilitates 使容易，使便利

  B. fascinates 吸引，使着迷

  C. immerses 沉浸，使专心，常和 in 连用

  D. indulges 沉溺，纵容，常和 in 连用

152. D 参考译文：通过耐心询问，律师从证人口中得到了足够信息。

  A. evacuate 疏散，撤离

  B. withdraw 撤回，取回 withdraw sb. / sth. from sth. 从……中撤回某人（取回某物）

  C. impart 传授，透露 impart sth. to sb. 将某事透露给某人，不与 from 连用

  D. elicit 诱出，探出 elicit sth. from sb. 从某人处探出（事实、反应等）

153. C 参考译文：乔治喜欢谈论别人的私事，是个爱拨弄是非的人。

  A. solicitor 事务律师   B. coward 胆小鬼

  C. gossip 爱说闲话的人   D. rebel 反叛者

154. A 参考译文：新秘书写了份简洁的报告，只用了几百个词，却包含了所有重要细节。

  A. concise 简洁的   B. brisk 轻快的，通常指行动、心情等

C. precise 精确的 D. elaborate 详尽的

155. D 参考译文：由于他从学校一路跑来，所以进来时脸很红。
    A. flared 信号弹，短暂烧旺 B. fluctuated 波动
    C. fluttered 拍翅膀 D. flushed 脸红

156. B 参考译文：钢不像铸铁那样脆，不容易断裂。
    A. elastic 有弹性的
    B. brittle 脆的，容易碎的
    C. adaptable 能适应的，常用作褒义词
    D. flexible 有弹性的，柔韧的，可变通的

157. C 参考译文：作为英语外语学习的一大问题是缺乏与精通英语的人的言语互动的机会。
    A. instantaneous 即时的 B. provocative 挑衅的
    C. verbal 口头的，言语的 D. dual 双重的

158. B 参考译文：在十年内他们把荒山变为绿色林地。
    A. vacant 空的，未被占用的 B. barren 贫瘠的
    C. weird 奇怪的 D. wasteful 浪费的

159. D 参考译文：伦敦之行最难忘的是参观白金汉宫。
    A. summit 顶点，最高点 B. height 高度
    C. peak 山顶，峰顶 D. highlight 重点，最精彩的部分

160. D 参考译文：Harold 称他自己是个严肃的、有名的艺术家，但事实上他是个骗子。
    A. alien 外星人，外侨
    B. client 客户
    C. counterpart 两方面地位、职务相当的人物
    D. fraud 骗子

Group 9

161. We don't _____ any difficulties in completing the project so long as we keep within our budget.
    A. foresee   B. fabricate   C. infer   D. inhibit

162. He is looking for a job that will give him greater _____ for career development.
    A. insight   B. scope   C. momentum   D. phase

163. The high school my daughter studies in is _____ our university.
    A. linked by   B. relevant to   C. mingled with   D. affiliated with

164. The Browns lived in a _____ and comfortably furnished house in the suburbs.
    A. spacious   B. sufficient   C. wide   D. wretched

165. A membership card _____ the holder to use the club's facilities for a period of twelve months.
    A. approves   B. authorizes   C. rectifies   D. endows
166. They have done away with _____ Latin for university entrance at Harvard.
    A. influential   B. indispensable   C. compulsory   D. essential
167. It is no _____ that a large number of violent crimes are committed under the influence of alcohol.
    A. coincidence   B. correspondence C. inspiration   D. intuition
168. One's university days often appear happier in _____ than they actually were at the time.
    A. retention   B. retrospect   C. return   D. reverse
169. She _____ through the pages of a magazine, not really concentrating on them.
    A. tumbled   B. tossed   C. switched   D. flipped
170. Any salesperson who sells more than the weekly _____ will receive a bonus.
    A. ratio   B. allocation   C. quota   D. portion
171. Many ecologists believe that lots of major species in the world are on the _____ of extinction.
    A. margin   B. verge   C. border   D. fringe
172. He could not _____ ignorance as his excuse; he should have known what was happening in his department.
    A. petition   B. resort   C. plead   D. reproach
173. By turning this knob to the right you can _____ the sound from the radio.
    A. intensify   B. enlarge   C. amplify   D. reinforce
174. The traditional markets retain their _____ to many Chinese who still prefer fresh food like live fish, ducks, and chickens to packaged or frozen goods.
    A. appeal   B. image   C. pledge   D. survival
175. _____ efforts are needed in order to finish important but unpleasant tasks.
    A. Consecutive   B. Perpetual   C. Condensed   D. Persistent
176. They couldn't see a _____ of hope that they would be saved by a passing ship.
    A. grain   B. slice   C. span   D. gleam
177. One of the attractive features of the course was the way the practical work had been _____ with the theoretical aspects of the subject.
    A. embedded   B. integrated   C. embraced   D. synthesized
178. This is a long _____, roughly 12 miles down a beautiful valley to the little church below.
    A. terrain   B. degeneration   C. descent   D. tumble
179. Apart from philosophical and legal reasons for respecting patients' wishes, there are several practical reasons why doctors should _____ to involve patients in their own medical care decisions.

A. enforce   B. endeavor   C. endow   D. enhance
180. Medical students are advised that the wearing of a white coat _____ the acceptance of a professional code of conduct expected of the medical profession.
   A. supplements   B. simulates   C. signifies   D. swears

Group 9　Detailed Answers (161–180)

161. A　参考译文：只要我们维持在预算内工作，现在还看不出完成项目会有任何困难。
   A. foresee 预见
   B. fabricate 编造，捏造
   C. infer 推断
   D. inhibit 抑制，阻止

162. B　参考译文：他在寻找一份能提供给他事业更大发展空间的工作。
   A. insight 洞察力，见识
   B. scope 范围，领域，常与 of 连用，表示发挥能力的机会或余地，常与 for 连用
   C. momentum 动力，势头，冲力，动量
   D. phase 阶段，时期

163. D　参考译文：我女儿上学的中学附属于我们的大学。
   A. linked by 被……连接
   B. relevant to 与……相关
   C. mingled with 与……混合
   D. affiliated with 附属于，并入

164. A　参考译文：布朗家住在郊区宽敞、布置舒适的房子里。
   A. spacious 宽敞的
   B. sufficient 充足的
   C. wide 宽的，宽阔的，单纯指某物的宽度，而不形容空间大小
   D. wretched 不幸的，可怜的，悲惨的，恶劣的

165. B　参考译文：会员卡授权持卡人使用俱乐部设施，有效期十二个月。
   A. approves 同意，认可 approve of sb. / sth. 同意某人或某事
   B. authorizes 授权，批准 authorize sb. to do sth. 授权某人做某事
   C. rectifies 改正，校正（及物动词，宾语常为错误、疏漏）
   D. endows 捐赠 endow sb. with sth. 资助某人某物

166. C　参考译文：他们已经废除哈佛大学入学对拉丁文必修的要求。
   A. influential 有影响力的
   B. indispensable 不可缺少的，绝对必要的
   C. compulsory 必修的，强制的
   D. essential 基本的，本质的

167. A　参考译文：大量暴力犯罪都是在酒精作用下犯的，这一点并非巧合。
   A. coincidence 巧合 it is no coincidence that...句型表示并非巧合
   B. correspondence 信件，对应
   C. inspiration 灵感
   D. intuition 直觉

168. B　参考译文：一个人的大学时光在回忆时经常比实际上更美好。
   A. retention 保留，保持

B. retrospect 回顾，追忆 in retrospect 是固定短语，表示回顾，回想起来

C. return 回来，返回 in return 是固定短语，表示作为回报

D. reverse 撤销，扭转，调换，翻转，倒挡，挫折，相反，背面

169. D 参考译文：她翻着一本杂志，并没专心看。

    A. tumbled 跌倒，翻滚，猛跌，倒塌

    B. tossed 抛，扔

    C. switched 切换

    D. flipped 翻动 flip through 快速翻阅，浏览

170. C 参考译文：任何销售人员能够卖超出一周的销售指标将会得到奖励。

    A. ratio 比率　　　　　　　　　B. allocation 分配

    C. quota 配额，定额，销售指标　　D. portion 部分，一份饭

171. B 参考译文：许多生态学家相信世界的主要物种正处于灭绝的边缘。

    A. margin 页边的空白，差数，利润，地域或水域的边缘

    B. verge 濒于……，即将……

    C. border 国界，边饰

    D. fringe 刘海，外围的边缘

172. C 参考译文：他不能以不知情为借口，他一定知道在他的部门发生了什么。

    A. petition 请愿

    B. resort 度假胜地，诉诸某种手段

    C. plead 恳求，解释，在法庭上承认或否认是否有罪

    D. reproach 谴责，批评

173. C 参考译文：向右拧旋钮就能放大收音机的声音。

    A. intensify 强化，加剧　　　　　B. enlarge 扩大

    C. amplify 放大声音，详细说明　　D. reinforce 增援军队，巩固关系

174. A 参考译文：传统市场依然保持着它们对许多中国人的吸引力，和包装和冷冻的食品比起来，他们更喜欢新鲜的食物，如活鱼、活鸭、活鸡。

    A. appeal 吸引，呼吁，上诉　　　B. image 形象

    C. pledge 誓言，抵押，典当　　　D. survival 生存

175. D 参考译文：要完成重要而不愉悦的任务坚持不懈的努力是必需的。

    A. Consecutive 连续的　　　　　B. Perpetual 永恒的，永久的

    C. Condensed 凝结，压缩，浓缩　D. Persistent 坚持不懈的

176. D 参考译文：他们看不到一丝希望能被过路的船只救助。

    A. grain 颗粒，谷物

    B. slice 片，削球

    C. span 范围，领域，持续时间，跨越

    D. gleam 微光，一丝

177. B 参考译文：这门课程最吸引人的特色之一就是实际操作与研究对象理论方面的融合。
   A. embedded 嵌入，深入的
   B. integrated 使融合，融入，合并
   C. embraced 拥抱，包括
   D. synthesized 合成

178. C 参考译文：这是一个很长的下坡路，沿着美丽的峡谷到下面的小教堂大概十二英里。
   A. terrain 地形
   B. degeneration 堕落，腐化
   C. descent 下降，出身，血统，下坡路，沦落，突然到访
   D. tumble 跌倒，翻滚，猛跌，倒塌

179. B 参考译文：除了因为在哲学和法律上的原因需要尊重病人的意愿，还有其他实际的原因要求医生努力去让病人参与到自身的医疗决策中。
   A. enforce 强迫
   B. endeavor 努力做某事
   C. endow 捐款，资助，赋予
   D. enhance 提高

180. C 参考译文：学医的学生被要求穿白色外套是象征着能够接受医疗职业所期待的职业准则。
   A. supplements 补充，增刊，附加费，补品
   B. simulates 刺激，激励，促进
   C. signifies 象征，意味着，有重要性
   D. swears 发誓，咒骂

Group 10

181. For many patients, institutional care is the most _____ and beneficial form of care.
   A. pertinent   B. appropriate   C. acute   D. persistent

182. Among all the changes resulting from the _____ entry of women into the work force, the transformation that has occurred in the women themselves is not the least important.
   A. massive   B. quantitative   C. surplus   D. formidable

183. Mr. Smith became very _____ when it was suggested that he had made a mistake.
   A. ingenious   B. empirical   C. objective   D. indignant

184. Rumours are everywhere, spreading fear, damaging reputations, and turning calm situations into _____ ones.
   A. turbulent   B. tragic   C. vulnerable   D. suspicious

185. The _____ cycle of life and death is a subject of interest to scientists and philosophers alike.
   A. incompatible   B. exceeding   C. instantaneous   D. eternal

186. She remains confident and _____ untroubled by our present problems.
    A. indefinitely   B. infinitely   C. optimistically   D. seemingly
187. Fiber-optic cables can carry hundreds of telephone conversations _____.
    A. simultaneously   B. spontaneously
    C. homogeneously   D. contemporarily
188. The police were alerted that the escaped criminal might be in the _____.
    A. vain   B. vicinity   C. court   D. jail
189. Whether you live to eat or eat to live, food is a major _____ in every family's budget.
    A. nutrition   B. expenditure   C. routine   D. provision
190. Now a paper in Science argues that organic chemicals in the rock come mostly from _____ on earth rather than bacteria on Mars.
    A. configuration   B. constitution   C. condemnation   D. contamination
191. There is much I enjoy about the changing seasons, but my favorite time is the _____ from fall to winter.
    A. transmission   B. transformation   C. transition   D. transfer
192. I think we need to see an investment _____ before we make an expensive mistake.
    A. guide   B. entrepreneur   C. consultant   D. assessor
193. The _____ on this apartment expires in a year's time.
    A. treaty   B. lease   C. engagement   D. subsidy
194. The elderly Russians find it hard to live on their state _____.
    A. pensions   B. earnings   C. salaries   D. donations
195. There is supposed to be a safety _____ which makes it impossible for trains to collide.
    A. appliance   B. accessory   C. machine   D. mechanism
196. After four years in the same job his enthusiasm finally _____.
    A. deteriorated   B. dispersed   C. dissipated   D. drained
197. No one can function properly if they are _____ of adequate sleep.
    A. deprived   B. ripped   C. stripped   D. contrived
198. For years now, the people of that faraway country have been cruelly _____ by a dictator.
    A. depressed   B. immersed   C. oppressed   D. cursed
199. Ever since the rise of industrialism, education has been _____ towards producing workers.
    A. harnessed   B. hatched   C. motivated   D. geared
200. The prospect of increased prices has already _____ worries.
    A. provoked   B. irritated   C. inspired   D. hoisted

Group 10 Detailed Answers (181–200)

181. B 参考译文：对许多病人来说，社会福利机构的照顾是最合适并且是最有益的一种护理方式。
A. pertinent 直接相关的，有关的 B. appropriate 适当的
C. acute 敏锐的 D. persistent 坚持不懈的

182. A 参考译文：在由于妇女大量进入劳动大军而引起的所有变化中，妇女本身发生的变化并非不重要。
A. massive 大量的 B. quantitative 定量的
C. surplus 多余的 D. formidable 可畏的

183. D 参考译文：当有人暗示史密斯先生犯了一个错误时，他变得非常生气。
A. ingenious 心灵手巧的 B. empirical 以科学实验（经验）为依据的
C. objective 客观的 D. indignant 愤怒的

184. A 参考译文：谣言四起、散布恐怖、诋毁名声，使平静的局面变得动荡混乱。
A. turbulent 动乱的，狂风大作的 B. tragic 悲惨的
C. vulnerable 脆弱的，易受伤的 D. suspicious 怀疑的

185. D 参考译文：生与死的永恒循环是科学家和哲学家们都感兴趣的主题。
A. incompatible 不兼容的 B. exceeding 超过，超出
C. instantaneous 瞬间的 D. eternal 永恒的

186. D 参考译文：她仍然保持信心，看上去不为我们目前的问题所烦恼。
A. indefinitely 不确定地 B. infinitely 无限地
C. optimistically 乐观地 D. seemingly 表面上

187. A 参考译文：光纤电缆可以同时传送数百个电话。
A. simultaneously 同时地 B. spontaneously 自发地
C. homogeneously 同种类地 D. contemporarily 当代地

188. B 参考译文：有人向警方报警说逃犯可能就在附近。
A. vain 徒劳 B. vicinity 附近 C. court 法院 D. jail 监狱

189. B 参考译文：无论你活着是为了吃饭，还是吃饭是为了活着，食物总是每个家庭预算的主要开支项目。
A. nutrition 营养 B. expenditure 支出
C. routine 惯例 D. provision 提供，条款

190. D 参考译文：《科学》杂志上刊登的一篇论文指出：岩石中的有机化学成分大部分来自地球本身的污染物，而不是来自火星上的细菌。
A. configuration 构造，布局，计算机设备的配置
B. constitution 宪法
C. condemnation 谴责
D. contamination 污染

191. C 参考译文：我很喜欢四季的交替，但我最喜欢秋冬之交的时节。
A. transmission 传播 B. transformation 变形
C. transition 过渡 D. transfer 转移

192. C 参考译文：为了避免犯代价惨重的错误，我认为我们有必要咨询一下投资顾问。
    A. guide 指南　　　　　　　　　　　B. entrepreneur 企业家
    C. consultant 顾问　　　　　　　　　D. assessor 估价员，评分人

193. B 参考译文：这套公寓的租约一年到期。
    A. treaty 条约　　　　　　　　　　　B. lease 租约
    C. engagement 订婚　　　　　　　　D. subsidy 补助

194. A 参考译文：俄罗斯的老年人觉得只靠国家发给的养老金生活非常困难。
    A. pension 退休金　　　　　　　　　B. earning 收入
    C. salary 薪水　　　　　　　　　　D. donation 捐款

195. D 参考译文：据推测那儿有一种安全机械装置保证火车不相撞。
    A. appliance 家用电器　　　　　　　B. accessory 附件
    C. machine 机器　　　　　　　　　　D. mechanism 机制

196. D 参考译文：相同的工作做了四年之后他的热情终于耗竭了。
    A. deteriorate 恶化　　　　　　　　　B. disperse 驱散
    C. dissipate 消散，挥霍，浪费　　　　D. drain 耗尽

197. A 参考译文：如果被剥夺了充足的睡眠，没有人能够正常工作。
    A. deprive 剥夺 deprive sb. / sth. of sth.; sb. / sth. be deprived of sth.
    B. rip 撕破
    C. strip 脱衣
    D. contrive 设法做到，发明设计

198. C 参考译文：这些年来，那个偏远国度的人民一直被独裁者残酷地压迫着。
    A. depress 使沮丧　　　　　　　　　B. immerse 浸入
    C. oppress 压迫　　　　　　　　　　D. curse 诅咒

199. D 参考译文：自从工业化兴起之后教育已经开始适应产业工人的需要。
    A. harness 马具，利用控制（自然力）
    B. hatch 孵化，密谋，舱门
    C. motivate 激励
    D. gear 使准备好，齿轮，汽车挡位，运动装备，使适应 gear sth. to sth.

200. A 参考译文：价格上涨的前景已经引起了人们的担忧。
    A. provoke 引发　　　　　　　　　　B. irritate 激怒
    C. inspire 启发　　　　　　　　　　D. hoist 升起

Group 11

201. The suspect _____ that he had not been in the neighbourhood at the time of the crime.
    A. advocated   B. alleged   C. addressed   D. announced

202. Although the colonists _____ to some extent with the native Americans, the Indians' influence on American culture and language was not extensive.
　　A. migrated　　B. matched　　C. mingled　　D. melted
203. E-mail is a convenient, highly democratic informal medium for conveying messages that _____ well to human needs.
　　A. adheres　　B. reflects　　C. conforms　　D. satisfies
204. The wings of the bird still _____ after it had been shot down.
　　A. slapped　　B. scratched　　C. flapped　　D. fluctuated
205. The disagreement over trade restrictions could seriously _____ relations between the two countries.
　　A. tumble　　B. jeopardize　　C. manipulate　　D. intimidate
206. When you put up wallpaper, should you _____ the edges or put them next to each other?
　　A. coincide　　B. extend　　C. overlap　　D. collide
207. Her jewelry _____ under the spotlights and she became the dominant figure at the ball.
　　A. glared　　B. glittered　　C. blazed　　D. dazzled
208. Oil companies in the U.S. are already beginning to feel the pressure. Refinery workers and petroleum-equipment-manufacturing employees are being _____.
　　A. laid out　　B. laid off　　C. laid down　　D. laid aside
209. We'll _____ you for any damage done to your house while we are in it.
　　A. compensate　　B. remedy　　C. supplement　　D. retrieve
210. She cut her hair short and tried to _____ herself as a man.
　　A. decorate　　B. disguise　　C. fabricate　　D. fake
211. Starting with the _____ that there is life on the planet Mars, the scientist went on to develop his argument.
　　A. premise　　B. pretext　　C. foundation　　D. presentation
212. After several nuclear disasters, a _____ has raged over the safety of nuclear energy.
　　A. quarrel　　B. suspicion　　C. verdict　　D. controversy
213. Their diplomatic principles completely laid bare their _____ for world conquest.
　　A. admiration　　B. ambition　　C. administration　　D. orientation
214. The director gave me his _____ that he would double my pay if I did my job well.
　　A. warrant　　B. obligation　　C. assurance　　D. certainty
215. The Christmas tree was decorated with shining _____ such as colored lights and glass balls.
　　A. ornaments　　B. luxuries　　C. exhibits　　D. complements
216. The two most important _____ in making a cake are flour and sugar.
　　A. elements　　B. components　　C. ingredients　　D. constituents

217. Cultural _____ indicates that human beings hand their languages down from one generation to another.
    A. translation   B. transition   C. transmission   D. transaction
218. We must look beyond _____ and assumptions and try to discover what is missing.
    A. justifications   B. illusions
    C. manifestations   D. specifications
219. No one imagined that the apparently _____ businessman was really a criminal.
    A. respective   B. respectable   C. respectful   D. realistic
220. If nothing is done to protect the environment, millions of species that are alive today will have become _____.
    A. deteriorated   B. degenerated   C. suppressed   D. extinct

Group 11　Detailed Answers (201–220)

201. B　参考译文：犯罪嫌疑人声称案发时他不在附近。
    A. advocate 提倡   B. allege 声称
    C. address 发表演讲   D. announce 宣布
202. C　参考译文：虽然殖民者与美洲土著人在某种程度上互相融合，但是印第安人对美国文化和语言的影响并不广泛。
    A. migrate 迁徙   B. match 使……匹配
    C. mingle 混合，应酬，交际 D. melt 融化
203. C　参考译文：电子邮件是一种便捷而又高度民主的非正式媒介，它传递信息，符合人类的需要。
    A. adhere 遵守   B. reflect 反映
    C. conform 遵循，符合   D. satisfy 满足
204. C　参考译文：鸟儿被打下来后仍然拍打着翅膀。
    A. slap 扇耳光   B. scratch 抓，搔
    C. flap 振动翅膀   D. fluctuate 波动
205. B　参考译文：贸易限制方面存在的意见分歧会严重危及两国的关系。
    A. tumble 跌倒   B. jeopardize 危害
    C. manipulate 控制   D. intimidate 威吓
206. C　参考译文：当你贴壁纸时你是把纸的边缘重叠起来呢？还是把它们平铺连在一起呢？
    A. coincide 巧合   B. extend 延长
    C. overlap 重叠   D. collide 碰撞
207. B　参考译文：她的珠宝首饰在聚光灯下闪闪发光，让她在舞会上大出风头。
    A. glared 闪耀，发出刺眼的强光，例如 The sun glared out of the blue sky.（太阳在蓝天上发出强烈的光），也可表示怒气冲冲地瞪着某人 glare at sb.

B. glittered 闪闪发光，闪烁，常指珠宝、星光等的闪光

C. blazed 强烈燃烧，发强光，光线或色彩的光辉

D. dazzled 使目眩，使眼花，美貌或技能等使人倾倒，眼花缭乱，例如 The bright light of the car dazzled me.（这汽车的灯光使我目眩）

208. B 参考译文：美国的石油公司已开始感到压力巨大，正在裁减炼油工人和加工石油的雇员。

A. lay out 设计，展开

B. lay off 解雇

C. lay down 正式声明，规定，放下武器

D. lay aside 把……搁置在一边

209. A 参考译文：我们居住期间对你房子所造成的任何损坏，我们会赔偿你的。

A. compensate 赔偿　　　　　　B. remedy 补救，药物

C. supplement 补充　　　　　　D. retrieve 取回

210. B 参考译文：她把头发剪短，试图假扮成一个男人。

A. decorate 装饰　　　　　　　B. disguise 伪装

C. fabricate 制作　　　　　　　D. fake 伪造

211. A 参考译文：以火星上有生命存在这一假设开始，那位科学家继续进行论证。

A. premise 前提　　　　　　　B. pretext 借口

C. foundation 基础　　　　　　D. presentation 陈述

212. D 参考译文：发生几次核灾难之后，关于核能安全的问题引起了一场激烈的争论。

A. quarrel 争吵　　　　　　　B. suspicion 怀疑

C. verdict 判决　　　　　　　D. controversy 争议

213. B 参考译文：他们的外交原则完全暴露了他们要征服世界的野心。

A. admiration 羡慕　　　　　　B. ambition 野心

C. administration 行政管理　　　D. orientation 定位

214. C 参考译文：主任向我保证，如果我工作干得好，他就会给我双倍的工资。

A. warrant 授权令，许可，正当理由　B. obligation 责任

C. assurance 保证　　　　　　　D. certainty 明确

215. A 参考译文：圣诞树上点缀着闪光的饰物，如彩灯和玻璃球。

A. ornament 装饰物　　　　　　B. luxury 奢侈，奢侈品

C. exhibit 展览，展品　　　　　　D. complement 补充

216. C 参考译文：制作蛋糕时所需的两种最重要的原料是面粉和糖。

A. element 元素　　　　　　　B. component 零件

C. ingredient 烹饪原料　　　　　D. constituent 选民，成分

217. C 参考译文：文化传承意味着人类将语言代代相传。

A. translation 翻译　　　　　　B. transition 过渡

C. transmission 传播，传承　　　D. transaction 交易

218. B 参考译文：我们必须看破那些幻觉和设想，努力去发现遗漏的东西。
    A. justification 理由　　　　　　　B. illusion 幻想
    C. manifestation 表明，迹象　　　　D. specification 产品说明，规格
219. B 参考译文：没有人想象到这位表面上受人尊敬的商人实际上是个罪犯。
    A. respective 分别的　　　　　　　B. respectable 可尊敬的
    C. respectful 尊敬的　　　　　　　D. realistic 现实的
220. D 参考译文：如果不采取措施保护环境，数百万的现存物种就会灭绝。
    A. deteriorate 恶化　　　　　　　　B. degenerate 堕落
    C. suppress 武力镇压　　　　　　　D. extinct 灭绝

Group 12

221. The _____ of the scientific attitude is that the human mind can succeed in understanding the universe.
    A. essence   B. texture   C. content   D. threshold
222. The old lady has developed a _____ cough which cannot be cured completely in a short time.
    A. perpetual   B. permanent   C. chronic   D. sustained
223. What the correspondent sent us is an _____ news report. We can depend on it.
    A. evident   B. authentic   C. ultimate   D. immediate
224. Having had her as a professor and adviser, I can tell you that she is an _____ force who pushes her students to excel far beyond their own expectations.
    A. inspirational B. educational   C. excessive   D. instantaneous
225. Some researchers feel that certain people have nervous systems particularly _____ to hot, dry winds. They are what we call weather sensitive people.
    A. subjective   B. subordinate   C. liable   D. vulnerable
226. Hurricanes are killer winds, and their _____ power lies in the physical damage they can do.
    A. cumulative   B. destructive   C. turbulent   D. prevalent
227. In some countries, students are expected to be quiet and _____ in the classroom.
    A. skeptical   B. faithful   C. obedient   D. subsidiary
228. In spite of the _____ economic forecasts, manufacturing output has risen slightly.
    A. gloomy   B. miserable   C. shadowy   D. obscure
229. Body paint or face paint is used mostly by men in preliterate societies in order to attract good health or to _____ disease.
    A. set aside   B. ward off   C. shrug off   D. give away

230. The international situation has been growing _____ difficult for the last few years.
    A. invariably   B. presumably   C. increasingly   D. dominantly
231. The prisoner was _____ of his civil liberty for three years.
    A. discharged   B. derived   C. deprived   D. dispatched
232. Small farms and the lack of modern technology have _____ agricultural production.
    A. blundered   B. tangled   C. bewildered   D. hampered
233. The Japanese scientists have found that scents _____ efficiency and reduce stress among office workers.
    A. enhance   B. amplify   C. foster   D. magnify
234. All the students have to _____ to the rules and regulations of the school.
    A. confirm   B. confront   C. confine   D. conform
235. He _____ his head, wondering how to solve the problem.
    A. scrapped   B. screwed   C. scraped   D. scratched
236. As soon as the boy was able to earn his own living he _____ his parents' strict rules.
    A. defied   B. refuted   C. excluded   D. vetoed
237. The helicopter _____ a light plane and both pilots were killed.
    A. coincided with   B. stumbled on
    C. tumbled to   D. collided with
238. To _____ is to save and protect, to leave what we ourselves enjoy in such good condition that others may also share the enjoyment.
    A. conserve   B. conceive   C. convert   D. contrive
239. Put on dark glasses or the sun will _____ you and you won't be able to see.
    A. discern   B. distort   C. distract   D. dazzle
240. In _____ times human beings did not travel for pleasure but to find a more favourable climate.
    A. prime   B. primitive   C. primary   D. preliminary

Group 12   Detailed Answers (221–240)

221. A 参考译文：科学态度的本质是人类的智力能够成功地理解宇宙的奥秘。
    A. essence 本质   B. texture 质地
    C. content 内容   D. threshold 门槛
222. C 参考译文：那位老太太患有慢性咳嗽，短时间内无法完全治愈。
    A. perpetual 永久的   B. permanent 永恒的
    C. chronic 慢性的   D. sustained 持续的
223. B 参考译文：记者发来的是一份可靠的新闻报道，我们可以依赖它。
    A. evident 明显的   B. authentic 真实的
    C. ultimate 最终的   D. immediate 立即的

224. A 参考译文：由于她是我的教授兼指导老师，我可以告诉你，她具有一种鼓舞力量，激发着她的学生超越他们自身期望的成绩。
    A. inspirational 有鼓舞力量的   B. educational 教育的
    C. excessive 过度的   D. instantaneous 即刻的

225. D 参考译文：一些研究者认为某些人具有易受干燥热风伤害的神经系统，我们称他们为天气敏感者。
    A. subjective 主观的   B. subordinate 下级的
    C. liable 可能的   D. vulnerable 脆弱的，易受伤的

226. B 参考译文：飓风是具有杀伤力的风，其破坏性的力量在于其能够造成的物质损坏。
    A. cumulative 积累的   B. destructive 毁灭性的
    C. turbulent 动乱的，狂风大作的   D. prevalent 普遍的，流行的，盛行的

227. C 参考译文：在某些国家，要求学生在教室里安静、听话。
    A. skeptical 怀疑   B. faithful 忠诚的
    C. obedient 服从的   D. subsidiary 附属的

228. A 参考译文：尽管经济发展前景不容乐观，但制造业的产量却稍有增加。
    A. gloomy 低迷的   B. miserable 痛苦的
    C. shadowy 阴影的   D. obscure 模糊的

229. B 参考译文：在史前社会，主要是男人文身或文面以追求健康或防止疾病。
    A. set aside 预留   B. ward off 防止，抵挡
    C. shrug off 对……满不在乎   D. give away 赠送，泄露

230. C 参考译文：最近几年里，国际形势日益严峻。
    A. invariably 不变地   B. presumably 大概
    C. increasingly 越来越   D. dominantly 支配地

231. C 参考译文：那个罪犯被剥夺了三年的公民自由权。
    A. discharge 释放   B. derive 派生，获得，源自
    C. deprive 剥夺   D. dispatch 派遣

232. D 参考译文：农场规模小和现代技术的缺乏束缚了农业生产。
    A. blunder 做错，办错   B. tangle 纠缠，混乱，争吵，打架
    C. bewilder 迷惑   D. hamper 阻碍

233. A 参考译文：日本科学家已经发现，香味能提高办公室工作人员的工作效率，能减缓压力。
    A. enhance 提高   B. amplify 扩大
    C. foster 培养，收养   D. magnify 放大

234. D 参考译文：所有学生都必须遵守校纪校规。
    A. confirm 确定   B. confront 对抗
    C. confine 限制   D. conform 遵循

235. D 参考译文：他挠着脑袋，思索着如何解决这个问题。

A. scrap 打架，报废，放弃，抛弃，碎屑

B. screw 旋，拧

C. scrape 刮，擦

D. scratch 抓，擦

236. A 参考译文：那个男孩刚能够养活自己，就公然违抗父母的严厉管教。

  A. defy 公然违抗   B. refute 反驳

  C. exclude 排除   D. veto 否决

237. D 参考译文：那架直升机与一架轻型飞机相撞，两个飞行员均遇难了。

  A. coincide with 巧合   B. stumble on 绊倒

  C. tumble to 猛跌   D. collide with 碰撞

238. A 参考译文：保存就是保留并爱护，把我们所喜爱的东西好好保留下来，别人也可以分享我们的快乐。

  A. conserve 保存   B. conceive 设想，构思

  C. convert 转变信仰   D. contrive 谋划

239. D 参考译文：戴上墨镜，否则耀眼的阳光会让你看不见东西。

  A. discern 辨别   B. distort 扭曲

  C. distract 分心   D. dazzle 炫目

240. B 参考译文：在原始时代，人类长途跋涉不是为了找乐趣，而是为了寻找更加适宜的气候。

  A. prime 首要的   B. primitive 原始的

  C. primary 主要的   D. preliminary 初步的，预赛